Rather His Own Man

———————————————

ALSO BY GEOFFREY ROBERTSON

Reluctant Judas: The Life and Death of the Special Branch Informer Kenneth Lennon

Obscenity

Freedom, the Individual and the Law

Geoffrey Robertson's Hypotheticals (Volumes 1 &2)

Does Dracula Have AIDS?

Robertson & Nicol on Media Law

The Justice Game

Crimes Against Humanity: The Struggle for Global Justice

The Tyrannicide Brief: The Story of the Man Who Sent Charles I to the Scaffold

The Levellers: The Putney Debates

The Statute of Liberty: How Australians Can Take Back Their Rights

The Case of the Pope: Vatican Accountability for Human Rights Abuse

Mullahs without Mercy: Human Rights and Nuclear Weapons

Dreaming Too Loud: Reflections on a Race Apart

Stephen Ward Was Innocent, OK: The Case for Overturning His Conviction

An Inconvenient Genocide: Who Now Remembers the Armenians?

Rather His Own Man

In Court with Tyrants,
Tarts and Troublemakers

GEOFFREY ROBERTSON

Biteback Publishing

First published by Penguin Random House Australia Pty Ltd
This edition published in Great Britain in 2018 by
Biteback Publishing Ltd
Westminster Tower
3 Albert Embankment
London SE1 7SP
Copyright © Geoffrey Robertson 2018

ISBN 978-1-78590-397-7

10 9 8 7 6 5 4 3 2 1

A CIP catalogue record for this book is available from the British Library.

Set in Adobe Garamond Pro

Printed and bound in Great Britain by
CPI Group (UK) Ltd, Croydon CR0 4YY

To the memory of my mother and father

'All change in history, all advance, comes from the non-conformists. If there had been no troublemakers, no dissenters, we should still be living in caves.'

A. J. P. TAYLOR

Contents

Preface

—

I remember – I cannot forget – my first case at the Old Bailey in 1974, when I was still possessed of the hardened vowel sounds acquired by growing up in Australia, the kind that nasalise the 'a' in words like 'Frānce' and 'brānch'. I was appealing the conviction of my client for wearing an indecent T-shirt, before a reactionary and sarcastic judge. Nervously, I stood to explain: 'This case is about an allegedly indecent T-shirt, m'lud. Its logo reads "Fuck Art, Let's Dance".'

There was a terrifying silence, and then a judicial boom: 'Fuck art let's WHAT, Mr Robertson?'

'Dānce, my Lord. Dānce.'

Another silence, then an exaggerated sigh.

'Oh. You're an Australian. What you need to say, Mr Robertson, if you want to succeed at the English Bar, is "Fuck Art, Let's DARNCE".'

There was sycophantic laughter from the well of the court, and Mr Justice Melford Stevenson was so pleased with himself at humiliating another young barrister that he acquitted my client.

Appearing at the Bar of the Old Bailey had been a far-fetched career goal inspired, during my school days at an outer-Sydney comprehensive, by reading a banned book. The Prime Minister, Sir Robert Menzies, had announced that despite the acquittal of *Lady Chatterley's Lover* in England he would not allow his wife to read it (Australians, at least, did not much bother about their servants). So the novel was banned, and for good measure his government also banned a Penguin Special containing the transcript of the Old Bailey proceedings, *The Trial of Lady Chatterley*. A samizdat copy fell into my schoolboy hands, desperate in those days for anything about sex, but entrancing me instead with the story of two QCs, Gerald Gardiner and Jeremy Hutchinson, whose forensic tactics and rhetorical skill had struck such a blow for liberty against an establishment almost as repressive as the one I was suffering in Sydney. To follow them into the lists at the Central Criminal Court became, at age sixteen, the dream that I followed, eventually to meet Lord Gardiner (who helped in the defence of *Spycatcher*) and to have the joy of being Jeremy's junior in Old Bailey triumphs like that over the spooks (the 'ABC' case) and the censors (*The Romans in Britain*, of which more later). I have given some account of these early cases in a previous memoir, *The Justice Game*, published in 1998, and have tried in this autobiography not to plagiarise myself (if that is legally possible), although there is some overlap – curious readers could treat the earlier work as a companion volume. Now, with twenty more years under my wig, I can emerge from the Old Bailey to tell of the struggle for human rights in courts around the globe.

Any autobiography is, by definition, an egotistical exercise. One of my clients, Julian Assange, was so horrified when he read his own that he tried to stop its publication, although his ghost-writer came back to haunt him. Most authors justify themselves by pleading a didactic purpose – look how I handle fame / love my mum / learn from my mistakes – and this may indeed help sales of their books. My reason for writing *The Justice Game* was that its exposure of the inadequacies in British law and practice would enhance the case for a Bill of Rights – vouchsafed by the Blair government shortly after its publication. In this book, I have tried to explain my concern for human rights not only in Britain but in the wider world. Through the arcane prerogative that comes from being a British QC, I have been able to parachute into Commonwealth courtrooms to assist defendants, sometimes saving their lives by taking their cases to the Privy Council – that curious court of last resort for men sentenced to death in the Caribbean. Then there are cases from the newly established UN tribunals (including the UN Special Court in Sierra Leone, where I served as President). This is all a far cry from the Old Bailey, but the international human rights circuit provides a dimension to a modern barrister's life that has not yet been the subject of a television series.

The Bar is a lonely profession: you live in your head, even when you are on your feet. Your trade is to juggle laws and precedents while reaching for scraps of old wisdom from the grab-bag of past cases to construct an argument to favour your client or your cause. You go into battle along with no army to lead or supporters to rally or speechwriters and researchers to back you up. Your efforts may influence social progress more effectively than other blatherers, like MPs or bishops or media commentators – but you must not expect to be loved, especially when those you defend are perceived, at the time, as non-conformists or troublemakers.

John Mortimer, who became my forensic father, created in *Rumpole of the Bailey* a barrister everyone could love, but I could never be that barrister. I took John to Strasbourg to show him the wonders of European law, but in the storyline that emerged for the next novel, Rumpole was not impressed and would, I expect, have voted for Brexit. He was the first truly 'Dickensian' character on British television, but is now an echo from the self-contained world of English criminal law that I entered in 1974, venturing later to the libel and public law courts and then, on wings of silk acquired in 1988, for a legal world beyond the Old Bailey.

There are plenty of books – both fiction and non-fiction – which portray advocacy under wigs and gowns in the setting of a jury trial, but few which describe the very different exercise of persuading an international court in Geneva, or The Hague or in war-torn Sierra Leone or even the Privy Council in London, to produce a verdict in favour of freedom. While I have reminisced about battles at the Old Bailey against police corruption, moral panic and unfair prosecutions, I have endeavoured to explain the purpose behind the establishment of Doughty Street, a barrister's chambers dedicated to human rights work, and how to invoke universal standards to protect not only the underprivileged in England but oppressed people elsewhere in the world.

Just as autobiographies of sports and movie stars and politicians tell stories of sports and movies and politics, so this account of a barrister's life must delve into the more arcane milieu of the law. Our memoirs are always in danger of sending non-lawyers to sleep because our tricks and our tragedies and our triumphs so often depend upon intricate rules that have taken us years to learn and which defy quick explanation to a general reader. I have consciously tried to write a book that will not take a law degree to understand. Readers who wish to find out more – and perhaps a different perspective – on the cases I recount, will find them in the footnoted references. Despite their factual complexities and legal technicalities, I have tried to be simple without (I hope) becoming simplistic.

Another word of warning. My pronunciation has changed through years of grovelling before English judges; I am what *Private Eye* has described as 'an Australian who has had a vowel transplant'. The British press never allows me to forget my antipodean origins. In order to fund return visits to see parents in Sydney I developed a television presence there, and have managed (with some difficulty) a career in both countries. I am a dual citizen, which has some advantages – I have my prostate felt in Harley Street and my teeth fixed in the Sydney equivalent (the English are not renowned for their smiles). I am not aware of any inconsistency in giving my loyalty to both counties – growing up in Australia was much like growing up in the Isle of Wight, without the pop festivals. The only time my allegiance is torn is by boyhood sporting loyalties, impossible to erase. For that reason I will always fail Norman Tebbit's 'cricket test' for Commonwealth citizens seeking nationality – I am psychologically unable to support England when it comes to the Ashes.

I have removed some accounts of local politics and politicians that feature in the Australian edition of the book, to give greater space for cases involving British identities ('no one here has heard of Arthur Scargill' came a plaintive note from my Australian editor, although everyone there had heard of Cynthia Payne). My neighbour in north London is Dame Edna Everage, and we sometimes talk about spending our 'dementia years' in an Australian 'Twilight Home', but at least it will open onto a warm beach, with cold beer. It is perhaps the highest tribute that Australian expats have paid to the genial and intellectually stimulating life in Britain, at least prior to Brexit, that we have chosen to forsake our sunburned country for the ice-age miseries of English winters.

I have now reached three score years and ten – the biblical allotment

of sentient life, so this book is written in my anecdotage. Barristers notice
the passing of time – the policemen get younger, the judges more polite. I
have done my best to produce reliable memoirs, but I warn – as I have had
frequently to point out to prosecution witnesses – that memory is always
skewed and self-selective. I make the occasional digression into what I am
told is the stuff of autobiography – family and favourite music and what
I like for breakfast – but have tried to hold to the thread of human rights,
which is the nature and content of my practice and my beliefs. I have tried
to explain how and why I have dedicated my workaholic life to this pursuit, although I do pay tribute – insufficiently – to friends and lovers who
have done their best to relieve the loneliness of the long-winded lawyer.

A word about the title, *Rather His Own Man*. Some years ago, a minister
in the Blair government decided to appoint me to an important European
judicial position. He told his permanent secretary, one of the breed so
accurately personified in *Yes Minister* by Sir Humphrey. 'What a brilliant
idea, Minister,' said the permanent secretary, with feigned enthusiasm.
'But… he is… rather his own man, isn't he?' In other words, I could not
be trusted always to do what the UK government might want. As the
minister explained to me later, he could not find a way around civil service
opposition. But I was rather taken with Sir Humphrey's tribute to my
independence, which would presumably for ever disqualify me from a government job. I thought then that I would have his remark engraved on my
tombstone, but since an autobiography is the literary equivalent, here it is.

Chapter One

Who Do I Think I Am?

The first Rhodes scholar to sell his semen to a sperm bank with the avowed purpose of propagating his intelligence (and the unavowed purpose of making money) was William Shockley, a Nobel Prize-winning scientist. His theory was that IQ was genetically inherited, though he had already fathered three exceptionally dull children. When asked how this squared with his theory, he replied that his wife was stupid.

I have always been a believer in Dr Spock rather than Dr Shockley. It is nurture, not nature, that shapes who we are, the qualities that really matter in our character – integrity, morality, decency, compassion, consideration for others and so on. This lifelong belief has not been shaken by developments in genetics: DNA obviously shapes our physiognomy, our health and may explain our predilections for our own or another sex, or for alcohol or nicotine, but we are essentially influenced by upbringing and education, by life experiences and by what we make of ourselves. Heredity is no guide – a hereditary monarch, as Tom Paine pointed out, is as ridiculous as a hereditary mathematician or (to update) a hereditary airline pilot.

My very first political instinct was republican, when as a sun-struck schoolboy I was crammed into Sydney Cricket Ground on a sweltering summer's day in 1954 to wave limply at Elizabeth II as she sped past in her royal jeep. The idea that she might be a distant relative (of which more later) never occurred to me. Heedless of heredity, I married into Australian royalty. My wife could boast an impeccable convict lineage: a drunken burglar from the first fleet who had married another convict

– a thieving lady's maid – who came out on the second. Kathy Lette had enough common blood – she really was *la crème de la crims* – to shock Dr Shockley.

I spent most of my life in a state of deliberate ignorance about my ancestry, uninterested in anyone I had not met. Knowledge of my forebears went back no further than to my dear, undistinguished grandparents, and nothing about my ancestors had piqued my curiosity until *Who Do You Think You Are?* made me an offer I decided not to refuse. This programme's trick is to take well-known people back to their roots, confronting them with the carefully researched behaviour of their distant relatives, who would turn out to be heroes or criminals or slaves, or whatever could elicit a great-great-grandchild's joy or tears, caught on camera. The show proved an absorbing way to understand history, in particular the social history of ordinary folk, and for that reason I agreed to be one of its first Australian guinea pigs. Its systemic weakness was that it concentrated on people with a degree of celebrity – actors, singers, sports heroes, newsreaders and the like, and rarely on surgeons or politicians or lawyers. The latter were in fact invited to participate, but usually declined for fear that researchers would turn up something unpleasant that would damage their self-esteem. My mother expressed a concern – 'What if they find a dark secret in our family?' I was aware of none, and, besides, rather wanted to bone up on any skeleton in our closet. A former girlfriend, Nigella Lawson, had done the show and been delighted to find herself descended from a minor criminal. Besides, the production company were offering all-expenses-paid travel not only to the Isle of Skye but (intriguingly) to Berlin and Potsdam. Which thread of DNA, I wondered, would trace back to Deutschland?

* * *

My last relatives in the UK were Alexander and Christine Robertson. They were poor Scottish crofters, who with others of their like came out to Australia from Skye in 1837. They had lived, and almost died from hunger, on this island of the Inner Hebrides which had been hit like the rest of the Highlands by the great potato famine of 1835. In desperate straits, they rented an acre of land from a rapacious absentee landlord, eking out their rent with a few sheep and goats, with whom they shared their hovel (literally – I was shown a small dwelling in which they would have lived, with their creatures at one end and they themselves at the other). Their annual potato harvest was stored to last them throughout the year. Except there were no potatoes in 1835, and by 1837 men, women and children were dying of starvation throughout the Highlands. The government of Britain – wealthy beyond measure as the industrial revolution churned out its profits – was well aware but entirely unconcerned until the Reverend Norman MacLeod, moderator of the Presbyterian Church, came down from Glasgow to challenge London society with a fire and brimstone sermon at London's Mansion House. Something had to be done, he threatened, or those in government would go to hell for their inaction.

This remarkable event became historic, thanks to the presence of a young Presbyterian clergyman from Sydney, the Reverend John Dunmore Lang. As he listened to MacLeod's speech, a profound idea came to him. He had been much exercised by the corruption that infested the exercise of power in Sydney: the officers of the 'Rum Corps' who had ousted Governor Bligh (of *Bounty* fame) were back in control, with the help of a gang of former convicts, mostly Irish. These were godless men, and Lang had already called for a 'Protestant immigration scheme' to counter their corruption. Now, he realised that this pool of poor, devout Presbyterians might, with government assistance, be brought to Sydney to combat the criminal Irish. These two goodly and godly men were observed in earnest conversation, and subsequently MacLeod used his influence to make Lang's hopes a reality. The government advertised for contractors to take impoverished Scots, as assisted voluntary migrants, to Sydney town, and in due course the *William Nicol* anchored in the harbour at Skye and Alexander and Christine Robertson embarked, with 300 other destitute Highlanders. The greedy contractors (paid per passenger head) had massively overloaded the vessel and did not stow sufficient food, water or medicine: on the two-month journey to Cape Town, ten children died from diarrhoea and other curable ailments. There were complaints, but the contractors brushed them aside – critics 'did not understand the habits of the peasants'.

It was with great relief that the Presbyterian pilgrims came ashore in Sydney, refugees from a country that preferred to get rid of them rather than to feed and clothe them. Dunmore Lang and MacLeod had planned for these shiploads of Bible-bashing Presbyterians to impose a measure of decency and civility on vice-ridden old Sydney town, but they reckoned without simple human psychology – the need felt by lonely émigrés, halfway across the world, to recapture at least the atmosphere of their homeland. Alexander and Christine and their shipmates were born and bred beneath mountains capped with snow, and they soon set off to find the equivalent – some 700 kilometres away from Sydney, by the Snowy River, in the shadows of Mount Kosciuszko. There they found fertile land, so much more impressive than their rack-rented acre in Skye. So Alexander and Christine built a makeshift house and raised two sons – 'Sandy' and 'Red Bill' – called after their hair colour. ('Red Bill', my great-grandfather, handed down his follicles: when I grew my hair fashionably long in the '60s, my sideburns came out red. Indeed, I was sometimes called 'Red Robbo' – but that was because of presumed left-wing tendencies.)

Sandy and Red became wild colonial boys, daredevil horsemen of the mountain ranges, cowboys saluted in Australia's wild west poem (and, later, movie) 'The Man From Snowy River'. The verse was handed down to me, almost as a folk memory, by Red Bill's son, my grandfather, and I can still flawlessly recite:

> There was movement at the station,
> For the word had passed around,
> That the colt from Old Regret had got away,
> And had joined the wild bush horses;
> He was worth a thousand pounds.
> So all the cracks had gathered to the fray...

And so on and on, naming the celebrated horsemen as if they were heroes on their way to Valhalla – which in a sense they were, for a small boy growing up in the Sydney suburbs. But horsemanship has to be taught rather than inherited: I was first seated on a horse when I was twelve, whereupon it bolted and my fear was such that I never wanted to sit in the saddle again. When they made *Who Do You Think You Are?*, they took me back to the Snowy River and dressed me as a cowboy – the viewer can marvel at my death-defying ride down the mountain, cracking a whip. In fact, I had a stunt double. Every respectable lawyer should have one – a doppelgänger who can live out the fantasies he dares only to dream.

Living was not easy in 'the Snowy'. The Robertsons had land, and some years of plenty counterpointed by years of drought. The house burned down, and Red went back into the flames to salvage a mirror. When asked why, he's said to have replied, 'So I can watch meself starve.' The house was rebuilt – I found bedsprings and perfume bottles among the ruins – but another drought convinced the Robertsons that their own children would have more luck in 'the big smoke'. So, half a century too late for the purposes of Dunmore Lang, they came back to the industrial suburbs of Sydney.

*   *   *

The Robertsons came to Australia out of necessity; my father's line began when they married into the Westons, who emigrated as a result of love. Squire Weston was a landowner in Surrey, with a large mansion outside the village of Horsley. The house was once owned by the son of Sir Walter Raleigh and remains resplendent, having reopened with much fanfare in 2017 as the site of Grange Park Opera, Britain's latest music festival. My ancestor, William Francis Weston, was the squire's second son, and the family's stately pile was bound under the laws of primogeniture to go to his elder brother. William was a gambler and a gamboller, squandering his share of the family fortune on the Paris gaming tables and returning to make hay with Elizabeth, one of the serving maids, who in due course became pregnant. At this time in England the unexpected progeny of the upper-middle classes usually suffered a cruel fate: illegitimate babies were quietly given to baby farmers, a clandestine profession whose sleazy practitioners pretended to place them for adoption but often killed them, or at best left them at the door of the Foundling Hospital in Bloomsbury.

But West Horsley was not Downton Abbey, thank goodness, and there a most unusual thing happened: the maid was delivered of a baby, named John, who was two years old in 1817 when his mother became Mrs Weston: William married her.

It has to be assumed that he acted out of love, but their union only inflamed the prurient prejudices of Surrey society. Once a bastard, always a bastard, in the eyes of these intolerant parishioners. William determined to take his young bride and their baby as far away from social shame as possible. They took ship to Sydney.

They were made welcome by its Governor, delighted to have a member of the English squirocracy as a free settler in what was still a colony of convicts and jailors. He asked no questions about the pedigree of Elizabeth or the birth date of John, and generously provided them with 500 acres of land. Like the Robertsons twenty years later, there was a certain pining for home, or at least for the mansion: William planned to build 'West Horsley Place' near Wollongong at the township of Dapto, along the Bong Bong Road (how I love these names), but died in 1826 aged only thirty-three. Elizabeth married a convict and built the house, modelled on the stately pile in which she had borne a child to 'him upstairs'. Horsley Place is one of Australia's earliest historic houses, its 'Georgian-style farm complex and garden' still visible from the Bong Bong Road on the 'Dapto and District Heritage Trail'.

Baby John grew up to marry the daughter of the crooked commander of the Rum Corps, George Johnston, and inherited some of his corruptly acquired land. They had a lot of children – John spread his seed whenever he could: there are horrifying tales (which fortunately I could not verify) that he raped several indigenous women. But one of his daughters married 'Red Robbo', and my grandfather, Harold Lancelot Robertson, was, at the turn of the century, the result.

*   *   *

On my mother's side of my family, there hangs a great question. Her father's ancestry is clear: Harry Beattie was one of fourteen children of a farming family first brought to Australian by the gold rush, a common demographic. But Mum's grandmother was Jane Dettmann, the daughter of a mysterious Prussian woman, Agnes, who had come to Sydney, first class, with her new husband, Louis Dettmann, in 1848. That was the year of European republican revolutions, especially in Berlin against the King of Prussia and the royal family. Could they be in any way connected?

The arrival in Australia of Agnes and Louis seemed at first blush to be another result of love. Agnes was the second daughter of Joseph Kroll, an impresario who ran a big establishment in Berlin – an opera house, no less, surrounded by pleasure gardens. Louis was Kroll's chief pastry chef, and it was said that he and Agnes had eloped, marrying in London and setting sail immediately for Sydney. There they opened the colony's first tea and sweet shop, selling delicious pastries that soon became the talk of the town. This culinary fame enabled them to branch out into a catering business that provided dinners and luncheons and sundry confections for Sydney society 'dos', frequently mentioned in the social pages of the newspapers. The Dettmanns provided a touch of European taste – in both senses of the word – to the boring 'meat and two veg' English cuisine of the colony. In 1865, this celebrated couple were offered the jobs of chief steward and deputy steward of the New South Wales Parliament. MPs, even in those days, wanted to put their snouts in the best available trough.

I am addicted to cakes and opera and must admit to being a bit chuffed when I heard of my relationship to the Kroll establishment. Pictures and early photographs show it as a magnificent palace, seating up to 5,000 in three concert halls, with fine restaurants and walks through flower-strewn gardens. The composer Johann Strauss – Joseph's wife, Caroline Strauss, may have been a relative – came from Vienna to provide music, and the 'Blue Danube' – the world's most famous waltz – had its premiere there. After Joseph's death in 1848, the Kroll Opera continued under one of his daughters, and in the late 1920s its music was famously supervised by Otto Klemperer, the resident conductor. In those Weimar years its operatic repertoire became world-famous, with avant-garde directors, sets commissioned from modern painters and works by contemporary composers. Klemperer's *Fidelio* was its last gasp of defiance against the Nazis. They took it over, alas, after the Reichstag fire in 1933, and used it as their make-shift Parliament: Göring presided and Hitler used its podium in January 1939 to give his wicked speech which first threatened 'the annihilation of the Jewish race in Europe' and on 1 September to make his declaration of war. The last session of the Reichstag, held in my family's opera house in April 1943, gave Hitler absolute power over the judges and the law. It deserved its obliteration by Allied bombing a few months later. But its posters and billboards, from the 1840s onwards, are preserved in German museums as a testament to the vision of Joe Kroll. I was rather pleased to learn that he was my great-great-grandfather.

Or was he? There are cracks in this story, which point to a much less likeable forebear. For a start, Joe's eldest daughter was born, so church records (which do not lie) tell us, on 15 November 1823. Agnes, so family records (normally reliable) say, was born on 30 January 1824 – ten weeks later. Some mistake, surely? If Agnes was his daughter, she was obviously not conceived by his wife. Then there was Joe Kroll's unbelievable good fortune. There he was in Breslau (the city was then located in Prussia, but is now Wrocław, in western Poland) with heavy debts, running a Winter Garden, which mainly consisted of swimming baths and one shabby restaurant. Suddenly, on the recommendation of Prince Wilhelm, he is vouchsafed by the King of Prussia the best piece of vacant land in Berlin and enough money to build an entertainment complex that today would cost the equivalent of many millions of pounds. He must have done a very great favour for the prince, or for the king, or for both, to become virtually overnight the city's cultural czar and one of its wealthiest citizens.

Nor does the 'elopement' stack up. In March 1848 came the violent revolution – hundreds killed on the streets of Berlin – and Prince Wilhelm was sent to take refuge in England with his cousin, Queen Victoria. It turned out that Louis and Agnes travelled comfortably to London from Hamburg shortly afterwards, accompanied by a diplomatic courier. Their marriage was immediately and efficiently arranged (difficult for two newly arrived Germans to manage) and a mystery witness at the wedding bore the name of a senior adviser to Queen Victoria's husband, Prince Albert. They travelled to Australia as first-class passengers, at a cost not normally affordable by a pastry chef. When, some years later, a member of the Anglo-German royal family arrived in Sydney (Prince Alfred, the Duke of Edinburgh, second son of Queen Victoria), the first thing he did was to look up Louis and Agnes, as if they were part of the family. He carried a letter of introduction from Prince Wilhelm, who had by now become King (Kaiser) not only of Prussia but of a Germany united by the genius of Bismarck. The very religious Jane Dettmann, at a time when she was likely to die and hence unlikely to lie, told her son (who is still alive) that her mother was a princess, the illegitimate daughter of Kaiser Wilhelm I, the King of Germany.

This was all very discomforting. I really do not fancy having any connection with kaisers, or even the English royal family, the Saxe-Coburg-Gothas, who changed their name to 'Windsor' during World War I to pretend they were not related to the enemy. (This produced the only joke the Kaiser is known to have made: 'Do they still perform at Windsor, the merry wives of Saxe-Coburg-Gotha?')

Before I could credit Jane Dettmann's dying declaration, I would need to know who and what Prince Wilhelm was up to back in 1823 when he allegedly fathered Agnes. There is evidence that he knew Kroll, and had visited his Wrocław establishment on hunting trips to the area. But was it likely – or even possible – that he could have produced at this time an illegitimate child who would be farmed out to the Krolls in return for a king's ransom – the cost of the Kroll Opera?

Unfortunately, it is altogether possible. A few years after the programme, a book was published which gave more credence to the theory, and suggested that I may have a double dose of royal blood.[1] It drew on the well-known fact that Prince Wilhelm – who later, under Bismarck's tutelage, became Kaiser Wilhelm I – was in 1823 conducting a passionate affair with the love of his life, the Polish princess Elisabeth (or Elisa) Radziwill. They were writing to each other every day, and many of the letters with the tell-tale details are publicly available to historians (although there are curious gaps in the 1823 correspondence). The two had been in love from 1822, giving each other rings ('ever true'). Elisa confessed to friends that she dreamed they were married, and that Wilhelm 'took the liberties of a married man'. Their idyll lasted seven years, as Wilhelm fought his father

and the Prussian court for his right to marry Elisa. But Hohenzollern politics were cruel and opportunistic: the Radziwills were not royal enough or
important enough for Wilhelm to marry into them. He lacked the courage
to disobey his father, who insisted on a union with Russian royalty, so in
1829 he married a better-qualified princess, Augusta of Saxe-Weimar. Just
before his nuptials, the King published a most curiously worded decree,
annulling 'any union of marriage that Prince Wilhelm may have entered
into' – leading to conjecture that his son had married Elisa secretly. Elisa
pined away, dying a few years later of a broken heart. Wilhelm kept a
picture of her (which looks uncannily like a picture of Jane Dettmann at
seventeen) on his desk throughout his long life, and asked on his deathbed
that it be placed in his hands so that he could expire while looking at her.

I despise Kaiser Wilhelm I, and sincerely hope we are not related. As a
young man he was a coward, unable to stand up to his father and the court
in order to marry, at least publicly, the woman he really loved. Contrast
him with William Weston, who had the courage to do the right thing no
matter what society might have said about his love for the 'lower-born'. As
king of Bismarck's Germany, Wilhelm was militaristic and imperialistic,
and his son (Kaiser Wilhelm II) was a war criminal who invaded Belgium and ordered unrestricted submarine warfare. I want nothing to do
with these pumped-up Prussians, however many researchers believe in my
royal genes! But their work illuminated the problem of royal (and other)
bastards at a time when shame over sex and class had morally calcified
Europe. There is now evidence that Elisa had two illegitimate children and
was most likely the wife whose secret marriage was annulled by the king
just before Prince Wilhelm began his loveless (but not childless) union
with the better-connected Augusta. In 1605, or thereabouts, Shakespeare
in *King Lear* gave illegitimate Edmund the great plea 'Now, gods, stand up
for bastards!' It took four centuries before it was heeded in the West, by
laws that repealed their stigma and inability to inherit.

That was the inconclusive end of my quest to find out who – or whom
– I was. Frankly, I do not much care whether I am descended from a
prince or a showman. Joe Kroll did strike a chord but so far science has
not discovered a genetic predisposition to musical appreciation. I do have

traits associated with emperors – pomposity, and an inability to suffer fools gladly (for which reason I have never attempted a political career) – but I doubt whether this derives from the Hohenzollerns; rather from life as a judge and QC in England. My family thought it most pronounced when I came home after a long day laying down the law to grovelling barristers and attended by clerks and ushers – my court servants. It comes, in other words, by immersion in the class system, and not naturally. As for ethics, those I have are derived from my mother – because she taught me them, not because I inherited them from her down a line of dodgy royal relatives.

* * *

My real family story – of the members of my family I can actually remember – begins with my grandmother Bernice, daughter of Jane Dettmann who had become in time a rather joyless member of the very joyless Plymouth Brethren. Bernice was high-spirited and, under the pretext of spending a weekend at a bible camp, headed instead for Sydney's Central Station, where the country troop trains were decanting the 'boys from the bush' who had volunteered for military service on the Somme. They were milling around the platform, talking loudly, and it was a simple trick for the girls to choose a target and bump against him. Bernice chose her man and moved towards him. 'Did you speak to me?' she asked. 'No,' replied the somewhat startled young man, a twenty-year-old teacher from the country town of Tumut, Harry Beattie. Bernice grinned. 'Well, you can now.'

And so he did, for the rest of the day, as they wandered the foreshore before his troop ship sailed for England on the morrow. The vivacious girl made such an impression on this rather staid and studious youth that over the next four years, until his return, he wrote her a letter every week, in unusually perfect copperplate handwriting. After the war they reconnected and married, on the strength of his perfectly sloping calligraphy and her need to escape the smother-love of the Brethren. Harry was a lapsed Catholic. He had been sent to St Patrick's College in Goulburn, where he was not sexually abused, but each night he observed from his bedroom window the line of priests visiting the maidservants' quarters to dishonour their vows of chastity. He decided, at the age of twelve, to have nothing further to do with these hypocrites.

Bernice's instinct at the railway station was right – bright young Harry Beattie was quite a catch. He and his brother Bob showed scholarly qualities and had been trained by the Education Department to serve at the one-teacher schools that dotted the countryside. They had heeded the imperial call and volunteered for the war: Harry with his educated voice and quick wit was selected for Australia's first air squadron – the Australian Flying Corps – but to his regret poor eyesight precluded him from becoming a pilot. Instead he became flight sergeant to the squadron and was awarded a Mention in Despatches for dragging a pilot out of a burning Sopwith aircraft. His was a good war, unlike Bob, who was blown up with nineteen other Australians by a German tunnel bomb at Bapaume, a town on the Somme.[2] On British ceremonial occasions to which I am sometimes summoned by an embossed card that says 'Dress: Medals', I clip on to my jacket the small golden wings that Harry bequeathed me – his medal as a founder member of the Australian Air Force.

After marrying Bernice, Harry was appointed schoolmaster at Marshall Mount near Dapto, a single-teacher school outside Wollongong, and not far from Horsley Place. The family occupied a large white house opposite the school – all seven children (my mother being the third) would be dispatched each morning to call their father 'Sir' rather than 'Dad' once they entered the school gate. They lived happily until a family tragedy. The second-born, Margaret, seemed inattentive and short-sighted aged around six. Her worried father bought her glasses, but they didn't help. Peg, as she was known, had an inoperable tumour on the brain, from which, doctors said, she would die.

She survived, attended a school for the blind and lived happily – she was always happy – until she was seventy-eight. She often stayed with us – my mother was closest to her in age and took most responsibility for her – and knitted us socks, jumpers and tea cosies. The subdued click-clack of her knitting needles orchestrated our house, and every Easter we would queue up to enter the Pavilion at Sydney's Royal Easter Show and radiate pleasure at all the prizes Auntie Peg had won in the 'Blind Knitting' section. She was an object lesson in overcoming the challenge of living with a disability, and I wore her blue-ribbon jumpers with a certain pride. Today she would be hailed as a champion, a role model and an example of why knitting should be a Paralympic sport, but in her time she was seen as a poor blind girl who was good at crocheting. Her prizes – never of money – were acts of condescension by people who did not realise that the disabled have real talent and are capable of superhuman efforts to show it.

My mother's name, Bernice Joy Beattie, was shortened to 'Joy' to avoid confusion with her mother. She gained top marks at high school, but at sixteen there was no money for further education. The country was in the grasp of the Depression and most people in Wollongong were un-employed. She took a low-paid job at a dental clinic for the poor, staying with a friend in town during the week and returning to the family home at weekends with a bag of sweets for Peg. The work brought her into contact with despairing victims of the Depression – unemployed men struggling to feed their families who could not afford 2/6d for a set of dentures. It aroused a concern for the poor that never left her.[3]

When the war came, Joy decided to volunteer for the air force – an obvi-ous choice given her father's membership of the original Australian Flying Corps. So off she went, with 140 other recruits, to train for the WAAAF – the Women's Australian Auxiliary Air Force (a third 'A' for 'Auxiliary' to emphasise, I suppose, the perceived inferiority of women). They would not be flying, of course – the war did not break down the sexism of the time quite so far – but these women would do more than pack parachutes. They would be permitted to help in the administration of the war effort, so they had to complete an intensive three-month training course. It was held in a town called Robertson. To Joy's surprise, she came first, and was quickly made a corporal and sent north to Townsville, the key administra-tive centre for pilots, ground-force soldiers, ships and aeroplanes en route to fight the Japanese in New Guinea and the islands of the South Pacific.

She arrived at a crucial time for Australia: the Japanese were still in New Guinea, threatening Port Moresby, and were making bombing raids on Townsville. She was placed in the personnel section and put in charge of pilot-debriefing records: she met – through their words, and then in person – the men who were flying in combat at this terrifying time, and she had to close their files when they did not return from battle.

* * *

Meanwhile, my uncle Ron had been the first-born (in 1918) of that branch of the Robertsons who had left the snowy caps of Mount Kosciuszko to find work in the big smoke. Ron's father, Harold, was the son of 'Red Robbo', the squatter who came to the city so that his boys could learn a trade. Harold had a bad chest, which kept him home from the war and limited the jobs available to him: the trade he chose, at fifteen, was that of a 'French polisher' – essentially, polishing the pianos of the upper classes in Sydney's wealthy eastern suburbs. He was employed by Beale and Co., the piano specialists, and rose to become its factory foreman, supervising fifty workers and apprentices. He met his wife Fol (some arcane allusion to 'Fol de Rol'), a farmer's daughter, at the Methodist Church.

Then, in 1929, the Great Depression hit and Harold lost his job – piano-polishing was a luxury even the rich could no longer afford. He would tramp the streets every day, finding a job here and there, earning just enough to pay one shilling and sixpence to the local 'rabbito' for a pair of the rabbits which kept the Sydney poor from starvation. Fol took a tailoring course and learnt to cut down Harold's suits to make presentable clothes for her three sons. The boys never forgot their father's anxious negotiations with a caring bank manager over the mortgage he could not afford to pay: suspending the repayments was the salvation of the Robertson family. In admiration, Frank aspired to become a bank manager, as did his younger brother Lance (who did indeed become one).

It was Ron who led the Robertsons to war, even before Pearl Harbor. He started at university, learnt about fascism and the need to fight it, and chose to leave to join the air force – more individual, more romantic and more chance of standing up to the enemy. Soon he was selected to go to England to navigate on the heavy Lancasters that were beginning to pound Germany. In the weeks before this lethal posting (half the wartime

Lancaster crews were killed), he was stationed in Queensland with a squadron flying Avro Anson bombers, on the lookout for Japanese submarines.

The threat from Japan increased, and Frank was next in line to volunteer. He chose the RAAF, for much the same reasons as Ron, and just before his twentieth birthday was accepted for pilot training. He had never flown before, but was soon doing aerobatics in a Tiger Moth. 'My first spin – nearly scared me to death and found myself trembling when the ordeal was over – don't think I'll ever master the queer sensation,' Frank recorded, frankly, in his new logbook. In no time he'd mastered the Tiger Moth, and moved on to the Wirraway (the Aboriginal word for 'challenge'), Australia's unique contribution to fighting aircraft, too slow and cumbersome ever to win a fight. Pilots likened it to a flying lawnmower.

It was in a Wirraway, on the night of 30 May 1943, that nineteen-year-old Frank Robertson (and, inferentially, his unconceived son) almost ceased to exist. It was his first solo night flight and he was caught in an unexpected and violent storm. He became lost in a plane without radar, and a few minutes of fuel in the tank. Bailing out was the best option, to climb to a height from which he could safely parachute, abandoning his plane to crash by itself. But the youth had seen the lights of the town below, and he was not prepared to save himself at the risk of civilian life: he would take his chances and go down with his aircraft. So he wheeled the aircraft around in a loop and descended, putting the wheels and flaps down, flying parallel to power lines. He threw a flare, which dazzled him momentarily but showed he was heading straight for a large telegraph pole. He stepped hard on the right rudder so the plane began to slew, but too late to avoid the impact, which tore away the engine and the left wing. The rest of the plane bounced high to the right, landing on the power lines. The fifty-six strands of rubber wire cushioned the craft for a second, then quite literally catapulted it into the air, from where it descended, almost sedately, onto the flat roof of a nearby house.

When Frank came round, he saw a vision – a lady with long white hair and a white nightgown. 'Oh gosh,' the young Methodist thought. 'I'm in heaven.'

He was in fact in the small bush town of Chiltern, and had landed on the roof of a house belonging to the local nurse. She was woken by the crash and had climbed to the roof in her dressing gown – and then fainted at the sight of the burning plane and its pilot. His epiphany over, the trainee gingerly hoisted himself out of the cockpit and slid down to the roof to embrace the recumbent nurse, at which point both lost consciousness – my father as much from the shock of surviving as from the pain of his bruised arm and broken ribs.

He came round as an army doctor and nurse were inspecting his injuries, and heard them say, 'We'll have to cut it off.'

'Be buggered,' he interjected, but they were talking about his sleeve.

Frank was back flying in three days, and was in combat three months later. The official RAAF investigation of his crash made no criticism: he had made a moral and honourable choice. As he told his debriefers, 'I had glimpsed a town beneath me and I was not prepared to let my aircraft go with the possibility of it causing damage and loss of civilian life.'

The story – and the photographs – were in all the newspapers and are now on display at the museum in Chiltern. I was pleased to read that the nurse had been compensated – the plane's impact had pushed her house a metre off its alignment.[4] The only effect the crash had on Dad's career was to supply his nickname: his mates in the air force dubbed him 'Home-wrecker'.

They marvelled at the newspaper photographs, which became the pictures I too held in my mental attic after I first discovered them at the back of my father's dresser, rooting around, as small children do, among the impedimenta of their parents' war experience. It is impossible to look at them without wondering how the pilot survived. On this photographic evidence, I was the by-product of providence, of what Claire Tomalin calls 'the randomness of things'. Contemplating these pictures may have influenced me to seek with determination and accept with gratitude whatever fortune this life would put in my direction.

* * *

Ron was first to congratulate Frank on getting his wings ('May they always bear you up and bring you home'). His letters told how the pilot of his Avro Anson would go on target runs over the Barrier Reef a few feet above the waves, so they could see schools of sharks, a whale and her calf, and a jumping marlin. He would pull back on the stick just in time. It may have been this kind of daredevil flying that caused the pilot of AX-471 to fly as low as he could over Heron Island, and then discover that he couldn't. The wing clipped a pisonia tree, the plane crashed (on what is now the tennis court of a luxury resort) and most of the young airmen on board died instantly. Ron survived, was rescued by a US 'subchaser' and was brought back with critical injuries.

It was a terrible time for the family. His mother, Fol, was flown to Gladstone to take up a hopeless vigil by his bedside, and Harold joined her the next day. My father, now practising aerial combat, received two telegrams from his parents on 30 July:

RON DANGEROUSLY ILL — PRAY HARD. MUM

RON SUFFERING INTERNAL INJURIES AND PNEUMONIA AS RESULT OF CRASH — CAN YOU COME TO GLADSTONE? DAD

Frank took compassionate leave and hitched a lift in a DC3 to arrive the day after the funeral: Ron had survived in a coma for a week, coming out of it only once to tell his distraught mother that he was in pain and could not feel his legs (both had been amputated). He was a remarkable young man, aged twenty-five, and it was my family destiny to be born to fill his legless shoes. He haunted my life, in the sense that I was middle-named (Ronald) to replace him, for my grandparents at least. Theirs was a private grief that lasted all their years — I went once with my grandmother to Ron's war grave and will never forget the anguish on her face. I grew up with them and imbibed this sense of hopelessness at how war can so arbitrarily destroy what is good.

*　　*　　*

Providence, having preserved my father in the Wirraway crash, brought me closer to existence because of his need for a pair of long socks. These

17

accessories – looking slightly ridiculous below the bare knees of the khaki shorts worn by fighting men in the tropics – were required of every young recruit. Fol, for all her trauma over Ron's death, had another son to groom for the air war against Japan, and her misery could not overcome her lower-middle-class need to send him forth to battle properly dressed. It was, of course, unthinkingly cruel of officialdom to send Fol's second son into harm's way a few weeks after the loss of her first, but such considerations do not bother officials. Frank was ordered to board the train to Townsville then fly to New Guinea and join in combat as a member of 75 Fighter Squadron. But first, insisted Fol, a trip must be made, from the grieving home in the suburbs to a city haberdasher.

And there, in the menswear department of the Cooee Clothing Store, Bernice Beattie awaited, ever ready to be the instrument of fate. She had taken the job for three days a week to supplement her husband's teacher's salary and to help the war effort. On this day she met a protective mother dragging a son who, although somewhat woebegone, had an Errol Flynn moustache and a courteous bearing.

'Long socks?' she enquired helpfully.

'Yes, he's off to Townsville tomorrow. He's to fly to New Guinea.'

Bernice leapt in: 'Townsville! I have a daughter in Townsville. He must look her up for me…'

The young man pricked up his ears. The word in the RAAF was that Townsville was a dreadful place with a severe shortage of women. You couldn't swim – the beaches were covered with barbed wire against the expected Japanese invasion – and for the same reason the local wives had been moved to Brisbane and the girls' school was closed. Having an intro-duction to a WAAAF – a blonde no less, as her mother hastily added ('but very reserved') – might be just the ticket. 'Perhaps I could give her a mes-sage from you?' offered Frank as he scented possibility. Bernice helpfully dictated Joy's name and telephone number.

When Frank arrived at Townsville, with an order to fly out to Port Moresby the next day, he dialled Joy's number from the train station. Per-haps they could meet that evening? Joy had no particular desire to step out, but at nineteen she was still a dutiful daughter: if her mother had vetted this stranger, she could at least meet him. She instructed Frank to collect her at the WAAAF barracks.

Frank Robertson turned up at the hostel at the appointed hour to request the receptionist to call Joy Beattie's room. There were other women in the badly lit foyer eyeing the evening's male visitors, and suddenly one of them let out a heart-rending scream. She fell to the floor, pointing at Frank. 'Robbie – Ron – Ron Robertson!' She thought she had seen the ghost of the man whose funeral she had attended a few weeks before and who now, as if resurrected, had walked through the door. Frank knelt down to the traumatised woman. 'No, I'm his younger brother. Tell me about him.' She had worked in the officers' mess and Ron had been her favourite – 'We all loved him.'

It was, on any score, a remarkable scene that greeted my mother – although in a war which was claiming so many lives it was not all that surprising. But it gave a certain unworldliness to my parents' first meeting, when Frank stood up to salute (really) and to introduce himself. It was not love at first sight, but you could say there was definitely emotion in the air.

Then fate took a hand, in the form of one of those bossy-booted, kind-hearted, no-nonsense alpha females who are at their best when organising and administering what would, if left to males, be chaos. She was responsible for transporting men and materials to Port Moresby and the islands, and must have had a soft spot for Joy and thought she needed a break. Her escort was gentle, well-spoken and genuine, and flying into battle the next day. Or was he? In an act of total defiance of her duty, which should have had her cashiered, she decided to remove Francis Robertson from the next day's transport roster. And the next. And the next.

So Frank and Joy were vouchsafed a full week to get to know each other and the city of Townsville, which they toured. There was barbed wire on the beach and the town was peppered with bomb craters – the Japanese were making night-time raids. There were, however, some of the attractions that followed American servicemen around the world: an open-air cinema with the latest films (*Casablanca*, inevitably), late-opening bars, and something that shocked the inner-city Methodist and Brethren-raised girl: brothels. Even more shocking was the fact that the American forces had segregated brothels – one for Negro soldiers, another for the whites. Frank and Joy took themselves off on the ferry to Magnetic Island, a pleasant sanctuary half an hour from the coast, to swim and talk and take tea at the Arcadia guesthouse.

The idyll could not last. After the week in which Frank's name had mysteriously disappeared from each day's transport roster, the commanding officer of 75 Squadron visited the main office. Joy introduced Frank – by now almost her boyfriend – to his commanding officer, who hit the roof: 'Frank Robertson! What the blue blazes are you doing here? You should have been with us a week ago! Get on the transport tomorrow, or there will be hell to pay!'

Pilot Officer Robertson was dispatched to war the next day.

Frank became a useful Kitty Hawk pilot, to judge from his reports, and he was soon promoted to flying officer. His squadron had an important late-war role, winkling the Japanese out of their redoubts up the northern coast of New Guinea and then from islands further to the north. The Kitty Hawk (the Curtiss P-40 Warhawk) was built for this role: its powerful cannon could rip through enemy aircraft fuselages or enemy armaments on the ground, and its missiles and underbelly bomb could rain havoc on enemy soldiers in dugouts and slit trenches. It was brutal, single-minded warfare: my father could never forget the smell of burning flesh as he came out of his cockpit onto a captured runway after an island assault. The Japanese, told by their demigod emperor to fight to the death and never surrender, had to be exterminated in their trenches.

They were – so much later – called 'the great generation' by their children, these fliers and fighters of the South Pacific. I have always been proud of my father for being one of them, although I suspect he was terrified much of the time, inconsolable over his brother, and simply found himself in a position where there was no alternative to courage. They had exotic women painted on their fuselages – Betty Boop was on the nose of his plane – and of course there were pleasures – the grass skirts and coconuts, swimming in clear mountain pools and coral-paved beaches, meeting the occasional infusion of nurses, and always the sunshine (which planted the melanomas that later killed many of them – sunscreen was not available).

But the war in the Pacific was as cruel as war anywhere, and as wasteful. These kids were not political: they were doing their duty, and in the moments before their deaths their minds filled with images of their mothers.

My father spent his time flying over islands occupied by Japanese troops who would have cut off his head with a ceremonial sword if he once again crash-landed. Malaria was endemic, as was dengue fever and gastroenteritis: pilots had an empty gumboot in the cockpit to serve as a toilet. His logbook is full of the hazards of flying in New Guinea – the low cloud, storms and rain squalls that would suddenly put pilots in peril over Japanese-occupied islands. Much of his work was on successful bombing and strafing raids on enemy positions, keeping a wary eye on the lethal Zeros that came out of the sun and onto their tails. The war at this point was not one-sided, although the US forces were slowly getting the upper hand. My father found the Americans fascinating, if rather naïve – they were always trying to barter their new automatic weapons for old Australian revolvers which reminded the Yanks of the guns their cowboys used in the movies. He got on well with them, and as an officer of an Allied force he was always treated generously. On one occasion he brought his flight into an American base, all four pilots low on fuel after battling with turbulent weather. He was welcomed in the officers' mess, but was surprised to find that his NCOs were sent elsewhere. Australian pilots did not pull rank and on the ground, as in the dogfight, all were equal.

Frank's tour of active duty ended when he was made an instructor – at the grand old age of twenty-two – and sent back to Australia to teach nineteen-year-olds how to handle their war machines in the tropics. It was in this last phase of the war that he experienced the thrill of flying a Spitfire. It flew like a dream, and he flew it like a dream from the first. I note in his logbook a certain number of solo flights which he would have taken for the joy of flying, in this craft that was so light to his touch after the ponderous Kitty Hawk.

It was on these private excursions that he lived the poem he later taught me:

Oh, I have slipped the surly bonds of Earth,
And danced the skies on laughter-silvered wings;

Sunward I've climbed and joined the tumbling mirth

Of sun-split clouds – and done a hundred things

You have not dreamed of – wheeled and soared and swung

High in the sunlit silence. Hov'ring there,

I've chased the shouting wind along, and flung

My eager craft through footless halls of air...

Up, up the long delirious burning blue

I've topped the windswept heights with easy grace

Where never lark or even eagle flew

And, while with silent lifting mind I've trod

The high untrespassed sanctity of space,

Put out my hand and touched the face of God.[5]

My father, tossed in the storm before his crash, had a vision of his mother – not of the Virgin Mary or a bearded man with a halo. These boys were fighting for their mothers and their families, not for religion or empire. Frank was a gentle youth deeply affected by the debriefing photos of all the bodies he had shot and bombed in his strafing raids on Japanese trenches – seventy years later he could still recall his recoil at the sight and the stench. But this was a war which threatened to destroy his family and had already taken the life of his beloved big brother: it had to be won. Which is why, midway through 1945, he was prepared to leave his comfortable and safe work as a Spitfire instructor to join the impending invasion of Japan. The word in the RAAF was that General MacArthur had no need of Australian squadrons to defeat the enemy: the only way to see action was to enlist as a naval pilot and fly off the British aircraft carrier that would be part of the invasion fleet. My father volunteered and was ordered to report to naval headquarters in Melbourne on 15 August 1945.

On that very day, he was saved by the bomb. Emperor Hirohito announced Japan's surrender, telling his people the reason – 'The enemy has begun to employ a new and most cruel bomb.' Without Hiroshima, my father would have been part of a bloody finale to war in the Pacific certain to have cost hundreds of thousands of Allied and Japanese lives – and possibly his own.

The war was over, and there was dancing in the streets. Frank Robertson decided that he would not report for naval duty. Instead, he telephoned Joy, the WAAAF corporal he had taken out in Townsville. Since the war had ended, he said, they might as well get married. She agreed, and they did. The photos show my mother in a full and flowing white bridal dress, my father in his blue RAAF uniform replete with medals, still sporting his Errol Flynn moustache.

There was nothing to stop me now: my potential existence had survived the Wirraway crash and been saved by the bomb. In due course I was born – on 30 September 1946. Coincidentally, on that day, 12,000 miles away on a foggy morning at Nuremberg, and at much the same hour, eight judges entered the courtroom to deliver their historic judgment on the Nazi leaders who had started the war. As they came in, I came out.

That is a crude way of saying that happenstance had me born on the day of the Nuremberg judgment, and that the length of my life still provides a precise temporal measure of the extent to which the international community has failed to deliver on the momentous promise of that day, namely that crimes against humanity would henceforth be deterred by punishment of their perpetrators. The judgment upon the Nazi leaders – perpetrators of the Holocaust – created the law that I came in time to practise, to judge, to write about and generally to try to develop. My textbook a half-century later was called *Crimes Against Humanity: The Struggle for Global Justice*. By a 'Crime Against Humanity', I meant a crime so heinous that the very fact a human being could commit it demeans every other member of the human race, wherever they live and whatever their culture or creed. From its iniquity arises an 'international jurisdiction' – i.e. a power in any country – to try and to punish those who command or organise it or abet it, whether they are Presidents and Prime Ministers or Generals or bureaucrats or ideologues or industrialists. Since these scoundrels are generally above or beyond the law in their own state, the Nuremberg legacy depends for its fulfilment on the establishment of international institutions of justice with power to end their impunity. My affinity with the day of the Nuremberg judgment was no more than a curious coincidence, but perhaps providence was once again at work.

Chapter Two

Baby Boomer

———————

My very first memory is of sitting in the sunshine on the sand of Bondi Beach, overlooked by the tall Norfolk pines that grew there in 1950. I heard a bell, and then saw a great wave of people erupt from the foam-capped breakers and swarm towards the shore. 'It's the shark bell,' my father explained, introducing me to the great Australian fear of death in the water. If you grew up in Sydney, the terror was magnified by the young Rupert Murdoch's afternoon tabloid, the *Daily Mirror*, with a series called 'Famous Shark Deaths', which would be rerun whenever the paper needed to boost its circulation. I can still recall the gory details – the actress taken (victims are always 'taken' not 'eaten') in two feet of water and so on. Hence the sense of relief and joy for Australians at their first plunge in the Mediterranean Sea, as they realise it is the only sea they can swim in without fear of people-eaters.

My parents managed to acquire a small flat in a dilapidated building in Bondi, overlooking a park, not far from the beach and close to the job to which my father had returned, as a teller at a branch of the Commonwealth Bank, where he earned a subsistence wage. My mother, in her later stages of pregnancy, became so worried about how they would cope with the cost of a baby that, for the first (and last) time in her life, she bought a lottery ticket. The Plymouth influence on her upbringing had inculcated the belief that all forms of gambling were evil – she would never in later life flutter on a horse race or buy shares (which she regarded as a form of gambling), but the impending cost of diapers drove her to this desperate extreme. She won £10, which would now be worth several hundred pounds, and put it aside to pay for my nappies.

I was delivered by the local GP, who also performed my circumcision. This male genital mutilation was routinely inflicted on baby boys at the time – 'Dirt might get under the foreskin,' doctors would say, or 'You must admit that the Jews know about hygiene.' The fact that it might diminish sexual pleasure in later life was not, in those prudish times, a worry.

On the subject of sex, I should mention my only memory of abuse. It happened when I was four, undergoing in hospital the unnecessary (but then routine) operation to have my tonsils taken out. It was worrying to be separated for the first time from my parents, although my handsome father would come from work every night and charm the nurses into allowing him to stay after visiting hours. There was no such thing as television, but he would bring with him a hand-held 'magic lantern' and project onto the wall the frames of a 'Tiger Tim' cartoon for the pleasure of all the children on the ward.

The next day, after I had emerged from the anaesthetic, an unknown doctor came to my bedside. I can recall him vividly – he was small, with black hair and glasses, wearing a brown cardigan. After a perfunctory chat, he put what seemed to be a leather finger-glove on his right index finger. Instinctively I felt terror and then unbearable pain as he violated me. Perhaps it was just another unnecessary medical procedure to which kids were subjected at the time. Perhaps it was not. I will never know. But I still recoil whenever a doctor suggests a prostate examination, and it may explain why I have never been drawn towards being made love to by a man. I was not assaulted again: although I walked past public toilets to and from school, I was an ugly, acne-strewn youth who was never invited in. Not until I went overseas was I solicited, with invitations I always refused – probably from the unconscious fear that gay sex would be like having my tonsils out.

All other memories of Bondi – where we lived until I was six – are unalloyedly happy. I did not realise that my parents were poor – their attention made me feel quite rich. I ran on the sand at Bondi Beach, and was taught to perform that ceremonial wriggle handed down by Australian fathers to their sons: how to hold a beach towel over your privates while extricating yourself from wet swimming trunks (on no account in the 1950s could a penis, however tiny, be displayed on a Sydney beach). I would paddle (holding my father's hand) in the rock pools, then venture with him into the old bathing sheds to inhale the warm tang of sun-burnished flesh. I would watch superbly muscled young men in posing pouches play hand-ball, then walk up to the local Oval and climb on the big World War I cannon gun. It was removed some years ago, by pacifist killjoys who foolishly feared that it would turn small children into militarists.

It was at that Oval I observed my first sporting hero, the fast bowler Alan Davidson, whose run-up was poetry in motion. Later, at age fourteen, I was thrilled to watch him attack the West Indies batting one late afternoon during the legendary 1961 Test series. There really was 'a breathless hush' – not in the close at Eton, but at the Sydney Cricket Ground. I listened to every ball bowled in that series, on the wireless. The first nail-biting Test had ended in a tie and the fourth was drawn after an incredible Australian last-wicket partnership against speed demon Wes Hall. Such were the joys for small citizens of a 'sporting nation'.

There was no preschool on offer for poorly off parents in those days, which was fortunate because mine occupied their spare time reading to me. My mother disapproved of comics, but found the money, at 2/6d a time, to buy the range of *Little Golden Books* in which I could follow the illustrations and hear of the adventures of Scuffy the Tugboat and the Five Little Firemen. We progressed to Enid Blyton's *Shadow the Sheepdog* and I became very fond of the local strays I would pat in the park, until a mastiff bit me, severely enough to induce a lifelong anxiety about big dogs. Then came larger books – notably the Australian classic *Blinky Bill*. I cried over his daddy's cruel death, shot by a man for pleasure, while Blinky the baby koala was hugging a gum tree. Such stories are thought to induce in children the desire to be kind to animals, but since the conceit was to create animals that are human, it may be that my sorrow over the pointless killing of a koala actually sparked an embryonic interest in human rather than animal rights.

Dorothy Wall, author of the *Blinky Bill* stories, could certainly pack a punch for a four-year-old.

The koala family lived so happily; never thinking of harm, or that anything could happen to disturb their little home, as all they asked for were plenty of fresh gum leaves and the warm sun. They had no idea such things as guns were in the world, or that a human being had a heart so cruel that he would take a pleasure in seeing a poor little body riddled with bullets hanging helplessly from the tree top.

Her precise description of the killing of Mr Bear, of the vigil over his body by his wife and child, then her decision to go 'far into the bush with Blinky, away from the man with his gun' was my first alert to the modern refugee experience. After that, I could never be interested in the milksop experiences of Rupert Bear, or even Winnie-the-Pooh.

Robin Hood's adventures came to me in a picture book from the Disney movie: Errol Flynn, with my father's moustache, and a photo of a large knight with a large sword, captioned 'Sir Geoffrey'. My namesake was, I was disconcerted to discover, on the wrong side of history, in the ranks of the Sheriff of Nottingham. Then, inevitably, came *The Wind in the Willows*, that anthropomorphic classic about character types I would later meet in England (with Jeffrey Archer or Alan Clark playing Mr Toad, and tabloid journalists taking the parts of stoats and weasels). I would beg my father to reread the chapter about 'The Piper at the Gates of Dawn', with its strangely comforting religiosity which could lull a small child to sleep.

When I learnt to read, I introduced myself to the unending struggle between good and evil through Biggles books, in which good – the British chaps – always triumphed. I worked my way through every volume, entirely unaware of the gay subplot debunked later by comedians or the racism which has caused librarians to remove the series from their shelves. The first pun that made me laugh, before my age reached double figures, was the suggestion that the next offering from Captain W. E. Johns would be titled 'Biggles Flies Undone'.

By this time I was talking, quite volubly, although until I was almost five my speech lacked coherence. When it did develop, it had an unmistakable English accent. 'Is his father an English migrant?' my mother would be asked in the street by people who had overheard us talking and assumed that I was the offspring of a 'ten-pound Pom'. I may have picked up these unwanted strains from announcers on the national radio (the ABC), who cultivated BBC accents, which were then thought of in Australia as 'educated'.

Frank's ambition at this point was one day to be a bank manager, and the Commonwealth soon recognised his potential and made him the assistant to a senior manager, whom he accompanied on a three-month tour of banks in America and Europe. Every day, scrupuously, my father would send us (my mother had by now, three years after me, produced a truculent baby brother, named Graeme) a postcard from wherever he happened to be. Thus my introduction to the wide world was through the rose-tinted lens of the picture postcard. The Eiffel Tower, the Waldorf-Astoria, the Rockies, the Colosseum, the Swiss Alps – places of legend and majesty I craved to visit when I grew up. Most picturesque of all were the bonnie banks and braes of Scotland, presumed to be teeming with trout, not to mention ladies of the lake and a monster in Loch Ness. I longed in daydreams to visit the land of Clan Robertson and to follow my father's slipstream to countries that, by the time I did set foot in them, were not quite so pretty.

Dad came back home straight from San Francisco with a precious gift – a genuine raccoon-skin cap, as worn by the celluloid hero Davy Crockett, king of the Wild Frontier. It was a sign of how crazes in America were beginning to rub off on Australia that small children, egged on by Walt Disney, were running around in this hairy headgear in the middle of summer, yelling 'Remember the Alamo!' as they fired their cap-pistols. Crockett helped to lose the Alamo, but the Disney film portrayed the disaster as a moral victory by courageous frontiersmen faced with a lesser breed, Zapata-moustachioed Mexicans. Donald Trump would have been taken in by the film at the same time: his memory of the Alamo may explain his obsession with fencing off the Mexican border.

When I turned seven, we moved to Eastwood, a nondescript Sydney suburb. My father bought a small brick-veneer house next to a power station, and it came – joy of joys – with a half-acre of land. A giant lizard was in occupation, which came out of its hole every year to sunbathe, flicking its blue tongue wickedly, and leaving its skin behind as a parting reptilian gift before it retreated for six months of hibernation. There was a small orchard, dropping apples and deliciously ripe peaches, and a field with a cricket pitch and a few feet to spare. I abandoned hope of emulating Alan Davidson, and shortened my run-up to bowl the sort of leg spin with which the young Richie Benaud had begun to take wickets. Beside the pitch ran a creek, the habitat for a million tadpoles and for bandicoot families in soggy burrows. The willow trees by the creek drummed in summer with cicadas. We would pour water down their holes to make them emerge for their brief earthly sojourn and shake them to make them sing. All over Sydney, wanton boys were pulling wings off not flies but cicadas – insects did not merit the regard we had for Blinky Bill's dad or Bambi's mum.

Best of all in this new house, beyond the creek was a grassy knoll that led to some tennis courts. This became my true sport, and I neglected my leg spin to work on my backhand. I soon developed a dynamite forehand and a serviceable serve, and started to hit, quite naturally, a hard and accurate double-handed backhand, in the hope of one day representing Australia in the Davis Cup (my first career choice). But this stroke was unacceptable to Australian coaches at the time: double-handed backhands were for girls (they used the ultimate put-down: it was 'sissy') and I had to be weaned off it. I have never forgiven them: my tennis career was subsequently blighted by a vulnerable, limp-wristed backhand, which I would run around whenever possible.

Nineteen fifty-three was the most exciting Davis Cup of all time. I listened, breathless, to every point, crouched over the radio by my bed on our glassed-in front veranda. The top Australian player, Frank Sedgman, had turned professional, and our defence of the cup against the might of America was dependent on two nineteen-year-olds, Lew Hoad and Ken Rosewall. On day one Rosewall lost to the American top gun Tony Trabert, and Hoad beat Vic Seixas; but the next day Australia's legendary coach Harry Hopman uncharacteristically miscalculated and pulled Rosewall from the doubles, which Australia lost, and was in consequence 2–1 down. The tension on day three was unbearable: Hoad eventually triumphed over Trabert, winning the fifth set 7–5, and Rosewall won the final match the next day. I have never felt prouder or more patriotic. I'd found a real sporting hero in Hoad: when his autobiography was published, I loitered in a bookshop to watch him sign copies. I was eight and had no money to buy his book, but I finally plucked up courage and asked him to sign a serviette. He looked down at me with his dreamy blue eyes and I was smitten. If only I'd had a mobile phone and could have asked him for a selfie!

Later, when I was sixteen, I watched Hoad play the match of his, and my, life. It was around the time Rod Laver, the reigning amateur champion, turned professional. Lew had lost his touch – he was overweight, out of condition, into drink and cigarettes. So the promoters of Laver's debut as a pro thought it would be a good idea for Rod to thrash Lew as a warm-up, then battle it out the next day with Ken Rosewall, who was the reigning professional champ. But Lew took himself in hand for three months, stopped drinking, lost weight, trained, and beat Rosewall in four terrific sets at White City. I was there, forever inspired to win against the odds, on court or in court. I did finally get to play with Lew, many years later at a charity gig. I warmed up like a demon, but in the doubles match we played together I muffed my volleys, double-faulted, and even failed to return an underarm serve from the aged Vic Seixas. In tennis, as in love, never partner your hero – you cannot help but let them down.

I am often asked whether anyone inspired me when I was very young. People always expect me to name Nelson Mandela or Martin Luther King or Clarence Darrow. When I'm feeling truthful, I tell them about Lew Hoad.

*　　*　　*

In 1952 I became aware – from the radio, although we were prepared for the news by our teachers at school – that King George was dying. He had been taken ill in London while Princess Elizabeth was in Kenya, at a luxury resort called Treetops. A clear but crazy image came into my dreams of a man with a crown, in bed in a tree, below which a pride of lions crouched – kings of the jungle paying their tribute to the King of England. I was a right little royalist, especially after the coronation, when I insisted that my parents buy me coloured picture books so I could be struck by awe at the solid gold coaches with their red plush seating, the bejewelled crowns and orbs and other impedimenta of royalty.

This changed just one year later when the young Queen came to visit her Australian dominion. 'Every woman's dream of beauty steps ashore' announced the *Sydney Morning Herald*. Every schoolchild was summoned to see her at the Sydney Cricket Ground, on a day of 35°C heat. We were made to wait six hours in this burning cauldron: kids all around me were fainting from sunstroke (there was no cover) or clutching diarrhoea-wracked little stomachs. I was eight but I could recognise torture when I saw it, even if I did not know the term for the deliberate and unjustified infliction of severe pain. The young Elizabeth passed in a closed car which sped around the track, her limp arm poking out of the window.

The day was a cruel farce: I felt cheated, but also slightly amazed. How could Australia go nuts for an English monarch to the extent of offering up to her its children in inhumane homage? I really did think republican thoughts, without being able to put that name to them. I could do that by the time I was twelve, when the whole disgraceful spectacle was repeated, this time merely to welcome the Queen Mother (who at least waved to us from an open jeep). I was critical of Prime Minister Menzies, an extreme Anglophile, who on a later royal visit looked at the Queen adoringly and emoted, 'I did but see her passing by and yet I'll love her till I die.' I did but see her passing by, but so quickly that it made me a lifelong republican.

Kathy Lette and I are sometimes invited to the palace, invitations which, as a rule, we graciously accept. We do our best to entertain Her Maj – I may, after all, be one of her more distant relatives, on the German side. On one occasion my wife wore a suit emblazoned with corgis, which was greeted with a broad royal smile. (As you can see from the dirty look on the face of the flunkey in the photograph, Brenda is not often allowed to be amused.) This was at a celebration for the Commonwealth, and I sat next to her while the orchestra played 'God Save the Queen'. I noticed that she tapped her feet to the tune. We all sang the words and she seemed to sing along – 'God Save Our Gracious Me', I suppose.

Our presence was publicised, and we were berated by some foolish commentators in Australia for betraying our republican principles. They don't seem to understand either the virtues of politeness or Kathy's point about accepting invites to Buck House: 'Of course they are dinosaurs, but who wouldn't want to see dinosaurs in their natural habitat?'

*   *   *

The Robertsons were a middle-class family in a middle-class house in a middle-class suburb. Eastwood was not exactly middle class, it was a mix, in those days when your 'class' in Sydney was deducible from your household newspapers. We took the Fairfax paper, the *Sydney Morning Herald*, while our working-class neighbours took the Packer *Telegraph*. Those with no class at all took Rupert Murdoch's evening tabloid, the *Daily Mirror*. My mother wouldn't have it in the house – she noted that the men in our street who read the *Daily Mirror* were the ones who beat their wives.

The only other reading material in our home was a series of *Reader's Digest* condensed books. I didn't understand the 'condensing' process (it sounded like condensed milk, which was also sickly sweet) but the stories were always meant to impart some high-minded moral. There was one that made a particular impact on me, about a Scottish general practitioner devoted to his country clients, visiting their far-flung farms without demur whenever duty called. One night he saved the life of a wealthy businessman, who insisted he take as a reward a block of shares in an obscure company. The price rose to a dizzying height and the good doctor realised he was rich. One day an urgent telegram came from his benefactor, which he put aside because he was rushing to an emergency. When he opened it the next day, he discovered it said, 'Sell shares immediately – market about to collapse.' He realised, as he went back to work a poor man, that he had saved the life of an insider trader who had repaid him in the same crooked coin. The moral was that virtue is its own reward, and this I actually believed and acted upon for many years, until I came to understand that my favourite boyhood story really means that no good deed goes unpunished.

My mother's favourite maxim, instilled from the cradle, was that money cannot buy happiness. This was consoling when we had none, and was given a particular emphasis on my impressionable young mind by Australia's first kidnapping, of a boy my own age whose parents had won the lottery. The police mishandled the ransom demand and the boy was killed. 'That's what can happen when you win the lottery. Money does not buy you happiness,' pronounced my mother, insisting she was glad that her one lottery win had yielded only money for my nappies, not the attractions and distractions of great wealth. The evidence for this proposition seemed overwhelming, and I went through most of my life believing it, despite my wife's elucidation of the proverb: 'Money does not buy happiness. It just buys yachts and five-star hotels and diamond jewellery – I quite like the sort of misery that money buys.'

My parents were not religious, but they thought I should have the chance to embrace the Anglican God. So off I went, every Sabbath, to Sunday school. I quite enjoyed this for a few years and routinely achieved first-class honours in state-wide Sunday school exams, picking up a working knowledge of the Bible which was later to become useful in defending *Gay News* at the Old Bailey on the charge of blasphemy. My father took me to a Billy Graham crusade – the biggest excitement in Sydney for years – and I observed the tricks of this over-the-top evangelist as he enticed the depressed and impressionable of Sydney (there were a lot of them) down the aisles to give him money and sign a book which declared they were now 'saved'. I was very young and very tempted to join them, but I was saved by my father, whom the hokum could not budge. It vaguely occurred to me, however, by the age of nine, that if there was any truth in religion, it logically followed that it should be the most important thing in one's life. Hence my second career choice: I would become a missionary. The job would entail foreign travel, death insurance (access to heaven) and plentiful opportunity to preach. There would, I gathered, be a certain frisson in converting cannibals – ending up in the cooking pot would be an ever-present possibility, but at least I would have a fast track to paradise through their alimentary canals.

In time, however, I had to choose, not between God and Mammon but between God and tennis. My game had progressed well enough for me to be selected in the district's Under-16 team, but our matches were on

Sunday, which conflicted with church confirmation classes. I was given a dispensation and was ready to be received into the church by the laying on of hands. The hands to be laid upon me were those of Archbishop Gough, the rather ridiculous upper-class Englishman who headed the Anglican Church in Sydney. Just a few weeks before the ceremony he had been quoted on the front page of the *Mirror* declaiming, 'The younger generation is wallowing in a mire of sexuality.' I was not doing much – or indeed any – wallowing, but the good archbishop certainly was – with a number of married parishioners within the range of his archbishopric. He was cited in secret divorce petitions and the scandal was hushed up by the media – even by the *Mirror*, as proprietors were 'leant upon' by an establishment that did not want the 'established' church to suffer embarrassment. The public was not allowed to know and the promiscuous primate was packed off to the smallest parish in England.

*   *   *

I went to Eastwood Public School – a venerable institution, as primary schools go, with the asphalt playground which left its marks on schoolboy shins, and a cricket pitch on which I experienced the thrilling sensation of thwacking a perfectly timed cover drive (though when I played for the school as opening batsman, I made more runs snicking through the slips than thwacking through the covers).

School life was uneventful. History, incredibly, was not taught at all, and English amounted to lessons in grammar rather than in drama or literature – deemed unnecessary and possibly corrupting, the state school syllabus reflecting the philistine values of the Menzies era. We did have a 'play festival' once – in 1955 – when I enjoyed the role of the wise and judicious Mr Badger in *The Adventures of Toad*.

There was the cane, of course, overused in all schools of the period, and routinely prescribed at Eastwood for the most minor infractions. It was administered by a kindly old ex-serviceman whose hand shook so much – probably from delirium tremens – that the beating rarely hurt. Had it done so, I might have been inclined to rebel. But the only trace of any sense of injustice that I can find in my prepubescent schoolbooks (loyally preserved by my mother) was in a composition on the subject of 'My School'. In it, I inveighed against the hypocrisy of teachers for disciplining children they'd seen 'scratching themselves' in the playground, 'as I often see teachers scratching themselves'. This scored a hit, and I felt a thrill of satisfaction when I saw a group of teachers passing around my essay and laughing – rather defensively, I thought. Tight underwear produced in the summer rashes that did bring on an urge to scratch one's balls and my criticism deterred the use of the cane as punishment for giving in to the itch – my first blow struck for human rights.

Eastwood did not lack culture. There was a cinema, where small boys could roll Jaffas (an orange-coated ball of chocolate) down the aisles and watch endless black-and-white adventures of Hopalong Cassidy, in which the ageing cowboy hero would embark on different ways of slaughtering Indians. I was never much attracted to this genocidaire on horseback – when we played cowboys and Indians, it was only fair that the Indians should sometimes win.

Much more excitement came when I was almost ten and Eastwood suddenly became the cultural capital of Australia. This was the new age of television, launched in 1956 when Bruce Gyngell (later, Mrs Thatcher's acolyte and founder of TV-AM) appeared on screen saying, 'Good evening, and welcome to television.' Channel 7 built its studios at Eastwood, around the corner from our street, and began to record game shows that entranced the nation. I went to some recording sessions – invariably with breakdowns in the primitive technology – and might well have imbibed the adrenalin and some of the techniques I was later to use for my own shows for British and Australian television. I cannot be sure whether those visits to the Channel 7 studios are responsible for my pleasure in performing on television, but I did feel a nostalgic delight when I returned there forty years later, by which time I was a UN judge, to make a cameo appearance in *Home and Away*. You can take the boy out of Eastwood, but you can't take Eastwood out of the boy.

As I think back to those formative years between eight and twelve, I have to acknowledge that the greatest influence came from ABC (the BBC equivalent) radio. I was never interested in their kids' programme, a riff on Jason and the Argonauts, although the legend of armed men springing from the bloody soil of an invaded land has been a useful metaphor in writing about the dangers of military intervention. I remember only one altercation with my parents in those years, and it was over whether I could stay up late to listen to the end of an ABC radio performance of *Hamlet*. My mother insisted it went on past my bedtime; I pointed out that it was said to be the greatest play ever written, and I wanted to hear how it ended. My father was called and I was physically removed to my bedroom, hurling imprecations about their ignorance. It was a bad call on both sides: they could have granted me this indulgence, and I should have taken their decision with some humility. But it brought home to me the important fact that those in authority – even those you love, with your best interests at heart – are not always right.

What brought my ear to the wireless at appointed hours on most evenings were the BBC comedies – *Take It From Here*, *Hancock's Half Hour*, *Educating Archie* and so on. I would note and venerate the names of the writers – Galton and Simpson, Muir and Norden, the latter two featuring in *My Word!*, a favourite show in which their wordplay was dazzling and their seeming ability to deconstruct well-known quotations amazing. It was my introduction to the art of rehearsed spontaneity, and these men were my gods of insightful comedy. Many years later, when I bumped into Denis Norden shopping in a delicatessen in north London I almost fell at his feet, and when I heard that a friend was to marry Frank Muir's daughter I envied his marriage to a goddess, although I had never set eyes on her.

Best of all was *The Goon Show*, with writer and star Spike Milligan. This was a wonderful world for a small boy growing up in an outer-Sydney suburb, although it was wonderful for those growing up anywhere (in palaces, for example, where Prince Charles became a fan). It was radio at its best, enabling the attuned listener to conjure in his imagination a surreal world of exploding puddings and the dolly mixture of the British Empire. There was nothing to rival it on television, at least until Monty Python, years later, made a brilliant attempt. I idolised Spike and dragged my somewhat uncomprehending father to the recordings of some of his

ABC shows. Milligan was a regular visitor to Sydney – his mother lived at Woy Woy (a name as far-fetched as any he invented) – and in due course he acquired an Australian stalker as in love with his imagination as I. Her name was Kathy Lette.

Later in life, through Kathy, I met many comedians, some of whom – Stephen Fry, Billy and Pamela Connolly, Rory Bremner, Barry Humphries – became friends. Comics rather than lawyers graced our dinner table with an anarchic ebullience that my own profession is trained to subdue. Delight in humour transcends politics – many comedians are conservative, but hours in their company never exposed political differences. They have a special insight into the absurdities of life for which they should always be valued – a point overlooked by Australia House in the years when it banned Barry because his caricature diplomat, Sir Les Patterson, was 'bad for Australia's image abroad'. In fact, it much enhanced that image in a Britain which loved the kind of self-mockery that did not come easily to those from other nations (Canadians or New Zealanders, for example).

School life took a turn for the better when I was selected to spend my last two years of primary education in what was called an 'opportunity class'. I was never quite sure what it was an opportunity for, other than to be educated by a remarkable young teacher, Lionel Phelps, who taught me to think. Phelps made us read the *Sydney Morning Herald* every day, and to criticise the doings of grand men with three names – like John Foster Dulles and Robert Gordon Menzies. 'Ming' was at the time an international laughing stock for his one attempt at world attention – he had allowed himself to be used by a dishonest British government planning with Israel and France to invade Egypt and recover the Suez Canal. Menzies's role was to threaten President Nasser to give up the canal, or else. It was a despicable role, and Nasser called his bluff ('You send this Australian mule to threaten me'). Menzies was ridiculed, particularly by the Eisenhower administration, which deplored this last throw of the colonial dice. Meanwhile, US Secretary of State Dulles was justifying CIA interventions (the CIA being led by his brother) in small islands in the Caribbean, while Khrushchev was preparing to khrusch freedom in Hungary. By age eleven, I knew what was happening in the world, but the

Cold War barriers seemed so immutable that it was impossible to think of making it a better place.

Mr Phelps encouraged other enthusiasms. He set inventive composition subjects such as writing *Goon Show* scripts, and urged us to try our hands at poetry. Only one of my efforts survives in my class notebook:

> There was a young lady named Helen
> Whose breasts were the shape of a melon
> But it also appears
> She had cauliflower ears,
> Which is why she was so meloncholy.

Helen would have been a figure of my eleven-year-old imagination – Eastwood was strictly segregated and the only girls in my orbit were those I met at Sunday school. One I did rather like was Meredith Oakes. We met up many years later when she was a distinguished musicologist in London, having written the libretto for Thomas Adès's opera *The Tempest*. Her mother produced a photo of us together in a class at St Philip's Sunday School in Eastwood, and I hope our learning of the Bible has come in as handy for her as a librettist as it has for me as a defender of blasphemers.

My primary schooling at Eastwood left me, by age twelve in 1958, with some degree of self-confidence but no clear ambition. I was losing interest in a missionary life and the single-handed backhand was not improving. I cannot recall any interest in law, although I have found among my mother's papers a copy of an Empire Day speech I gave the school when I was eleven. It eschewed the usual grovels to the Queen and noted that 'the true spirit of the British Empire' was shown when 'its people combined to defeat the Kaiser'. (I did not know then that he might be a relative.) I went on to make this point:

> British justice, envy of the world today, dates back to 1215, when King John was forced to sign the Magna Carta. Its main clause is the basis of British law today. It states that: 'No free man shall be taken, or imprisoned, or deprived

of his property, or outlawed, or exiled, or in any way harmed, save by the lawful judgment of his equals.'

There, at this young age, I was unconsciously piping a principle I would later intone in Commonwealth courtrooms around the world. That, of course, would have gone over the heads of my schoolmates and their parents – and probably myself – when piped in my unbroken voice in the Eastwood Odeon in 1957.

* * *

The attraction of being in an opportunity class was that your card was marked for onward transmission to a selective grammar school. But by the time my turn came, the New South Wales education department had changed its policy, and kids in my year were streamed off to a new and very unselective comprehensive that had just opened in Epping, a suburb next door to Eastwood. My parents were inconsolable and offered to pay for me to go to Sydney's top private school. I refused. I would like to be able to think of myself at age eleven a precocious progressive, firm in my support for state education, but this political principle had nothing to do with my decision. I simply worked out that I could spend an hour longer in bed if I went to Epping Boys High School. I went to this comprehensive school out of youthful laziness, not youthful idealism. So it happened – for better or worse – that the next five years were spent in a rustic atmosphere of fields and gum trees at a school with no history, no old boys, no girls and no reputation to live up or down to.

Epping's motto was 'Strive to Achieve', but with the emphasis very much on 'Strive'. We were mainly from hard-working families with fathers who had returned from the war and mothers who dutifully described their occupation as 'domestic duties'. Our faces and races were monochrome: the White Australia policy precluded any other colour (freckles were allowed). We were expected to learn how to become useful members of society, a step up from our parents, whose ambitions were for us to earn more money than they did, perhaps as engineers or solicitors or accountants (actuaries were a popular aspiration, since they were reported by the *Sydney Morning Herald* to be in the best-paid profession). The notion that a son might become an actor or a poet or a ballet dancer would have been viewed with horror, although a top sportsman would have been very acceptable.

Our school, which had only been operational for two years, was still in the process of being built. In my first year, we were all ordered to bring from our gardens some samples of kikuyu grass, which we proceeded to plant on the sports field (it remains there sixty years later – my proud contribution to my old school). My father became the mainstay of the P&C (Parents and Citizens Association): by this time he had been made registrar of the Commonwealth Bank – a title that gave him some heft with the Education Department, which he badgered to provide us with a teacher of Latin. This was regarded as a luxury for state schools, although every wealthy private school had one, but he thought the ancient language might be useful if his son ever chose a career in law. It wasn't, as it happens, although five years of its study did help my sex life by enabling me to translate the erotic poetry of Catullus.

My sex life needed all the help it could get. Puberty brought the teenage equivalent of the scourge, the acne that was Black Death to social life, and which scarred me until university. Red pustules covered my face: each morning I would take a blackhead extractor to the overnight pimples, covering the bathroom mirror with ejaculations of pus. I was sent repeatedly to a 'skin specialist' – an avuncular doctor who prescribed a sulphurous solution which I had to apply every morning and which made my face raw and stained purplish-white, and even less sightly than before. It left the indelible impression on my mind that I was ugly and unfit for female company, so I retreated to my books and rarely accepted invitations to parties. In any event, the girls I met on the train displayed no interest in me whatsoever. In Australia, to paraphrase Dorothy Parker, girls never made passes at boys with A passes. Intellectual achievement could not get me a partner to the school dance. It was then that my mother decided I must learn some social graces: she enrolled me in a course at Miss June Winter's Academy of Dance.

There, in a converted shed near Epping Station, I had the most excruciating experience of my teenage life. It was soon clear that I got no rhythm, and had two left feet. The moment of truth arrived with the 'Ladies' Choice'. The boys were lined up against one wall, with the girls about to venture, like heat-seeking missiles, towards their target. My friend Roger and I quaked with apprehension – there was one beautiful and rather forward girl whom we both fancied and she made a move in our direction. To my brief delight she selected me rather than my rival, a generosity I repaid by treading on her toes. She did not make the same mistake again.

I could never get the hang of ballroom dancing, and my embarrassment was only relieved because a fat American named Chubby Checker had made a dance called 'the twist' so popular that Miss Winter had to include it in our repertoire. It enabled you to distance yourself from your partner and gyrate within your own space, without contact with your partner's body, or with her toes. A few years later, at university balls, I would manage to sway and smooch to 'Hey Jude' and other Beatles standards, but any other form of dance still eludes me. I am probably the only person in the UK never to have watched *Strictly Come Dancing* – the very sight of it would, I fear, bring back excruciating memories of Miss Winter.

As for sex, in the '50s it really was a terrible business for sensitive teenagers. There was no sex education, apart from a ludicrous quasi-evangelical group called the Father and Son Movement, which was invited to the school for one evening each year. Embarrassed fathers were required to sit with their even more embarrassed sons to watch magic-lantern slides of tadpoles swimming towards a cartoon uterus, and endless close-ups of sores on male groins and organs – the consequence, we were assured, of sex with any woman who was not our wife. The wages of sin were death, and we were inculcated with paranoid fears of venereal disease. The Father and Son outfit was also militantly opposed to masturbation – their literature hinted that it might cause eye-sight loss, mental derangement, general ill-health and, worst of all, perpetual prepubescence. Hence a cartoon of a grown boy riding a child's rocking chair, with the caption 'Growing up means leaving childish things behind' – only primary school boys would pay any attention to their willies, which could thereafter curl up as if in hibernation but spring back into action on the wedding night. It was all too silly for words.

Nor was it the only absurdity. Australia was the most censorious society in the free world, keeping out books with the same determination as it kept out black people. *Lady Chatterley's Lover* was acquitted at the Old Bailey obscenity trial in 1960, but not even Robert Menzies's Anglophilia would allow him to permit it into Australia. The story I later heard from his Minister for Air, Fred Osborne, who lived nearby, was that the Cabinet all assumed that Menzies would respect the British decision and allow the book entry. They were taken aback when he stormed into the Cabinet meeting to declare, 'I've read this dreadful book. And I am not going to allow my wife to read it.' They did not have the courage to disagree so the Dame Pattie Menzies protection test determined in my youth our federal level of sexual tolerance for imported literature.

I wonder now what drove these moral paragons – were they somehow trying to conceal their own depravity by pretending to electors that they were saving us from sin? Nobody ever called them out, and the incidence of rape kept on increasing (although not in the statistics: as a result of their stigmatising of sex, most rape victims were deterred from report-ing the assaults against them). Liberation of a kind, at least for men, had come to America in the '50s with the publication of *Playboy* – it was, of course, banned from Australia. Film censorship was just as stringent: I recall the loud-mouthed moderator of the Methodist Church describing cinema-going as 'like travelling through a sewer in a glass-bottom boat'. More evidence, I think, that the dirt was all in the minds of the men who set Australia's moral standards.

Angry though I still am about those wowsers, I must admit that cen-sorship did me some good. It forced me to hunt out literature the censors were too stupid to have banned. I had read that Rabelais, for example, was pretty ... well, 'Rabelaisian', and I found a copy of *Gargantua and Panta-gruel* on the innocent shelves of Eastwood Public Library. It had enough scatology to last a lifetime. There was Boccaccio (*The Decameron*) and Chaucer (*The Canterbury Tales*), with rude sections you had to read into the books to find. And, immortally, *Ulysses*, which I forced the school to buy me as a prize for coming top in maths. Who could have a more erotic love affair than with Molly Bloom, or with Joyce's own wife, the blowsy barmaid Nora Barnacle, on whom she was based?

My lifelong aversion to censorship – both in ideological terms when it amounts to denying the right to information or opinion, and for the practical reason that it is usually counterproductive – really began at Epping when I discovered how it was being used to disadvantage all comprehensive school kids in my year. The background to this scandal was that we were all studying, in 1962, aged sixteen, for our Leaving Certificate – the equivalent of A-levels and our passport to the future. English was a compulsory subject and *The Tempest* was our set text. We were issued with a cheap edition which, on first reading, struck me as a play that was deeply flawed, inhumane and racist. It was the story of Prospero, Duke of Milan, being exiled to an island with his daughter, but taking books that enabled him to learn sufficient magic to confound his enemies and create a brave new world. Except that his seemingly cruel and unjust treatment of his own servant – the indigenous Caliban – undercut the whole message of this apparently humourless text. Then one day on the train, I noticed some private schoolkids of my age with a larger book – a different edition of *The Tempest*, with more pages. I hastened to buy their edition, which was published by Methuen in London, and discovered a different, rather wonderful and funny play.

It turned out that some idiot in the New South Wales Education Department had determined that state schoolboys were only fit for the bowdlerised edition, in which the absurd Dr Bowdler had removed not only all the comedy and rude jokes ('This ship is as leaky as an unstanched wench', 'Monster, I do smell all horse piss') but any reference to a main fulcrum of the plot – Caliban's attempted rape of Prospero's daughter. State school kids would therefore have no understanding of Prospero's motivation for punishing Caliban, a handicap for analysing the play that would not afflict our wealthy school rivals.

I wrote an angry denunciation of the Education Department – my first piece of investigative journalism – in the school newspaper, and the very fact that educators could betray education in this way still rankles. But what made this censorship not only stupid but actually absurd was that surgically removing all – and even inferential – references to sex meant that state school kids would never read a word of Prospero's speech in favour of premarital chastity, as he warns his daughter's suitor in terms that a seventeenth-century Father and Son Movement would have applauded:

If thou dost break her virgin knot before
All sanctimonious ceremonies may
With full and holy rite be ministered,
No sweet aspersion shall the heavens let fall
To make this contract grow, but barren hate,
Sour-eyed disdain, and discord shall bestrew
The union of your bed with weeds so loathly
That you shall hate it both. Therefore take heed,
As Hymen's lamps shall light you.

Hymen's lamps had to be dimmed and virgin knots left untied for my exams in 1962. And this was just one small example of the hypocrisy that was characteristic of the city in which I was growing up. It was a strange experience, reading newspapers and watching television that presented a political and social world so different from the real one. Cover-ups were commonplace: in the Anglican Church, Archbishop Gough preached against promiscuity while secretly indulging in it himself; meanwhile, Catholic confessors ignored or excused the paedophilia that was rampant in their own priesthood. The state government was irredeemably corrupt, yet not a word was mentioned in the media until a politician was stupid enough to be caught (like the Minister for Prisons, who had been accepting regular bribes to release prisoners early).

The New South Wales police force was thoroughly corrupt as well, with senior officers, praised by the media for putting down anti-Vietnam demonstrations, doing a nice line in protection rackets with abortionists or setting up serious crimes with their friends, the serious criminals. These were subjects that would never be mentioned in the newspapers because of defamation laws inherited from England, which awarded large sums in damages to anyone whose reputation was lowered by published criticism. I later spent much time trying to reform these laws, in England and the Commonwealth – there is no doubt the catalyst was my schoolboy disgust at how they had whitewashed the news during my youth in Sydney, a city of dirty secrets.

There was no obvious outlet for political views in school, other than through debating in competitions with other schools. This was quite a big deal, as teams of three would vie for this cup or that shield. I was third speaker (or 'whip') for the school team, which meant engaging in off-the-cuff criticism of the other side. We were doing very well in the main competition until we met the top grammar school – an engagement in which we were beaten by a bad adjudicator. We had to propose the motion 'Melbourne needs 50,000 Negroes'. This had recently been suggested by a visiting American sociologist who was vilified by the press for this implied criticism of White Australia.

I had not thought much about the White Australia policy until we began our one-hour preparation – all we could think of at first was to argue that Melbourne was so boring it needed some jazzing up. But as the minutes ticked on, and we talked about our monochrome existence – no coloured faces in the school, not even a Chinese restaurant in Eastwood – we began to understand and agree with the viewpoint of the alien sociologist. The racist assumptions in 1901 of Australian's founding fathers – kick the Pacific Islanders out of Queensland, forbid the entry of slanty-eyed Chinese, treat Aboriginals as subhuman (in 1962 they could not even be counted in the census) – had consigned us to a dull incomprehension of what amounted to humanity. We convinced ourselves, if not the adjudicator, and I like to think of the moment as some sort of turning point in our thinking about the racist mindset of the nation in which we had, by happenstance, been born. It also aroused the interesting thought that radical, non-conformist ideas might be right – or turn out to be on the right side of history.

As for the politics of the school playground, Epping was a small, struggling school and I could not find anyone who would bother to help set up a student council. The headmaster, H. E. (Hector) McGregor, was as good as they came in state schools: a grave and serious man with a prominent hearing aid, he had published a book on English grammar that we all had loyally to study. I could never thereafter split an infinitive, and it had a permanent influence on corrections to girlfriends and my children: 'Don't say "quite unique" – something is either unique or it is not'; '"Disinterested" means impartial, not uninterested'. Kathy dubbed me Conan the Grammarian.

Like most ambitious teenagers, I was dogged by the question – from teachers and relatives and everyone I met – of what I wanted to be when I grew up. I had by now abandoned interest in becoming a missionary or tennis player, but the school was good at careers advice, subjecting pupils to numerous 'aptitude tests'– and it turned out that my perfect occupation would be that of an orchestra conductor. I liked the idea, but I could not read music. I had lost interest in maths, which ruled out accountancy or the preferred profession of an actuary, and despite my attraction to the *Reader's Digest* doctor, I wasn't sure about trying my unsteady hand at surgery. I began to wonder whether my facility at debating meant that lawyer might be an attainable career choice, although I had never met one.

At age fourteen I did a speed-reading course and obtained a list of the world's best books. I borrowed them from libraries and began to enjoy the pleasure of literature uncondensed. The most impactful was *Great Expectations*, the story of the convict Magwitch, who returns from Botany Bay to confront, in a memorable scene, his unwitting beneficiary at Pip's flat in the Temple (by a coincidence that could be called Dickensian, the very flat allocated to me after I became a Master of the Middle Temple forty years later). The character in the book who most intrigued was the lawyer, Mr Jaggers, the *deus ex machina* of the plot. Most readers find him slightly sinister and he is not one of Dicken's popular or inspiring characters (if you want a hero, try Sidney Carton). But I was gripped, from the moment he appears at the Three Jolly Bargemen pub to explain the presumption of innocence to bar-room readers of a tabloid who have presumed the guilt of a client suspected of murder. He remains in the book a figure of self-controlled power and professional purpose, dedicated unemotionally to saving the lives of wretches at the Old Bailey who manage to pay his fees. For all the guilty secrets he keeps as a counsellor, it is his good deed that is the wellspring of the plot. Mr Jaggers was the first lawyer I met, through the imagination (grounded in his early life as a court reporter) of Charles Dickens. He was someone I thought, at age fourteen, that I might like someday to be like.

It was censorship that finally determined my career. In my final year at school I got hold of a book that influenced me profoundly: *The Trial of Lady Chatterley*. The Menzies government, not content with banning Lawrence's novel, had banned this account of the trial, published as a Penguin Special, as well, on the grounds that a transcript of the celebrated court case might 'deprave and corrupt' Dame Pattie Menzies and the wives of Australia's ruling classes. This idiocy provoked a courageous Sydney bookseller to arrange for friends in England to transcribe by hand every word of the book – legal arguments, witness cross-examination, judge's summing up and all – onto thirty-two tightly spaced 'air letters', the fastest means of communication in those days. The pages entered Australia as personal mail and so eluded the censors. *The Trial of Lady Chatterley* was then reconstituted and printed in a samizdat edition, and a copy fell into my schoolboy hands. What I found exciting was not the surplus of four-letter words, nor the erudite debate over D. H. Lawrence's place in literature, but the conduct of the trial by the book's defenders, Gerald Gardiner QC (soon to be Labour Lord Chancellor) and Jeremy Hutchinson QC. Their court tactics replaced those of Lew Hoad in my pantheon, and by the end of my final year my ambition had settled. I was now a prefect, with a particularly cheeky first-year class to oversee (and no power to cane them, as they usually deserved). 'What you going to be when you grow up, sir?' they asked me in assembly line.

'I am going to be a barrister, at the Old Bailey in England,' I replied, to my own surprise as much as theirs.

They burst into disbelieving laughter. 'Some hope, sir,' said one. 'How many pimples you got on your face, sir?' said another.

I smiled: thanks to censorship, I had found my vocation, just as (many years later) I found Gerald Gardiner to help with *Spycatcher*, joined my learned friend Jeremy Hutchinson for censorship trials heard in the Old Bailey, and accepted the invitation of Penguin Books to write a foreword to a new edition of *The Trial of Lady Chatterley*.[6]

Meantime, some cultural interests were developing: I could neither sing nor play an instrument, and had no knowledge of music other than the Top 40, which I would listen to with Auntie Peg – 'Volare' and 'How Much Is That Doggie in the Window?' One day I walked into the school assembly hall when a rehearsal of *Trial by Jury* was in process, and was smitten by the wittiness of the words and the rum-te-tum of the music. I became an instant Gilbert & Sullivan fan. Records (long-playing discs, in those days) were too expensive, but providentially an EMI cut-price operation, the World Record Club, offered some G&S operas that had been recorded in East Germany (to avoid D'Oyly Carte copyright) by good British casts. I soon knew all the words, and moved on to the sexier Offenbach, in clever translations rendered by the Sadler's Wells opera company. I was excited when the company brought their version of *Orpheus in the Underworld* to Sydney's Tivoli Theatre and I persuaded our Latin teacher that she had to attend – she was quite shocked that in Offenbach's version the reason for Orpheus turning round to Eurydice (and thus losing her to hell) was not the magnetic pull of his love but her thrust of a candle up his posterior.

Love of operetta led to love of opera – a matter of logic, I think, rather than any genetic inheritance from Joe Kroll. For my twentieth birthday, my mother took me to see *La Traviata* so I could thrill to the trill of Joan Sutherland, who was accompanied by a striking and actually quite slim Italian tenor named Luciano Pavarotti, in the days before he became, in every sense, great.

Orchestral concerts never enthused me, perhaps because attendance was compulsory for school concerts at the Town Hall, but also because they did not have words. The Sydney Symphony Orchestra had previously had one of the world's best conductors, Englishman Sir Eugene Goossens, to whom Australian music owes two crucial discoveries: Joan Sutherland (working in a typing pool) and the need for Sydney to build an opera house. He was, alas, another victim of censorship – disgraced and deported after the vice squad (egged on by the *Daily Mirror*) arrested him at the airport for importing indecent photographs secreted beneath the score of *Salome*. When he claimed that his butler must have done it, by packing some Continental porn before he left Europe, he was confounded by the fact that the face on some of the photographs was that of Rosaleen Norton, a habituée of Sydney's red light district, Kings Cross, who had introduced him to what they called 'sex magic'. It was the perfect tabloid story – the grand maestro brought low by the 'witch of the Cross'. Although her magic was no more than the practice of fellatio, this struck puritanical Sydney as demonic. The finest pervert ever to raise his baton to conduct the Sydney Symphony was thrown out of the country.

Theatre offered much more thoughtful entertainment. By good fortune, a close friend had a younger brother who had won the part of the Artful Dodger in the stage version of *Oliver!* His mother took us to see it, and to other shows, including a memorable *Saint Joan* played by the remarkable actress Zoe Caldwell, who hooked me on drama for ever. My own debut came in the school production of Douglas Stewart's *Ned Kelly*, in which I played the manager of a bank robbed by the outlaws. I had to appear without trousers (the gang had arrived while I was in the bath), so my mother made sure the shirt I had hastily to put on was long enough not merely to cover my manhood, but almost to cover my kneecaps.

School, like everything else in Australia, broke up for long Christmas holidays. I spent these at Harrington, a little fishing village on the north coast to which my grandparents had retired. It took six hours, with the state of the roads at the time, to make the journey, with a break for lunch. At a café on one trip I had the quintessential Australian experience of peeling back the cheese topping on my veal steak to watch half a dozen flies emerge and slowly flutter away. It is the kind of memory that lingers. Others were happier, especially of the oysters my father could expertly extract from the breakwater rocks, the prawns we would pick up in nets at night and the fish I learnt to catch and would bring back to my grandmother to cook for dinner. I came to know the breaks in the seaweed surrounding the sandbanks where flathead would lazily bask, the rocks from which I could cast at sunset in hope of bream, and, best of all, the beach where I could wade into the waves and pick up some of the sand whiting feeding beneath them. There were big rods stacked underneath my grandparents' home, with hoods and sinkers that I learnt to tie on to nylon lines, and the pleasure almost made up for the daily sensory torture of sitting on the unsewered toilet.

Catching fish was exciting – the choice of bait (I could thread a mean worm), the feel of the bite, the jerk to hook the fish, the careful reel-in to ensure it did not escape, and so on. But as every good fisherperson knows, the true pleasure of the sport can be experienced without catching fish. It comes from the feeling – as you watch hypnotic patterns in the water while fingering your taut line – that you are doing something, even though you are not doing anything except wave watching and waiting for the bite that never comes. It was a common dream of my grandparents' generation of Australians to 'head north' before they reached three score years and ten, retiring to fish in the sunshine, and I shared it at the time.

Holidays at Harrington did put me in touch with old people, and really poor people. My grandparents were happy enough in a home they had bought and then part-rented. I would play bridge and cribbage with them and listen to the cricket – the wonderful commentaries of John Arlott and Michael Charlton and others who not only knew what they were talking about but how to talk, unlike the current crop of ex-players, who drive me mad with their fatuities. As for the town poor – the aged and the disabled, who would struggle to the post office for a pension that barely allowed them to live – I felt some stirring of political feeling. In a land of plenty, with a mining boom beginning, the care of the old and unfortunate – I called them 'down-underdogs' – should have been a priority for all politicians and political commentators. It wasn't and it isn't – I am still annoyed at how little politicians and the media (especially the 'commentariat' I read in Murdoch-owned papers in Australia and Britain) care about the poor. The Calvinism that has shaped the Protestant religion holds that although you cannot earn your way to heaven, concern for the poor is a sign of your election as a saint; lack of concern is an indication that death will mean a one-way ticket to Lucifer-land. For Christians, the great thing about dying – if there is a God, that is – will be to watch all the politicians and journalists going the other way.

We did not study politics at school – I did English and history honours, together with economics, French, Latin and maths. Nevertheless, at age thirteen I developed a short-lived political theory, which I would propound to my friend the school librarian. The trouble, I explained, with Australian democracy, where voting was compulsory, is that so many dumb people get to vote (my evidence for this was the 'donkey vote', by which many compelled electors simply voted down the card, on which candidates were listed alphabetically, so that parties would strategically select candidates with names beginning with A or B). My solution was simple: we should not deny the vote to the unintelligent, but we should give an extra vote to all those with an above-average IQ. 'I don't think that's likely to find favour, Geoff,' said the librarian, over-kindly.

I might have suggested that we simply make voting voluntary – Australia is the only democracy in the Commonwealth where it's a crime not to vote. But voluntary voting has its problems – in the Brexit referendum, 37 per cent voted to leave, 35 per cent voted to stay, and 28 per cent didn't bother to vote at all (many of them because they believed the opinion polls, which said the remain side was assured of victory). Compulsory voting might have saved the British from the Brexit disaster, in which the impressionable, the over-patriotic and the racist, stirred on by opportunistic politicians, propagandist tabloids and Russian bloggers, produced a result against which most of the intelligent members of society – teachers, professionals, university students, businesspeople – had voted. There should be some guard against short-term populism, but I have to doubt, like the librarian, whether my youthful idea of an IQ test at the polling booth would be the answer.

My favourite day of the week was Saturday. At the time, people worked on Saturday mornings. I would catch the train from Eastwood with my father, raid his office fridge, then take myself to visit the City of Sydney Library. This was my mecca: it had a vast range of books, all covered by cloth glued with a substance which gave off an aroma that had the effect of a drug. In some strange way, I think it turned me on as I sniffed the covers before setting off for the heady delights of the city. First stop was a film theatre which had a weekly programme of Movietone news reels, interspersed with The Three Stooges and Charlie Chaplin. The black-and-white coverage of a world before television news was narrated histrionically, by a voice rising to repeated crescendos as it spoke of war, communists, car rallies[7] and (inevitably) the royal family. I vividly remember the white flowers on the coffin of Ethel Rosenberg, executed with her husband, Julius, for spying. Her children were my age and I wondered – I still do – how Americans could bring themselves to kill a mother. Executions were always good news for Movietone: they were covered with grisly fascination. But comedy invariably followed, or Australian news that would end with a joke or a homely salutation: the rest of the world was there to be gawked at, but should not be allowed to intrude on our love for cricket and football, the royal family, car rallies and Mr Menzies.

Out in the sunshine, I would press my small face against the windows of shops selling model aeroplanes – how I longed for the money to buy one – and then cross the road to the main bookshop. In this shop, at age thirteen, I committed my first – and only – crime of dishonesty. There was no one looking on the first-floor display of Latin textbooks, and a racy translation of Catullus, at the cost of 1/6d, was just sitting there. I had the money, for a change, but became overwhelmed by curiosity – how would it feel to break the law? It felt guilty, of course, and the buzz of excitement as I liberated the book fizzled out as soon as I left the shop without being apprehended. The guilt did not come because of the deterrent effect of the criminal law, or from remorse, or the eighth commandment, but because I had done something of which my mother would have disapproved. That has always been my ethical standard, as I suspect it is for so many others of my generation. In my case, it even stops me from fibbing on my tax return.

Nineteen sixty-three was a febrile and frenetic year. I attempted special honours courses in my Leaving Certificate while captaining tennis, squash and debating teams, sneak-reading *The Trial of Lady Chatterley*, gleaning some sex education from news reports of Stephen Ward's ordeal at the Old Bailey and listening to early Beatles melodies. There was also the distraction of those two essential requirements of being Australian: sport and 'mateship'. Everyone had to have 'mates' – mine were half a dozen of the brighter kids, those who shared a degree of cynicism about power (whether of teachers or of government). My first experience of what mateship meant had come at the end of the previous year, after we had performed a play I had written to entertain the boys in the departing year. They enjoyed it, and when we were summoned to the headmaster's office the next day we assumed it was to receive his thanks. Instead, fingering his cane, he told us it was an obscene and criminal libel on various teachers, himself included. 'Who wrote it?'

There was a long and (for me) quite painful silence – would they 'dob me in'? Eventually, one stepped forward and said, 'We all did, sir.' And the others slowly nodded. This, I realised, was what mateship meant.

But something was wrong – I didn't want the cane but I did want the writing credit. Ego got the better of discretion and I owned up. It turned into a Monty Python-esque moment as we all vied for punishment:

'We all wrote it, sir.'

'No, I wrote it!'

'No, we all did.'

'No, sir, I wrote almost all of it…'

The confused headmaster shelved the cane but ordered me – his prime suspect – to apologise to all the teachers.

The experience – I was quite astonished at the overreaction to satire – taught me that discretion might be the better part of valour when it came to credit for our final schoolboy stunt – a plan to disrupt the headmaster's final address to our year. This was a solemn speech that would be larded with Polonius-like precepts about how we should behave in the big wide world. My idea was to interrupt it with a broadcast from a 'Rebel Radio', mixing seditious reflections on our education with readings from a new satirical magazine called *Oz* (a Sydney equivalent of *Private Eye*). Several of my mates were budding engineers and they worked out how to rig the assembly hall sound system so that at the flick of a switch, the headmaster's microphone would be cut off and the rebel broadcast would be heard through the loud-speakers. A courageous classmate was prevailed upon to record the subversive content (I did not want to be expelled after voice recognition of my 'Pommy' accent). The switch was flicked just after the head began his speech. He stood in frozen fury. 'It must be Robertson,' he spluttered.

'No, it's not!' I shouted as I jumped from my seat in the hall, unwilling this time to take the credit. My engineering mates had wired the hall so cleverly that none of the teachers could work out how to stop the broadcast, and the headmaster eventually gave up. It proved, I suppose, that we were now old enough to outwit the authorities. I doubt whether they went on like this at Eton, but perhaps that was their loss.

There was no time to gloat: we had to hunker down for the Leaving Certificate – an external examination, the result of which would be the key to winning a scholarship to Sydney University. Your future depended on how much memory you could cram into three hours of speed writing, and how well your teachers had tipped the questions. I cannot now remember what causes I attributed to World War I, or my answer on the economics of autarkies, although I do recall mentioning the rape of Miranda and analysing the scansion of Prospero's injunction to chastity.

A few nights before the results, we went to the theatre, to laugh manically at a young comedian from Melbourne, whose Edna Everage (long before she was made a dame) resembled all our grandmothers. To open the show, Barry Humphries came on stage with a long flaxen wig and a surfboard, singing:

> I was down by Manly Pier
> With a tube of ice-cold beer,
> And a bucket full of prawns upon me knee.
> When I swallowed the last prawn,
> I gave a Technicolor yawn,
> And chundered in the Old Pacific Sea.

Fifty years later, I was able to recite it back to Barry, our neighbour in north London, on the occasion of his eightieth birthday.

The interesting thing, looking back, is that we state school kids had absolutely no idea how good – or how bad – we were academically. We came from a new, fly-by-the-seat-of-your-pants comprehensive, without a notion of how we would fare against kids from the massively funded private schools based on British models, who had bigger and better textbooks. Our teachers seemed good enough, but perhaps they could have been better. My favourite, a charming but anarchic history master, had once told me to wag school and spend my days in the State Library. I took his advice, but did not know how it would pan out for my history honours effort.

Our results sent us into a state of shock – my friends and I had attained first class in almost all our honours subjects. And, *mirabile dictu*, I had come second in the state in history. I was so overwhelmed at this achievement that it was several hours before I began to wonder why I had not come first. Later, I put this down to the fact that the other kid's father was a history professor who had set the honours paper. Ironically, we became rivals again in 1975, when our first books were published by the same London publisher. Mine was about the mistreatment of Irish Republicans by the British, and it did not sell well except in Ireland. His book was a hagiography of General Pinochet: many thousands of copies were bought by Chilean embassies around the world. Once again, I had come second.

*   *   *

We were not really disadvantaged by attending a comprehensive school – we weren't bullied or buggered or forced to join cadets. But we were not led to believe we were any good. The lack of confidence came out in university tutorials – old school ties, for no rational reason, induce self-confidence and self-assertiveness. That should not be the case: public education should compete much more effectively in the parental marketplace. Not only is it free, it has the great advantage of secularity. In a world where dogma has become the greatest threat to rationality, I still think that this is the most important form of education. Something only comprehensive schooling can produce is diversity – the value of children and teenagers mixing with a wide variety of fellow human beings from different social classes, different ethnic and religious groups, and different levels of advantage and performance.

I am inclined to think, however, that schools make little difference to the adult we learn to be at our mother's knee. Years later I defended A. S. Neill's famous school Summerhill from David Blunkett and his education inspectorate, who were trying to close it down. One of Neill's basic beliefs was that children come to embrace education – but only when they want to. Hence they must not be forced to attend class. Of course, Blunkett's government inspectorate had decided to close the school because its pupils were not being forced to attend class. The case (which became a TV movie) challenged the bureaucrats who could not tolerate difference and could not abide parents who genuinely believed their children would thrive under different conditions.[8] I called evidence from former Summerhillians – an astrophysicist, a philosopher and a Hollywood actress – whose free schooling had done no harm. That, I think, is the best thing that can be said about a school, and it could probably be said about Epping Boys High School in my day.

These days when I talk to teachers, I advocate courses in human rights, which should be introduced (perhaps in the space allocated to religious studies) in all secondary schools. I recite the story of the headmistress who sent all her new teachers this letter:

> *Dear teacher,*
>
> *I'm a survivor of a concentration camp. My eyes saw what no man should witness, gas chambers built by learnt engineers, children poisoned by educated physicians, infants killed by trained nurses, women and babies shot and burnt by high school and college graduates. So I'm suspicious of education. My request is to help your students become human. Your efforts must never produce learned monsters, skilled psychopaths, educated morons. Reading, writing, arithmetic are important only if they serve to make our children more human.*

It's surely time to put that insight back into and onto the school curriculum. Human rights are not history, because they aren't past; they're not law, because they're still in flux; they're not philosophy, although they do provide ethics for our time. Nor are they religion, because they pay no heed to the supernatural; and they're not politics, because they're not populist. They are, however, drawn from all these disciplines, and more, in their efforts to define and enforce human values. Values which a democratic society can't be neutral about. For students in our state schools, and teachers as well, they serve to show that privilege is an anachronism, dogma a distraction; freedom is a birthright and discrimination a wrong that should never be suffered. To the advantages of comprehensive education with its secularity, diversity and locality, let us now add humanity.

Chapter Three

Student Power

In 1964, aged seventeen, my acne on the wane, finances secured by a scholarship and confidence boosted by my Leaving Certificate results, I entered the Gothic archway to the main quadrangle of the University of Sydney. I was bewitched by the promise of intellectual excitement for the next six years (I had signed up for a course in arts followed by law). The place had a colonial whiff of Oxbridge, in its architecture and its motto, *Sidere mens eadem mutato* ('The same spirit under a different sky'). The sandstone lions at its entrance were said to roar at the approach of a virgin (this joke might have seemed funny to a seventeen-year-old male virgin). The place was full of recent ghosts – an orientation revue had scripts by one Clive James, recently departed to Cambridge, and my philosophy tutor arrived very late for his first class, explaining as he wiped away a tear, 'I've been at the airport, farewelling Germaine.' Whoever she was, I felt sorry to have missed a woman who could have such an impact.

All the excitement in our first weeks centred on a young leather-jacketed English lecturer newly arrived from Manchester, who looked and sounded just like a Beatle and was lecturing on D. H. Lawrence. It was a hot summer and the large lecture theatre was filled with hundreds of partly clothed females in open-mouthed adoration of Howard Jacobson (now a grizzled Booker Prize-winner), who could not believe his beginner's luck.

English was a joy to read, although the faculty was savagely split between the Leavisites – disciples of the Cambridge don F. R. Leavis, who believed that the text must speak for itself without reference to the author

– and everyone else, who favoured putting literature into some kind of context. Leavis had a black mark in my mind because he had refused to give evidence for the defence in the *Lady Chatterley* trial, but the bearded and intense lecturers he inspired (Jacobson was one) were the more entertaining. Professor Goldberg, the head Leavisite, revitalised the student literary society and I will always be grateful to him for introducing me to *The Uses of Literacy* by Richard Hoggart, who had been the star witness for *Lady Chatterley*. I thought the division all a storm in a literary teacup, although it split the faculty down the middle. Of course you should be able to appreciate *Saint Joan* without bothering about Shaw's liking for Stalin, or read *Mrs Dalloway* without knowing that Virginia Woolf wanted to exterminate the mentally handicapped. But context can add meaning and understanding and enjoyment to a text, as I had to point out, at risk of failure, to my examiners in my BA honours exam. They had set a paper requiring the appreciation of two unattributed and anonymous poems – one clearly superior (it was W. B. Yeats's 'An Irish Airman Foresees His Death'); the other the verses my father had taught me, which had inspired fighter boys throughout the war (Magee's 'High Flight'). I could not imagine them ever reciting the dour Yeats poem as they went into battle, so I felt almost duty-bound to point out to the examiners that the less accomplished verse at least offered some meaning and hope to those experiencing war in the air. My paper, presumably marked by an anti-Leavisite, received a distinction.

The study of literature, once past *Beowulf*, never seemed a chore. I marvelled at Marvell (even more, many years later, when I studied the Civil War era during which he wrote), while John Donne's sensual images (and he a priest!) superseded the crudities of Catullus in my erotic imagination. Then the poets of our twentieth century – Auden, of course, and T. S. Eliot, whose ageing Prufrock still comes to mind whenever I walk on a beach (I shall never wear the bottoms of my trousers rolled) or dare to eat a peach (was it, I wonder, a fear of dribbling, or of indigestion?). I was much taken with George Orwell, although my admiration for this hero of the British left has been somewhat dimmed by the recent revelation that he was an informer – on his fellow writers – for MI5. When speaking at the

George Orwell Memorial Prize recently, I joked that he was 'just another Blair'. It did not get many laughs from an audience now largely unaware that Orwell's real name was Eric Blair.

The subject that fascinated me was philosophy, in which Sydney University had a notable pedigree by virtue of the lengthy tenure of John Anderson (from 1927 to 1958), who had given his name to a description – 'Andersonian' – which I never fully understood, although its remaining disciples, by the time I arrived, seemed to be pissant libertarians. But much as I enjoyed the study of philosophy, the artificiality of the arguments eventually irritated me. I wanted a discipline that offered concrete and common-sense rules at a level of generality that could be applied to solve real problems with an outcome that was not necessarily good but could at least be said to be fair. In history we studied revolutions, through the spectacles of an American author, Crane Brinton, who likened them to fevers, with early symptoms, high temperatures and long periods of recovery. His metaphors never convinced me, although later they struck me as a useful analogy for litigation, which can become a kind of disease. I immersed myself in the French and Russian Revolutions, and the 1848 eruptions, from which my great-great-grandmother had fled Berlin.

My first essay, I decided, would be on an early French revolutionary, perhaps the first socialist, one Gracchus Babeuf. I took myself, as had been my school-day wont, to the State Library, from whose bowels I extracted what appeared to be the only book ever published on Babeuf, and indeed one of only two copies of this rare book which had ever reached Australia. I thought I was safe, and I copied it prodigiously. When I visited my lecturer to receive his congratulations on my erudite essay, I noticed with some horror the other copy of the book on his desk. It turned out that he was finishing his own work on Babeuf, and he read me a lecture on plagiarism. It had the desired effect, and by the end of the second year I had an offer to do an honours course.

But by this time I was anxious to help make history rather than to study it. The reactionary government of Sir Robert Menzies (we called him 'Ming' – he reigned imperially from 1949 to 1966) was conscripting my generation to fight a real war in Vietnam, where the 'yellow peril' was waiting to descend, as if by gravity, on our whites-only civilisation. National service was conducted as fairly as a lottery: only those whose birthdates were drawn out of a barrel were called up, and then only if they could not make it to university, where you were exempt. An old friend from Epping High, Bernard (*aka* 'Judy') Garland, became the first of my school mates to be blown up in South Vietnam. I remember him as a kind and decent mate, always willing to help, and now he is just an entry on the wall at the War Memorial. There were 580 others, and 3,000 wounded (included my cousin from Dapto, whose kids bear the consequences of Agent Orange). I suspect that Menzies did not give a proverbial toss for the South Vietnamese, whose leaders included the hideous Madame Nhu, who exulted in what she called 'Buddhist barbecues'. He just wanted to do what he thought America wanted – although, ironically, as it now appears (from Robert McNamara's memoirs and other sources), America thought that Australia truly wanted the US there. Menzies misled America and he had no insight into Asia and no concern for the kids he put in harm's way.

It was censorship, as ever, that propelled me onto the student political stage. Nineteen sixty-four was the year of the infamous conviction of the editors of *Oz* magazine, Richard Walsh and Richard Neville: they were jailed by a moronic magistrate for publishing satire he did not understand, and some weak puns ('Get folked', a pun advertising a folk festival, was one the magistrate thought obscene). Even more obscene, to his perverse mind, was a savage cartoon by artist Martin Sharp (who was jailed as well) titled 'The Word Flashed Around the Arms', which satirised drunken and loutish behaviour by privileged hoons in Sydney's eastern suburbs. This was the same idiocy that had censored Prospero's adjuration against pre-marital sex in *The Tempest*, and now in this crazily conformist country it was putting artists in jail for condemning immoral conduct by their peers. I made my first public political speech, on the front lawn of the main quadrangle, where protest crowds gathered, in order to raise money for the *Oz* appeal.

*   *   *

Inexorably, I was drawn to student politics, and was elected as president of the Students' Representative Council, 1966/67. In that office I found myself regularly in the papers denying absurd allegations or hosing down provocations. When the *Telegraph* reported that 'Methods of contraception are described in detail in a three-page supplement in the student newspaper *Honi Soit*' (only in Australia could this be news, or a sensation, in 1967), I had to explain that 'students stand four-square behind the publication of information about contraception ... they come to university with no real sex education [so much for those Father and Son evenings] and the problem of the unmarried mother is a real one at the university.' It was – and I dared not mention that I had authorised our welfare services to pay for impecunious students to have illegal abortions.

The SRC supported more than eighty clubs and societies, and those concerned with drama and music actively promoted the new, the classic and the avant-garde – the latter, in the case of works by Pirandello and Alfred Jarry, often occasioning visits by the New South Wales vice squad, whose members sat stoically through *Ubu Roi*, with its chorus singing loudly the refrain 'Arseholes to you'. The student revues were brilliant, building up a tradition of acerbic, sledging satire very different from *Beyond the Fringe*, but just as funny.

My own efforts at satire were confined to *Oz* magazine. There was much to lampoon, but my wordplay was laboured, over-intellectual and unmemorable – it was a joy to meet Kathy, years later, whose puns are effortless and survive in quotation dictionaries ('Monogamy is what men think dining room tables are made out of' etc.). My work for *Oz* did garner one particular accolade, thanks to Garry Shead (now a famous Australian artist), who illustrated my 'Birdwatchers' Guide to Vietnam' (politicians as doves, hawks etc.) by putting genitals on several ornithological caricatures. This could not be allowed in the backward state of Victoria, so the *Oz* distributors put a large black line over the testicles before they crossed the border.

Honi Soit, the SRC newspaper, provoked a lot of controversy during my term as SRC president. It caused shock and horror in right-wing newspapers by sending a correspondent to Hanoi (which any good newspaper should have done) and in the wider population by raising funds for medical assistance to the Vietcong. It was humane, I suppose, for Australian students to pay to save the lives of jungle fighters, but paradoxical if, thereby nursed back to health, they were to kill more Australian soldiers. I spent some time quoting Voltaire ('I don't like what you say but I will defend to my death your right to say it') in defence of the editors, but eighteenth-century French philosophers did not carry much weight in a country that supported this war against gravity (i.e. against the yellow peril descending inexorably from the north) and dominoes (Asian countries would collapse towards Australia if Vietnam fell over).

I look back with amusement now at my address to students at a ceremony in the Great Hall in 1967, filmed for a *Panorama*-style documentary on education.[9] I wore my mortar board while speaking (a breach of academic protocol) and mispronounced the word 'orgy' – no doubt because I was not indulging in any. I did by this stage have a regular girlfriend, who lived near Dobroyd Point, which has the most romantic view from a high cliff over Sydney Harbour. We would contemplate the starry heavens from my father's Valiant of a late evening, until puerile policemen would sneak their paddy-wagon behind us and switch their lights on to high beam. Once, I parked the car at midnight a little too close to the edge, over which it partly slid and needed tow-truck recovery the next morning.

Another development in my romantic sensibility came from a dawning liking for opera. It is difficult to think of Sydney without its iconic Opera House, but the building did not open until 1973, and the art form was hitherto provided by the curiously named Elizabethan Theatre Trust. It had an amazing scheme (I have not heard of it anywhere else) involving 'youth nights'. During its seasons, every opera would be performed on a Monday 'youth night', which youths (defined as anyone under twenty-six) could attend for the impossibly low cost of 5 shillings. The casts were generally good – the principals were usually Australian returns from Sadler's Wells or Covent Garden – and when Donald Smith was singing, the high notes were as high as any tenor in the world and even sweeter. Smith was a small, plump man with a hare lip, who preferred to perform at rugby league clubs rather than La Scala, but in costume and make-up his plangent voice transformed him into the most romantic of stage heroes. (I can never forget his appearance as Cavaradossi in the second act of *Tosca*, igniting the audience with 'Vittoria' – the victory over the torturers). I soon discovered an interesting thing about the 'high C' which Smith would effortlessly hurl from the stage, whence it would enter at the base of my backbone and run tingling up my spine to explode in my head: it had a mysteriously erotic effect on a female partner. I would wait until just before I knew the note was in the offing and then hold and gently stroke my partner's hand. It worked every time.

* * *

The great battle of my student political life was against the university itself, to ensure that it took student concerns into account in major decisions. Australian universities in the '60s, like those in Britain, were run by powerful administrators responsible to the vice-chancellors: student representation on committees and disciplinary tribunals was unknown and unwanted – indeed, actually feared. 'Student power' had erupted on American campuses, the slogan originating in the free-speech movement at Berkeley and spreading like wildfire along with anti-Vietnam protests. The vice-chancellor at Sydney, Sir Stephen Roberts, saw it as a dangerous threat to his authority, and to that of all vice-chancellors. They were ready to nip in the bud any form of US-style protests, sit-ins or occupations. So when the first challenge to their absolute power arrived in early 1967, in the unlikely form of a postgraduate student, Max Humphreys, who organised a protest at the university library against an increase in fines for overdue books, Roberts and his star chamber – called the Proctorial Board – grossly overreacted. They suspended Humphreys, without any form of due process, despite his first-class degree in psychology.

It may seem bizarre that a revolution should begin as the result of a fine for overdue books. Nonetheless, it was a 400 per cent hike, imposed arbitrarily and without any consultation with the student library committee. And what soon became the real issue was the high-handed and obviously unjust behaviour of the proctors. Humphreys had undoubtedly been present at the sit-in, which had disbanded peacefully on the arrival of the Yeoman Bedell – the absurd Oxbridge name given to those we termed 'the campus cops' – sixteen armed guards commanded by our main enemy, Assistant Principal. He was the head of the administration and the real power behind the vice-chancellor, and he regarded students as mere inconveniences who should put up or be shut up. When Max the next morning attempted to distribute a hastily written pamphlet protesting against the fine increase, the Assistant Principal had him arrested by the campus cops and dragged to his office, where his pamphlets were confiscated and Max was charged with 'gross contempt of the university authority and inciting such contempt in others'. I tried to remonstrate with Sir Stephen, a nice enough old man who chain-smoked with trembling hands, but he remained adamant: he had been to a vice-chancellors' conference where they had all agreed on the need to prevent 'student power' from taking hold of Australian universities, and he had a weird sense that history had destined him to be the first to stop this menace in its tracks.

These heavy-handed actions provoked widespread anger and demonstrations by students who would never have thought of protesting about Vietnam. As SRC president, I accompanied Max to his hearing before the Proctorial Board – Sir Stephen and the deans of four university faculties. The hearing was a farce – we arrived to find his accusers, the Assistant Principal and the librarian, taking morning tea with these 'judges'. They refused me permission to call no fewer than twelve witnesses who had been present at the sit-in and whose testimony would have refuted the charge that Max had incited them. We were ushered out – the Assistant Principal and the librarian being asked to remain in order to 'advise' the judges. They returned, half an hour later, with their sentence: Max, for his contumely, would be 'rusticated' for a year.

Max's friends on the far left began to mutter about the need for sit-ins and occupations of university property. They called a lunchtime meeting on the front lawn, and to their – and my – amazement, several thousand students turned up with banners demanding 'Justice for Humphreys'. I stood there, undecided, while they revved up the angry audience to various forms of violent protest. I realised the opportunity really belonged to the

SRC, so I grabbed the microphone and solemnly pledged that it would fight the university to reinstate Max Humphreys, but any violence had to be postponed. I kept speaking – a long diatribe against the Proctorial Board and the need for student representation on it – until 2 p.m., by which time I knew the audience would have to melt away to attend classes. They did so, seemingly content with my promise that the SRC would fight the university and win. But how? We had no access to any form of power.

When I made that promise, I was thinking about the law. I had not been studying it for long, but I had picked up enough knowledge to realise that it could rectify injustice, even at a university. I had already come across the 1610 case of Dr Bonham, a Cambridge don restored to his lectureship by the Chief Justice after his unfair dismissal. And I had by this time commenced my articles of clerkship at the most prestigious (or so it described itself) solicitor's firm in Sydney. The partner I was working for thought it would be fun to sue his alma mater – so long as I did all the work, and we found a QC prepared to take it on. The silk who accepted the brief with great pleasure was Gordon Samuels, a saturnine Englishman who had cut his teeth debating at the Oxford Union against Kenneth Tynan and was a dab hand at civil procedure, in which he was a part-time lecturer at the law school. His name on our pleading was calculated to strike fear into the vice-chancellor's heart, and it did.

Sir Stephen and his proctors – all eminent professors in disciplines other than law – had no defence to our claim for Max's reinstatement and damages, and the last thing they wanted was a trial which would expose their ignorance and unfairness. They offered to settle by restoring Max to his seat in the library after a 'retrial' at which he would merely be reprimanded. I drove a harder bargain – we wanted two seats for students on the Proctorial Board and on other key university committees. Sir Stephen gave in – even paying the SRC its legal costs and cancelling the increase in library fees. Both he and the Assistant Principal were ridiculed, not only by the left but in right-wing journals, while the *Sydney Morning Herald* suggested that the Main Quad be turned into a 'penitentiary for naughty students'. This was a crucial learning experience: how 'lawfare' could win battles for just causes, on behalf of those who had no other kind of power.

The 'Humphreys Affair' was my SRC's finest hour. I am all in favour of student protest, including, as a last resort, occupations and sit-ins – but not if they can be avoided by sensible compromise or, as a second-last resort, legal action. The importance of the action we took was that it created a precedent: it served notice on all Australian university administrations that they must deal with students fairly. I had come to university expecting to find 'a community of scholars', but had found instead a community organised largely in the interests of its professors and administrators. Students were to be seen but not heard. A good example was provided by the resignation of Sir Stephen, which we forced by our legal action: the university gazette dedicated an entire issue to reminiscences about him from everyone – except, of course, any student. No one thought to ask me: I was merely the representative of the 16,000 people for whom the university was meant to exist. When Sir Stephen's replacement arrived – an emollient economist from Manchester University – he made a point of including me and my successor in his counsels. I like to think that this period in student politics did force the university's 'community of scholars' to include scholars in their community.

It was a triumph of sorts, in its time and place. When my student activist daughter teased me – 'What did you do in the '60s, Daddy? Were you arrested at anti-Vietnam demos? Were you on the barricades with the students in Paris in '68?' – it was deflating to have to reply that I was suing the university and arranging legal defences for protesters. But our legal initiatives in some ways had more lasting effects. When reminiscing with Tariq Ali and other '60s protesters from the US and Europe, and we go round the table to tell of the outrages that provoked our battles, 'a steep increase in library fines' brings forth incredulous laughter. But, ironically, because we used the law rather than broke it, we had success.

Soon enough, our triumph had the practical result of requiring the appointment of two student proctors to join the board for its next big case: 'Who threw the tomato at the governor?' The governor was the imposing figure of Sir Roden Cutler, a VC winner no less, who had come to campus to inspect the university regiment. He had lost a leg in the course of winning his Victoria Cross, which did not stop him supporting conscription for Vietnam, where many more legs, and lives, were being lost. That justified, perhaps, a demonstration against his visit, though not the act of someone in the crowd who had hurled a rotten tomato, accurately, at his medal-bejewelled chest. But who? The indefatigable Sergeant Longbottom, charged with policing student demonstrations, came up with the tiny figure of Nadia Wheatley, who had certainly been in the crowd, although in those days there were no CCTV cameras nor any other photographic evidence to convict her.

I was appointed a student proctor to advise the distinguished professors of medicine and science and engineering. They certainly needed advising – I could hardly believe how insouciant these great men were about the rules of evidence, and how anxious they were to convict someone – in this case, young Nadia – to satisfy the media thirst for blood over the splattering of a war hero. I found it necessary to argue that the charge, which would have ended Nadia's academic career, had to be proved beyond reasonable doubt – I even brought one of my criminal law books to read to them about 'the golden thread of the criminal law'. Eventually, Nadia was acquitted and went on to write acclaimed children's books, but the case provided a first insight into judicial psychology – people who want to be appointed as judges think they have a duty to find someone guilty.

One benefit of life in student politics was to participate as delegates to the National Union of Australian University Students (NUAUS) conferences, held at different campuses around the country, and most often upstairs in a Melbourne pub. After one conference in Tasmania, a friend and I decided to spend a week hiking through the state's fabled wilderness, along with a female delegate named Gayle. We didn't have much money, so at the end of each day I would go alone to a country pub to book a room – they usually had two or three beds – and having paid and taken occupation would nip outside to my friends waiting around the corner to invite them in for the night. This seemed to my partly formed forensic mind to be perfectly legitimate – I had purchased the room as overnight occupier and there was no express condition about not inviting guests. It was at a grungy, empty hotel in Launceston that the three of us were arrested, after a complaint from a very grumpy publican. His wife had found Gayle's sanitary towel in the toilet and deduced that it did not belong to me. We were taken to a police station and fingerprinted before I could expand upon my legal theory about my innocence. It convinced my friends, who urged me to run it when we were brought to court the next day, but it did not convince the police. Having learnt at school that discretion could be the better part of valour, I paid the grim-faced hotelier for three rooms to avoid the danger of a conviction from a Launceston beak. The cops drove us to a local stadium, where we slept on concrete benches, with my companions complaining that we would have been much more comfortable in a warm police cell.

*   *   *

The other task for the SRC president was to arrange legal representation for students arrested for demonstrating against sending Australian troops to Vietnam. These demos were frequent in 1966/67, as conscripts of our own age who had not managed a university exemption began to be killed in provinces with unpronounceable names, fighting people of a colour that they would not have seen at home. My younger brother Graeme became a conscientious objector (it surprised me that he had a conscience, but his plea was upheld). The government's lickspittle support for America's folly (the Prime Minister, Harold Holt, went to Washington and actually said, 'Australia is all the way with LBJ') was opposed by Labor (for obscure reasons, the Australian Labour Party is spelled without the 'u') and by trade unions, but there were not many dissident voices from the business or legal establishment. One of them came from Sir John Kerr, then a distinguished judge, whose florid features became internationally famous in 1975 when, as Governor General, he sacked the Whitlam government. In 1967, however, he called me up to offer advice about handling the legal case for a hundred students arrested at a big anti-Vietnam demo. His son had been one of them, and he suggested we take his case first as a test for the rest, and he would come to court and glare at the magistrate to make sure he saw through the concocted police evidence. I was grateful for his help and sad, later, that he became a leper in his own land for dismissing – on a mistaken theory as to the legal powers of a British regent – a democratical-ly elected Labor government.

Kerr in 1967 struck me as genuinely progressive, although in later writ-ings I used him as an example of liberal lawyers who had a fatal tendency to go weak at the knees when given access to power. Another example was Ramsey Clark, who when made Attorney General by LBJ proceeded to authorise the prosecution of Dr Spock for encouraging opposition to the draft. Another was Sam Silkin, the Labour Attorney General in Britain who initiated oppressive actions against journalists (my clients) under the Official Secrets Act. I came to detect in the minds of these men a cer-tain craving to be accepted as 'responsible' by the establishment they had hitherto been happy to criticise – their proclaimed commitment to 'civil liberties' faltering whenever security services told them (often mistaken-ly) that 'national security' required an oppressive prosecution. The Phil Ochs folk ditty 'Love Me, I'm a Liberal' neatly skewered the hypocrisy of 'small-l' liberals, like – I began to worry – me. So I began to describe myself as a 'Gladstonian liberal', unwavering in carrying through domestic reform and taking humanitarian action against atrocities abroad (well, at least atrocities against Christians, in Gladstone's case). Gladstone did not, however, have to deal with the Cold War, nor with the CIA.

By this time, that agency had me in their sights. In 1968 I received a strange letter from the US embassy: would I care to apply for what they called a 'Far-East Student Leader scholarship' – a three-month all-expenses-paid tour of America? I would – I was a student leader, Sydney was in what must have seemed, from the vantage point of Washington, the 'Far East', and I had never been out of Australia (other than to New Zealand, which didn't count). I did not smell a rat, or have any inkling that this seeming-ly educational trip, run by a pleasant-sounding foundation in Vermont, was in fact a CIA front – part of its long-term plan to win friends and influence people to believe in the American dream, or least to be wary of the communist nightmare. They were secretly funding, for this purpose, Radio Free Europe and *Encounter* magazine. (The latter's editor, Melvin Lasky, who later became a friend, defended taking CIA money for the benefit of Europe's liberal intelligentsia – it prevented them having to earn their money by writing for right-wing propaganda sheets.) I was awarded the 'scholarship', apparently because I had been 'spotted' by the CIA as a future Prime Minister of Australia. The CIA made many mistakes in the '60s.

It was very exciting. I could not wait to Pan-Am across the Pacific, landing in Fiji at night and watching as friendly brown faces approached from the tarmac. I had left White Australia. I remained in Suva for a few days, staying with an Indian family, who explained their fears about the discrimination against them, imposed by indigenous chiefs (an issue which was to bring me back to Fiji as a QC many years later). Then it was off to Hawaii to join my group of Asian student leaders.

There were thirteen of us, assembled under the wing of a benign Scout-leader type called Phil. Some were not very political, and I suspected they had been chosen because of a familial relationship with corrupt rulers. I remember the sad face and sage advice of Hien from South Vietnam, who after the fall of Saigon was probably sent for 're-education', and Shig, a jolly Japanese youth who was later to make a fortune in steel. My best friends were Kiwi, an obsessively nationalist Singaporean, who rose high in Singapore Airlines before falling out with Lee Kuan Yew, his former idol, and Sarwono Kusumaatmadja, a grave Indonesian given to frequent laughter which showed the gaps in his teeth. He became a particular friend, and in years to come I watched with admiration his political career in Golkar (the ruling party) as he fought to combat the corruption that had become endemic in his country.

Then it was onwards to California, to begin our three-month indoctrination into the values of the 'greatest country in the world'. Our first stop was at the Santa Cruz campus of the University of California, set in the mountains and, unlike Berkeley and UCLA, not known for student activism. The CIA doubtless reckoned it was a safe place, not realising that the reason for its lack of protests was not so much the conservatism of its students but the fact that most were spaced out on drugs. The very first night of our arrival featured a lecture on the subject by none other than Timothy Leary, the Harvard professor who had become the guru of dropping out. He spoke about the 'philosophy of ultimate pleasure' and how psychedelic drug-taking resulted in the 'suspension of conditioning' so that the individual could enjoy 'real thought, real decisions, real love and real life'. He struck me as a salesman, of no great intellectual rigour (too many fried brain cells?), but what was extraordinary was the street erudition of his audience. Their questions – sometimes of a technicality that even he could not answer – showed that drug culture had permeated this centre of learning, with no obvious ill-effects. By early 1969, 'Timothy Leary Dearie' (as he had been saluted by 'Let the Sun Shine In' in *Hair*) was becoming passé. I introduced myself after the lecture and begged an interview for my student paper. He agreed: no doubt this Johnny Apple-seed of hallucinatory drugs saw Australia as fertile territory for propagating mind expansion. I bothered him the next lunchtime with questions that he thought naïve (they probably were) while he ate a steak that had been specially prepared for him by his acolytes, 'peppered' with some undoubtedly illegal substance. Later he had to flee America after escaping prison, and took refuge in Algeria for some time. On his death, his ashes were put in a satellite and released, appropriately enough, in space.

Leary was the first famous American I had met – the CIA would have been appalled. It did not control our movements, however, and Phil, who was very relaxed, did not attempt to direct them. Thus it came about that in Atlanta, Sarwono and I spent some time with Black Panthers, listening to their grievances, which were real enough, and allowing them to introduce us to hash. We inhaled as deeply as we could, for some time, but abjectly failed in our first attempt to 'turn on'. In the end everyone collapsed with laughter, not because of the drug but because of our hilariously inept attempts to get high.

We were soon whisked to Washington, where CIA connections brought us an audience with the House Minority Leader, Gerald Ford. We were unimpressed: he had a face out of a gangster movie and seemed a bit slow – he did not know where or what 'Far-East Asia' was. But three nights in New York were well spent: I went to a performance of *Hair* (which had just been banned in Sydney by the reactionary state government) and I discovered the Met. *Il trovatore* was playing, an opera which, as someone remarked, needs only the five best singers in the world. The Met could afford them – Leontyne Price, Grace Bumbry, Luciano Pavarotti, Sherrill Milnes and not forgetting Ezio Pinza, for me the most thrilling of all because he had been the dubbed voice singing 'Some Enchanted Evening' in the movie of *South Pacific*. The Met, with its amazing Chagall stained glass, was my New York mecca ever after. On my last night I had a ticket for another opera, with Renata Tebaldi and the reigning tenor, Franco Corelli. Alas, he had to cancel to fly to his father's sick-bed in Italy, to be replaced at the last minute by an unknown, Plácido Domingo. I heard him there first!

The CIA tour took us around the country – from the bears of Yellowstone to the Colorado canyons to the wooden bridges of New Hampshire. We marvelled at the beauty of America, and occasionally at the ugliness of some of its people – when we came across Ku Klux Klanners in the South and visited the Texas A&M (Agricultural and Mechanical) University, alma mater to George W. Bush, with its massive collection of guns donated by old 'Aggies' – an example of how deeply entrenched the Davy Crockett instinct is in American culture.

The planned highlight of our visit was the one-month 'homestay' with a typical American family in a typical American town. The place the CIA had carefully chosen, to impress on us the virtues and superiority of the American way of life, was Sarasota on the Mexican Gulf shore of Florida. This was indeed a pretty nice place – lots of spacious houses with motor launches on its numerous quays. It had a famous circus museum (it had been winter home to the Ringling Brothers), a nice little opera company, innumerable tennis courts (and later the celebrated Bollettieri Tennis Academy, where my son was to train) and plenty of fast-food delights to dazzle we Far-East Asians, who had yet to be colonised by McDonald's.

My 'typical American family' was that of Milt and Judy Rubenfeld, proprietors of the local light shop. It comprised Paul, a quirky seventeen-year-old, whose bedroom I shared for the month; Abby, his very serious teenage sister; and a somewhat fractious younger brother. The latter, in this typical American family, later did time for armed robbery in the local penitentiary. Abby became a distinguished attorney with a lesbian partner with whom she produced children in Texas. But I like to think of Paul, my bedroom mate, as the most typical of all.

Paul Rubenfeld became an actor, *aka* Paul Reubens. He appeared in some Cheech & Chong movies and then developed his own almost immortal character, Pee-Wee Herman, to the delight of children around America, and indeed throughout the world. But Pee-Wee's biggest adventure came when he returned to Sarasota to see his parents, dropped into one of its gay cinemas and was arrested by an undercover cop for – well – scratching himself. His career immediately came to a total and cataclysmic end. He was treated as if he had betrayed a generation of American children. Some time after Paul's fall, I reconnected with Judy. Hugh Grant had just been caught, at the height of his Hollywood fame, picking up a sex worker on Sunset Boulevard. 'Times have moved on – it hasn't ended Hugh's career,' I said. 'Maybe they can now forgive Paul.' She cackled with laughter and shook her head. 'Geoff, you still don't understand America!'

Did the CIA get its money's worth out of my three-month 'indoctrination'? Not if you believe the *Washington Times*, in which I was listed in 2000 (by John Bolton, no less, Bush's ambassador to the UN and now Trump's national security adviser) as one of his country's enemies because of my arguments that the US should be bound by international law. But however forcefully I may criticise its foreign policy, the ugliness of its gun culture or its responsibility for some of the world's inequality, poverty and conflict, I have never faltered in my general support for America's leadership of the free world – a result, I suspect, not of my youthful CIA sponsorship but of my knowledge about the alternatives. As for Paul, he is a delightful man who has entertained my actor son and may soon make a comeback. I hope he does, although it will be too late for me to retitle this book *How the CIA Made Me Sleep with Pee-Wee Herman*.

Chapter Four

Learning the Law

Sydney University Law School was in the city centre, in a grim, squalid old building opposite the courts. We had a dean who was a drunkard, teaching Roman law at an early hour before delirium tremens set in. Our most memorable character was Ron, the disabled lift driver, who told dirty jokes as he navigated his vehicle to the higher floors of the narrow building. His stories were often interrupted by a male shout from the back: 'Lady in the lift, Ron' – the few women who ventured into law at the time had to be protected from smut. They were on their way to 'the ladies' common room' – the smallest room in the building, converted from a men's toilet, which had four chairs and a settee.[10] Australia did not have a single female judge until Roma Mitchell was appointed in South Australia in 1965, although Britain was no better. I have enormous respect for the women who did suffer this suffocating sexism in the legal profession and came through: the two finest examples are Mary Gaudron, the first woman on the Australian High Court, and Brenda Hale, until 2017 the only woman on the Supreme Court. They have long been my legal heroines, and they needed psychological strength as well as intellect to cope with constant belittling.

The first surprise about Australian law circa 1966 was its Anglo-centricity. English judges were venerated, and their (often narrow and narrow-minded) decisions always followed. This was because English Law Lords, who sat in England's highest court (the House of Lords Judicial Committee), also sat as Australia's highest court, the Privy Council, the Supreme Court for most countries in what was then the British Commonwealth (now just 'the

Commonwealth'). Traditionally, on granting independence, Britain would insist on retaining control of a new nation's legal system by requiring it to allow a final appeal to the Privy Council. It did so with Australia in 1901, and with Canada, which got rid of the ridiculous colonial arrangement in 1949. Why did Australia not finally pull the imperial plug until 1986? It was beloved by generations of top corporate solicitors and barristers, whose clients paid large fees for them to travel first class to London, stay at the Savoy and spend a few days inviting English Law Lords, who knew nothing about Australia, to reverse a decision already expertly made by its own High Court. Although I was subsequently to appear frequently in the Privy Council, rubbing shoulders in its robing room with leaders of the Sydney Bar, I never felt that the justice they obtained from bored English Law Lords was half as good as the justice they had already received back home. It was a genteel scam, really, that top Australian lawyers connived in for too many years.

So far as teaching was concerned, the law school was really a dictation factory. Its students, after a full-time first year, had to do three years as an 'articled clerk' with a firm of solicitors in order to be permitted to practise after getting their law degree. They took lecture notes before rushing off to their offices, later regurgitating them for examiners, whose marks depended on how many of their own words they could recognise in the exam papers. In contrast, a good lawyer must have the ability to apply statutes and reports available to hand to a particular case. The true test of legal ability is not how much law you can remember, but how you devise arguments and solutions in applying it. I took up the cause of 'open book' exams, which would require creative thought rather than regurgitation. This was, I noticed when I visited on my CIA trip, how Harvard Law School was beginning to teach. There, instead of force-feeding submissive students dictated lecture notes, these were supplied a week before each class, which took the form of a role-playing exercise in which students were assigned parts and required to participate in unfolding scenarios, displaying their reasoning faculties as well as their understanding of the law. It was a way of teaching the most important lesson of all – how to apply book-learnt knowledge. This 'Socratic' method of teaching did not catch on in Sydney, however, where lecturers preferred to stand and deliver their wisdom by reading from typed notes, or from textbooks they happened to have written. They might just as well have sent us a tape recording.

I learnt the bread-and-butter subjects in this way, about contracts (the bargains that the law will enforce), tort (civil liability – in car-crazy Australia, mainly how to recover compensation for negligent road accidents) and real property (i.e. conveyancing land and houses). As for legal history, it stretched from Anglo-Saxon times to 1485: nothing about the fundamental (and fascinating) developments in legal principles in the seventeenth century, when battles against royal absolutism secured, among other things, the independence of the judiciary, the abolition of torture and the emergence of parliamentary sovereignty. When I came to study this period many years later, I found it so fascinating that I wrote a book – *The Tyrannicide Brief* – about the achievements of regicides and levellers – the brave and inspired people who turned England, briefly, into a republic. British legal historians had largely ignored this crucible period (1649–60) and Australian academics had followed their royalist lead.

For all these failings, the law school had two internationally renowned departments that did offer some inspiration. One was the school of jurisprudence, headed by Professor Julius Stone, which leavened the school's obsession with teaching black-letter law by introducing students to the modern American 'realist' school of jurisprudence, which argued that law is what officials do in fact rather than what law books say they should do. Stone was a genial, pipe-smoking, patriarchal figure when I arrived, by which time his own had passed – he gave us only one lecture, to remind us to read his books. They were enormous – his footnotes took up half of each page – but his work on 'sociological jurisprudence', i.e. that law has social consequences, had an impact at schools in the US, although not so much in England. His questioning spirit pervaded the study of jurisprudence and its teaching by Tony Blackshield and Upendra Baxi: to them I owe much of my understanding of legal theory. Stone was a great figure, shamefully treated by the university because he was Jewish – its professorial board deliberately held meetings on Jewish holidays so he could not attend.

The other department with international recognition was criminology, headed by a warm, down-to-earth Englishman, Gordon Hawkins, and his student-friendly assistant, Duncan Chappell. Gordon had run a borstal back in Britain, and promulgated a ready cure for much of the crime in New South Wales: remove all the criminal laws that punished matters of private morality.[11] There were many of them at the time – against abortion, homosexuality, gambling, drunkenness, vagrancy, drugs, prostitution, pornography and any form of artistic licence – and they spawned real crime when corrupt police took bribes – as they regularly did – to allow them secretly to flourish. I had, while studying philosophy, become an adherent to the views of John Stuart Mill and the principle of his book *On Liberty*: 'The sole end for which mankind is warranted in interfering with the liberty of action of any of their members is self-protection ... the only purpose for which power can rightfully be exercised over any member of a civilised community against his will is to prevent harm to others.'

The range of victimless crimes on the statute book had made Sydney a sick and secretive city, full of 'two-up schools', abortion clinics paying off the police, public toilets where nice young constables scratched themselves and arrested anyone who showed an interest, and so on. The ironies abounded: Sydney's leading abortionist, Geoff Davis (a distant relative), and others of his trade flew to Bangladesh at the behest of the World Health Organization and the International Planned Parenthood Foundation in 1971 to perform late-term abortions for thousands of local women who had conceived through rape by Pakistani soldiers during the genocide in Bangladesh. Davis and his colleagues were hailed there as heroes and awarded medals, before they returned to Sydney to pay off police to avoid prosecution.

It was particularly galling as in Britain, where these laws had originated, they were being dismantled by the Labour government elected in 1964, largely by my *Lady Chatterley* hero, now the Lord Chancellor, Gerald Gardiner. But in Australia we remained more British than the British wished to remain, partly through the malign influence of Christian churches and churchmen. They had no direct political power, but politicians were in awe of their influence over voters and dared not upset them. If you want just one example of the idiocy that I raged against, take the case of *Hair*, the smash-hit musical I had seen on Broadway, with lyrics touching upon sex, drugs and rock 'n' roll, and thirty seconds of on-stage nudity at the close of Act I. A Sydney impresario bought the rights and hired the innovative Jim Sharman to direct it. The churches and public moralists of the time manufactured outrage and in 1969 the chief secretary of the massively corrupt state government announced that *Hair* would be banned. He thought that this would win approval, and votes, from an electorate in which churchgoers outnumbered theatregoers.

But just a few weeks after his threat, Princess Anne, the eighteen-year-old daughter of our beloved Queen, saw the show in London and went on stage to dance with the cast. There were photographs of her in all the newspapers. The government went into crisis mode – to maintain the ban on *Hair* would imply serious criticism of the morals of the royal family, something even more unthinkable than on-stage nudity. Calculating, no doubt correctly, that there were more royalists than there were prudes in the state's electorate, the government withdrew the threatened ban and the impresario made a fortune from Jim Sharman's production, which played for years to plane-loads of sex-starved Melburnians at a theatre in Kings Cross.

When, some time later, I had the opportunity, I told Princess Anne (no one else would) how she had struck a blow for artistic freedom in Australia, and she could scarcely believe it: 'Can people really be so silly as to ban a musical?' In Australia in the '60s, they certainly could.

Imbued with my new-found knowledge of criminology, showing how prohibition drives up the price of harmless pleasures, profits a criminal sub-culture and corrupts law enforcement, I joined the Council for Civil Liberties, an engaging group of liberty-conscious lawyers and academics who would spend weekends roasting pigs (wearing policemen's hats) at a country property and distributing information, in a badly typed newsletter, about the latest police atrocities. It was the cops, of course, who were making most money out of the legislature's inability to distinguish between sin and crime: the vice squad operated as God's police, punishing various forms of immorality outside lawful matrimony, while on a vast subterranean level actually allowing it to flourish – for a fee, which was incorporated into its cost. We had laws against drinking in pubs after 6 p.m. (which was time for 'the six o'clock swill') but everyone knew where to buy a drink after hours; we had laws against prostitution, but in laneways off Kings Cross hundreds of sex workers were permitted to ply the trade, molested only by policemen they hadn't paid.

There was so much wrong with the law I studied in the '60s that it seemed impossible to practise it without agitating for its reform, or else going into politics to try to change it. Perhaps the worst aspect, in the sense that it affected so many law-abiding people, was the difficulty of ending a broken-down marriage. Thanks to the pernicious influence of the churches, especially the dogmatic teaching of the Catholic Church that marriages were made in heaven to last for ever, divorce was difficult, lengthy and expensive, and destructive of any post-separation collaboration (e.g. over the kids) because it required proof of a 'matrimonial crime' – in most cases, adultery. There had to be evidence of stains on the sheets, weekends with a blonde in Surfers Paradise or illicit passion in a car parked on a bush road and photographed in grainy silhouette by a private detective up the nearest gum tree. Relationships rarely recovered from this sort of divorce, unless both parties collaborated (which they frequently did) in committing perjury. There were lots of unhappy marriages, until 1975, when the Whitlam Labor government took divorce (but not consequent financial arrangements) out of the courts and made it a formality after one year's separation – a process much more civilised than family law in Britain today, which still requires in most cases an admission of a 'matrimonial crime' of adultery or unreasonable behaviour. (The failure of British politicians to remove the requirement to make allegations of fault in order to obtain a divorce within reasonable time is not just evidence of sloth or pusillanimity: it demonstrates a deliberate refusal by representatives of the people to recognise the needs of people they are meant to represent.)[12]

The major flashpoints for Australian university protests in the '60s were capital punishment, Vietnam and discrimination against Aboriginals. The death penalty was by now confined to Victoria, where truculent politicians had to be threatened by the High Court with imprisonment for contempt before they forbore, in 1962, from hanging a mentally ill man. They succeeded, five years later, in marching an escaped convict to the gallows. He had been captured in New South Wales, and we protested somewhat vainly outside the Victorian Tourist Office in Sydney (for Victorians in the '60s, the world was small). Books written about these cases, and the work of the courageous counsel who fought to save their clients' lives, lodged in my mind – they became sources of learning and of inspiration when I became the leading death row defender in the Privy Council between 1975 and 1995.

The case which had the most lasting influence on me was that of Rupert Max Stuart.[13] It took place in 1959 in South Australia, fiefdom of another long-serving reactionary premier, Thomas Playford. I briefly recount the Stuart story to explain why it fascinated a student who encountered many of its problems when he came to practise law in Britain and elsewhere. In particular, the problem of how to tell whether 'confessions' made in police cells are true.

The raped and murdered body of nine-year-old Mary Hattam was found in a beach cave near Ceduna, in far-west South Australia, in 1958. Rupert Max Stuart was arrested two days later. He was an 'outsider', briefly in town for work on a travelling carnival, and he was Aboriginal – a peripatetic member of the Aranda people of Central Australia. During an interview with police – unrecorded – he was stripped naked and at the end signed a typewritten statement in precise, educated English, confessing to the crime. This was the only basis for his prosecution.

The local press was hysterical about the awfulness of the crime and shared the police confidence in Stuart's culpability; the judge summed up for a conviction and the South Australian Court of Appeal dismissed Stuart's appeal. The prosecutor was so convinced of Stuart's guilt that he later said, 'I would have hanged him myself; he's nothing but an animal.' The young defence lawyer was a solicitor inexperienced in murder trials, without legal aid to obtain expert testimony. The most important evidence came after the trial, from anthropologist Ted Strehlow, a professor who knew more about the Aranda people and their language than any other white Australian. He said that Stuart could not possibly have used the language or the sentence structure of the so-called confession. The High Court refused to order a new trial because the evidence had not been obtained in time, and the Privy Council showed no interest in the case (it never did at this time in cases involving capital punishment). However, when dismissing the appeal, the High Court did note that 'certain matters in this case give us cause for concern', a statement that inspired Rohan Rivett, editor of Adelaide's *The News*, to launch a campaign to reprieve Stuart. His proprietor, the young Rupert Murdoch, approved. The campaign increased circulation and increased the pressure on Playford to stay Stuart's execution until after an inquiry. Playford decided that this should take the form of a three-judge Royal Commission, chaired by Sir Mellis Napier (the Chief Justice of South Australia, who had rejected Stuart's appeal) and including the trial judge. This was outrageous – two of the three judges were being invited to review their own decisions – but it shows the complacency of reactionary figures like Playford, who believed he could get away with appointing the Adelaide legal establishment to investigate its own behaviour.

In the meantime, Stuart's supporters had paid for Sydney's top QC, Jack Shand, to appear before these biased judges. As he was cross-examining a policeman, suggesting that the confession had been bashed out of the naked and terrified Aboriginal, Napier refused to allow his questions. Then, in the most electrifying moment in Australian legal history, Shand dropped his books loudly on the desk, said that he would no longer by his presence lend legitimacy to a biased tribunal, and walked out. (This is something I have always wanted to do, and have occasionally been tempted.) Shand took a risk – he was lucky not to have been jailed for contempt of court. His action actually saved his client's life – by emphasising to the world that the tribunal was a fix. It surprised no one when it upheld Stuart's conviction, but because Shand had demonstrated its bias, its report did not provide the excuse for Stuart's execution that Playford had intended when he set it up. He was forced by a public outcry to commute Stuart's sentence.

The main casualty of the saga was its hero, Rohan Rivett, who then began a campaign for Stuart's release from prison. This would not boost the circulation of *The News*, reckoned young Rupert, so he sacked one of the great heroes of Australian journalism. As for the other Rupert, he served many years in prison before he was let out, but he went on to become an elder of the Aranda people and chair of the Central Land Council, in which capacity he welcomed Queen Elizabeth when she visited in 2000. Asked on television whether he'd murdered Mary Hattam, Stuart replied, 'Some people think I'm guilty and some people think I'm not. Some people think Elvis is still alive, but most of us think he's dead and gone' – which most people took to mean 'no'.

The Stuart case lodged in the minds of law students of my generation through a remarkable and moving series of paintings by David Boyd. For my money (literally – I bought one of them, as did John Mortimer), they are among the most important pieces of Australian political art, confronting, as they do, ashen-faced judges with the Neolithic masks of defendants to whom their system cannot deliver justice.

The lessons of the Stuart case were, firstly, that you could not try Aboriginals by the procedures of the law of England. Stuart could not read or write, yet at no stage had he been supplied with an interpreter, in court or in the police station. Whether or not he had been bashed, his word-perfect confession was obviously unbelievable. No lawyer, social worker or Aboriginal protection officer had been present at his interview and the very fact that he had ended up naked in the interview room demonstrated the need for a tape recording of his alleged confession. There was no 'equality of arms' – his defending solicitor was inexperienced and outclassed by the senior Crown prosecutor. And, most fundamentally, both in police station and in court, a defendant was overwhelmed by white authority figures asking aggressive questions to which the easiest response was to acquiesce.

By the time I came to practise law, a decade after the Stuart case, those problems remained, not only for Aboriginals but for vulnerable people in Britain and elsewhere. We urged solutions such as tape recordings (and, later, video recordings) of police interviews, improvements in legal aid and support for Aboriginal suspects when they were questioned about serious crimes. The need for these reforms was exemplified by a case we took up in 1969 – that of Nancy Young, an Aboriginal woman convicted by an all-white, all-male jury and sentenced to three years in prison for the manslaughter of her baby, who died – probably of scurvy – on the insanitary

Aboriginal reserve in Cunnamulla, a town serving the rich cattle country of south-west Queensland.

The trial was in many ways a grave miscarriage of justice, from the moment bail was set at a ridiculous amount ($1,000 when Nancy was earning $6 a week), to the judge's summing up, which invited the jury to convict because Nancy had not given evidence (on her counsel's advice, who feared she would be overawed and overwhelmed and simply acquiesce to questions asked in cross-examination by a white authority figure). There was no credible evidence that she had malnourished her four-month-old child, who appeared to have died of disease, and the prosecution failed to obtain expert medical evidence which might support its case of deliberate neglect. This case was weak enough – the local hospital had not provided prompt or proper treatment when Nancy had brought the child in from the squalor of the reserve where Aboriginals were obliged to live, out of sight and out of mind. Aboriginal child mortality was six times that of white children, and Nancy's prosecution was a reflection of racist attitudes in the town, which assumed that the fault belonged to Aboriginals for the refusal by authorities to provide them with proper housing and health conditions.

I was outraged, and organised public protest meetings.[14] The public defender belatedly obtained some expert evidence from the state's top paediatrician, who concluded that it was reasonably possible the death had been caused by a birth deficiency that was no fault of Nancy's and had been hastened by incorrect treatment at the hospital. This, we thought, would be fatal to a conviction that had to be proved beyond reasonable doubt, but, almost inconceivably, three cloth-eared judges on the Queensland Court of Appeal refused to hear it. It was a shameful performance, and it attracted the attention of an ABC programme, which proved that the baby's death was not caused by Nancy. The chairman of the local council expressed sentiments that would have been shared by other whites, both in the town and in the jury room: 'Aborigines, I think, have the motto "Something for nothing". They don't get very much for nothing, I'll admit that too. I think you'll find if you poke down there in their reserve, they are pretty happy in their environment.' The programme ended with a close-up of the baby's rough grave, with a table of unacceptably high Aboriginal infant mortality rates superimposed.

The effect was so powerful that the disgraced Queensland judicial establishment had to act: a new Court of Appeal bench was hastily rustled up and a petition for Nancy's pardon referred to it, with a statement by another expert confirming the evidence disregarded at the earlier appeal. Nancy was declared not guilty and released from jail a week before she would have completed her sentence – with no compensation for her wrongful imprisonment.

The Nancy Young case, and the extraordinary behaviour of the Queensland judges, was too outrageous to be allowed to rest in the obscurity that the second Court of Appeal verdict was designed to secure. I wrote articles which drew comparisons with the Stuart case and stressed the need for Aboriginal legal services and changes in court procedures to give Aboriginal people a chance of a fair trial. It was an important lesson: justice will not be done unless injustice is seen to be done. Judges are experts in twisting facts and manipulating legal doctrines and at giving good impressions of fairness that can fool the public – when they go wrong, it takes journalists working with lawyers prepared to speak out to unravel the errors.

My efforts to highlight the deficiencies that produced the wrongful convictions of Nancy Young led me to meet Faith Bandler, a warm and wonderful woman of Islander heritage who invited me to join the board of the Federal Council for the Advancement of Aborigines and Torres Strait Islanders (FCAATSI), which was leading the struggle to end nationwide discrimination in wages and employment, and beginning to talk about land rights at a time when state and local governments, ever receptive to the demands of developers, were moving Aboriginals off their historic homelands to make way for white settlers. At the 1970 FCAATSI conference, I gave a paper on 'Aborigines and the Law Courts', in which I had become something of an expert as a result of Nancy's case; it surprised me that, notwithstanding the large numbers of Indigenous people processed by the law courts over the twenty-three years of my life, there were not more lawyers to have made this injustice their study.

By then I had begun acting *pro bono* for some Aboriginal families at Botany Bay who'd been threatened with eviction for non-payment of rent, writing letters repeatedly assuring the Minister for Lands that these families were earnest in their promises to pay rent in the future. In reality, of course, they saw no reason to pay to live on land they believed was their own, and I came to see their point of view. I was also asked to act for Aboriginals arbitrarily arrested by police, but the problem was that my prestigious law firm made a point of not doing criminal work. I raised this with its senior partner; he sucked his pipe for a moment and then explained the facts of legal life: 'Why, lad, it's like this. We just couldn't have criminals sitting in our waiting rooms alongside corporate clients like Mr Packer and Mr Murdoch and the Board of Mineral Securities.' He intended no irony, but in a few years' time, when the mining bubble burst and many of its corporate clients were threatened with prosecution, the firm learnt to do criminal law quickly enough to keep them.

*   *   *

The law – and its practitioners – gave the poor no access to justice, so with like-minded colleagues in 1970 I drew up plans for a legal service, to be operated by law students under the supervision of a qualified solicitor. The plans were submitted to the Law Society, to no effect: the editor of its journal sarcastically called for cartoons to illustrate our efforts. Such was the resistance of a wealthy, uncaring profession. The society pointed out that its members did a lot of charity work – which was true, though usually for their churches or golf clubs – and they saw no reason to change their rules to allow the establishment of a legal aid clinic for poor people.

The fact that the law was thought – by lawyers – to have no business help-ing the poor was partly because there was no movement in this direction at Oxbridge, where narrow-minded dons showed no interest in the social role of their discipline. America – Harvard, in particular – was another matter. The 'War on Poverty' in the US had already produced 850 neighbourhood law centres which helped the unemployed to deal with rent demands, hire-purchase commitments and immigration disputes, while thirty-six US law schools were offering precisely the community legal aid services that we were proposing. We sent some photographs of them to the *Law Society Journal*, suggesting that they might be more informative than cartoons.

For all these well-meaning efforts, I should not give the impression that fun was off the agenda. The student Law Society organised balls – grand events at Luna Park, where dinner-jacketed judges of the future drunkenly bumped each other in dodgems or swung wildly over the harbour in aerial rides. When our guests were real judges, we would hold balls at the Trocadero and moodily smooch to restrained cover versions of Beatles hits. Then there was the infamous law dinner, where inebriated students bawled out songs about the slavery of articled clerkship and threw bread rolls at the distinguished speaker.

The star performer, the greatest celebrity in the common law world ever to grace a student dinner, was Lord Denning. He was, by the time he visited Australia in 1967, a jurisprudential phenomenon whose decisions updating old laws of contract and tort we had all read (they were, unlike most legal judgments, eminently readable) and admired. By this time he was Master of the Rolls, i.e. head of the civil division of the Court of Appeal, and at the height of his powers. He was also an impressive speaker. At the dinner, he opened by announcing, 'I am Master of the Rolls, so you can throw your bread rolls at me now.' This disarmed his audience, and he proceeded to tell a number of weak jokes before elaborating on his controversial credo: 'I must do justice, whatever the law may be.'

I must say that he seemed a charming old English gent, and I was regretful that if I ever made it to the English Bar it would probably be too late to appear before him. He toured the Australian legal circuit like a popstar, soaking up the adoration of a colonial profession still in awe of every word in his judgments.

When I did start appearing in the English courts, a decade later, Tom Denning was still Master of the Rolls. He was in his eighties, but not bound by a retirement age: 'I have every virtue except resignation,' he had announced. That was because, sadly, all the adoration had gone to his head. The after-dinner credo 'I must do justice whatever the law may be' was irresponsible enough (judges are there to apply the law as it is, not as they think it should be), but he had started to twist it to suit his own prejudices, which turned out to be extremely reactionary. He could never allow a trade union to win,[15] or a prisoner or a gay person or even a woman

(El Vino's wine bar that refused to serve women was not discriminating against them; it was merely showing 'gentlemanly courtesy'). He adjudged that a trainee schoolteacher could not complain about unfair expulsion when found to have a man in her room, since 'promiscuous girls' were not fit to teach. He had gone from being the great ornament of the common law to its great embarrassment.

When I did appear before him, it was usually for a client he disliked: before they could get justice according to law his sanctimonious judgments had to be appealed. Eventually, in 1982, I had the sad but necessary task of taking an action that forced him to resign. He wrote a book in which he repeated some scuttlebutt about black jurors being untrue to their oaths by acquitting black defendants in a political trial, and on their behalf I wrote a 'letter before action', threatening to sue him for libel. He admitted the offence and resigned immediately.

* * *

By the end of my academic studies, I had to decide just what sort of law I wanted to practise. I was aiming for the Bar but was wary of legal argument as a means to establish truth. My final-year dissertation took the form of a Socratic dialogue, set 'in a meadow in some jurisprudential cloud-cuckoo land' between Chaïm Perelman (a philosopher who thought legal rhetoric had metaphysical value), Clive Cicero QC (an amalgam of the great Roman advocate and Clive Evatt, the most cunning QC at the Sydney Bar), and Jerome Frank, an acerbic US judge renowned for his scathing attacks on lawyers and their courtroom tricks. The other participant in the play (which was heavily influenced by *Waiting for Godot*) was 'the reasonable student', i.e. me. It analysed the common forensic fallacies and wondered whether they might nonetheless help juries towards a justifiable verdict. It would never make it into production, but at least I seem to have discerned that the art of judging is the ability to reject arguments that are good in favour of arguments that are better.

It was a burden to do articles of clerkship at the same time as your university course, and the student law society urged the abolition of articles and their replacement by a six-month 'skills course' after you took a degree. Nonetheless, I had an interesting few years working for Allen Allen & Hemsley, which served the nation's corporate titans, its newspaper moguls (notably Sir Frank Packer and Rupert Murdoch) and its commercial giants: they sought the firm's services to raise share capital, satisfy prospectus requirements and, above all, to avoid tax. Articled clerks worked from strip-lit cubbyholes, running errands for partners who worked in large offices with unimpeded harbour views (in Sydney, your rank in the legal profession may be judged by how much of the harbour can be seen from your office window). It was a privilege to be given the opportunity to grasp the lower rung of this establishment ladder – the competition was intense, and some thought it amusing that a leader of the campaign to abolish articles of clerkship should be so keen to accept them when offered by the best firm in town. But there was no alternative, and I listened intently to my first lesson on professional behaviour: never talk in lifts, or in lavatories.

My first year was taken up with the duties of a filing clerk, running all over town to deliver documents. I developed the ability to cross a busy road, irrespective of traffic lights, without being run over. This skill – the first an articled clerk learns – has become an irrepressible instinct, to the terror of partners, children and old ladies I have helped across the street. Other tasks were easier and sometimes instructive. For three months I was seconded to sit as the most junior member of the Allens team, billed at many times my menial salary, on the case of *American Flange v Rheem Australia*, the nation's longest-running lawsuit. It was all about the 'flange' on a drum, with our American clients holding a patent which Rheem had allegedly infringed. The evidence was mind-numbing and I would occasionally nod off, to be shaken awake by an American Flange executive who feared that my drowsiness might be fatal to his company's case. The only memorable moment came from the habit of the opposition silk of consuming half a bottle of champagne at the mid-morning adjournment. His solicitor solicitously kept it in a specially cooled bag under counsel's desk: one morning the cork popped and hit the startled judge on the nose. At this point, everyone woke up.

More courtroom enjoyment was to be had in defamation trials. We acted for Consolidated Press, Sir Frank Packer's mouthpiece for the conservatives, curiously in Australia called the Liberal Party. Its role was to defame Labor MPs, who would sue with the help of Clive Evatt, the go-to QC for 'defo' (defamation) plaintiffs. Sir Frank insisted on being represented by Antony Larkins QC, the monocled epitome of upper-class English taste: I would run with the brief to his junior, who did all the work. Evatt was cunning, and 'the Lark' would fall into the traps he carefully laid before working-class juries. For example, when addressing them, Evatt would deliberately misquote Shakespeare: 'A rose by any other name would smell the same.' Larkins would jump up to correct him – '"Would smell as sweet", Your Honour.' Cue Evatt telling the jury that he was just a poor Australian worker, like them, who did not have the literary learning of his colleague, but who did know a libel when he saw it. In those days, newspaper defendants not only had to prove the truth of their allegations, but also that they were published for the public benefit. In one case, I heard Evatt persuade a jury that making true allegations of corruption against a Labor candidate was not for the public benefit because it was only a small electorate.

In due course we were allocated to work for a partner, and mine acted for Gordon Barton, an eccentric businessman I dubbed 'the fast buccaneer'. He had left his law course to run a trucking company, then an airline, and now was setting up mutual funds and other financial products to finance radical newspapers and a political party that urged withdrawal from Vietnam. He was one of the very few – perhaps the only – multimillionaire in the country who could qualify as a radical libertarian. My role in his empire was street-level but not insignificant. I had to take the prospectus for each new company or fund for registration at the Companies Office. The officials on the desk had to be persuaded that the glossy brochures with front-cover pictures of the Harbour Bridge and part-finished Opera House were not in fact representations that Barton's 'Fund of Funds' actually owned these prime pieces of real estate. I was successful in over-the-counter advocacy and soon Gordon and I were meeting for coffee. He did his best to seduce me away from the law, offering me the editorship of one of the newspapers he was planning. I resisted Gordon's blandishments – I still had starry-eyed trust in law as a lever for social progress.

I did not stay long in Gordon's turbulent corporate milieu, but he and his partner, Mary-Ellen, were warm and generous friends over the years. They bought Ken Tynan's large house in Kensington, where the *Spycatcher* conspiracy was plotted (see Chapter Thirteen). For some years they ran an almost overnight delivery service – TNT Air Express – between Sydney and London, and they came to my fortieth birthday party at my home in Islington with forty dozen reasonably fresh Sydney rock oysters. The guests, who had not experienced the delicacy, were overwhelmed – as was I, by their kindness. They had a Sydney home – a mansion on the harbour with a large and comfortable boathouse said to have been used for assignations by Prince Philip. They made it available for me to use for some weeks when my assignations with Kathy Lette excited the interest of gossip columnists: we could look out on the loveliest view in the world, without the world looking in. Back in the late '60s, my work during the day for Gordon had to be balanced with student political activities and – I had almost forgotten – attendance at law school.

Busy practitioners were in the main too busy to impart much learning by lectures. One exception was Trevor Martin, a civil liberties barrister who taught the law of evidence and was fascinated by its intellectual challenges. He would obsess over the 'best-evidence rule' – an archaic principle developed before the invention of the photocopying machine which prohibited the introduction of a copy if the original – the 'best' evidence – was available. It did not seem relevant and after I left uni I never thought of it again, until a quarter of a century later, in London, when I found myself defending some American musicians with odd names – Dr Dre, Ice Cube and so on – who were members of a group called N.W.A. – Niggaz Wit Attitudes. The tabloids called them 'Niggaz Wit Mansions' and incited Scotland Yard to seize their album, which had reached Britain in the form of 100,000 cassette tapes. The police were pretty confident of their case under the Obscene Publications Act, and they served us with their evidence in the form of a transcript of N.W.A. songs – 'To Kill a Hooker' and so on. My wife almost threw up – 'How can you possibly defend them?' This must never be said to a barrister, because it will always elicit the response 'Just watch me.' In no time I had found an expert witness who opined that N.W.A. was producing 'street journalism' for the public good. I doubted, however, that the three elderly magistrates would have the street wisdom to appreciate it, and Scotland Yard were already preparing to have the cassettes crushed and dumped somewhere in the North Sea.

The point when the prosecutor proffered to the court the transcript of the lyrics was the moment when memory suddenly flashed back to Trevor's lectures twenty-five years before, and I jumped up: 'Objection. This evidence is inadmissible. Under the best evidence rule, you cannot find N.W.A. obscene by reading a transcript of their lyrics: you must listen to the original article – the cassette tape – which is the best evidence.'

After a mad scramble in old textbooks, the court had to agree, and called on the prosecution to play a confiscated cassette. So confident were the police of victory that they had not bothered to bring a cassette player to court, and a ghetto-blaster had to be borrowed from a passing black youth. The N.W.A.'s cacophony resounded through the court for about ten minutes, until the chairman, hands over his ears, shouted, 'We can't understand a word! Case dismissed. With costs.' (The last two words are always the sweetest.) N.W.A. – Ice Cube, Dr Dre and the others – went on to chart-topping success in the UK and everywhere else. This case is still the source of my street cred: when I visit youth centres, kids sidle up to me and ask with awe, 'Didn't you defend Ice Cube?' The case did not make it into the movie *Straight Outta Compton*, but perhaps it will be seen in the sequel.

*   *   *

I made, quite unconsciously, my greatest contribution to changing Australian minds about human rights while editing my last edition of the law school magazine. One of the most heated questions of the moment was whether Australian sporting bodies, particularly rugby union and cricket, should continue to play against racially selected teams from South Africa. Opposition came from small anti-apartheid groups, whose demands were dismissed by sports administrators and politicians alike, with the mantra 'We don't mix sport and politics.' In 1970, Australians were looking forward to rugby Tests the following year – a rematch after the Wallaby tour of South Africa in 1969, and then a Test cricket series. That was when I bumped into James Roxburgh, a law student from my final year who had played in the Australian team on the 1969 South African tour. He said that he had been deeply shocked by apartheid, and expressed some qualms about playing against the all-white Springboks again. Maybe we could discuss it? He seemed keen, and then reluctant, and then asked if he could bring a friend. In fact, he brought four more Wallabies. I settled them down in the Law School Library, took out a tape recorder and asked some questions.

The session lasted several hours, and the information they vied with each other to impart was chilling. Their four months' experience of apartheid went beyond the segregated 'whites only' and 'blacks only' signs which met tourist eyes in buses, lavatories, hospitals, post offices, restaurants and park benches. These young men had witnessed the personal degradation of apartheid. The secret police had been on their tail whenever they attempted to meet non-whites; they had been carpeted by the team manager, who'd passed on a warning from the police that they would only harm black people by trying to fraternise with them. Whenever they played, the blacks and 'Cape Coloureds' would be herded into the worst seats, behind the goalposts, from where they would barrack loudly for Australia. The players were left in no doubt that South African government officials and sporting bodies were using the Australian tour as propaganda, as an Australian endorsement of apartheid. They had discovered that not only were blacks prohibited from selection for international sporting teams, but they were denied the opportunity to participate even in rugby-club training. One of the players put the case succinctly: 'An Australian tour hardens existing attitudes and strengthens the hand of advocates of sporting apartheid, because it implies Australia's approval of that system … You have to understand how big sport is there, how much it means to the country's image.'

I came to the crunch – would they play against racially selected South African teams again? They later said they had not decided, before the interview, to make any sort of joint declaration, but when put on the spot they were driven by the logic of their earlier answers to say 'no'. It was a big statement – it would mean sacrificing their places in the next Australian side. But all of them said it, firmly and individually.

They had presented the most powerful case for stopping political football, emphasising their sincerity by ruling themselves out of selection. It was a decision that had news value, and the editor of *The Australian* got to hear of it and offered to publish. The interview was given headline publicity, and it shocked Australian rugby union to the core. Its officials threatened to blacklist the young men and end their careers, and tried to suggest that words had been put in their mouths by some communist agitator. The boys stood by their opinions I had recorded in the interview and accepted speaking engagements to repeat them. For the first time, Australians were provided with information about sporting apartheid from those whose views about it deserved the greatest respect – players who had directly experienced it and had sacrificed their own future in an attempt to end it.

The rugby tour went ahead at the insistence of Australian officials without action by a lily-livered conservative government. On the other side, the leader of the Labor Party, Gough Whitlam, announced that he favoured a ban, and the leader of the trade unions, Bob Hawke, actually imposed one on the Springboks' travel arrangements, forcing them to charter planes, trains and automobiles to get around the country. Peter Hain came out from England to inspire the protests, and my dear friend Meredith Burgmann (many years later, president of the NSW Legislative Council) was in the forefront of the disruptions, showing extraordinary courage: she was dragged from the pitch by police, beaten up by angry fans and actually jailed by a benighted Sydney magistrate.

It took a great Australian sportsman – indeed, the greatest – to end the sordid business of supporting apartheid. Sir Don Bradman was chairman of the Australian Cricket Board: he read my interview with the Wallabies and began a curious correspondence with Meredith Burgmann, arguing out the case for and against sporting contracts with Africa. She seemed to convince him, because he cancelled the Test series due to be played later in 1971, writing, 'We will not play them until they choose a team on a non-racist basis.' Australia did not officially play cricket with South Africa for the next twenty-two years, until it allowed the selection of black sportsmen.[16]

In campaigning against racism and advocating the end of apartheid, withdrawal from Vietnam and lifting of censorship, as with so many other causes in the '60s, we were on the right side of history. It didn't feel like it at the time: we'd grown up in a society with its mind firmly closed and a police-bashing in store if you wanted to open it too far. Fast forward half a century, from the stultified post-war era to our present multiracial, multi-cultural, vibrant society, and perhaps we students can take some credit for the change, although success came in large measure because of the moral bankruptcy of the conservatives. Progressive reforms were welcomed by most and turned out to have none of the dire consequences our enemies had predicted. Dinosaurs still roam the earth, with an instinctive inhuman-ity that prevented progress for so long on gay marriage or, in Australia, the constitutional recognition of Indigenous people and ending the sufferings of refugees in offshore detention centres. They are, however, much less for-midable than the opposition we faced in the '60s. Had we been vouchsafed, as students in 1967, a view into the society of 2018, we would have been amazed and delighted – there has been real change as well as *plus ça change*.

*   *   *

In 1962, my parents had acquired a small block of land in Longueville, a quiet bayside suburb in Sydney, inhabited mainly by doctors and elderly but comfortably-off widows. Tennis ace John Newcombe lived around the corner, Nicole Kidman would later live up the road, and overlooking the ferry wharf was the house of Jane Perlez, a girl of my own age with whom I bonded on the city bus. She was to become one of the world's best journalists. She began as a cadet on the *Australian* newspaper, working there until its proprietor, Rupert Murdoch, sacked the editor for writing anti-Vietnam editorials. She left for New York, vowing never again to work for a Murdoch paper, and soon made her name as city editor and ballet critic for the *Post* and media columnist for the *Village Voice*. Then Murdoch came to town and took over both papers and, true to her vow, she resigned, giving up fame and power for a column in the small-circulation *Soho News*. Eventually she was taken on by the *New York Times*, where she still reports from Kenya, Pakistan, China or wherever – her by-line on a story is a guarantee of its accuracy. I would later spend a lot of my working life defending journalists and became friends with the older generation of Australians – Phil Knightley, Bruce Page, Tony Delano (whose daughter married my brother Tim) and Murray Sayle – but I always admired Jane, the girl on the bus.

Our small family house in Lucretia Avenue is still there: it was where I would always come home, several times a year, for forty-five years, to kiss my parents and go to sleep in a small bedroom full of memories. I was at its desk, working on an essay one fine afternoon in 1967, when the ABC radio news announced that 'a very important frogman' had disappeared off Portsea, a beach near Melbourne. It was some hours before it could bring itself to verify the frogman as Australia's Prime Minister, Harold Holt, whose body was never recovered (he was probably 'taken' by a shark, although conspiracy theorists still claim he was taken aboard a Chinese submarine). It was in the room opposite – the laundry – where I heard from my ashen-faced father of John F. Kennedy's assassination. JFK had saved us from the Cuban Missile Crisis and I can't think of any politician for whom I have had such total trust – I was only sixteen, and far away from his faults.

Longueville has changed now – the widows have been winkled out and replaced by lawyers, and the big houses at the end of the point are being bought by wealthy Chinese, but it still radiates the calm that comes from water and gum trees and genteel prosperity. In my teens I would venture along the wooden planks of the harbour pool, watching the vapour trails of the big jets landing and departing, their engine *whoosh* punctuated by the tinkling of masts in the bay. I had no doubt I would depart on one of them – but I had yet to decide how, and whence.

*   *   *

In my final year, something surprising happened: I came top in tax. The intellectual chess played between taxpayer and taxman intrigued me. There were ethical dilemmas – the distinction between tax avoidance and tax evasion, for example; there were sociological and economic implications, for governments which believed that growth would come through tax cuts or else that a more equal redistribution of wealth would result from tax hikes on the wealthy; but most interesting were the implications for international businesses operating in countries with different tax regimes, or none at all. The subject that was novel was 'blue-sky law', over large areas of the globe where the taxman had no jurisdiction. I toyed with the idea of doing a doctorate on the subject, publishing it as the first book in the field, and becoming a barrister expert in international tax law, a subject that would be lucrative enough for me to spend time, free of charge, defending Aboriginals and dissidents and others in peril in the courts. It was a nice idea, adapted from Robin Hood, but would require a further course of study, preferably at an overseas university.

Harvard was the obvious choice, as it led the world in analysing the sociological impact of law. The easiest and cheapest way to get there as a postgraduate was to win a scholarship, and, serendipitously, a new scholarship had just been announced, with requirements that seemed to fit perfectly. A successful career in student politics was said to be a qualification, whereas the venerated Rhodes scholarship was usually confined to those who played rugby, had attended private schools and did not cause trouble. In any case, Rhodes led you only to Oxford – this brand new scholarship would take me directly to Harvard Law School. The drawback? It was called the Robert Gordon Menzies scholarship. I asked myself whether I could really go through life bearing the name – a Robert Menzies scholar – of the man responsible for sending my schoolmates off to be killed in Vietnam? In a rare moment in which I put ideology above self-interest (and which I have since sometimes regretted), I decided not to apply for a Menzies scholarship. I would take my slim chance with Cecil Rhodes: a name, so I thought, I could proudly bear throughout my life.

There was much in the study of law in Australia that was also tempting me to England. Certainly there were more exciting developments in the

US, but London was where judges made our law, and where the English Law Lords decided our final appeals, in the quaint old Downing Street courtroom of the Privy Council. Interesting, to my juvenile legal mind, was the fact that the Privy Council's reach extended to most other countries in the Commonwealth – it was still the final Court of Appeal for Singapore, Hong Kong, Malaysia, New Zealand, Mauritius and most Commonwealth countries in Africa. That meant it had a broad death-penalty jurisdiction, as capital punishment was still in full swing in most former colonies of the British Empire.

John Kerr introduced me to Garfield Barwick, the Chief Justice who had been Australia's premier advocate before becoming Menzies's Attorney General. It was a small dinner party, and Kerr encouraged Barwick to tell this wide-eyed student about his exploits in Downing Street before the judicial time lords of the Empire.

Sir Garfield told me what appeared to be his favourite story, the one about 'thirteen little Malaysians'. They were all communists sentenced to death for subversion, who had appealed to Her Majesty's Privy Council to stop their executions. Twelve of them had the sense to retain Barwick, who appeared for them in Downing Street to take a very short and very technical point about the validity of the arrest warrant, which the barrister for the thirteenth appellant, who made a florid appeal about the iniquity of the death penalty, did not bother to take. When the judgment came down, Barwick's argument had succeeded and his twelve clients were released. The thirteenth, whose case was the same in every way, failed in his appeal and was hanged. Everyone at the table laughed – that's what happens when you don't retain Barwick. I found the story shocking but also intriguing – so you win human rights cases not by emotional rhetoric but by becoming a good lawyer. Maybe one day I could persuade these mighty lords of English justice to strike down death penalties because they were legally as well as morally wrong? That would mean I would have to go for postgraduate study in Britain.

The Barwick story did make a necessary point, for those who seek to practise human rights law. It is that a solid grounding in common law and professional practice is essential equipment for success. So many bright-eyed and bushy-tailed idealists think they can jump into human rights work after a quick law degree, but if they want to make a difference they really must first learn techniques and technicalities, and all the tedious precedents which may eventually be shaped by the advocate into arguments for change. They must be able to absorb the history of the subject, and be solidly grounded in the ethics that animate legal practice. They must learn how to interview potential witnesses, how to keep a case file in order and how to keep themselves from penury – and to keep their lips sealed in lifts and lavatories.

*　　*　　*

The scholarships funded by the will of Cecil Rhodes were meant to identify 'the best men for the world's fight' – not the best women, who were not allowed to compete in those days. Cecil had a dubious background, initially having made his fortune by starting a rumour that a company (in which he held shares) had found gold, and then selling his shares before the rumour turned out to be untrue. His behaviour contributed to the Boer War and his subsequent conduct in the Cape was politically questionable and morally unscrupulous, but he had won posthumous acclaim by donating his fortune to bring to Oxford scholars from countries as diverse as America, Australia, India, Jamaica and Germany – by 1970, about seventy a year in all, including one from each Australian state. A Rhodes scholarship was well funded, and came with guaranteed entry to an Oxford college. I decided to try for the New South Wales scholarship. The word around town was that my state's selection committee was overly impressed by the 'manly' sport of rugby union and avoided 'political' candidates. I had played tennis for the university and I had played student politics, so I applied without any great expectation of success. I was, however, short-listed and summoned to attend, with other candidates, the seven-man selection committee, which would convene at Government House under the chairmanship of Sir Roden Cutler.

My recent part in the acquittal of Sir Roden's alleged tomato assailant did not bode well, and as the appointed hour approached I lingered over urgent corporate work in the office and misjudged the time it would take to walk to Government House. I was not aware that the selection would involve seven candidates rotating around the seven selectors, ten minutes with each, before being asked to withdraw while the committee deliberates on their choice. (These days, candidates are forced to eat a four-course meal with their selectors, presumably so their table manners can be taken into account.) The panel comprised three former Rhodes scholars, three leading businessmen and Sir Roden, who was tapping his wooden leg in impatience as I arrived a minute or so after the musical chairs had started. I had to think quickly to explain my tardiness. The excuse worked in my favour. I had this important commercial client, you see, who needed immediate and urgent advice, and although it might mean ruining my chances of a Rhodes, I was bound by my professional code to put my client's interests first. The businessmen certainly liked this explanation, which had an element of truth. Another selector was a professor of English, with whom I had a hilarious conversation about the Leavisite split in the English department at Sydney – it was he who characterised it as a fight between 'the maddies' and 'the dullies'. His was the only laughter in the large, lounge-chaired sitting room of Government House, and I felt I had one definite ally. But last came a man I knew only by reputation, and his reputation, as a university vice-chancellor, was not favourable to student politicians. His name was Zelman Cowen.

To my surprise, he was a delight, and we struck up a most animated conversation about the role of law in improving society. He was obviously testing me but I saw no reason to dissemble – my goose, I assumed, had already been overcooked by my tardiness. He was provocative and I allowed myself to be provoked. When the whistle blew to signal the end of the last inquisition (Sir Roden was nothing if not military), the seven candidates lined up and trooped out, leaving the selectors to decide over tea and cakes. I felt annoyed with myself – had I not underestimated the walk to Government House, I might have been in with a chance. But I need not have worried. I learnt later that Sir Zelman had been my greatest advocate, his arguments overcoming what I assume were Sir Roden's doubts. Many years later, when Zelman was appointed chairman of the British Press

Council, his most ardent critic would, ironically, be the man he had sent to Britain. The Press Council was paid by the press barons to pretend to discipline tabloid journalists. I wrote a book denouncing it as 'a confidence trick which now fails to inspire confidence', to which Zelman replied, 'Mr Robertson shouts with reason.' Neither of us, however, managed to reform the body before a committee of inquiry came to the same conclusion, and it was wound up.

My scholarship elicited some comment in the press about the selection of an 'unorthodox' candidate, by which they probably meant a state schoolboy who did not play rugby. The main news was about the Queen's next visit: she would be sailing into Sydney on her yacht *Britannia*, and Princess Anne would be with her. There would be a royal luncheon on the boat, and to the usual array of state ministers always eager to suck up to the royals were added a number of gold-medal-winning sportsmen and the 1970 New South Wales Rhodes scholar. I was intrigued by my first gold-embossed invitation, and, my republicanism notwithstanding, I brushed aside my younger brother Tim's insistence that I wear a political anti-pin – anti-apartheid or anti-Vietnam or anti-conscription, I cannot remember which. I was not going to exploit the royal visit, like everyone else. I was going to graze with the dinosaurs, and I did not want to frighten them off.

The guests were arranged in a semicircle in the *Britannia* stateroom for the fabled meeting with the Queen. There were fifteen of us, and she stopped at each person to ask a few of her trademark questions: 'Have you come far?' 'Isn't the weather nice?' I was at the end of the semicircle and watched her performance: the smile, for which she had injections to strengthen her cheeks, was a marvel. It would stay in place for five minutes, then it would start to slip. When it reached a certain level, she would make a movement with her shoulders, and literally hitch the smile up. The exercise was repeated a few times as she progressed around the semicircle. I thought her a real pro.

At lunch I was seated next to Princess Anne, and we discussed LGBT rights. Seriously, forty years before that acronym came into being. Our topic was a recent English court decision in the case of April Ashley, née

George Jamieson, who had joined first the Merchant Navy and then a Parisian drag cabaret before having gender reassignment surgery and becoming a model. She wanted the gender on her birth certificate changed, but the judge refused. It caused a lot of controversy, and Anne was on the side of reforming the law to uphold trans rights. I suggested she might undergo a transgender operation herself so that she could inherit the throne (she was last in line below her wimpish younger brothers, Andrew and Edward). She quite liked this idea. We compared notes about *Hair*. She could not believe the stupidity of the state government in threatening to ban it, and laughed when I told her that by dancing on stage during the London run she had influenced the turn-around. If Charles did eventually lose the throne – by becoming a Methodist or Catholic or plant-worshipper of some kind – I thought for a moment that Anne would make a very acceptable head of state for Australia.

After the lunch, we were escorted out to the wharf for what was, for some guests, the really important part of the occasion: having our photographs taken for the gossip pages of the Sunday newspapers. I could scarcely believe I would be pictured along with the socialites I had pilloried and satirised for years. 'If you can't lick 'em, join 'em,' I joked to the Olympic gold medallists on either side as we posed for the *Sun-Herald* photographer, who assured us that the picture would be in the next edition. It was, I have to admit, with some anticipation that I opened his paper a few days later. The gold medallists were pictured all right, guests of the Queen on *Britannia*, but there was no sign of the man in the middle. The Rhodes scholar had been carefully airbrushed out of the photo: presumed intellectuals did not belong on Sydney's social pages. It was a neat reminder of my nation's real priorities.

Leaving Australia was always a matter of contemplating return – my generation did not have the despair with which some expatriates renounced the dreary country of the '50s. The leading silk at the Sydney Bar, Bill Deane, offered me the chance to 'read' with him on completion of the Rhodes scholarship, and I gratefully accepted. He invited me to dinner at his house, and showed me an Aladdin's cave of books – his ambition was to become a novelist, rather than to go on to become a judge. So, actually, was mine, and I watched his career with interest as he became instead a federal and then a High Court judge and then Governor General. It is likely that his brilliant judicial career, exploring 'implications' in the Australian constitution favouring democracy and freedom of political speech, has been more important to the nation than any additions he might have made to its literature. The instinct of the cobbler, to stick to his last, is right for most of us. I have sometimes been tempted to do something different – to make a home on an island and write a novel, to become a TV chat-show host, possibly to become an honoured placeman in some establishment or other. The fact, sad but true, then hits home: I am nothing more or less than a jobbing barrister, and should content myself with that lot. It's not a bad one.

But it can be a hard one. Bill pulled from his library a book for me to read on the voyage to England. It was *QB VII*, by Leon Uris, the lightly fictionalised account of the defamation case that was brought against him by a former Auschwitz doctor he had exposed in his earlier work *Exodus*. It contained one of the most glowing tributes ever to be paid to a member of the Bar: in the middle of the trial the author walks at midnight in the Temple, where barristers in London have their offices, worried sick about the outcome that could lose him his money and his reputation. He suddenly sees the lights on in the room of his own advocate, and is filled with awe at a professional who could so relentlessly dedicate himself to another's cause. Gerald Gardiner, *Lady Chatterley's* great defender, was that counsel (his junior, Louis Blom-Cooper, was burning the dawn oil). His room was known as 'the lighthouse' long before Uris saw its beams and identified with awe the obsessive commitment which is a barrister's most overlooked yet most valuable quality. Did I possess it? The book left me in no doubt that the course I had chosen would not be easy, and that sacrifices made for a good client would need a different rationale when made for a bad one. That I had yet, in my own mind, to find.

And so to farewell. There would be no tears at my departure: brother Graeme was glad to be rid of me, brother Tim excited at my prospects, and my parents proud that I was leaving as a Rhodes scholar. My girlfriend seemed resigned – she had, I suspect, a more reliable prospect in mind.

There was one piece of parting advice, from my mentor Michael Kirby (an older student politico and later a High Court judge), which made an indelible impression. He took me aside and wagged his finger. 'Let me make this prediction. You will stay in England and be a great success at the English Bar, until the day you appear in the highest court – the House of Lords. As you address the Law Lords, you will not be able to resist that temptation of yours to make a joke. And that will be the end of your career.'

I lived in fear of Michael's Delphic warning for many years, and never made jokes when appearing in the House of Lords. But in 2010, when the Law Lords were transferred to the new Supreme Court and I was called upon to address them in their first case, I could not resist. I was appearing for *The Times* and *The Economist* and other papers concerning an appeal against secret justice – the use of acronyms to hide the identity of parties to litigation. As I came into the court I noticed its list for the next three months, full of ABCs and XYZs. So I began by saying, 'Your first-term docket reads like alphabet soup.'

It wasn't a very funny joke, but it caused a flutter in the audience and the sound of indrawn breath. It was hard to tell the judicial reaction until they handed down judgment some weeks later. It began, 'Counsel challenged us in opening by saying that our first-term docket read like alphabet soup...' It was official: the Law Lords, now they are Supreme Court justices, appreciate humour. The case is known as the 'Alphabet Soup' case, and it has served as a precedent for the occasional joke from the Bar table, although not yet for a funny one.

Chapter Five

Must Rhodes Fall?

I remember the streamers – the great multi-coloured tangle of ribbon which encased ocean liners as the voyage began. The Rhodes scholarship paid only for a sea passage, which is why I found myself, in August 1970, on a castellated tub which would take me to Durban, so I could see a little of Africa en route to England. The ship stopped for an afternoon in Melbourne, where I went to the Arbitration Commission to observe the currently 'hot' ex-Rhodes scholar, trade union advocate Bob Hawke, in action. His tactics were to call for regular adjournments, whereupon he would repair with his clients to the next-door pub and quickly down a schooner or two. As the afternoon wore on, his advocacy improved although his clients became too sozzled to notice. By the time we reached Perth the ship had lost a stabiliser, but that did not deter the shipping company from sending us, wallowing and listing, across the Indian Ocean. Never again have I been able to contemplate a sea voyage longer than, say, the ferry ride from Piraeus to Mykonos.

South Africa was exactly as described by my rugby interviewees. Petty apartheid was everywhere, in segregated buses, park benches and urinals, although in Durban the facilities were triply segregated – for 'coloureds' as well as for blacks and whites. I'd had a debate on television, a few weeks before departing, with Dr Christiaan Barnard, the smooth-talking South African playboy surgeon who had done the world's first heart transplant. He denied my allegation that his country segregated not only hospitals but also ambulances. Of course it did, and I took photographs proving (if only to myself) that he had lied. I was invited to dinner by some wealthy liberal contacts: the hostess and her friends were clever and cutting about the stupidity of the Afrikaners and their apartheid policies, but I couldn't help noticing the absence of black faces – until she tinkled a little silver bell, whereupon black waiters and maids emerged to clear the plates and serve the next course. Apartheid seemed a congenial system for white liberals, offering endless opportunity to laugh at the Boer while enjoying the benefits of cheap labour. In time I would return to South Africa to meet liberals risking their lives to dismantle a system that brought benefits they could no longer accept. But I had little time before my first Oxford term and had to crack on, overland to Nairobi.

My first stop was in the Matopo Hills, to contemplate the grave of Cecil Rhodes, invariably known to his beneficiaries as 'the Founder'. It was a serene beauty spot, where his ghost could survey hundreds of miles of colonised country that then bore his name – Rhodesia. I did not actually pay my respects – I knew enough about the Founder to realise that he was too devious ever to qualify for one of his own scholarships (he had written home to his mum about the joys of having 'land of your own, shooting when you like and a lot of black niggers to do what you like with, apart from the fact of making money'). I might, however, have had a sneaking suspicion that the trip could earn a few brownie points at Rhodes House. Who knows? A photo beside the Founder's remains might induce the Warden to extend my scholarship for a coveted third year.

Then I drove to Great Zimbabwe, a magnificent and mysterious ruin, evidence of a highly intelligent civilisation as early as the eleventh century. Rhodes had looted it, of course: one of the noble 'Zimbabwe bird' statues was installed at his house (Groote Schuur) in Cape Town and another stands atop Rhodes House in Oxford. When I passed through Rhodesia in 1970, Ian Smith's racist government had banned archaeologists from suggesting that Great Zimbabwe had been built by Africans, lest people might get the idea that they could be clever: they were ordered to speculate that it was the work of wandering Jewish or Arab architects. Actually, it was almost certainly built by ancestors of the Shona people with the profits from trade in gold and ivory.

After a tedious three-day drive through the monotonous countryside of Zambia came the thrills of the Serengeti, a World Heritage environment second only to the Great Barrier Reef. Revhead that I am, the experience of racing a cheetah travelling at 60 mph against the backdrop of Mount Kilimanjaro stays with me still. So does the experience of being charged by a short-sighted rhinoceros, who pulled up a few paces from our jeep when he realised that we were not, after all, a love rival. Going over the top of the Ngorongoro Crater and descrying hundreds of thousands of flamingos on the lake in the centre of the extinct volcano surrounded by trees full of monkeys and clearings full of elephants and zebras was another never-to-be-forgotten experience. But this was Tanzania, and despite the Christian socialism of its leader, Julius Nyerere – the gentlest man ever to preside over an African country – there were human rights abuses from which animals could not distract me for long.

They were taking place offshore, in Zanzibar – the 'zan' in Tanzania (the old British colony of Tanganyika). Dr Nyerere, who had translated two Shakespeare plays and the Bible into Swahili, was by 1970 regretting the amalgamation which made the island's ruler, Sheikh Abeid Amani Karume, his vice-president. The sheikh was the caricature black despot to whom South Africans liked to point their attempts to justify apartheid: he announced that there would be no elections on the island for the next sixty years, since democracy was a Western luxury that impoverished Africans could not afford. Then he took it into his head to require local Arab virgins to marry black Africans. He decreed that any unmarried Zanzibar girl must accept a marriage proposal from a 'physically sound male citizen' – and shortly before I arrived, a number of unwilling Persian women were forcibly married to his party officials. When the parents objected, they were jailed. Then, to emphasise his point, he himself married a nineteen-year-old Persian virgin, said to be unwilling (although it was a criminal offence to speculate). I ignored the beaches and the picturesque Arab dhows on the placid emerald waters and wrote a story intended for publication when I was safely in London. My suggested headline was 'Democratic Marriage on Zanzibar', although it was retitled 'The Sheik and the Single Girl'. Nyerere was applauded by the international left; I admired him, but did not think it right to cover up a scandal for which he had democratic responsibility.

Nyerere's promise of 'democratic socialism' would soon be betrayed, not only in Tanzania but also in Kenya, Malawi, the Seychelles and elsewhere on the continent, by new constitutions drawn up by Marxist lawyers establishing one-party states. Much later, I would be involved in the task of trying to unravel them. For the present, my problem was how to parachute into England in time for Michaelmas term – the arcane description of the first of three eight-week sessions that make up the Oxford University year. Air travel in 1970 was prohibitively expensive, unless you joined a 'club' that was entitled under some obscure rule to organise cheap charter flights. For this reason only I joined a sports organisation – the sport in question being the hunting of big game – which entitled me to fly in an old jumbo from Nairobi to Benghazi (refuelling while surrounded by soldiers of the newly empowered Colonel Gaddafi, pointing their guns at our plane) and thence to Stansted, in the Essex countryside, where I was vouchsafed my first sight, on coming in to land, of the green fields of England.

As a naïve Australian, I headed for Earls Court (my knowledge of London was limited to this 'Kangaroo Valley' and the places that appeared on the Monopoly board) and spent a week feeding unfamiliar coins into spluttering gas meters – although it was still summer, the temperature reminded me that in England, summer's lease had all too short a date. But there was no time to be disappointed – the West End beckoned. First stop was a play that would be banned in Sydney for its blasphemy, although *Abelard and Heloise* (starring Keith Michell and a briefly, if memorably, naked Diana Rigg) deserved to be banned for its banality. Next I hammered a hire car around little England – I drove to Penzance, in honour of Gilbert & Sullivan's pirates, and thence in the same day up several motorways to watch the late sunset ripples on Loch Ness. The places in the postcards sent by my father seemed less impressive close up: Stonehenge, for example, was just an array of rocks compared to the ruins of Great Zimbabwe.

Finally, the entrance to Oxford. It still provokes a warm tingle of wonder whenever I reach the roundabout at Magdalen Bridge and drive up the long, question-mark curve of the High Street, to see the jutting façade of

University College leaning towards Queen's and All Souls on the other side of this yellow brick road. Oxford, like Cambridge, is a collection of colleges with centuries-old reputations (most were there during the English Civil War) with which students are expected to bond more closely than with the department teaching their subject or with the university itself. Whenever you mention that you studied at Oxford to anyone who also attended the university, their invariable response is 'Which college?' – a question much more significant than the identification of your subject or your supervisor. It evokes an old-boy network unlike any other, epitomised years later when I came face to face with Lord Diplock, the brilliant but reactionary judge who delighted in tearing my arguments to pieces in the House of Lords judicial committee. We were at a BBC seminar on terrorism (I was there to represent the terrorists) and afterwards, to our mutual horror, found ourselves face to face at the bar. Thinking quickly, I recalled seeing his name on some books that had been donated to the college library, so I ventured to thank him. His death's-head face creased into a wide smile. 'Ahh,' he said, making an appreciative noise. 'You're a Univ man, are you?' It was open sesame – he bought me a drink – several, indeed – and told me all about his secret work (he was commissioner for national security) until very late in the evening. This is how Philby, Maclean, Burgess and Blunt came to infiltrate the security services on behalf of the KGB – they were hired and advanced by chaps who had attended their colleges.

My alma mater was University College (invariably known as 'Univ'), which had been founded at some point in the thirteenth century. That made it the oldest, but not the richest, college. Australians generally made the mistake of choosing Balliol (where, in the unlikely event that they were admitted, they would be housed in small, newly built rooms alongside American postgraduates) or Magdalen (beautiful, certainly in the rooms that overlooked the deer park, but noisy during the rutting season). I had chosen Univ not so much for its celebrated socialists (William Beveridge, architect of British post-war social reconstruction, had been a master, Harold Wilson a don, and Bob Hawke a student) but because it was currently the college of two liberal legal philosophers I greatly admired –

H. L. A. ('Herbert') Hart and his successor as Professor of Jurisprudence, Ronald Dworkin. These men were intellectual lodestars, providing principles against the law tangling with moral standards which chimed with my Sydney criminologists and their practical reasons for abolishing laws against abortion, homosexuality and obscenity.

Hart in particular had been the proponent in a celebrated debate with Lord Devlin about the continued existence of the common-law offence of 'conspiracy to corrupt public morals', a law so vague that it permitted judges (as one had declared) 'to guard the moral welfare of the state against attacks which may be more insidious because they are novel and unprepared for'. That the job of preparing for and punishing new forms of misbehaviour belonged in a democracy to Parliament, and not to judges, was precisely Hart's point.

Dworkin, a former Rhodes scholar from America, agreed but took up the further argument that judges had a power, and indeed a duty, to interpret legislation according to certain fundamental principles which could be derived from the very concept of law, including respect for human rights. It required no personal propinquity to agree with these ideas, but it was certainly a privilege to dine and discourse with these famous jurisprudes. Ronnie supervised my thesis, which in due course became a book (*Obscenity*), and his philosophy was to be a lifelong inspiration. We sat together at a seminar organised by the *Times Educational Supplement* shortly before his death in 2013, where I opined that the UK would never achieve equality until Oxford and Cambridge Universities were abolished. He was less shocked than everyone else.

I meant it, although the thought would not have crossed my mind while I was at Oxford: the university had cast its spell over the thinking world. Here I sat a few feet from the pitted moonface of W. H. Auden and the noble if ruined visage of Robert Graves, listening to them declaim their verse. I heard Mikis Theodorakis bemoaning the Greek junta, John Kenneth Galbraith and Ralph Nader expanding on the arguments in their books – all, I think, in my first term. It was a time when the most famous people would go out of their way to speak at the Oxford Union, although this was really a juvenile debating society where students with political pretentions honed their blunt wits. Self-important politicians graced its benches so that they could report the fact in their autobiographies.

It is ironic that the union gained its historical significance from a vote in 1933 that it 'would no longer fight for King and Country' – a support for appeasement that doubtless reflected the refined apathy that privilege engenders. Certainly, its law faculty lacked all initiative and imagination – I had actually been better off at Sydney, where by the time I left we had finally begun to think about law as a tool to achieving social justice. Oxford was a city with a car industry, and increasing numbers of its employees were being thrown out of work by the policies of Ted Heath's new Conservative government. It had problems of homelessness, drunkenness and delinquency. Yet no one in the faculty was interested: the dons flowed quietly, teaching property law. Of human rights law, they had not heard. When a young don, Bryan Gould – a former New Zealand Rhodes scholar and later a Labour shadow minister – called a meeting to set up a legal advice centre for unemployed car workers, I was the only person who attended and we had to abandon the project. The lack of interest might have been defensible if traditional subjects had been taught with any creativity – as they were at Harvard, for example, lectures there having long been abandoned in favour of the case-study technique. At Oxford, the most celebrated professor in the faculty, who had written the textbook on private international law, turned up to read it, line by line, for sixty minutes. He wore a long black gown and announced at his first lecture that students would not be admitted in future unless they wore gowns as well. I read his book but refused to gown-up to attend his lectures.

There were other unattractive aspects of the Oxford experience. On my first morning in my 'rooms' (we had two, unlike redbrick students with a single room), I was roused by an elderly retainer: 'I am your scout, sir. I shall wake you with a cup of tea every morning, make your bed and do your washing...'

'You shall do no such thing,' was my immediate response, as I explained that I did not want to see him again until I gave him the traditional tip at the end of term. I should like to think that this was an Australian's rejection of upper-class privilege – it was absurd that young men should be cosseted by a superannuated slave – but it might have been more to do with the fact that his early arrival would interfere with my John Donne-induced fantasy of having bountiful English undergraduettes soundly sleeping with me until lunchtime.

My friend Julian Disney, the South Australian Rhodes scholar, was at Univ as well, occupying rooms recently vacated by Bill Clinton (we later joked about the stains still visible on the sheets). It was not thought, by the Univ Middle Common Room, that Clinton would amount to much. The American we voted 'most likely to succeed' was Paul Gambaccini. For a reason we could not initially fathom, we were both called 'Bruce' by undergraduates. Then we noticed how on Tuesday nights they all de-camped to the television room (there was only one TV in the college) and we followed, to enjoy the lumberjack song in one of the early episodes of *Monty Python*. It had featured the sketch about the fictitious Woolamaloo University Department of Philosophy, where everyone bears the name of 'Bruce', so we laughed along with our would-be sledgers. The show was hilarious – at least it was in 1970, before all the repeats.

I did my bit for the college, at rowing (Rhodes scholars, heavier and heartier than weedy English undergrads, were good for ballast) and at tennis, in which the team did well in a competition called 'Cuppers' (for a cup, presumably), although rain usually stopped play. In order to in-dulge my interest in journalism I sought out the offices of *Cherwell*, the university newspaper, named after the slim stream that serves for summer punting and evokes memories of the riverbank in *The Wind in the Willows*. They immediately appointed me features editor. From this portentous position I was able to arrange meetings with those of the university's philosopher-kings who were prepared to submit to my interviews. Stuart Hampshire, the Warden of Wadham, pointed out the importance to the Oxford college system of the physical architecture – how the beauty of the buildings, their shape and disposition, provided an intimate environment for learning and reflection.[17] I conceded the point – the gardens at Univ were great places to sit and think, surrounded by buildings that had cast shadows over scholars for centuries – but I was not sure (at least not in my case) of the quality or worth of the thoughts that came to mind. I have always had more inspiration when looking at a brick wall – beauty is a distraction, as I found a few years later when I took a flat with a magnificent view of Sydney Harbour in order to write a book. Words did not come, just the yachts and ocean liners followed by my mind's eye.

Another editorial initiative of mine was to expose the scourge of alcoholism in Oxford and, I suspected, in other towns in Britain, where so many jobs were lost in this austerity period of a Conservative government. We demanded that the town 'spare a thought for Oxford's shambling brigade of alcohol-poisoned beggars whose request for "a couple of bob for a sandwich and a cuppa" regularly touch student hearts and purse strings'. My reaction, at twenty-four, was puritanical: 'The only truly charitable response to a beggar's plea for food money is to take him to the nearest shop and to buy him the food he so obviously needs – NOT to give him money, which is invariably spent on alcohol.' These days I'm less judgemental and hope my grateful beggars buy – and enjoy – a good whisky.

It was a time when the popular press was headlining the horrors of drug addiction (when are they not?), so with the help of Oxford's scientists I compiled comparative tables to prove that alcohol and cigarettes were more harmful than marijuana. My own experience of drugs was limited, and still is. I became drunk once at a teenage picnic and hurled my heart out beneath a gum tree, and have never imbibed alcohol immoderately since. (As for British beer, I have never imbibed it at all since the first sip of that insipid room-temperature brown water.) Nicotine has never held me in its thrall (remembering my mother, who fell for my father because he was the only fighter pilot she met who did not smoke). LSD I have never touched – my brain is difficult enough to unscramble without chemical complications. Cannabis, of course, should be legalised, at least if they develop a 'potalyser' that can catch those who ingest the weed and then drive. Bill Clinton was unusually truthful when, in answer to the question of whether he had ever taken marijuana at Oxford, he replied, 'Yes, but I did not inhale.' The mode of ingestion at the time was via hash cookies.

As for cocaine (which, let's face it, has had some terrible consequences), I have sampled it on three occasions. The first, with *Oz* magazine editor Richard Neville, was in New York, in the approved way – through rolled-up hundred-dollar bills provided by one of his millionaire friends. It did produce a portentous feeling of invincibility, so I immediately went walking at nightfall in Central Park, then the mugging capital of the world. After forty-five minutes the effect wore off: I had lost my way and felt incredibly stupid and quite frightened. I resolved not to yield again to this temptation, but on the second occasion it was impossible to resist. I was at the house of a wealthy lawyer at Palm Beach, on the occasion of the legendary 'gonzo journalist' Hunter S. Thompson's visit to Sydney. The legend and I were ushered into a room where white lines of powder had been generously laid out on the table. Snorting them seemed to be the right thing to do, under the tutelage of this drug-promoting ne'er-do-well, who looked and sounded like an accountant both before and after he snorted what appeared, at least, to be cocaine: it had no effect on me at all. Perhaps it was washing powder, provided by a host who hadn't the connections to indulge his famous visitor. The third occasion was in a London hospital after I'd had a wisdom tooth extracted, and a grinning Australian anaesthetist said he would pack the cavity with coke. The effect was to make me want to talk volubly, so I rang my wife at a dinner party to chat to our friends. She reported that they all thought me uncharacteristically charming.

Back at Oxford, there was still no interest in human rights, in the law faculty or anywhere else. In Londonderry, 'civil liberties' had started to matter as the Catholic minority in Northern Ireland began to chafe under Protestant repression, but the major reforms of the Wilson government in legalising abortion and homosexuality and abolishing theatre censorship had lulled people in England into thinking that they lived in the best of all liberal worlds. A small book by Harry Street, *Freedom, the Individual and the Law*, which I was later to rewrite, said otherwise, identifying the failures, for example, to hold over-powerful policemen to account, but there was a popular television cop – Dixon of Dock Green – who was so utterly benign that his public charisma covered up the deep and dark corruption at Scotland Yard.

Internationally, of course, concern about Vietnam abounded, and there was hostility to racism in Ian Smith's breakaway Rhodesia and apartheid South Africa. But human rights were being abused throughout the world, and the only organisation doing anything about it was Amnesty International. I joined its group in Oxford, only to discover that all its members could do was write polite – indeed, grovelling – letters to dictators, begging them to desist from torture and mass murder and to set free those whom Amnesty considered to be 'political prisoners'. From this class it excepted those political prisoners, like Nelson Mandela, who refused to renounce violence. There were endless terminological disputes: I felt we should support prisoners who advocated violence only as a means of overthrowing a violent dictatorship rather than the sort of violence which would take civilian lives, but the distinction was still not clear. At least we could concentrate on dictators who killed dissidents irrespective of their views about overthrowing the state. So I took up my pen – so pathetically less mighty than the sword – and began to write.

> *To his Excellency Idi Amin Dada, VC and Bar,*
> *Amnesty (Oxford) respectfully requests that you might graciously be pleased to hold an inquest into the deaths of the three judges of your Court of Appeal, whose bodies (headless) were found floating in the river outside Kampala after they had delivered a judgment to which, perhaps on reasonable grounds, you took exception...*

Later I would write:

> *Dear General Pinochet,*
> *Amnesty is very concerned at reports of torture chambers in Santiago...*

This would have pleased the general, had he read it, because he wanted to encourage reports about his torture chambers in order to deter those who might otherwise have to be placed in them. But of course those letters were never opened, as I discovered years later when bored bureaucrats in apartheid South Africa showed me their drawers of unopened letters from Amnesty members, including one of my own. It proved my instinct that the human rights movement would never get very far by begging tyrants to be less tyrannical. But just twenty-five years after I had written the letter to General Pinochet, he was placed under arrest in London for torture and I acted for Human Rights Watch in the case against him. In the 1970s this turn of events would have seemed fantastical: talk of actually holding heads of state accountable for their crimes was the most far-fetched of pipe dreams.

* * *

A colossus first struck by time's arrow in 1970 was Cecil Rhodes. The problem that arose when I arrived at Oxford, and which should have been appreciated long before, was that the nine scholarships allocated annually to South Africa had been subject to the most outrageous race discrimination: of all the hundreds of scholars sent to Oxford since the scheme had begun in 1903, not a single one of them had been a black student or even a 'Cape Coloured'. Not a single member of any selection committee for South African Rhodes scholars had been non-white. This was truly a scandal, uncovered by American scholars in our year, who issued a fact sheet setting out the statistics and pointing out that four of the nine scholarships were tied to schools that did not accept black students anyway, and the South African selectors had kept the other five scholarships confined to whites.

Julian Disney and I tramped angrily through the rain to furious meetings in smoky Balliol common rooms, and eighty-five of us – the majority of Rhodes scholars in residence – signed a petition threatening to give back our scholarships unless the trustees took immediate action to ensure the appointment of black scholars. Bill Williams, the rather slippery Warden of Rhodes House, pretended to be sympathetic, although in private apparently he snidely remarked that 'the present generation of students have found South Africa the cushiest "demo" available'.[18] There was nothing cushy about this demo – we were appalled that complacent men like Williams, the Rhodes trustees and the selectors in South Africa had let our scholarships fall into such disrepute, and we were sincerely prepared to give them up. I remember some agonising, with Julian and others, over the decision – we did not want to make a futile gesture like John Lennon, who had returned his MBE in protest against the war in Vietnam. But if only a few of us sacrificed our scholarships it would be big news and a public blow to the trust, and the trustees knew it, so they made a public statement promising reform.

It is fair to say that change did not come easily. Rhodes had provided in his will that 'No student shall be qualified or disqualified for election to a scholarship on account of his race...', which seemed clear enough, although by 'race' he probably meant to include Jewish scholars and members of European races rather than black South Africans, whom he had worked as a legislator to exclude from voting rights.[19] He had anchored four of his scholarships to all-white schools in South Africa, and in 1971 the trust asked the UK Minister for Education to alter this provision of the will. Mrs Thatcher (for it was she) refused. Education throughout South Africa was in the grip of the Bantu Education Act of 1953, which legalised several forms of segregation. Its architect, Dr Hendrik Verwoerd, had explained that this act aimed to stop black South Africans from harbouring 'unhealthy white-collar ideals'.

'There is no place for the Bantu', he announced, 'in the European community above the level of certain forms of labour ... it is of no avail for him to receive a training which has as its aim absorption in the European community ... and mislead him by showing him the green pastures of European society in which he is not allowed to graze.'

This was the pernicious thinking which the Rhodes trustees knew about and had played along with for so many years. They would have done better to suspend the South African scholarships on the basis that apartheid made fair competition for them impossible. How could you demonstrate 'ability at manly sports' when you were denied the right to play in South African teams, or demonstrate 'qualities of leadership' when membership of the African National Congress was banned?

We expended a lot of emotional energy in protesting against the exclusion of black men, but without giving much thought to the fact that black and white women were ineligible for selection. Rhodes himself probably gave no thought to it either. The sexist clause in his will was abrogated by the 1975 Sex Discrimination Act and needed no Rhodes scholar revolt to speed its passage. I am proud nonetheless of my small part in that revolt and surprised now, looking back, by my willingness, as a matter of conscience, to walk away from Oxford if necessary after only a year, without taking a degree. In due course I obtained one – a postgraduate Bachelor of Civil Laws – although it may be a measure of Oxford's irrelevance to my future that I have never bothered, to this day, actually to 'take' it by turning up with gown and mortarboard and rusty Latin to a degree ceremony.

As for Cecil Rhodes, the evil that he did lived after him: his statues have recently been taken down at universities in South Africa and Zimbabwe, and in 2016 the 'Rhodes Must Fall' campaign demanded the removal of his effigy which stands in the wall of his old college, Oriel, his head sheltered by gauze to stop pigeons getting a toehold for their toilet. The campaign was widely ridiculed – the first publicity-seeking 'scholar' (I use the term loosely) to condemn it was Tony Abbott (who had gone on to become, briefly, an Australian Prime Minister), who thought it had something to do with rewriting history. It did not: it had much to do with a university where very few black students are selected to study, where very few dons are black, where black history is not taught, where the prime object of the education on offer is to produce a white professional elite and where black students are routinely stopped and refused entry to their colleges until they produce identification.[20] The 2016 campaign was led by black Rhodes scholars from South Africa – the very people we sought to bring into existence by our revolt in 1970. Unlike Abbott, I welcomed their iconoclasm – pulling down statues, whether of Stalin or of Saddam, can be cathartic as well as symbolic.

The 'Rhodes Must Fall' question reflects debates throughout the world about how to preserve the memory of those whose historical claims to greatness require revision. In 2017, the US was in uproar over Donald Trump's apparent sympathy for neo-Nazi protests against tearing down a statue of the Confederate General Robert E. Lee in Charlottesville – erected a century ago by racists as part of the push for 'Jim Crow' laws, a fact that now justifies having such statues torn down or moved to a museum where the racism behind them (although Lee himself was against slavery) can be fully explained. People are entitled to change their view of historical heroes: in 2015, Ukrainians cut to pieces a Soviet-era statue of Marx's collaborator Frederick Engels to protest against Russian aggression; the following year it was retrieved and reassembled in the city of Manchester to celebrate his contribution to the socialism newly popularised by Jeremy Corbyn. Both actions were fair enough.

This question came to mind on holiday recently, while swimming off Villefranche-sur-Mer, arguably the most beautiful environ on the French Riviera. From the warm and shark-free waters of the bay, I looked back at a majestic villa, its walls luminously white, its tropical vegetation lush green with crimson foliage (for movie buffs, it was the setting for the shenanigans of Michael Caine and Steve Martin in *Dirty Rotten Scoundrels*). It happened to be the summer home of one of history's dirtiest rotten scoundrels, namely King Leopold II of Belgium, who built it on the proceeds of his rape of the Congo, which cost ten million (that's right, ten million) lives. Knowing that fact did not spoil the beauty of the view, but I would not have been sorry to see, scribbled in red paint on the white walls, some reminder ('*génocidaire*', 'assassin' or such like) of the character of the mansion's former owner. The monument to Leopold, just up the road, makes no mention of the wickedness of a life that did no good at all, other than for property prices on the Riviera.

The test for tearing down a statue should be whether it has been erected merely as a reminder of the former presence of the bad person on its plinth, or whether it is intended to celebrate that bad person. In the latter case, it deserves destruction, unless the statue itself has architectural interest, in which case it can be permitted to stand so long as some reference to his or her (invariably 'his') crimes is inscribed on its plinth. As for mausoleums, I have no strong views: they engage a certain ghoulish fascination – Lenin's body shows the inadequacy of Soviet taxidermy, while a visit to Mao's resting place enables you to meet in the hours-long queue the children of those he liquidated by execution or starvation but who nonetheless revere his remains. All very primitive – and yet it is a nice surprise to pass, on visits to UCL, the body of Jeremy Bentham – his mind, I hope, will be with students as long as his mummified corpse. As for names – on schools and hospitals and civic centres – they can always be changed, if enough people care.

As for the Rhodes statue (I must have walked the cobbled street hundreds of times without noticing its niche in the wall), there is nothing celebratory about the impression it gives. It is there because Rhodes was there, and he gave the college a lot of money – a charitable action to which no objection could be taken. The 'Rhodes Must Fall' campaigners would do better to climb the north face of Rhodes House to hack off the Zimbabwe bird that nests on top, and return it to the mysterious site in former Rhodesia from which it was plundered. That would make a point about colonialism robbing civilisations of their legacy, and about the return of cultural property, as well as about Rhodes's imperialist mentality. So I would leave Cecil in his niche, but remove the gauze that protects his head from the bird droppings of history. I can claim in support of that position no better race warrior than Robert Mugabe. When faced with demands that Rhodes himself should be dug up from the scenic grave that I visited in the Matopo Hills, he ordered instead that the grave should be protected and kept as a tourist attraction. 'The bones do no harm, but we want to make them pay taxes.'[21]

The Rhodes Trust had a remarkable eightieth anniversary in 1983, by which point the Trustees calculated that they had more money than the university itself. So they spent it, not (as they should have) on endowing more scholarships, but on a lavish celebration in which we were invited back to our Oxford colleges for a weekend of festivities, to be capped by an audience with the Queen herself. For this purpose the ancient wall between Wadham College and Rhodes House was dismantled for a day, at vast expense, to accommodate the conga-line of ex-scholars who would pay respects to Her Majesty, as if they were medieval knights subject to her command, and afterwards the wall was reassembled and re-cemented. It was an outrageous waste of money, and the more republican scholars among us decided to disdain the opportunity to bow and chat with the monarch. We had to book for the event a year in advance, and I was asked whether my wife would accompany me – I said yes (I was single, but you never know what might happen in a year) and took Jeananne Crowley, an Irish actress of republican sympathies who joined me with the other refuseniks – Ronnie and Betsy Dworkin and a dozen or so self-styled republicans, on a mound that overlooked the royal queue. But the majesty of Majesty worked its spell, and as the Queen neared the end of the line (giving every few paces that trademark shoulder shrug that hitched up her smile), they started to defect, eventually leaving only the Dworkins and the make-believe Robertsons in lonely but principled splendour.

Otherwise, it was an enjoyable event: Harold Macmillan had been lured out of retirement to make the best after-dinner speech I have ever heard – a reminder of just how super 'Supermac' must have been in his heyday. Back at college there was a reunion with Bill Clinton, then Governor of Arkansas, who was trying out his handshake – he would stretch out his hand as if it were a tentacle from his heart, and hold yours long enough to drain away any resistance to whatever he was selling – invariably, himself. After he had stepped down from the White House we did have another reunion at Univ, on some pretext (I think it was Chelsea's graduation – she had studied there without any of the usual difficulties of getting admitted). Bob Hawke was invited back, for good measure – the measure being the yard of ale he had once drunk in eleven seconds in college to enter the *Guinness Book of Records*. He repeated the feat, because that night the ale was even more watered down than is usual for English beer.

*   *   *

The Rhodes scholarship, at the time I held one, was most accommodating: it provided a reasonable stipend and there was no immediate need to settle on any particular course of study. I had a year to make up my mind, which could be spent getting to know Oxford, or England, or indeed the Continent. I decided that the best thing about Britain was its proximity to France, and was soon venturing to behold Paris and the splendours that survived through collaboration with the Nazis, who did not, in consequence, subject it to a blitzkrieg. At the famous Shakespeare and Company bookshop, I was offered a bed for as many nights as I liked, although it had fallen on hard times and the rat droppings under the proffered palliasse disinclined me to spend any night in this literary shrine. Further afield lay the Côte d'Azur, where I first experienced a shark-free ocean swim and found a small fishing village – Bouzigues – with oysters that rivalled in taste my favourite Sydney Rocks.

University holidays were long, which left plenty of time to explore Europe. Winter meant skiing in Austria (only once: I never got past snow-ploughing) and in summer the inevitable charter flight to the glory that was a Greek island. At Easter, Julian Disney and I explored Spain at a rapid speed, observing with pleasure the economic cost of fascism – the peseta had hit rock bottom in the last stultifying years of Franco's reign, and we stayed in great style for peanuts at *paradores*, castles from the days of Don Quixote de la Mancha. Some years ago I wrote rudely of American Rhodes scholars that they 'regarded the university as little more than a five-star refuge from the draft: a place for post-coital punting and a base for touring Europe'. I can't imagine now why I was disparaging – everyone can benefit from a gap year or two, and Oxford has stood for many centuries without requiring input from anyone until after they leave, when it is avidly sought in the form of donations. I did the right – or at least the expected – thing by my college for many years, in the form of an annual tax-deductible charitable bequest, but then, on principle, I stopped. Oxford is a phenomenally wealthy citadel of privilege, which even in the twenty-first century helps mainly the children of the upper and middle classes to take those privileges into adulthood. I became a trustee of the School of Oriental and African Studies (SOAS), part of London University, and redirected to it what time or money I had to spare. On its students, not Oxford's, the world's fight will depend.

My own efforts to fight the world's fight had not proceeded far during my first term at Oxford: my letter to Idi Amin had not been answered and the only fight that looked like being a success was against the Rhodes Trust itself. The Conservative government had started to make life difficult for Australians in order to make it impossible for black students from former colonies: those of us from the Commonwealth who could not boast a British grandparent would be out on our ears once our course had finished, so my hopes of appearing at the Old Bailey would be dashed. I had an English girlfriend – Jane Turnbull, from St Hilda's – and wondered whether marriage might be a way out – or, at least, a way to stay in. Academically, I was still toying with the idea of doing a doctorate on blue-sky tax havens, but then along came a small bear with a large penis to decide my career trajectory. It was Rupert Bear, in 'Schoolkids' *Oz*, whose head had been placed on a body in a state of high erection drawn by underground cartoonist Robert Crumb. This had shocked the authorities, and *Oz* editor Richard Neville had been charged with 'conspiracy to corrupt public morals'.

One evening, Richard came to Balliol to talk about his impending prosecution and, having raised money for his first trial in Sydney seven years before, I offered to defend him, and his fellow editors Felix Dennis and Jim Anderson, in this new ordeal, promising to make the *Oz* trial an obscenity trial to end all obscenity trials. The defence team had a vacancy – in fact, it had a yawning gap, with hundreds of supporters and hangers-on and no full-time lawyer to prepare the defence. I took the role, armed with my free-speech philosophy, and threw myself into constructing arguments that depictions of sexual conduct neither depraved, corrupted nor debauched the morals of young persons within the realm, and in any event, even if they did, the magazine had enough literary and artistic merit to justify its publication. This last defence would be difficult, but I persuaded Marty Feldman, David Hockney and Feliks Topolski to testify, and visited London's leading psychologists and psychiatrists – Hans Eysenck, Edward de Bono and others – who were prepared to say that reading mischievous rudery does no real harm.

I was installed in a solicitor's office in Bond Street (which featured, in that era of the miniskirt, more flesh than I had seen since leaving Bondi Beach) and provided with a 'crash pad' – Richard's basement in Notting Hill Gate – under 24-hour surveillance, it later emerged, by Scotland Yard's Special Branch. They must have been surprised to see this clean-cut Australian in an unfashionable brown suit and tie, but no doubt recorded the degeneration in my dress sense as my hair lengthened and I acquired the mandatory velvet suit. In a fast Fiat I would thrash up the motorway in the early hours of the morning to make a 9 a.m. tax lecture or play inter-college tennis or edit my sections in *Cherwell*, before thrashing back down at night to Notting Hill. I ran up, I am told, more parking tickets than any other Rhodes scholar in history.

The *Oz* trial, held at the Old Bailey over the summer of 1971, was a trial like no other.²² The police had been gunning for *Oz* since it first started in Britain in the mid-1960s, as part of an 'underground press' devoted to personal liberation. They pounced on *Oz 28: The Schoolkids Edition*, put together by guest editors – a dozen or so bright but bored teenagers from north London comprehensives (some grew up to work for the *Sunday Times* before moving in middle age to *The Independent*). They were alleged to be co-conspirators in a plot to undermine the nation's morals, and the three editors – Richard, Jim and Felix – were to be made scapegoats for the permissive society of the '60s, charged with 'conspiracy to corrupt public morals', which carried a maximum sentence of life imprisonment.

Eventually, another explanation emerged for why Scotland Yard had chosen to prosecute. The police force at the time was riddled with corruption: its drug squad dealt in confiscated drugs, its serious crimes squad arranged serious crimes and the 'dirty squad' – eighteen constables charged with policing Soho – ran what the judge who later jailed them described as 'a vast protection racket', taking bribes to facilitate the sale of pornography of the hardest core. As a pretence that the police really were concerned with the nation's morals, the much-publicised raids on the underground press served as a decoy. Our defence evidence was directed to show that porn did not deprave and corrupt its readers, but it certainly did corrupt those charged with enforcing the laws against it.

To understand the *Oz* trial, you have to understand Rupert Bear's beloved place in the British nursery, and the horror when one of Richard Neville's youthful guest editors gave him an erection. To my astonishment, several of Britain's leading barristers were so shocked they refused the defence brief. There was no '*Je suis Rupert*' in those days – these self-regarding silks made their excuses and left. One, who had notably defended the German radical Rudi Dutschke, initially accepted the *Oz* brief, but after a two-hour conference called our solicitor, David Offenbach, and said he 'could not take the risk'. He became a Liberal peer, and doubtless feared that representing Rupert would put such a bauble in danger.

This was my first experience of the British Bar. Promoted as an independent and courageous profession, here it was quailing at the prospect of defending the editors of a rude magazine. We had only four days to find another QC: the next morning someone mentioned that John Mortimer was defending an axe murderer at the Old Bailey. He had successfully argued the appeal for the publishers of *Last Exit to Brooklyn*, and was our only and last hope. Richard and I tracked him down, lunching with two young women of my own age. 'What exactly is the case all about?' he enquired. Nervously, and somewhat shamefacedly, Richard unfurled Rupert the Bare, shielding him self-consciously from the ladies. To our enormous relief, John giggled – and showed it to them. Penny (later Mrs Mortimer) and her sister laughed too. I produced the brief, crossed out the names of the QCs who had become mysteriously unavailable and inserted his. 'Goody,' he said, 'when do we start?' On Tuesday. 'I must just finish my poor axe murderer,' he cautioned. 'The blood stains are not running our way.' He left us to his dessert and his companions, and he shuffled over the road to cross-examine a forensic scientist on a subject he – and years later his fictional character Horace Rumpole – knew everything about: how to deduce a reasonable doubt from the pattern made by splashes of blood.

We clung to John like a plank in a shipwreck, as for six weeks of the summer the majestic engine of British criminal law was rolled over these unruly Australians. It was driven by Michael Argyle, an excruciatingly polite and excruciatingly savage Old Bailey judge who took out on defendants his frustrations at being repeatedly rejected for preselection as a Tory MP (notwithstanding his urgent calls to bring back the death penalty). The cultural incomprehension was apparent from the start, as Detective Inspector Luff gave evidence of interviewing Felix Dennis:

> LUFF: When the interview ended, my Lord, the defendant said loudly, 'Right on.'
> JUDGE: 'Write on' – but you had already finished the interview?
> LUFF: Not 'write on – W-R-I-T-E-on', my Lord, but 'R-I-G-H-T on'. This is a revolutionary expression.

Most of the trial concerned the Rupert Bear cartoon, a collage from Robert Crumb and the Rupert annual, by a Hampstead teenager who explained to John Mortimer that 'Subconsciously, I wanted to shock your generation.' When Jim Anderson, a gay Australian who had left the Bar to write novels, took the stand, we were treated to a vintage example of Old Bailey cross-examination by Brian Leary, the Treasury Counsel, who prosecuted:

LEARY (*reading from Anderson's editorial*): '*Oz* was hit with its biggest dose of creative energy for a long time. Have a look at the Rupert Bear strip. Youthful genius.' Did you write this, Mr Anderson?

ANDERSON: Yes, I did.

LEARY: Is it still your opinion that Vivian Berger's cartoon of Rupert Bear is the work of 'youthful genius'?

ANDERSON: Yes, I think it was an extremely clever and funny idea.

LEARY: Did it amount to youthful genius?

ANDERSON: Well… maybe I was a little bit generous in my praise, but…

LEARY: The youthful genius set to work by snipping out of the Rupert Bear annual the head of the bear. That's right?

ANDERSON: Yes… er… I suppose that's what he did.

LEARY: And then if we were keen to watch a genius at work, we would see him sticking it on the cartoon already drawn for him?

ANDERSON: Yes.

LEARY: Wherein lies the genius?

ANDERSON: I think it's in the juxtaposition of the two ideas, the childhood symbol of innocence…

LEARY (*shouting*): MAKING RUPERT BEAR FUCK?

ANDERSON (*after a long pause*): … Er… Yes.

LEARY: Is that what you consider youthful genius?

ANDERSON: Yes, I thought it was extraordinary, even brilliant.

LEARY: Extraordinary it may be, but whatever it is, it's not genius, is it?

This is how you demolish overstatement: have the witness endorse it and then pull it apart with a dramatic climax. Leary produced an electric shock by shouting the unthinkable. The trial became even more surreal when the lateral-thinking Professor Edward de Bono took the stand:

LEARY: What do you suppose the effect is intended to be of equipping Rupert Bear with such a large-sized organ?

DE BONO: I don't know enough about bears to know their exact proportions; I imagine their organs are hidden in their fur. But if you had a realistic drawing I think you would miss the point of the drawing entirely.

LEARY: Mr de Bono, why is Rupert Bear equipped with a large organ?

DE BONO: What size do you think would be natural?

JUDGE ARGYLE: Well, forgive me, but you mustn't ask counsel questions.

LEARY (*another tack*): A success, do you think, this lavatory drawing?

DE BONO: If one considers it a success to have it published in *Oz* then I dare say it would be a certain measure of success.

LEARY: The success being this. That the lavatory wall is only available to those people who use the lavatory for the purposes of nature and this particular magazine has, as we are told, a circulation of up to 40,000.

DE BONO: I find that question difficult to answer, Mr Leary, unless I knew the turnover of a normal lavatory wall, which I would expect to be in the region of 30,000.

JUDGE ARGYLE: What, one lavatory, 30,000?

DE BONO: If you stop to calculate it, I expect so.

You may not believe it, but while this was going on, the judge was taking out his magnifying glass to stare at the small bear with the big erection. It was difficult – sometimes impossible – to keep a straight face, despite the awesome and oppressive surroundings of the Old Bailey's oldest courtroom. There had been some mention of oral sex in *Oz* – a taboo subject, before the movie *Deep Throat* – and to explain it I had to call a great British character – formerly an able seaman, then a jazz singer, then a sociologist. His name was George Melly, and he started to talk about the harmlessness of cunnilingus. The judge was genuinely puzzled. 'For those of us without a classical education, what do you mean by this word "cunnilinctus?"' (pronouncing it as though it were a cough medicine). Melly beamed at the judge: 'Oh, I'm sorry, my Lord. I've been a bit inhibited by the architecture. "Sucking" or "blowing", your Lordship. Or "going down" or "gobbling". Another expression used in my naval days, your Lordship, was "yodelling in the canyon".'

That brought the house down, and there were shouts of 'Silence!' 'This is a courtroom, not a theatre,' bellowed the judge for the umpteenth time.

To my great relief, after six weeks of this farce (the longest obscenity trial in British legal history), the jury acquitted Neville, Dennis and Anderson of conspiring to corrupt public morals, but convicted them – on the judge's misdirection – of obscenity. He remanded them in prison for psychiatric reports, which was an outrage – they were stark-staring sane. This misuse of psychiatry to demonise dissidents was what was happening in Russia. And as soon as they entered the prison gates, they were given a haircut. The atavistic revenge of the state, the short back and sides. This shearing of their long locks was front-page news – mothers and fathers throughout the land may have exulted, but their sons and daughters were furious. There were more letters to *The Times* about the *Oz* trial than there had been about the Suez crisis. As if enraged by the controversy, when they returned to court Argyle sentenced Richard to eighteen months' imprisonment and deportation (back to Botany Bay!) and Anderson to one year. Felix Dennis received only nine months 'because you are very much less intelligent' – a comment that inspired Felix to become, in time, one of Britain's wealthiest philanthropists.

With Marcel Berlins, a friend working at *The Times*, I stood on the court steps to watch as hundreds of demonstrators, encircled by as many policemen, lit a bonfire: an effigy of the judge was going up in flames. British justice (Marcel studied law in South Africa) had been a lodestar for us both: it now seemed there might be more justice on offer back in the colonies than at the Old Bailey. In search of some kind of sanity, I took a taxi to the offices of *Private Eye*, where Paul Foot was foaming at the mouth and comparing the infamy of the day to that on which Shelley was sent down from Univ for blasphemy. He ushered me into the presence of an ashen-faced Lord Gnome – at least that was how the proprietor, Peter Cook, introduced himself. 'I always believed they would get me, that I would be the one they would put inside. Now it's happened to Richard Neville. I feel I should be in his shoes.' I left the licensed jesters at work on their *Oz* trial edition (the cover was a savage caricature of the judge by Gerald Scarfe, captioned: 'This Justice must be seen to be done') and went off to consider whether I really wanted to stay in Britain. I had been here for less than a year, but this was certainly not the land of liberty I had fondly imagined back in Sydney, from reading Penguin Specials and the *New Statesman*.

It was a moment of real doubt – but a resolution to stay and fight was not long in taking hold. A sensible High Court judge granted bail, a group of MPs led by Michael Foot and Tony Wedgwood-Benn deplored the judge's behaviour, and Bernard Levin produced a magnificent polemic in our defence in *The Times*. Richard was accorded a deferential interview by David Dimbleby on BBC2 and given a regular column, by-lined 'The Alternative Voice', in the *Evening Standard* (the inspiration for *Private Eye*'s long-running column of the same name, by 'Dave Spart'). To prevent his dispatch to Botany Bay, the young Anna Wintour (in the days when she wore Primark, not Prada) offered to marry him. Fortunately for *Vogue*, the conviction and the deportation order were quashed on appeal.

It was such an astonishing case that I wrote a play about it, which was performed by the Royal Shakespeare Company (Ben Kingsley played Richard) and later remade for television as a BBC/ABC co-production. Leslie Phillips was the judge, Nigel Hawthorne the prosecutor and Simon Callow was John Mortimer. The ABC wanted Jason Donovan to play Richard, but the BBC insisted on using a completely unknown English actor named Hugh Grant. My stage direction called for the judge to bring out his magnifying glass and peer at Rupert's erection, as he had in the courtroom. The RSC director, Buzz Goodbody, wouldn't have it. 'But he did – I was there,' I insisted. 'Of course it happened,' said the director, 'in court. In a theatre, however, the audience won't believe it happened in court.'

I had prepared the grounds of appeal, identifying seventy-eight legal errors in the judge's summing up, although only two were necessary (a lesson: concentrate on your best points). It felt good to play a small part in changing the law: the Old Bailey acquittal meant that 'conspiracy to corrupt' would not be used against publishers again, and the Court of Appeal decided that they should not be prosecuted for obscenity if their publications were merely offensive or indecent. The *Lady Chatterley* trial in 1960 won freedom for great literature and the *Oz* appeal in 1971 won freedom for bad literature, or at least for writing and cartooning that was amateurish and provocative but was being used in the 'underground press' of the day to lampoon reactionary opponents of progress. The immediate beneficiary of the successful *Oz* appeal, however, was Rupert. Not Rupert the Bear, but Rupert Murdoch, fortified in his launch of page 3 of *The Sun*.

*   *   *

The very least of the trial's consequences was to provide me with a career path, by confirming my earlier ambition to practise law as a barrister at the Old Bailey. Although much about criminal justice in London had appalled me – the bent coppers and savage judges, for a start – they could be challenged and exposed, and there was always a jury to appeal to, and then a Court of Appeal. It was not exactly 'the world's fight', but jury verdicts at the Old Bailey could have an impact around the common-law world – they could reject political prosecutions, official censorship, discriminatory persecutions of minorities. And the 'justice game' itself was full of stratagems and tactics based on rules of evidence which I knew all too well. It had been my arguments, filtered through John Mortimer's silver tongue, which had persuaded the *Oz* judge to allow our expert evidence – years later the Law Lords said he had been wrong to do so, but there were other imaginative arguments where that one came from, and I was anxious to make them. I wanted to expose dishonesty through cross-examination, to stand up to judges and appeal to jurors to follow their consciences and acquit. I wanted a career in which my success or failure would hinge on my own ability, and no one else's – the independence of the Bar was its greatest attraction.

There was just one problem: money. The British Bar was so insular that it did not accept Australian qualifications: I would have to do a year's study of the same subjects I had passed with honours at law school in Sydney. The Rhodes Trust would extend its stipend to pay for a third year if you were doing a doctorate, but not, hitherto, if you wanted to do a law course in London. I had to blaze a trail, and it took me to the office of the Warden of Rhodes House. Bill Williams was no fool, at least in his own estimation (he was forever boasting that, as Montgomery's intelligence officer, he had won the battle of El Alamein), but he was kindness itself. He did not seem to mind that I had been a publicity officer for the Rhodes revolt, or had upset the establishment by staging the *Oz* trial. 'Your destiny is obviously to be a *consigliere* for causes that may or may not succeed: I think the Founder would not object to you obtaining a professional qualification at his expense.'

Perhaps I had misjudged the Warden – he did have a twinkle in his eye which can betray an inner anarchist beneath an ultra-conservative exterior. I did not need to boast of my pilgrimage to the Founder's grave in the Matopo Hills; Williams awarded me a not-inconsiderable sum of money to enjoy a year in London and obtain the requisite professional qualification. I did not have the heart to tell him that I had already arranged to spend part of it defending my next troublemaker, Peter Hain, the anti-apartheid demo supremo.

Peter had been charged with 'conspiracy to trespass' on sporting arenas, thus disrupting games against racially selected South African rugby and cricket teams. He was a youth of about my own age, then head of the headstrong Young Liberals and architect of their 'direct action' tactics of running on the field during play and being carried off without a struggle – this was 'peaceful-ish protest' (peaceful until the police arrived). The Conservative government did not have the gumption to ban these racist tours, and some sports-loving South Africans were so angry when 'Hain stopped play' that they invested in a private prosecution, brought by a company called 'Freedom Under Law Limited'. The offence of 'conspiracy to trespass' was controversial: it was being used against striking miners to turn what was essentially a civil matter (trespass on someone's property) into a crime carrying up to life imprisonment, merely because the trespass was the result of an agreement (the 'conspiracy') between two or more people. Peter's QCs advised him that under this draconian law he was guilty – he had made no secret of his agreements with other Young Liberals to invade cricket and football pitches – and so they could not defend him. He did not feel guilty, of course, and defended himself, with the help of an NCCL (National Council for Civil Liberties) solicitor and myself. I helped to write his speeches ('It's your parts that infuriate the judge,' he complained) and rehearsed his witnesses, who said they were so outraged by apartheid that they acted on their own initiative. My own leanings towards British liberals were not advanced by one well-known MP, who promised me in the court's coffee shop that he would say that his conscience would have impelled him to run on the pitch, but when in the witness box five minutes later he reneged and said he would never break the law – he would merely have held up a banner in the stands. My best witness was our last – a Church of England bishop, no less, in velvet vestments and shiny cross. He stuck to his script:

HAIN: Did you conspire with me to stop the rugby tour?
BISHOP WINTER: Yes, I must confess that I did.
(*Shock in court*)
HAIN: And how did you do that?
WINTER: I prayed to God, as a fellow conspirator and accomplice, to help you disrupt the tour.

The judge ordered him out of the witness box, but the whiff of sanctity left its impact on the jury, which acquitted Peter of all the serious charges and convicted him only of organising a brief trespass at Wimbledon, for which he received a small fine. Freedom Under Law Limited went into liquidation without achieving its stated objective of 'Pain for Hain', and a new Labour government abolished 'conspiracy to trespass' – a judge-made law used to chill political protest. It was a good result, which helped to prevent the rule of law being misinterpreted to mean the rule of lawyers.

Chapter Six

Down at the Old Bailey

It had been my boyhood dream to appear, wigged and gowned, address-ing a jury beneath the Old Bailey dome, on which stands its iconic golden statue of Lady Justice. Her right arm brandishes a sword to punish the wrongdoers found wanting in the scales held in her left hand. All other representations show the goddess wearing a blindfold, giving rise to aph-orisms about justice being blind. What few notice about the goddess atop the Old Bailey is that her eyes are wide open – as if to see through all the perjury that goes on in the courts beneath her skirts.

Working as a solicitor during the *Oz* trial had given me an insight into the production of perjury over the greasy Formica tables of the Rex Café, opposite the court. There, each morning, I watched the bottle-blondes being coached by solicitor's clerks over fried bacon and eggs to recite their alibis about being in bed with the defendant at the precise time the bank was robbed or the mansion was burgled. They were amateurs – at the other tables, police constables were rehearsing the lines they had made up in the police canteen, after they had arrested a suspect. This was where he was 'verballed' – a confession he had never made (usually 'It's a fair cop, Guv', or 'You've got me bang to rights') would be attributed to him and writ-ten down retrospectively in their police notebooks. Many coppers were bent (and so were some solicitor's clerks) but the conviction rates were reasonable, white-collar criminals were rarely troubled, and the public was happy watching *Dixon of Dock Green* on television and believing this impeccable constable was every-cop. I thought of ways to expose what a

Royal Commission, ten years later, called 'the Vaudeville routine of the police verbal', but first, I had to finish that tedious professional qualification course in London, and complete my pupillage (an apprenticeship to a practising barrister). I did both at the same time: you were not meant to, but I was impatient and saw no reason why not (there is now, of course, a rule against it).

Then there was the nagging question of money. My Rhodes stipend saw me through my first year in London, and my Oxford bank then extended a large line of credit in the belief that Oxford chaps came good in the end. I had hopes of discharging it when my play about the *Oz* trial was acquired by a Broadway producer, Van Wolf, who had been involved in a notorious film about the Rolling Stones, *Gimme Shelter*. He was dying of cancer and wanted to leave my play to posterity. I was regularly summoned from the side of my pupil-master at Stoke Newington Crown Court to Van Wolf's bedside at Mount Sinai Hospital in New York, where text changes were discussed while his friend Allen Ginsberg, in lotus position, said mantras and played a Peruvian flute to keep his cancer at bay until opening night.

At Van Wolf's request, the play was turned into a musical, and songs were donated by John and Yoko ('God Save Oz') and Mick Jagger ('Cocksucker Blues'). It had Jim Sharman's inspired direction and Brian Thomson's creative sets, and when it opened on Broadway every review was favourable, except for the only one that counted, in the *New York Times*. A surly Englishman named Clive Barnes, whose reviews at the time made or unmade shows in the city, hated *Oz* and it closed after six weeks, leaving me without royalties and with only one of those free Broadway show programmes, to impress visitors to my toilet, where it remains on framed display.

Jim Sharman, in town for his next musical, *Jesus Christ Superstar*, generously allowed me to share his Robert Stigwood-owned apartment in Swiss Cottage and I was joined there by an insanely attractive twenty-year-old, whom I'd last seen in a thong diving into a tank on a tabloid television show in Australia. When I came back the day after her arrival in London from Melbourne to find Dudley Moore edging towards her on the sofa, it occurred to me that Lyndall Hobbs would never have much trouble

finding accommodation. We chummed up and enjoyed free accommodation at a number of salubrious addresses in Kensington and Chelsea
provided by her boyfriend Michael White, the film and theatre producer
(of *Oh! Calcutta!* and other ground-breaking shows). Lyndall went from
strength to strength: she was hired by ITV as an on-camera news reporter,
and as a fashion and arts presenter (*Hobb's Choice*). She introduce me to
her friend Gael McKay, a Melbourne model, who later, as Gael Boglione,
became a family friend.

Our frequent changes of address caused a traffic offence notice to go
astray – I had incurred a ticket for parking outside a court. A particularly malevolent magistrate named MacDermott (a former deputy DPP)
issued a warrant for my arrest, which was fine, but did not back it for bail,
which was outrageous. This meant that when this first offender turned up
one evening at Chelsea police station, I was greeted by a semi-apologetic
policeman who pointed out that since the courts were closed they would
have to keep me in custody overnight. I was escorted, in a state of some
shock, to a dingy cell. Left in it for over an hour, the white walls and filthy
mattress and smell of urine and boiled cabbage began to work their magic:
I was prepared to confess to the Ripper murders, the Lindbergh kidnap,
whatever, just to get out. 'Don't I get one free phone call?' I had the nerve
to ask – I didn't (I had been watching too many American movies) but the
coppers let me use the payphone to contact my astonished pupil-master.
Jonah Walker-Smith, scion of a fine old Tory family, was scandalised that
police would dare to arrest his pupil. 'Hold on, I'll be right there,' he
promised, not that there was any prospect of my going anywhere. I was led
back to the cells and so did not witness his superhuman effort of borrow-
ing the arrest warrant from the police station sergeant and taking it late
that night to the home of another magistrate, Eric Crowther, whom he
persuaded to give me unconditional bail. 'I am not sure I should be doing
this,' the beak is reported to have said over his dinner table. 'It should be a
requirement for every young barrister to spend a night in the police cells.'

He was right, of course, and had this been a qualification for the Bar it
might not have been so hard for judges to realise how the oppressive atmosphere of custody can conduce to false confessions. A few hours inside

was quite enough for me, although when I came as a defendant to court next morning I was hailed as Houdini and my traffic violations were dismissed by a fine of £1. I could pay little more: my money problems had become increasingly severe.

By the end of 1973 I had a massive overdraft and even my Oxford bank was becoming worried. I began a second string in journalism, becoming a commentator on legal matters for the *New Statesman*. The *Statesman* did not pay much, and *The Guardian*, for which I also began to write, not much more, although the payments kept my overdraft from ballooning further. I needed, for example, a dark suit – my wardrobe of brown and velvet could not, by the rules of the Bar, be worn under a black gown. Lyndall took me down the King's Road on the day before my first court appearance and selected a charcoal-striped three-piece suit for which I paid £33 – the exact payment for my first *Guardian* article on the flaws in the government's draft Indecent Displays Bill, which threatened art gallery nudes ('How to Catch Rubens in a Draft' was how *The Guardian* headlined it).

At last, I could begin my chosen career. Not, at first, at the Old Bailey: I had to grub around magistrates' courts, taking whatever briefs a kindly solicitor might put my way, to help me 'get on my feet'. David Offenbach sent me off to Watford Magistrates' Court for a four-week committal proceeding concerning a conspiracy to make blue movies in divers fields, barns and houses in the suburbs of Rickmansworth. I was representing two of the actors, a spray-painter and his girlfriend: he appeared with some thirty partners in the course of the making of dozens of short films, but she refused to have sex with any partner but him. Their pièce de non-resistance was entitled *Santa's Coming*, in which he emerged in Father Christmas attire from the chimney to kiss and copulate beneath the mistletoe. They married shortly before the committal, and held hands every day in court. I could not resist asking the police officer in charge of the case, 'Would you accept that my clients are very much in love?' He accepted, just before the deadline for the final edition of the *Evening Standard*, where I made my first reported appearance as counsel under the headline 'Porn Couple "Very Much In Love"'. In court the next day, a man in a grubby raincoat sidled up to me and pressed a calling card into my hand. 'I'm from the *News of the World*,' he explained. 'We'll be hearing more of you.'

The fact that they did, as well as all other newspapers, was the result of acquiring an ex-Cabinet minister as my next client – John Stonehouse, the former Postmaster General in Harold Wilson's government. The MP had disappeared after walking into the water off Miami Beach, leaving clothes, money and passport in a locker to help the five insurance companies, with which he had recently taken out policies in favour of his wife, to deduce that he had drowned. Six weeks later he was discovered washed up in Melbourne, opening bank accounts and planning a long stay there with his secretary, Sheila Buckley – to the bewilderment of his wife, and his constituents in Walsall North. His had been a dramatic arrest by the Melbourne vice squad, who hoped the mysterious but imperious Englishman would turn out to be Britain's other famous fugitive, Lord Lucan. Scotland Yard had wired them that Lucan had a large mole on his upper right thigh: the arrest at gunpoint began with the order 'Pull yer trousers down!'

Stonehouse came back to face criminal charges and, having formed the view that he was being persecuted by the establishment of which he once had been part, asked his solicitor to instruct the young 'anti-establishment' lawyer who had defended *Oz* and Peter Hain. Summoned to meet him at Wandsworth prison, my task initially was to obtain bail so he could return to the Commons. 'But this is the face that launched a thousand headlines,' I exclaimed when the sour-faced magistrate expressed fears that he might slip out of the country unnoticed. After lengthy committal proceedings, we prepared for what the media were describing (they often do) as the 'trial of the century' at the Old Bailey. I would be led by Richard Du Cann, one of the finest and most professional silks then in practice. The day before the trial opened, as we were engaged in last-minute preparations, the news came through (on a BBC news bulletin) that we had been sacked – Mr Stonehouse had decided to represent himself. This may have been simply a politician's refusal to share the limelight, although he later told me that it was because Du Cann had never evinced any belief in his innocence. Given the evidence, this was hardly surprising, but what John did not understand was that Dick belonged to that old school of advocacy that suspended judgement, never descended to first-name terms with a client and insisted upon a personal distance that gave a false impression of disdain. Dick's early death from cancer was attributable to the cartons of cigarettes (I called him 'the Silk Cut silk') that he burned in his all-consuming anxiety over the cases of his clients. John was convicted: I had told him that he might receive three years if he pleaded guilty and showed some contrition, or five years if convicted after Dick and I had fought every point, but if he defended himself and got up the nose of the judge, he might get seven. He got seven.

He called me back to argue the appeal and then (with Louis Blom-Cooper QC) to take his case to the House of Lords, where we had some success but not enough to reduce his sentence.[23] It was a case which raised (and settled) some important points of law, and was my first experience of appearing in the highest court in the land – the House of Lords Judicial Committee. It was just that – an ordinary committee room in the House of Lords, into which would shuffle in lounge suits five very old Law Lords, to take their place at a green-baize horseshoe table. Appearances were deceptive – some of them could be quite ferocious. Louis 'blooded' me by allowing me to make a difficult legal argument, and to be torn to pieces by Lord Diplock. Still, it was a thrill later to see my name for the first time in the printed law reports and to scale the appellate heights – most counsel never reach them – in my first years of practice. At this rate, I might attain silk quite early and even be in line for a High Court judgeship – if that was what I really wanted.

I did feel a little sorry for John: he was a socialist MP who had come to disbelieve in socialism (a condition provided for a few years later by the foundation of the Social Democratic Party) and he became caught up in the middle-aged *Moon and Sixpence* dream of abandoning the pretence of power in favour of an invisible life playing chess, listening to jazz (his pursuits during his secret sojourn in Melbourne) and being looked after by Sheila, having done what he saw as the decent thing by his wife – of leaving her the insurance money. It was, of course, an appalling and selfish dream, and he paid heavily for the six weeks he enjoyed it. He sent me, every year, a Christmas card – it was, rather pathetically, a House of Commons Christmas card.

*　　*　　*

My career at the Bar had commenced in 1974, when I was admitted to practise as a member of the Middle Temple, one of the four Inns of Court spiralling down to the Thames from High Holborn, to which all who practise must belong. Their halls and gardens and the stately buildings (mostly rebuilt after the Blitz) offer a quiet, Oxbridge-like retreat from the noise of Fleet Street and Chancery Lane. Barristers work from 'chambers' (but independently of colleagues, who share rent and resources but are not allowed to be partners). They took their tone from the barrister who was 'head' of chambers although the real power was wielded by the head clerk, usually a venal character from the East End who negotiated (or extorted) very high fees from solicitors and decided (often on grounds of sex, race or politics) which of his barristers should receive the briefs sent to chambers by solicitors, unless they were marked for a particular recipient. There was one absurd qualification: to become a barrister you had to eat no fewer than thirty-six dinners at your Inn, to ensure that you 'dined well' and knew to pass the port in the correct direction. I survived the ordeal thanks to Arthur Scargill – his miner's strike in 1974 forced the Heath government to call a three-day week, and our dinner load was reduced to twenty-four.

The next step was to obtain a 'seat' in chambers, impossible for most women ('We don't have the toilet facilities,' said the clerks) and for almost all black counsel, although a few formed their own set – 'ghetto chambers' snarked the pin-striped Old Etonians (or at least Oxbridgeans), from which privileged pool 90 per cent of judges and barristers were drawn. They would select new members of their chambers by a cloning process that held out a hand to those applicants who most resembled themselves. Many graduates – from redbrick universities, or who had no family connections with the law – simply failed to find a 'seat' from which they could set up their shingle (the names of members had to be fancily sign-written, in order of seniority, on an outside door). I had to find a chambers which did the sort of work I wanted to do, and would want me to do it with them.

I had done my pupillage with Jo at Garden Court, but Arthur, its clerk, disliked all the calls I was taking from what he termed 'the National fucking

Council for Civil fucking Liberties'. I had to look elsewhere if I wanted its work. My *Lady Chatterley* idol Gerald Gardiner had retired (he had become chancellor of his own idea – the Open University – and was enjoying himself doing one of its undergraduate arts courses). Jeremy Hutchinson, my other hero, was in practice with Richard Du Cann at Queen Elizabeth Building, but their chambers only did crime and I wanted to spread my wings and practise constitutional and media law. Cloisters was the most left-wing choice, but its reputation had been earned in the '30s when it was the fiefdom of D. N. Pritt QC – a counsel who was a communist (to which I did not object) but one who whitewashed Stalin's show trials (to which I did). I made it my third choice. My first was to join the chambers of a man whose brain and courage I already admired – Louis Blom-Cooper QC. He had been Gardiner's junior in the *Exodus* case, had edited books on law and literature, and was always available to do death penalty cases – unlike Pritt, free of charge. His large, ground-floor room opposite the Temple Church was always open to young barristers wanting help on how to make creative arguments for civil liberties – it became more fashionable, many years later, to call them by a less aggressive title, 'human rights'. Louis's enthusiasm for novel points of law was infectious, at least until you put them before a judge. The first case we did together was at the instance of Amnesty International, which had discovered that one of Ian Smith's lickspittle Rhodesian judges, notorious for passing death sentences on black opponents of the Unilateral Declaration of Independence (UDI), was taking a holiday in Britain. We applied for a warrant for his arrest for incitement to murder, on the basis that his death sentences were void under UK laws passed to deprive Smith's regime of legitimacy, and so operated as an incitement to prison officers and the hangman to kill unlawfully. The Chief Justice granted the arrest warrant, and the judge quickly ended his holiday and scarpered back to Bulawayo.

Louis was delighted that I applied and promised his full support, despite – or perhaps because of – which (chambers politics are obscure) I was rejected. His clerk had heard from Arthur that I was 'too radical'. So I had to obtain my second choice of 'seat' in the traditional way, through connections. I called John Mortimer, who insisted I join him at Dr Johnson's

Buildings, and introduced me to the head, Emlyn Hooson QC MP. He was a delightful man (somewhat unfairly caricatured in *Rumpole* as Guthrie Featherstone QC MP), a Welsh Liberal steeped in the taxi-rank tradition of the Bar (he had defended Ian Brady, the Moors murderer) and encouraged my defence of controversial clients. I had my name hand-painted on the noticeboard, and took up residence in a small room with a view of the Temple Church, lit eerily at night by gas lamps. I stayed at Dr Johnson's (taking silk in 1988) until I left to found Doughty Street Chambers in 1990.

* * *

Now that I had the makings of a career, I needed to position myself – politically and intellectually. I was elected to the executive board of the NCCL, which fought against the illiberalism of James Callaghan's Labour government, forever trying to cut back on the right to trial by jury, increase police powers in response to IRA terrorism, and censor books (it actually prosecuted *Inside Linda Lovelace* and tried to stop publication of Richard Crossman's diaries). The government rejected our campaign for a Freedom of Information Act – 'Only two or three of your constituents would be interested,' sneered its Home Secretary Merlyn Rees. The NCCL's executive board was a diaspora of political views, ranging from young Tory Clive Landa (who later married into the Thatcher ministry) to old Trotskyite Paul Foot. Our monthly meetings did little more than approve the decisions of our General Secretary Patricia Hewitt (daughter of the Australian government's Cabinet Secretary) and her legal officer Harriet Harman, a bold and skilful solicitor who was niece to Lord Longford. MI5 was for no good reason tapping our telephones, as we discovered some years later from one of the MI5 phone-tappers, Cathy Massiter. (She had also been tasked to intercept calls to the Campaign for Nuclear Disarmament, and through listening to its conversations became so convinced of the dangers of nuclear weapons that she resigned from MI5 and joined them.) I took an action for breach of Pat and Hattie's privacy to the European Court of Human Rights – it was an easy victory, since the government at this point was pretending that MI5 did not exist. It paid compensation and more importantly passed a law that put MI5 (and later MI6) on a statutory footing. One of many examples of how the European Convention on Human Rights has enhanced the rule of law in Britain.

My journalistic efforts were beginning to flourish – *The Guardian* gave me a regular weekly column, 'Out of Court', which ran for some years, with either my fulminations or those I could persuade other lawyers to write. One newly qualified barrister who did produce some columns was David Pannick, brilliant even at that age (he had already been elected a fellow of All Souls). He came to me ashen-faced after one of his articles was published: he had just been carpeted by the chairman of the Bar for writing it. He was bewildered, as was I, at a profession that could not cope with well-intentioned criticism by its own members. (David's fortnightly columns are now the ornament of the legal pages of *The Times*, enjoyed by the nation's judges, whom they sensibly instruct.)

Nonetheless, the profession and the practice of law in the '70s, with its suffocating complacency, its sexism and racism and classism and denial of entry to minorities, its monopoly of advocacy and lack of interest in human rights, could not much longer be tolerated by a generation that had done its share of protesting as students in the '60s. A group of us met conspiratorially in various flats in north London, pondering how it might be changed – by setting up chambers outside the Temple, for example, which seemed then the most radical step possible (it had never been done before). One member was Tony Gifford, who was through ancient descent actually a member of the House of Lords – much to his embarrassment, although it provided him with a platform to urge the support of the Law Centre movement (he had started the first one, in north Kensington). Another member was Helena Kennedy, later author of *Eve Was Framed* and a doughty baroness who was to contribute much to law reform; another was Mike Mansfield, developing a talent for cross-examining perjurous policemen. Our intellectual leader was Stephen Sedley, who was older and had already established a reputation in public law. The most determined was Robert Hazell, a young Etonian who was so appalled at the Bar that he decided to leave it, but not before editing the book that in 1978 provided our manifesto – *The Bar on Trial*. It had a chapter by Helena on discrimination against women in the legal profession – the first time, incredibly, that this issue had been raised.

One result of our meetings was a proposal to set up barrister's chambers outside the Temple. Was this even ethically possible? Tony and I went to consult the General Secretary of the Bar Council, the legendary Mr Boulton of *Boulton on Ethics* (full title, *Conduct and Etiquette at the Bar*), the slim volume of biblical stature presented to every student on their call to the Bar. With the trepidation of ancient messengers approaching the shrine at Delphi, we asked the oracle – a kindly, owlish man, who had the volume at his fingertips. He slowly thumbed through its pages, and then pronounced, 'I find nothing in *Boulton on Ethics* against a set of chambers located outside the Temple.' We made another revolutionary request. Clerks were always employed on a percentage, which emboldened them to demand excessive fees from solicitors – could we employ our clerks on a salary instead? Again, the sage consulted his own book: 'I find nothing in *Boulton on Ethics* against a barrister employing a clerk on a salary.' Finally, a truly radical proposal: could we share our fees equally? Mr Boulton raised his eyebrows at this idea, but followed the same procedure before at length declaring, 'There is nothing to be found in *Boulton on Ethics* which precludes fee-sharing.' We left his office feeling as excited as Lenin on leaving the Finland station: permission had been given for the revolution to begin. Had we asked Mr Boulton's permission to make bombs in the basement, he would doubtless have gone through the same procedure before declaring, 'There is nothing in *Boulton on Ethics* against the making of explosive substances in barrister's chambers.'

This was heady stuff in 1976: it seems absurd now, when many chambers have moved out, together with the Bar Council itself, and most clerks are on fees rather than percentages. But fee-sharing for barristers never worked, and I am not sure that it should – we must be scrupulously independent, free of pressures from partners or from fee-sharing collectives. Tony went ahead, with Mr Boulton's permission, to set up the first 'outside' chambers, in Covent Garden – several of its members joined me when I set up Doughty Street Chambers, outside the Temple, in 1990.

The legal profession that my generation joined in the 1970s was a secretive, class-calcified body of men who exercised power without accountability – law-power – when sentencing convicts at circuit courts and when interpreting statutes and developing common-law doctrines in the High Court, Court of Appeal or, finally, the judicial committee of the House of Lords. Not only did the privileges of private schooling and Oxbridge speed you to a 'seat' in chambers: thereafter, any career promotion – appointment to silk, or to the judiciary – was swathed in utter secrecy. It was in the hands of the Lord Chancellor, who took 'soundings' (which never reverberated) from senior judges to ensure that 'radicals' or 'socialists' were not recruited to dine with the legal establishment at Temple dinners. As Lord Jowitt, the post-war Labour Lord Chancellor, explained to an American academic who wondered why British judges were all so conservative, including his own appointments, 'How do you think I would have felt, from all the cold looks I would have received when next I dined at the Inn?'

The over-powerful Lord Chancellor I had to endure for most of the '80s, when I was breasting the junior Bar, was no liberal, although Lord Hailsham could be quite engaging (as I discovered after his retirement, when we had some enjoyable jousts on breakfast television). I was critical of the fact that he sat as a Law Lord while a member of the government (Gardiner never did so) and detected ways in which his political beliefs had influenced his interpretation of the law, especially in a judgment which had turned trespass – a civil wrong recompensed by damages – into a serious conspiracy crime when committed by two or more persons. This was in order to jail protesters and flying pickets and (potentially) Peter Hain. I accused Hailsham of playing politics with the law in an article for the *New Statesman*, which had to be written under a pseudonym. 'I've called you John Paine,' said the editor, Tony Howard. 'I imagine you as Tom's brother.' It became less amusing when my article elicited an explosive response from Hailsham – letters written in furious fountain pen strokes on his headed notepaper, threatening to sue for defamation. Tony cleverly mollified the great man by offering to publish a sympathetic portrait of him by Paul Johnson, entitled 'The Old Steam Kettle'. Hailsham was delighted, and the letters threatening action against Tom's brother ceased.

Incredibly, judicial appointments were never advertised until 2005, nor discussed by the media: US Supreme Court candidates were invigilated in public hearings by Senators, reported on the front page of the *New York Times*, whereas appointments to the English equivalent received a small entry in the 'Court circular' page of *The Times*. John Paine, in the *New Statesman*, did demand that Anthony Lester and Louis Blom-Cooper be appointed to the High Court (which was doubtless the kiss of death to their chances). Prospects were blighted by personal or political animosities from existing Law Lords, and by poison pen letters sent in secret to the Lord Chancellor's department by other judges and barristers, detailing malicious scuttlebutt. This was quite an industry – I was once shown a nasty note by a circuit judge about something I had said. Instead of facing me in court when I said it, like a school sneak he sent his complaint privately to the Lord Chancellor. It was a false allegation and I wondered why he would even bother to make it. He was gay and hence insecure about his position (even in the 1990s), which may be why he sought to show he was a sound chap by tittle-tattling (I only discovered he was gay in the way you did in those days – by reading his obituary in *The Times*, which mentioned his partner).

There were lots of examples, used to pressure young barristers to conform. My head of chambers at Garden Court, Lewis Hawser, was a brilliant and dedicated criminal silk who deserved to be appointed to the High Court, but never made it. According to Arthur, 'This was because he took telephone calls from the National fucking Council of Civil fucking Liberties.' Hawser himself was mystified and shortly before his death asked me if I knew why – I did not, although I had heard a rumour that a powerful judge had disliked the vigour with which he had secured the acquittal of a client – which is, of course, the role of defence counsel, although some senior judges, mostly recruited from the commercial Bar, did not seem to understand it. 'The Old Bailey is hardly the SW3 of the legal profession,' one eminent Law Lord snarkily remarked. It betrayed the mentality of the judiciary of the time, brought home to me in 1976 when I appeared before a High Court judge en route to becoming a Law Lord who had recently served as head of the Bar Council. In the middle of the trial, he summoned me into his chambers. 'I've taken rather a shine to you,' he said (to my surprise – his interventions all seemed intended to take any shine off my arguments to the jury). 'Let me give you some advice. You must stop doing this class of case.' (I was defending a reputable bookseller, on an obscenity charge that could have cost him his liberty.) 'If you are not careful, you could end up doing bomb cases.' Bomb cases were what I very much wanted to end up doing and I could not believe the contempt in which the upper echelons of the English Bar and bench held barristers who defended Irish men and women accused – often wrongly – of planting bombs. Eventually, of course, the dreadful miscarriages that had innocent people jailed for many years – the Birmingham Six, the Guildford Four, Judith Ward – took the shine off the reputation of British justice.

It was a mentality that had to be changed, but not until after the Human Rights Act in 1988 did it really diminish. Typical of the time was the case of *Home Office v Harriet Harman*.[24] The Home Office decided to introduce a cruel and unlawful regime for 'difficult' prisoners, involving lengthy and solitary confinement in a 'control unit'. A prisoner subjected to the treatment sought help from the NCCL, whose solicitor (Harriet Harman) brought a case against the government forcing it to disclose the policy documents that had led to the unit's establishment. Her counsel was Stephen Sedley, by now leader of the junior public law Bar, who read out most of the documents in the course of his opening, to which they were obviously relevant. Hattie therefore saw no reason not to give the bundle to David Leigh, a reporter from *The Guardian*, which published several to illustrate how the Home Office had turned its back on human rights. The government, in a fit of pique, turned on Hattie and prosecuted her for contempt of court for disclosing its documents to the media. I acted as one of her counsel, and our case came before Lord Denning, who decided against us. We lost 3–2 in the House of Lords, but with a splendid dissent from Lord Scarman, who pointed out that if freedom of information meant anything, it meant that a document read out in public must be a public document. Off we went to Strasbourg, where the government was again held in breach of freedom of expression and had to amend the rules of the Supreme Court to allow documents to be publically disseminated once they had been read in open court.

I'm glad to say that the case did Harriet no harm – she was applying to be a Labour candidate, and Denning was so disliked by the trade unions (he always ruled against them) that when he convicted her for contempt it served as a badge of honour, and ensured her selection for a safe Labour seat.

There did come a point, quite early in those dispiriting first days at the Bar, when I seriously considered giving up the fight. I was contributing a lot to the *New Statesman*, with cover stories on miscarriages of justice and police corruption, and the atmosphere when I visited its offices in Great Turnstile were a good deal more congenial than the Temple. I would meet Chris Hitchens, James Fenton, Claire Tomalin and Bel Mooney and I confided my doubt about the Bar to Tony Howard, the editor. He urged me to stay where I was: 'Your articles have authenticity that comes from first-hand knowledge – you would be less use as a journalist or academic.' He was not going to offer me a full-time job, so I consoled myself with the thought that the long-term advantage of the Bar was that the older you get, the more distinguished you are assumed to be: with journalists, the opposite seemed to be the case. Tony was never quite sure about me – he confided to Bel (not realising that clandestinely we were 'an item') that this young whistle-blowing Australian was a bit too goody-goody to be true: maybe he was a 'sleeper' (a communist spy sent to infiltrate the British establishment). Bel suppressed her giggles and expressed some doubt over whether I was a 'sleeper' (or so she told me in bed that night).

Peter Preston, the *Guardian* editor, had no doubts about my allegiances and it was he who gave me the 'Out of Court' column in *The Guardian*. He was a shy workaholic, always serious but always genuine. One of the saddest of my memories is of rushing from the Old Bailey to tell him that Sarah Tisdall – the source the judges had forced him to expose by threatening to put the paper into liquidation if he didn't – had been jailed for six months for breaking the Official Secrets Act. He winced and almost collapsed in mental agony when I brought him the news – I sat with him for an hour as we talked through the case, and the bad legal advice that he had received from a City solicitor which stopped him shredding the incriminating document before the court injunction arrived.

Having renounced the attractions of a louche life as a journalist, I determined to make Dr Johnson's Buildings at least a home for like-minded civil libertarians. It already had some home-grown experts like Chris Sallon and Stephen Irwin. My most endearing recruit was Helena Kennedy. We had lots of friends in common and co-defended in some of the terrorist trials of the era. She was my heavily pregnant junior when we defended an art gallery charged with public indecency for displaying earrings made from freeze-dried foetuses – I hoped that the sight of her cross-examining with hands over her big baby belly would persuade the jury that we were on the side of fecundity. In this case we had a serious obstacle (apart from the evidence), namely a drunken and incoherent QC who was appearing for the artist – he was actually a head of chambers, and his junior, as was a common practice in those days, had brought in his head to lead him despite his unfitness for that or any other trial. It was a practice which I would never countenance when I became head at Doughty Street. We held some planning meetings for this new chambers at Helena's home, which had featured in one of my first successful cases when it was owned by the celebrated psychologist Ronald (R. D.) Laing. He had been licensed to prescribe LSD to patients and when the drug was banned he desisted, but absentmindedly left some capsules in the back of his fridge, where they were discovered by a very thorough burglar. He called the police, who made a quick arrest – but then prosecuted Ronnie for having possessed the LSD found in the burglar's possession. It was a ridiculous case, which the Hampstead justices threw out. With Helena now in residence at Laing's former home, with her husband Ian, it's always a pleasant pleasure to return to the scene of this non-crime.

I also managed to recruit Peter Thornton and Michael Grieve (Peter became the Chief Coroner; Michael a judge), but my persuasive powers failed in the case of Clive Anderson, a friend I had met when he was doing barrister imitations at the Edinburgh Comedy Festival. Despite my glowing assessment of his potential, my colleagues turned him down: 'No one has ever heard of him,' they said. I had more luck with Andrew Nicol, my first pupil (now Sir Andrew, a High Court judge) who was a great boon to have at my side, once he got over the embarrassment of being reported by

Treasury Counsel for wearing brown shoes – banned by Bar etiquette and never to be seen below a black gown. He remained a part-time lecturer at LSE, from which vantage point he was able to talent-spot my next pupils – Heather Rogers and Heather Williams, who both went on to be successful silks. Pupils have no job security, and live in perpetual dread of not being 'taken on' after they finish. Neither Heather need have worried.

One afternoon I had a call from a friend at Cloisters: 'My pupil has just been turned down for a tenancy,' he wailed. 'Let me send him round to you now – I think you'll like him.' I opened my door to Edward Fitzgerald, whom I did like, so much that I prevailed on Emlyn to take him. 'He'll have to smarten up a bit first,' said Emlyn after meeting this wild and woolly youngster who had just finished a Master's degree in criminology. 'He'll have to do a pupillage with one of our prosecutors.' Ed duly read up on the powers and duties of prosecutors – never to pursue a case they thought without merit – and, when left alone with the prosecution brief while his pupil-master was in another court, frequently made the decision that it was indeed without merit, and withdrew it. 'I have decided, my Lord, that it is my duty in the public interest to offer no evidence.' His pupil-master would return to an empty court, and the Metropolitan Police solicitors became concerned. So it was decided that Ed was cut out to be a defender, and he was sent off to Snaresbrook Crown Court to plead for a burglar with a long string of convictions who had been caught red-handed. To our surprise, we heard that he was pleading not guilty, and that Ed was running the defence, little-known outside criminology texts, of automa-tism – the defendant was sleep-walking at the time he was pocketing the loot. The judge is said to have told the jury, 'This is the most ridiculous defence I have ever heard in my life,' but they acquitted and Ed's fame among criminals and their solicitors quickly spread. He went on to act for Myra Hindley, Abu Hamza, one of James Bulger's killers, Abu Qatada and Silvio Berlusconi, as well as for many virtuous clients, and is now reckoned the best public lawyer in the land (and in other lands where he is pressed to defend the demonised). He remains a dear friend and is now my co-head of Doughty Street Chambers.

Another potential recruit looked good to me on paper, probably because his qualifications were similar to mine at his age – a state school, a redbrick university, some published articles, topped off by a goodish BCL from Oxford. Given that cloning is an inevitable temptation for an interviewer, I was predisposed in his favour, although he looked about fourteen, was nervous and awkward in the interview and (worst of all, for my colleagues on the panel) was poorly dressed ('We can't take someone who wears a cardigan,' said one, her nose crinkling). Well, we could, but it needed all my powers of persuasion to get Emlyn to accept him. I owed Emlyn a lot, and was only sorry that he did not live long enough to turn on the television today, almost every day, to see Sir Keir Starmer QC MP, shadow Brexit Secretary, make mincemeat of his government opponents. From the start, Keir was the finest of colleagues and an example of how interviews should never be relied on as a sole guide to ability.

Keir was really, I guess, the protégé that Emlyn wanted me to be. Emlyn was always urging me to stand for Parliament: he even approached his friend Bob Mellish, who was retiring from his Labour stronghold of Bermondsey, to promote my prospects of replacing him. I did not apply (to be perfectly honest, I could not bear to live south of the river) and an Australian friend, Peter Tatchell, was selected. The local party reckoned without the militantly anti-gay feeling in the dockyards, and after a disgusting homophobic campaign by the Liberals, their clean-cut and apparently heterosexual candidate, Simon Hughes, won the seat (it was some years before he could bring himself to admit that he was bisexual). My own political career never took off: when I congratulated Harriet Harman on her selection (I was defending her at the time) and wondered whether she would like me to join her on the green benches, she pulled a face: 'Don't be ridiculous. You could never suffer fools gladly.' The prospect never again crossed my mind.

I had some success in building up Dr Johnson's as a chambers specialising in civil liberties, but this was a limited objective. If we wanted to change the culture of the Bar (and of the bench), we had to start by educating lawyers of the future, in the universities. There, as Bryan Gould and I had discovered at Oxford, there was really not much interest: I met the occasional academic who was interested – like the brilliant Cedric Thornberry – but he and others quickly departed for greener fields in the US, leaving as his contribution to the left only a few insightful articles and a young daughter, Emily (now shadow Foreign Secretary). Go into a law library today and the shelves groan with textbooks on human rights (*aka* civil liberties), but in the 1980s there was only one – a slim Penguin paperback with the ungainly title *Freedom, the Individual and the Law*. When its author, Harry Street (a professor of commercial law), died, Penguin invited me to pick up his baton, so I rewrote the book (and tripled its size). I began with a quote from *Animal Farm* (which Orwell's left-wing publishers had refused to include because it was critical of Stalin): 'If liberty means anything at all, it means the right to tell people what they do not want to hear,' and opened by pointing out that 'Liberty in Britain is a state of mind rather than a set of legal rules' (I had yet to learn that in many quarters it was not even a state of mind, and legal rules in a Human Rights Act were required to induce one). After a few hundred pages cataloguing the yawning gaps in British law's protection of fair trial and free speech and the rights of minorities, I concluded with a heartfelt call for a Bill of Rights and a Freedom of Information Act. The book was prescribed at law schools for some courses on civil liberties and 'law and society' taught in the '80s and '90s, and may have made some small contribution (one never knows) to engaging future lawyers in the subject.

The Bill of Rights question (The European Convention? A British Bill? Or no Bill at all?) flares up from time to time. The Convention was drafted by British lawyers in 1950 and promoted by Churchill as a bulwark against fascism and encroaching communism in Europe, but it had no effect until Gerald Gardiner in 1966 allowed individuals to petition the court in Strasbourg, and no real impact until they started doing so in the '80s (notably the *Sunday Times*, under Harold Evans, when the Euro court condemned British judges for banning his attempt to expose the thalidomide scandal). Meanwhile Leslie Scarman, at the Law Reform Commission, had been studying all those gaps in the British common law, and began a campaign to plug them with a Bill of Rights. Support briefly came from one curious quarter – Lord Hailsham, the once and future Tory Lord Chancellor. Out of office during the Wilson and Callaghan years, he acutely analysed how democratic governance tended towards 'elective dictatorship' as the Prime Minister and Cabinet could rule to their heart's content over a tame civil service, a majority of docile MPs, and a powerless parliamentary opposition. A Bill of Rights was necessary, he said, to protect liberty against an extreme government – a view he ceased to promote as soon as he started to wield power again as part of Mrs Thatcher's extreme government ('elective dictatorship' is always less objectionable when you have been elected to power and are doing the dictating).

You would think – I certainly did – that this was the time for progressive lawyers to embrace a Bill of Rights. But the Labour Party soon split over the issue. One faction (and in Labour, factions speak louder than words) had taken fright at the behaviour of the judges in Mrs Thatcher's union-bashing National Industrial Relations Court. The other legal contributor to the *New Statesman*, LSE Professor John Griffith, wrote an influential book, *The Politics of the Judiciary*, tracing the right-wing views and decisions of English judges over the centuries, and arguing that they could not be trusted to interpret a Bill of Rights progressively – indeed, they would use it to strike down initiatives of a socialist government. By this stage I knew more judges than John, and did not find them (Denning and a few others excepted) to be dyed-in-the-wool reactionaries. Moreover, they were men who were ruled by law and conditioned to obey it. Put our liberties into a law and they would – with difficulty at first – come round to implementing it, and future judges – barristers and law students – could be trained to obey it. I dug out a quote from John's LSE predecessor, the left-wing luminary Harold Laski, to confound him:

> Bills of Rights serve to draw attention to the fact that vigilance is essential in the realm of what Cromwell called 'fundamentals'. Bills of Rights are, quite undoubtedly, a check upon possible excess in the government of the day. They warn us that certain popular powers have had to be fought for, and may have to be fought for again. The solemnity they embody serves to set the people on their guard. It acts as a rallying point in the state for all who care deeply for the ideals of freedom.

Like Laski, I thought it was the educative potential of a Bill of Rights that would make it most effective – and not only for judges. My children, going through school, were learning that civil rights began in Alabama with

Martin Luther King: they were given no appreciation of how the English were first to abolish torture and allow comparative religious tolerance and representative democracy and the independence of the judiciary – rights that were fought for in the muddy fields of Naseby, and by the Levellers and Chartists, whose struggles were not included in the school curriculum. A well-drafted Bill of Rights, referring to those won since Magna Carta, might be something our kids could recite with pride.

Nonetheless, the NCCL was split down the middle – with Stephen Sedley supportive of the Griffith line. The Haldane Society of Socialist Lawyers joined in the chorus of 'You Can't Trust the Judges'. The debate bubbled on during the Thatcher years, although it was noticed that the judges were her only real opposition, winning back some trust by 'judicially reviewing' and overturning some of her government's more unreasonable decisions. The Society of Labour Lawyers, of which I had become a member, turned in favour and after Neil Kinnock's strong showing in 1987 we pressed for a promise of a Bill of Rights and a Freedom of Information Act to go into the Labour manifesto. John Smith and his successor, Tony Blair, were not opposed, but left the decision to the shadow Home Secretary, Roy Hattersley. Figuring that the way to Roy's heart was through his stomach (he was a notorious glutton), a small dinner party was organised for him at Rules, the upmarket Covent Garden restaurant. We berated him about the atrocious record of the last Labour government – prosecuting pacifists and journalists; vetting juries; even, I expostulated, trying to ban Richard Crossman's diaries. Hattersley later said that his dinner with the Labour lawyers was the worst dining experience he had ever endured. And the food was excellent.

So a pledge to introduce a Bill of Rights went into the manifesto, and after the Labour triumph in 1997, we were quickly vouchsafed (with no opposition from disconsolate Tories) a Freedom of Information Act, which Tony Blair later said was his worst ever mistake (evidence of just how necessary it was) and a Bill of Rights. The judges, in some panic, asked for time to learn about it and were given eighteen months to be educated, under the guidance, ironically, of Mr Justice Sedley. Stephen had by now been elevated to the High Court, and did a fine job of ensuring that his dire predictions at NCCL meetings many years before did not come true.

Most lawyers would agree, twenty years on, that the Human Rights Act 1998 has measurably improved the state of civil liberties in Britain. The main problem has derived from the decision to 'bring rights back home' immediately, by adopting, off the peg as it were, the European Convention on Human Rights. Although drafted by British lawyers and embodying such rights as could be extrapolated from the English common law circa 1950, it was easy for Europhobic politicians and newspapers to present it as somehow alien to our traditions. It was a wonder of its time, but in fact its time had passed – it was a lowest common denominator declaration of freedoms that had consensus in Europe in 1950. Hence it did not have any provision for trial by jury (the most basic English right, but Napoleon had abolished juries on the Continent); it had a weasel-worded privacy provision that too often was allowed to trump free speech, and it had no provision for social or political or environmental rights, or for the protection e.g. of the disabled. These were not, of course, the reasons why the anti-Europe Tories came to oppose it (they wanted fewer rights for immigrants, or preferably none at all), but David Cameron responded to their Europhobia by promising a 'British' Bill of Rights.

Legal lobbies went into overdrive to preserve the European Convention, but the 'British' Bill would have to include all the rights in the Convention anyway (we were bound by treaty to include them) and would be an opportunity to expand free press and open justice and to add trial by jury, plus rights for the disabled, rights to education, to well-being, to work and to a healthy environment. I actually drafted a full-blooded British Bill to this effect, published in the High Tory magazine *Standpoint*, and wrote articles in support of David Cameron's idea in the *Daily Mail*.[25] When Shami Chakrabarti chided me for not toeing the line, I replied that the best way of protecting the Convention from the Tories was to scare them with the 'full English' alternative. At any event, their junior ministers and departmental lawyers wrestled for months to try to agree on a British Bill, and failed so abjectly that they have never dared to release their drafts. I was sorry to disappoint old friends from Liberty (the rebranded NCCL) by endorsing the idea of a 'British' Bill – perhaps they too now think of me, like Sir Humphrey, as 'rather his own man'.

Chapter Seven

Trial by Jury

———————

I had become a fully-fledged barrister in wig, wing collar, bands and gown, purchased from the tailor to the Bar, Messrs Ede & Ravenscroft in Chancery Lane. I made the mistake of being measured for my wig just after a haircut, and it is still forever slipping down my cranium; as Clive James said, 'You don't need a wig; you should just powder your hair.' I recently appeared with Amal Clooney in the European Court of Human Rights in Strasbourg. It was a serious case about genocide, and the British papers all sent their correspondents – their fashion correspondents, that is – who asked her, 'What are you wearing?' 'Ede & Ravenscroft,' she replied drolly – a couturier unknown on the catwalks of Paris.

The robes and wing collars that barristers must wear in Britain are constant irritants, especially the stud that must be attached to fix the starched wing collar to the white shirt. Indeed, it may be said that the only danger to a barrister's life comes in the robing room, when too-vigorous pressing of the collar stud may touch that gland in the neck, just below the carotid artery, which if pressed too hard will cut off the blood supply to the brain and cause unconsciousness and possibly death. (This knowledge comes in handy when you defend a strangler – 'He did not realise, members of the jury, that he was pressing just a little too hard.') I have always been in favour of abolishing the pantomime flummery of wigs and gowns, but the Bar Council took a consumer survey of the consumers of our services – i.e. of criminals – and they all said they wanted us to keep them: 'I like my brief dressed proper.'

There was only one occasion in my forensic life when I have been glad to have worn a gown. It was when I defended the movie *Deep Throat* the first time it was prosecuted at the Old Bailey. In those days in England they still had all-male juries for sex cases. The prosecutor opened the case very moderately: 'You are about to see a film, gentlemen of the jury. It will be for you to say whether it is an indecent importation.' The courtroom lights went down, and Ms Lovelace came on the makeshift screen. Ninety minutes later, the lights came up. Nobody moved. The judge then announced it was lunchtime and made his exit, in a crouching position. The all-male jury remained stock-still in the jury box. 'Come on,' said the elderly lady usher. 'It's lunchtime.' Still they did not move. 'Come on,' she said, 'I've got to get me lunch.' Still they did not move, those red-faced and sweaty twelve good men and true. We barristers left court, our gowns wrapped loosely around us, thinking that on occasions like this there was some point in being robed. Incidentally, you probably won't believe this but I swear it's true – the jury could not agree. It was what we call a 'well-hung jury'.

For all of the professionals – judges, QCs and barristers, solicitors, policemen and clerks – who inhabit the large court complex of the Old Bailey (four of the austere original courtrooms, and fourteen modern additions), it is the jurors who make the vital decision. It is a curious, somewhat irrational system, but it's been with us for 800 years – the notion that what lawyers condescendingly call 'ordinary people' (by which they mean people who are not lawyers) should hold the sword and scales, and substitute, in the flesh, for the goddess. No one in Britain can be sent to prison for more than a year without the opportunity to obtain the judgment of his or her peers. It is a clumsy and costly system, abolished in some countries (Lee Kuan Yew's Singapore, for example) in the interests of efficiency – and of verdicts in the government's favour by compliant judges. The Europeans simply cannot understand our affection for it – surely a defendant has a right to a *reasoned* verdict before they lose their liberty, rather than an inscrutable grunt of 'guilty' from the jury foreman? Yes, and no – I am in favour of defendants having the right to waive their entitlement to trial by jury and elect trial by (preferably three) judges if, for example, they fear a jury may be infected by racial prejudice or media prejudice. But for all the inconvenience and expense, the faith invested in this group of citizens chosen by lot is in my experience generally justified, and the right to an independent and impartial adjudication is the most fundamental of our 'fair trial' rights.

As if to illustrate this point, in the high-domed hall of the old building there are statues of William Penn and William Mead, two Quakers who were tried in 1670 for preaching sedition. Their jury refused to follow the judge's direction to convict, so he had them locked up for two nights without food or water or even a chamber pot. When they still insisted upon returning a verdict of 'not guilty', the judge sentenced them to prison. Their foreman, Edward Bushell, challenged the legality of their punishment by the great writ of *habeas corpus* (which requires the state to prove that imprisonment is lawful), and the Chief Justice ruled that it was not: every English jury was entitled to act according to its own conscience and appreciation of the evidence, irrespective of judicial direction or expectation. Bushell's case is the most important decision for Anglo-American criminal law, because it is the foundation of the constitutional independence of the jury: it can do justice, whatever the law may be. I have often told juries about Penn and Mead and invited them to contemplate the statues of the two Quakers, and to remember the astonishing courage of Bushell. Thanks to him, they will suffer no inconvenience or reprisal when they acquit my client.

*   *   *

There is something special about jury advocacy: I have in the course of a long professional life been privileged to address many appeal judges in many countries – benches of seven in the Privy Council, House of Lords and the High Court of Australia, not to mention judges in the Supreme Courts of Malaysia and Mauritius and Florida, Courts of Appeal in Hong Kong and Mozambique and Singapore, and a large semicircle of seventeen or so judges in the European Court of Human Rights. These are intellectual exercises, defining principles and gathering precedents in order to persuade judges who have probably already made up their own minds. (My judicial nemesis, Lord Diplock, boasted that only on two occasions had he been influenced by advocacy, and on one of them he had convinced himself.)

It is an altogether different experience to address an Old Bailey jury, arguing for the liberty of a person in peril in the dock. You feel, as you stand before them to deliver your final speech, a portentous rush of power – the power of persuasion. You grab the sides of your green-baized stand and talk to them without interruption and for as long as you like on the subject of how they should go about finding your client 'not guilty'. You have to shred the case presented by the prosecutor who has spoken before you, and booby-trap the judge, who will have the last word in his summing up. But for most of the time – and these speeches can last for days, although my preference is for two to three hours, with a short break – you must interpret the evidence they have heard and weave it into a scenario in which your client was, for example, absent when the fatal blow was struck, or else struck it in self-defence. Factual situations are infinite: what matters is that the advocate must leave the jury with a credible version of events as they might (not must) have happened, in such a way that the defendant would bear no criminal liability for his or her part in them.

Styles of advocacy vary, and have changed with developments in courtroom architecture and jury composition. Addressing all-male juries in murder trials in the sombre and intimidating pre-war courtrooms with death sentences always in prospect, advocates such as Sir Edward Marshall Hall KC could get away with emotional appeals that would not work in modern strip-lit courtrooms with young male and female jurors. Marshall Hall secured the sympathetic acquittal of a wretched woman who had killed her abusive lover by ending his final speech: 'Look at her, gentlemen. God never gave her a chance. Won't you?' They did – but such cheapjack appeals would be laughed out of a modern court. My own preference, in the all-important last minutes of a final speech, is to play upon the rule (which the judge is obliged to lay down to the jury) that the prosecution must prove its case 'beyond reasonable doubt'. 'How many "reasonable doubts" hang over the prosecution case, ladies and gentlemen?' I list them (observing meanwhile the jurors who are taking notes) and try to find at least ten. Some may depend upon forensic fallacies; others may be of the kind 'Well, suppose he had committed the crime, he certainly would not have acted like that afterwards.' (Although, in fact, criminals frequently act stupidly or illogically after their crime.) As the jury members retire to their room with ten or fifteen 'reasonable doubts' listed in their notepads, there is a good chance that they will think that one or two might be true. Finally, I give a quick reminder that 'This verdict will be yours and yours alone' (i.e. don't listen to the views of that prejudiced old judge) and 'Don't make it something that will trouble your conscience afterwards' (i.e. remember Penn and Mead). 'I invite you to acquit.' And, quite often, they do.

Some years ago the government, in the hope of increasing the conviction rate, decided that judges should be eligible to be called for jury service. I was by this time a Recorder – a part-time judge – and shared the concern that a judge-juror might have an undue influence on fellow jurors. The Lord Chief Justice sent all judges a letter advising that if you were called for jury service, you should not let on that you were a judge. I was one of the first judges to be called up, and of course as soon as we sat down in our jury room some bright spark said, 'Let's go round the room and tell each other what we do for a living.' I described myself as a 'grievance counsellor'. Nonetheless, the truth quickly slipped out, and I was elected jury foreman. The defendant was obviously guilty, although our number included two anarchists who did not think anyone was guilty – society itself bore the responsibility for crime. After fruitless argument, with only ten minutes to go until lunchtime, I am afraid I did use a little undue influence by reminding my two recalcitrant colleagues that unless we reached a unanimous verdict we would be locked up for lunch without access to alcohol or cigarettes. This had not occurred to them and they agreed immediately. We returned to court and I loudly announced our unanimous verdict of 'guilty'.

*　　*　　*

My wife had a very strange experience when she was called to be a juror for a trial in which the defendant was charged with a particularly vicious, Trump-like grab of the genitals of a young woman. It had been in a narrow laneway – the plaintiff had screamed and the defendant had run, straight into the arms of a policeman. The victim gave her evidence in a way that my wife thought was truthful – why would she accuse a random stranger of such a crime? – although the judge, who was a recently appointed upper-class commercial solicitor, told the jury in sexist language that this was a 'tuppenny-ha'penny' assault and the defendant could be acquitted because he had no previous convictions and because there really wasn't any evidence (ignoring, of course, the best evidence – that of the victim).

Back in the jury room, it was a case of 'one angry woman' as my wife battled unavailingly for a 'guilty' verdict. They returned to court to acquit, and my wife watched the victim, who collapsed when she heard the verdict. Kathy was really upset by her failure to deliver justice, and worried about the accuser's mental health – she was obviously gutted by the thought that the jury had disbelieved her. After she had suffered several sleepless nights, I decided to take a very unusual action. I was sitting, at the time, as a judge in another court. I told Kathy to write a letter to the victim, which I had to edit carefully (it's a crime to reveal the secrets of the jury room) but still getting across to her that she had not been condemned as a liar – the jurors had just felt that they must follow the judge's direction. I then arranged to deliver the letter to the police officer who'd worked on the case, who agreed to pass it on to the victim.

Kathy received a long letter from this young woman a few days later, saying that she had felt suicidal after the verdict and the letter had helped her pull herself together. We forgot about the case for a few years, until flowers and a large cheque advance came from the managing director of Kathy's new publisher, with a note from the director's personal assistant saying how happy she was to be sending it – she was the crime victim who had recovered with the help of Kathy's letter.

So far, so good. But the tentacles of this case continued to spread. The judge – a commercial conveyancer elevated to the bench to placate the solicitors' profession, which had been moaning that only barristers were made judges – was arrested for having committed a massive mortgage fraud. His trial at the Old Bailey lasted a year and the jury could not reach a verdict. He claimed to be too ill to face a retrial, but that did not prevent him from decamping to Florida, where he married an American heiress, to the indignation of the *Daily Mail*, which pictured him walking with her on the beach, quite miraculously recovered.

But wait – there's more. Fifteen years after the indecent assault trial on which my wife had sat as a juror, a criminal was sentenced to life imprisonment for having committed over 100 rapes and sexual assaults – a British record. At his first trial fifteen years before, he had been acquitted of indecent assault: a conviction might have stopped his sex-crime spree in its tracks. A smart reporter obtained the jury list at the original trial and spotted the name of my by then well-known novelist wife. If only she had convinced her fellow jurors! She has been writing about this extraordinary chain of events ever since.[26] I guess the moral is that you should always do jury service if you are lucky enough to be called – it could be an experience you may never forget.

*　　*　　*

In jury trials, the final speech is the defence advocate's most powerful weapon, and requires the skill of marshalling complex facts and weaving the evidence into a picture consistent with innocence. There is also skill in cross-examination. John Mortimer taught me that the art of cross-examination is never to examine crossly, especially when dealing with prosecution experts. He would read up on their publications, congratulate them, cosset them and soon enough have them eating out of his hand, changing their evidence – about bloodstains, for instance – by that fraction which could make all the difference for his client between freedom and a life sentence.

It is in dealing with expert evidence that barristers show their real ability, which is to absorb and master in a few weeks the relevant discipline or science and go head-to-head with experts who have studied it all their working life. I once had to learn how to make a nuclear bomb in order to defend a man accused of selling 'nuclear triggers' to Saddam Hussein. It was information I had forgotten within a week of the trial's end: the barrister's mind simply empties of hastily absorbed information, and moves on to the science called for in the next case. It's like wiping clean a computer disc stored in the brain and saving the next case over it.

You often read in books or see on television examples of dramatic, devastating cross-examination. This rarely happens – the worst (i.e. best) liars are charming conmen who readily convince jurors with the confidence of their answers. The witness who hesitates is often the witness who is most concerned to remember the truth. Judges, even, do not understand how hesitation in a witness can indicate an effort to remember truthfully. My favourite example comes from the obscenity trial of a book called *The Mouth and Oral Sex*, as writer Margaret Drabble was testifying to its merits before an aggressively puritanical judge:

> JUDGE KING-HAMILTON: We've got along without oral sex for over 2,000 years. Why do we have to read about it now?
> DRABBLE: (*hesitates*)
> KING-HAMILTON: (*pounces*) Witness, why do you hesitate?
> DRABBLE: I am sorry, my Lord, I was just trying to remember the passage from Ovid.

I did once – but only once – cross-examine a witness so effectively that he fainted in the witness box. He was manager of a once-fashionable band, whose roadie (my client) was accused of importing drugs. This manager had been rewarded with immunity for giving prosecution evidence, and I was able to demonstrate from his own diary that he was the prime offender, a man who had incriminated even his own younger brother. He struggled to explain the morality of his conduct, and when the accusations mounted, he collapsed – fell backwards out of the witness box – from (or so it seemed) horror at being confronted with his own depravity. It was a climax to a cross-examination that can be balanced by the disasters which come from breaking the golden rule – never ask a question to which you do not know (or strongly suspect) the answer. I was defending a London bookshop, Gay's the Word, on charges of importing indecent literature, after a massive operation by British customs officers, who seemed to think that homosexuality was an alien custom. They called this homophobic exercise 'Operation Tiger', and I went for the customs officer in charge of it: 'You called it Operation Tiger, I suggest, because the name is redolent of swaggering machismo.'

'Well, no, sir,' he meekly replied. 'Actually, I named it after my cat.'

*　*　*

One question barristers are always asked is: 'How can you defend someone you know is guilty?' It's very simple – you can't. If a defendant is honest enough to admit guilt, I tell him or her I will take any available legal points on their behalf but I will not defend them on the merits. I will do a great mitigation speech, if they're willing to plead guilty; otherwise, goodbye.

A follow-up answer for all other cases is that you never really know. That can best be illustrated by the arms-to-Iraq affair. In 1992 I was briefed to defend the managing director of Matrix Churchill, a company accused of supplying bomb-making equipment to Saddam Hussein which had been used against British soldiers in the first Gulf War. I read the prosecution papers, and the evidence of arms smuggling by making false customs declarations was overwhelming. 'How can you possibly plead "not guilty"?' I asked my client, Paul Henderson, at our first meeting. 'Well, I was shown how to make the false entries by Alan Clark [Mrs Thatcher's trade minister],' Paul said. 'And every time I went to Iraq I reported back to MI6.'

This story seemed ridiculous – there was not a skerrick of support for it in the prosecution papers, and Alan Clark signed a witness statement denying that he had ever given such advice. I embarked on a massive disclosure exercise, which the government strongly opposed, with four Cabinet ministers signing certificates claiming that disclosure of the documents would imperil national security, but in the end I obtained the release of some documents suggesting my client's story might be true. But to succeed, I had to break Clark, or at least show him to be a liar. It was a difficult exercise (described in *The Justice Game*)[27] but after fifty minutes of intense but friendly questioning, he eventually admitted that his statements were false. An erudite and fastidious historian, Clark could not admit that he had done anything as crude as telling a lie, and he disdained to confess, as the Cabinet Secretary had to Malcolm Turnbull at the *Spycatcher* trial, that he had even been 'economical with the truth'. This had to be perjury on an elevated plane – Clark had, he confessed, been 'economical with the *actualité*'.

The prosecution was immediately dropped, the Conservative government (which had secretly sold arms to Saddam and tried to send an innocent man – my client – to jail as a scapegoat) survived by one vote and the case mired it in 'Tory sleaze' from which it had not recovered by the time of Tony Blair's Labour election triumph a few years later. It is my best-known cross-examination, one which not only saved my client from jail but which had vast political repercussions, yet it had been conducted civilly enough for Alan Clark and I (and especially my wife) to become friends and later to enjoy picnic lunches at Saltwood Castle, his stately home, from which in 1170 the knights had set out to rid Henry II of Thomas à Becket, the turbulent priest. I tell this story to make the point that the most effective examinations are not angry or bullying: they can be quite amicable. I paid Clark the compliment of treating him as an intelligent historian who did not really wish to be as dishonest as his government required: after fifty minutes, he returned the compliment. My advice to young barristers is to try being nice to hostile witnesses, rather than to browbeat them as seen on television. Insults and sarcasm can be counterproductive: they put the witness's back up – he or she becomes more hostile, and perhaps more convincing.

The Matrix Churchill trial and the subsequent exposure of 'arms-to-Iraq' had another consequence which led to a reform in the law, although a reform which did not go far enough to protect against a class of wrongful convictions which continues to this day. It concerns the most important strategic weapon in the hands of the defence – the right to disclosure of potentially supportive evidence from police and prosecutors. This right had not been acknowledged before the mid-1990s: requests to judges to order disclosure of relevant files would be met by prosecutors chorusing that 'Mr Robertson is going on a fishing expedition'. I never saw this as a sensible objection – as a fisherman, I always went on any expedition in order to catch fish. But judges often upheld it.

Then came some IRA convictions – the Guildford Four, Judith Ward – which were undermined by evidence that the police had not handed over. And then came Matrix Churchill, with the spectacle of the Attorney General (Nick Lyell QC), the Home Secretary (Ken Clarke QC) and the Defence Secretary (Malcolm Rifkind QC) all signing Public Interest Immunity certificates to stop disclosure to me of evidence embarrassing to the government, but which they should have realised would help to prove the innocence of my client. Piquantly, the only minister who did realise it and refused to sign was Michael Heseltine, who was not a lawyer. If QCs could not be trusted to hand over vital evidence, neither could police or prosecutors, and an inquiry held by Lord Justice Scott recommended a change in the rules. There was much public debate on what form it should take – the authorities wanted merely a duty on police to disclose information if they thought it would help the defence. This was ridiculous, I would always say. How would police know? They had no motive to look, and were psychologically wedded to the guilt of the defendant they had investigated and charged. How would prosecution lawyers even know what to look for? They were not privy to the defence, and would rely on police assurances that there was no exonerating evidence to hand over. My contribution to these debates, at public and law profession meetings, was a heart-felt mantra: only the defence knows what can help the defence. The reform should therefore be constructed as a right in the defence to inspect all evidence gathered by police. Regrettably, thanks to self-interested opposition from police and prosecutors, who had the ear of weak-willed Tory law officers, the 1996 reform was framed in terms of a duty to disclose only evidence which 'in the prosecutor's opinion might undermine the case for the prosecution against the accused'.

This became increasingly unrealistic: given the storage capacity of smartphones and CCTV cameras, policeman did not bother to look at all the evidence, and even when they did they could not always recognise evidence which might support the other side. The Crown Prosecution Service (CPS), understaffed and underfunded, did not make the necessary checks, and prosecution counsel, often instructed only a few days before trial, did not see it as their job to go through all the unused material in the possession of the police. The only solution to avoid injustice is to allow defence lawyers to inspect all prosecution material. Especially the social media material in rape cases, where amid voluminous texts on the accuser's iPhone, some messages might tell a different story – consistent only with innocence. That was the case with several rape prosecutions which collapsed in 2017, exposing a scandal in which hundreds of innocent people were estimated to have gone to prison since 1996 because the police and prosecutors had failed to disclose (in fact, had failed to find, or else to analyse or to understand, rather than deliberately to hide) evidence which would undermine their case.[28] It is incumbent on every defender to demand to see all the evidence in the possession of police and to challenge in court any denial of access. Colleagues point out that this is a counsel of perfection where legal aid does not pay properly – or at all – for your time spent doing the police's job, in which case I can only reply that this is what we have to be: counsel of perfection.

That said, I must point out that the legal aid system in Britain today is in deep crisis, thanks to underfunding and under-appreciation. It should stand as a proud achievement – access to justice, like access to health care, effectuates a fundamental human right. But the cry 'What about the nurses?' will always have more political traction than 'What about the lawyers?' and successive governments have downgraded and diminished legal aid's claim on the public purse, so much so that a continuing refusal to index-link payments for legal aid has reduced them almost by half over the past twenty years, and now means that many young barristers are required to take cases for a remuneration that does not even cover their expenses. By 2018, a third of them were thinking of quitting the independent Bar, and working in government service or in some other trade entirely. One consequence will be to end the progress we have made in diversity, as many will be financially unable to contemplate a career, and those who can will be culled from the privileged classes who once monopolised the profession. The solution is not just more money, but a means of distributing it so that legal aid lawyers are fairly paid for their work, including their work of investigating 'unused material' in the possession of the police to prevent the wrongful conviction of their clients. I picketed the Ministry of Justice to endorse the Bar strike in 2014: it is very likely that I will have to do it again.

*   *   *

The most nerve-racking time, at least for defendants, is when the slightly bewildered citizens who will ultimately decide their fate are first brought into court. For most of my time in practice in England, defendants could challenge jurors, but unlike the practice in US courts, barristers could not ask questions to probe their prejudices. You could take a close look at them, but, as Shakespeare pointed out, 'There's no art to find the mind's construction in the face.' My only art was to find its construction in the reading matter under their arm. In a case with reasonable doubts, I really believe that intelligent jurors are more likely to find them than those who, for example, read tabloid newspapers. I would bump them off with a quick 'I challenge this juror, m'Lord,' while any with *The Guardian* or the *Financial Times* or, better still, a non-fiction book, were welcomed. So were those who asked to 'affirm' rather than to take the oath: people just assume that they should swear on the Bible, and I like free-thinkers who are sceptical about the deity – they might also be sceptical about the prosecution case.

Jury-rigging was common in England in the days of George III when the government wanted convictions for sedition, and they secretly brought back 'jury-vetting' in the 1970s in cases involving the IRA and some concerning national security. Led by Jeremy Hutchinson QC, we exposed this malpractice in a trial, known as the ABC case, of journalists accused of discovering an 'official secret': the eavesdropping role of GCHQ.[29] It was one of the many liberties that governments thought they could take with the law at a time of terrorism, but it undermined the principle of random selection of juries if the state could investigate and challenge any juror it discovered – through its surveillance apparatus – to have anti-establishment views. In my next 'political' case, I prevailed upon a fair-minded judge to extend legal aid to permit the defence to vet the jury as well. We obtained their names and addresses, but did not have the powers of the security service – all we could do was hire private detectives, who reported on, for example, the length of their hair and the number of locks on their front doors. The information was useless: the only answer was to demand an end to vetting by the state.

* * *

There is an unsettling and strange period in every criminal trial. It begins when the jury is sent out to consider its verdict. Until then you are on professional autopilot, scoring points that come instinctively to a mind immured in the law of evidence. It still falls so suddenly, that solemn moment when the talking has to stop, the summing up ends, and the palpable silence is broken by a Bible-bearing usher, as it has been broken at every criminal trial in Britain for centuries: 'I swear to take this jury to some private and convenient place, and to suffer none to speak to them this day, nor speak to them myself touching upon this case, except only to ask them whether they are agreed upon their verdict.' The courtroom soon empties, and so does the advocate's mind. There is nothing to do but wait. Sometimes, for a sign: a friendly usher will come up and whisper, 'The jury have ordered lunch,' and you feel free to leave the building for an hour and do likewise. (Although a friendly usher once had to pursue me with an update: 'The jury have just seen their lunch, and have decided to bring in a verdict immediately.')

Courts offer few retreats for barristers during this limbo in their practising lives. Passive smoking in the cells with a keyed-up client would soon pall for both parties, and cups of weak tea in the court canteen, with the police officers you have so recently accused of perjury joking at the next table, has limited attraction. The Old Bailey has a barristers' common room where copies of the morning's tabloids offer mindless diversion, but all too briefly: what you really crave is a pinball machine. I was always drawn to the library at the end of the common room, where the shelves groaned under the weight of 'Famous Trials', a series that chronicled the proceedings against the spies and poisoners and murderers of yesteryear, the people whose effigies were found in Madame Tussauds' Chamber of Horrors.

It took the tannoy to bring me out of my reveries and back to court for the final act – the delivery of the verdict. The courtroom is tense as the jurors file in: if they do not look at the prisoner, it generally means a 'guilty' verdict, but you never can tell. Reactions depend on the case – an acquittal may be met with applause from family or political supporters in the gallery, and I have seen defendants cry more often when they are found 'not guilty' than when they are convicted. The atmosphere is not conducive to displays of great emotion, and lawyers are trained never to show it when the verdict is delivered. One memorable exception was at the Persons Unknown trial back in the '70s, when defendants (including the author Ronan Bennett) were accused – on the strength of their possession of weedkiller (for their garden), sugar (for their tea) and a copy of *The Anarchist Cookbook* (for their jokes) – of planning to make a bomb. They faced twenty-seven charges, a prosecutor who vetted their jury and a biased judge (King-Hamilton again) who more or less ordered the jury to convict: after a trial lasting three months I can remember a sense of dawning wonderment as the foreman said 'not guilty' twenty-seven times. Even more amazing was the reaction of my solicitor, who leapt up and kissed me – in front of a press gallery which reported the incident as if it were without precedent, which it probably was. For all the unusual cases – official secrets, blasphemy, anarchist conspiracies and censorship – coming my way at the criminal Bar in the 1970s, there were also conventional defences for people accused of drug dealing and fraud and, occasionally, of murder.

*   *   *

The most sought-after client of a criminal barrister in his early years of practice was a professional criminal – an East End villain who would loyally call on your services throughout his and your career, generating legally aided work until you both retired (or until his children, following in his footsteps, would continue his trade). It was not long before I acquired one – Steve Jory. It was in an antiques fraud that I 'got him off' – as barristers like to say, although as Patrick Hastings pointed out, in nine out of ten cases the result is all to do with the evidence – counsel's ability makes a difference in only 10 per cent of trials. Soon, and for many years afterwards, briefs to defend in *R v Jory* were marked for my attention. Steve was a gentle, wryly amusing pirate – he could counterfeit anything, especially expensive perfume. In Mexico he produced hundreds of thousands of bottles of Chanel No. 5, indistinguishable in aroma and in the printed cartons that he also counterfeited, and then brought them back to the UK and sold them in pubs for £5–£10, to men whose girlfriends were temporarily delighted (the perfume went off after a while) by a gift that retailed in the shops for £45.

A lengthy trial took place: in those days there was no specific law against counterfeiting – the police had to charge conspiracy to defraud, which carried a maximum sentence of life imprisonment and required the CEO and the directors of Chanel to be called into the witness box to establish that Steve's operations had defrauded the company, i.e. that his operations had reduced its earnings. I quickly established that the net cost to Chanel of producing a bottle of No. 5 was merely £1, so its profits (even taking advertising and wholesaling into account) were immense. The jury was not impressed. Then it turned out that all the profits went to a company in a Caribbean tax haven – the Netherlands Antilles, as I recall – and that company's ownership was secret and undisclosable.

'So you don't know who actually owns you?' I asked the CEO.

'No, it's a holding company, I am not allowed to know the identity of the beneficial owner.'

'You do not know who receives your profits?'

'No.'

'You know that Coco Chanel was a Nazi sympathiser, in love with a German general?'

'I have heard something of that, yes.'

'And for all you know, these profits that you say Mr Jory has reduced could be going to an organisation that looks after old Nazis in Latin America?'

'Well, I wouldn't know if that was the case.'

The long-suffering prosecution QC could see the way the jury was scowling at the Chanel executives (and grinning at Steve), so I offered a deal: the defendants would plead guilty to a charge under the Trade Descriptions Act, with a limited term of two years in prison, if he dropped the conspiracy charge. He agreed, with the judge's approval: Steve and his co-defendants pleaded and were given short prison terms, and everyone was happy. But a week later, my client was even happier, and the prosecutor distraught – we had overlooked a sub-sub-section in the Act, which said that these new charges could only be dealt with in a lower court. The defendants were all released, and we had to present ourselves to the Lord Chief Justice to explain why the case had ended in this mess. It was the fault of the judge and the prosecutor, who were responsible for failing to check the statute carefully, but I felt a bit embarrassed because the deal was my suggestion. I was busy excusing myself when the Chief Justice, Geoffrey Lane, interrupted with some advice: 'Don't go on, Mr Robertson, or we will begin to think you have something to apologise for.' It was advice – 'the less said, the better' – that long-winded barristers find hard to swallow, but not when it comes from the Lord Chief Justice.

Steve was of course overjoyed and went back to counterfeiting expensive perfumes and other luxury goods. He called me to many a Crown Court (his operations moved about), usually to mitigate (he was an honest villain, confessing whenever arrested by police). I would sit with him in cells around the country, imploring him to use his talents for lawful ends, but he got a kick out of 'taking a rise' from the rich and helping the poor – at least, to think they were exuding the aroma of expensive perfume – and he had been born and bred in the criminal culture of the East End.

Our final meeting was at the Court of Appeal, after I had won a reduction of his latest sentence and met his wistful teenage daughter – for her sake, he promised to go straight. He did, and wrote a book about his exploits (self-published, by Pirate Publications) but died of a heart attack shortly afterwards. I missed him, but so had his wife and child during his years in and out of prison. He was an old-fashioned villain, never into violence, whose East End haunts are now trendy residences and restaurants for City bankers. Movies and books still romanticise the East End of the Krays and the Richardsons, but they were not romantic: they were stupid and vicious and, ultimately, pretty pathetic.

Briefs to handle drug cases were common in my early years at the criminal Bar, usually mitigation pleas for kids caught possessing or supplying drugs for which they had acquired a habit – often, in prisons that were full of drugs. In such cases, the barrister was a glorified social worker, who had to understand the human dimension and then bring advocacy to bear on unsympathetic judges who might – if moved – pass a non-custodial sentence. This could be a matter of life or death – prison sentences could destroy addicts who might otherwise be rehabilitated. Most judges were decent enough to allow themselves to be persuaded, but I recall one case of a heroin addict who in the year between his arrest and trial had pulled himself together, and all his reports were optimistic. He should have been put on probation or given at most a suspended sentence, but bad luck brought us before the Old Bailey's most heartless sentencer – Michael Argyle – who gave him five years and destroyed a life that might otherwise have flourished. I could forgive Argyle for the *Oz* trial – his stupidities were comic and his ignorance of the law was remedied on appeal. In run-of-the-mill cases, however, his inhumanity did damage that could not be rectified.

When I became a Recorder in 1992, youngsters were still being prosecuted when found with small amounts of cannabis for personal use. I would fine them £25 and tell them that the worst damage done by the drug was the risk of being caught with it and acquiring a criminal record. I did manage to do something to change this – not in court, but in a television studio, by conducting a *Hypothetical* for Granada Television which examined policing policies. In a scenario involving a black youth with a budding career, caught with a tiny amount of cannabis, three hardline chief constables were prevailed upon to caution rather than prosecute him. This became a news story, and the new policy was supported by other chief constables and welcomed by the Home Office. One strike, and you were not out.

I had been a counsel in the two most notorious drug busts of the 1980s. 'Operation Julie', subsequently the subject of books and a television movie, involved several clever young chemists who went over to the dark side and used their talents to manufacture many gallons of LSD. My client was Dr David Solomon – an older American author and academic who was said to have been their 'guru' – a Cambridge version of Timothy Leary. The story is always told as a police triumph – how clever detectives outwitted brilliant scientists – but in reality it showed how the young chemists became more interested in making money, and for all their academic abilities left their finger-marks all over the manufacturing process and the distribution arrangements – it took little detective work to put them behind bars.

Of more sociological interest, even today, was the case I called 'Drugs-head Revisited' – the fallout from the tragic death from a heroin overdose, at Christ Church College, Oxford, of Olivia Channon, daughter of Mrs

Thatcher's Trade Secretary. She was celebrating her finals with Sebastian Guinness (an heir to the brewing dynasty) and Count Gottfried von Bismarck, descendent of the Chancellor who had made Prince Wilhelm the King of Germany. Guinness and von Bismarck were charged along with my client Rosie Johnston, Olivia's best friend, sent to London with the money to purchase the drug from Olivia's dealer. They were all jailed, by a judge who declared that prison sentences were necessary to refute 'a notion in our society that it is acceptable for the rich and privileged to dabble in hard drugs'. Rosie was neither rich nor privileged – just best friends with a girl whose parents had given her access too soon to too much money, and who did something fatally foolish to celebrate the end of her studies. They had tried their best to revive Olivia and were anguished by her death, but there was no mercy on offer from the courts – policy required that Rosie must go to prison. It was full of drugs, of course, and drove her to alcohol on her release, but she always struck me as a good person with two attributes important to survival: a sense of humour and a loving family. She wrote an insightful book about her life behind bars and became involved in prison reform – after a period as an opera producer and a businesswoman, she married a churchwarden and now, a feisty grandmother, lectures children and prisoners on the dangers of drugs that are so much easier to obtain than in her days at Oxford.[30] I wish all my clients had Rosie's resilience.

It is always a temptation for law enforcers to try to punish conduct they do not like, but against which Parliament has not legislated. They try to stretch any vague or ambiguous statute to cover the situation. An example from the '90s was the challenge to the right of potheads (and anyone else) to read colourful manuals bearing titles like *How to Grow Cannabis Indoors Under Lights*. The law of obscenity, punishing publishers of material 'with a tendency to deprave and corrupt', was by now a dead letter regarding sex, which after the *Inside Linda Lovelace* acquittal (see later) was no longer viewed as corrupting. However, it occurred to some bright spark in the Home Office that the definition might cover encouragements to cultivate cannabis, if ingestion of the weed 'tended to deprave and corrupt'. That was the view of their distinguished, if somewhat old-fashioned, adviser, Dr Griffith Edwards. In consequence, a major operation was mounted by

Scotland Yard, raiding the publisher (a '60s survivor, Knockabout Comics) and hauling its directors into the Old Bailey on charges of distributing obscenity. They were fortunate in their solicitor, Anthony Burton, perhaps the best practitioner in crime, whose experience went back to the early 'drug bust' days: he amassed the defence evidence from experts explaining that smoking marijuana did not, by itself, corrupt anyone's moral values. The trial lasted a month at the Old Bailey: I cross-examined Dr Griffith Edwards pleasantly enough, having read all his publications and found in them no support for his theory that ingestion of the substance could rot one's moral backbone. The judge, as usual, was on the side of the prosecution, but the jury (I imagine there were a few pot-smokers among them) did not take long to acquit, another blow for the non-conformists.

* * *

The Old Bailey trial that always intrigued me was that of Stephen Ward, prosecuted in 1963 for 'living off the immoral earnings' of Mandy Rice-Davies and Christine Keeler. The newspaper reports of the case were avidly read in Sydney – indeed, all around the world – and provided my generation with an education in sex (with whips and two-way mirrors) far more interesting that those evenings with the Father and Son Movement. We would sing in the playground 'Mandy Rice, Mandy Rice, twice as nice at half the price' and other ditties based on the guilt of an apparently perverted osteopath – a profession we had never heard of before and a name which its practitioners hastened for a while to change to avoid the jokes.

My closer study of the case, many years afterwards, showed it to have been a massive stitch-up: Ward was not guilty (the women had actually lived off his professional earnings), but he had been driven to despair at the unfairness of the judge and committed suicide at the end of a poisonously prejudicial summing up. The behaviour of the government of the day had been outrageous. Its Secretary of State for War, John Profumo, had been forced to resign after lying to Parliament about his relationship with Keeler, to whom he had been introduced by Ward. The evangelical Home Secretary determined to make Ward a scapegoat, and ordered the head of

Scotland Yard to find some – any – grounds to prosecute. Police pressured vulnerable street-walkers to make false allegations, the Chief Justice suppressed evidence that would have exonerated Ward and at the Old Bailey the trial judge artfully persuaded the jury to convict Ward as he lay dying in hospital.

Fifty years later I wrote a book – *Stephen Ward Was Innocent, OK* – to expose the manipulation of legal processes that could happen again if the stakes are high enough.[31] It was launched by Mandy herself, who by 2013 had made 'a long descent into respectability' but was still as witty as ever; she had contributed to English literature with the withering reply, when asked by a bullying barrister if she did not know that Lord Astor had denied her claim that they'd had sex, 'Well, he would, wouldn't he?' Jeremy Hutchinson, who had defended Christine Keeler and had now reached his century, made a rumbustious speech decrying the unfairness of the trial, and Andrew Lloyd Webber joined in – he had just written a fine musical, *Stephen Ward*, to illustrate the injustice melodically. My book was placed on sale in the Aldwych theatre foyer, along with whips and masks and other impedimenta from upper-class orgies in the '60s.

Published in 2013, this book stirred the embers of a case the legal and political establishment still wishes to hide: incredibly, the government has banned release of some case files until the year 2046. The reason is, I believe (having been told on excellent authority), that some of the embargoed witness statements suggested that Ward had allowed his apartment to be used for an illegal abortion performed on a woman who'd been made pregnant by none other than the Duke of Edinburgh. In the course of my research I concluded that this was an entirely false allegation against Prince Philip, and did not even mention it in my book. I regret not doing so. In 2046, when Philip is long dead, along with Mandy and Christine (both now recently deceased), the files will be released, and the lurid allegation will no doubt feature as fact in whatever newspapers still exist and in whatever version of *The Crown* is remade by Netflix. Another example of the absurdity of censorship: had the file been released at a time when memories were still alive, the story would have been refuted. In 2046, it will emerge from the official records to embarrass King William and Prince George.

*   *   *

So there I was, reading about these 'Famous Trials' in counsel's library in the Old Bailey in the mid-1970s: I had made it to the epicentre of criminal practice. I had reached a position from which I could fight the English vices of hypocrisy, censorship and secrecy, not to mention police corruption, discrimination against women and people of colour and gay people and so on. Now was the time to test my theory that justice could be achieved through due process. Techniques and technicalities might be the rules of a game, but the game could be played in ways productive of liberty, where liberty was the just result.

In criminal cases, this game was against the state, represented too often by corrupt police and overbearing prosecutors and biased judges, but the advocate could stand between his client and these powerful forces and appeal to the jury. At the Old Bailey, David could sometimes slay Goliath. Jury trial and due process provided the possibility of victory against the state leviathan, and from victory in an important case might come political and social consequences which would enhance the liberty of the subject.

This had been the case with the *Oz* trial, where victory – ultimately on appeal – had done more than secure Rupert Murdoch's liberty to put nudes on page 3 of his tabloids. It had changed the law so that henceforth nobody could go to prison just for shocking or offending others. Of course, the repressive instinct of British authority continued for a while, for example by making use of local indecency prohibitions to confiscate art. This ended with the most ridiculous case I ever did, which was to defend Richard Branson, when Virgin Records released the album *Never Mind the Bollocks, Here's the Sex Pistols*. Richard was prosecuted on the grounds that 'bollocks' was an indecent word, although it was obviously being used in its modern meaning of 'nonsense' or 'rubbish'. John Mortimer and I called a professor of English language to explain to the court the etymology of the word 'bollocks' – he traced it right back to one of the earliest English bibles in print, Caxton's Bible, where it had been used with the meaning of 'testicles'. But then, he explained, in the King James edition, it had been replaced by the word 'stones'. At this point Johnny Rotten passed me a note that said,

'Don't worry. If we lose the case, we'll retitle the album *Never Mind the Stones, Here's the Sex Pistols.*'

Inevitably, we won: I have never seen a defendant vault out of court as quickly as Richard Branson, who led the press to the nearest record shop window to photograph him grinning in front of a display of the cover. The photo featured on every front page and greatly propelled the album's sales. That was how the authorities had to be taught the lesson that they should have learnt from *Lady Chatterley*: prosecute a book or a record and the results will be counterproductive – the publicity will almost always serve only to increase sales. This was also the result of the most significant censorship case I conducted at the Old Bailey, in 1979, defending a publisher prosecuted for obscenity for bringing out a grubby little paperback, *Inside Linda Lovelace*. It had sold a handful of copies at station bookstalls until the trial: after the publisher's acquittal, it sold a million. I had called, in the book's defence, some leading feminists and the Oxford Professor of Jurisprudence to testify that it had 'sociological merit' – if only the merit of describing the US porn industry, which was by then grossing (literally) more than Hollywood. The jury was young and half were female – the property qualification for jury service, which had meant that British jurors were usually male and middle-aged, had recently been abolished. The judge made the mistake of asking the jury, 'If this book is not obscene, ladies and gentlemen of the jury, you may ask yourself, "What is?"' After the verdict of 'not guilty', the Director of Public Prosecutions immediately announced that the written word would no longer be prosecuted in the UK. From such seedy acorns do great oaks of freedom grow.

There is a maxim of Equity – 'The law should not concern itself with trifles' – that should have been applied to all the attempts in the '70s to censor and suppress sexual explicitness. The Old Bailey at times resembled a porno cinema palace, with *Deep Throat* and other early examples of the genre playing before bewildered juries in various courtrooms. It really is no business of the law to impose moral standards, certainly where there is no popular consensus (as there is, of course, in relation to child pornography and jihadi incitements to violence). As a defence barrister, I was forever quoting John Stuart Mill ('The only purpose of the criminal law is to prevent harm to others'); Voltaire ('I don't like what you say but I will defend to my death your right to say it'); and Mrs Patrick Campbell ('I don't mind what they do, so long as they don't do it in the street and frighten the horses'). The *Inside Linda Lovelace* acquittal was the last straw for the DPP. There were no more obscenity trials, and sexually explicit films and publications were regulated and licensed (i.e. confined to the top shelves of newsagents, and to licensed sex shops and cinema clubs) rather than prosecuted. John Mortimer and I had ended an era of attempts to use the criminal law to ban discussion of sex, an era which had begun with Gerald Gardiner and Jeremy Hutchinson successfully defending *Lady Chatterley* in 1960. When Ken Tynan called to congratulate us on the *Inside Linda Lovelace* acquittal, I thought my youthful ambition to end censorship by criminal law might finally have been fulfilled.

I reckoned without Mary Whitehouse and her abiding hostility to homosexuality, shared by many judges at the time. It may be lawful, said the Law Lords, but it is in no way to be encouraged. In the '70s there was still a nasty stigma attached to this sexual orientation: nobody 'came out' (not even Liberace, who collected large libel damages from the dreadful suggestion that he was 'effeminate') and there were no openly gay MPs. (One gay MP was 'outed' by the *Daily Mail* and in consequence 'outed' from Parliament.) Mary Whitehouse pretended to be 'just a Colchester housewife' but she was in fact a front for the well-funded Moral Re-Armament movement, and she pounced in 1977 when *Gay News* published a poem 'The Love That Dares to Speak Its Name', which suggested that Christ's love for humankind had extended to a gay centurion. She brought a private prosecution for the arcane crime of blasphemy. Christianity, her counsel argued, was part of the law of England, and since its tenets held that homosexuality was a sin and Christ was without sin, imputing any gay attraction to him was, ergo, the crime of blasphemy, punishable by imprisonment for life. Mary's counsel was a red-faced, tub-thumping, gay-bashing barrister named John Smyth, who described the decorous metaphors of the poet (a fellow of the Royal Society of Literature) as 'so vile it would be hard for the most perverted imagination to conjure up anything worse'. Mark Twain had noted the phenomenon: 'To the pure, all things are impure.'

It was the craziest trial the Old Bailey had ever seen. The judge (King-Hamilton once again) ruled that Christianity was part of the law of England, and later admitted that he had been biased against us and that his summing up (a direction to convict) had been dictated by God (if it had, it would have been fairer to the defence). He allowed Mary and her followers to hold prayer meetings outside the court to pray for a conviction, and refused us permission to call any evidence from the defendant – the intention of the poet and of the editor who published the verse was, ruled the judge, utterly irrelevant.

I had taken the Bible away on holiday before the trial, rereading it as if studying for those Sunday school exams, and actually had no difficulty interpreting it inclusively. After all, the only way to beat Mary Whitehouse was to be holier than her. In two of her autobiographies (she wrote four) she praises with not-so-faint damns my efforts to become the angel's advocate:

> I shall never forget the dreadful sense of despair which overwhelmed me after hearing Geoffrey Robertson sum up for the defence. It was a truly remarkable performance. His manner was gentle and persuasive. In the silence that fell upon the court Robertson talked about God's love for sinners and for homosexuals, who, like everybody else, must have the hope of salvation and redemption … After Geoffrey Robertson's address to the jury, the phrase 'the devil's advocate' took on a whole new meaning.

This was not meant as a compliment. The judge (or his divine amanuensis) ended his summing up by reminding the jury that they had all taken their oaths on the New Testament, so they might ('It's a matter for you, of course') feel obliged to convict. John Mortimer and I were amazed that they took a long time and that two of their number dissented. We believed we should succeed on appeal because of the mistaken ruling that the publisher's intention was irrelevant. But one of the vices of laws like blasphemy is that judges have difficulty putting their own moral and religious views aside. When it came to the five Law Lords, one was a reactionary Tory ex-Lord Chancellor whose judgments were guided by prejudice, and another was a committed Catholic who ostentatiously refused to read the poem. That was 2–0 against us. Another judge was my nemesis Lord Diplock, and another was religious (Welsh Chapel) and conservative. But the latter, Lord Edmund-Davies, was the best criminal lawyer in the country. Both men must have hated the poem, but they had true fidelity to law, sticking scrupulously to its principles, and refusing to bend them in order to uphold a conviction the merits of which they would otherwise have approved.

With the game at 2–2, my favourite judge, Lord Scarman, shot an own goal. He was the leading advocate for a Bill of Rights and a supporter of free speech, but he was at this time particularly anxious to have minority races protected from insult and offence. He wanted laws that would protect all religions, otherwise attacks on Islam would become a veiled form of race-hate. He was well intentioned, but mistaken, in using this argument to uphold the *Gay News* conviction on the basis that blasphemy should be a strict liability offence covering insults to all religions. As a matter of law, this was not the position, because English law confined its protection to the Christian religion – as a group of Muslims discovered some years later when the High Court threw out their attempt to bring a private prosecution against Salman Rushdie for blasphemy for writing *The Satanic Verses*.[32] This ridiculous remnant of religious persecution protected only Anglicans, and in due course Parliament came around to abolishing it. Christianity was no longer a part of the law of England.

The law and the legal profession still discriminated against homosexuality, and this took longer to dispel. The forensic fight-back against Mary Whitehouse began when she privately prosecuted the National Theatre for staging *The Romans in Britain*, a play by Howard Brenton which in one scene depicted the rape of a young druid priest by a Roman soldier. Mary and her legal adviser, John Smyth, were determined to fight any depiction of the 'evil' practice of homosexuality, despite the fact that the play was a jeremiad against the brutality of war. Their motive may also have been political – at the initial hearing Smyth tried to injunct the whole play, no doubt because the Roman soldiers turned after the interval into British paratroopers and the druids into the Catholics they had recently been killing in Northern Ireland.

Theatres were protected from prosecution under the obscenity laws, but Smyth (who mysteriously disappeared shortly before the trial) found an obscure law against acts of gross indecency in public places, hitherto used only against people accused of masturbating in public lavatories. Sir Peter Hall, the National's director, instructed Jeremy Hutchinson and myself to defend, but the prosecution was a cock-up. Mary's solicitor, the only prosecution witness, testified that he saw an actor dressed as a Roman soldier take off his tunic, hold his penis in his hand with the tip protruding, walk across the Olivier stage at the National and place that tip against the buttocks of Greg Hicks, the actor playing a young (if ancient) druid.

The solicitor gave this evidence sincerely, and obviously believed that he had seen it with his own eyes. We were faced with the cross-examiner's nightmare: how to make a jury disbelieve an obviously truthful witness. We conferred in agitated whispers, as I urged Jeremy to ask the solicitor where he had been sitting. But experienced counsel hate asking questions to which they do not know the answer – 'He will tell us he was sitting in the front row, and all will be lost.' 'But, if he had been in the stalls, he would have told us in his evidence in chief. It's worth the risk.' 'No, it's a trap.' As our whispers became louder, Sir Peter Hall, sitting behind us, flourished a box office plan of the Olivier Theatre.

'All right,' said Jeremy to me with resignation, 'on your head be it.' The plan was shown to the witness. The judge, biased in favour of the prosecution, became excited and proffered his pen – 'Mark where you were sitting.' Like everyone else, he assumed that if you go to a theatre to collect evidence against a play, you would sit in the front stalls. But this was an honest – and, as it turned out, frugal, solicitor (or, perhaps as a religious man, he just wanted to sit in the gods). Jeremy choked back an expression of delight: 'The back row. You sat in the back row! You go to the theatre, knowing your task is to collect evidence for a very serious prosecution of my client, a man who has never committed a single offence in his life, on a very nasty charge, and you sit in the back row?'

Jeremy's high-pitched Bloomsbury voice, rising in pretended horror, detonated little explosions of ridicule, but the witness still maintained that he had seen the penis tip from this distance.

Q: Do you know that theatre is the art of illusion?

A: If you say so, Lord Hutchinson.

Q: And as part of that illusion, actors use physical gestures to convey impressions to the audience?

A: Yes, I would accept that.

Q: And from the back row, 90 yards from the stage, can you be certain that what you saw was the tip of the actor's penis?

A: Well, if you put it that way, I can't be absolutely certain. But what else could it have been?

There is a wise adage for a witness – never ask counsel a question. The QC stood to his full height, 6ft 3in. in his wig, and held out his clenched fist. 'What you saw, I suggest, was the tip of the actor's thumb … [he slowly raised his right thumb, until it stood erect, protruding an inch from his fist] as he held his fist over his groin – like this.'

The QC flung open his gown with his left hand, while placing his right fist, thumb erect, over his own groin. The jury stared transfixedly at the QC's simulated erection, the judge was struck dumb in horror, while the crestfallen witness opened and closed his mouth a few times before admitting that yes, he had a reasonable doubt about whether he had descried the glans of the actor's penis or the tip of the actor's thumb.

The case collapsed (the 'thumbs up' defence was used by gays thereafter caught by police in public toilets) and Mary was ordered to pay substantial costs. ('God will have to provide,' she said miserably as she slunk out of the Old Bailey.) We heard no more of her courtroom crusades against the permissive society.

My last defence of the gay community against state prejudice came from a UK customs operation which attempted to close down Gay's the Word, a little bookshop in Bloomsbury, on the grounds that the homosexual-themed novels it was bringing into Britain from Europe infringed the ban on indecent imports. By this time (1984) we had openly gay MPs: Chris Smith led demonstrations against this homophobic prosecution. It collapsed, to some public merriment after it turned out that they had seized, on the strength of the author's name, some books by that very heterosexual

American author Gay Talese. The bookshop became the launching pad for the gay and lesbian campaign to support the striking miners, and it stars in the delightful movie *Pride* (with Dominic West, Bill Nighy and Imelda Staunton), which illustrates how, towards the end of the twentieth century, Britons came not just to tolerate but to appreciate those of their number with a different sexual orientation.

The cases that fought prejudice against homosexuals were led in court by this heterosexual. Back in the '70s I had no help from any of the hundreds of gay barristers – they were afraid to come out in support, including two gay members of my own chambers. Now several senior judges are proud to be homosexual – Australian High Court judge Michael Kirby deserves acknowledgement for giving a lead to his English counterparts – and gay marriage has increased human happiness and actually strengthened the institution of marriage (or at least made it more widely popular).

The *Gay News* trial was disinterred by the media in 2017, forty years on, because of what they reportedly discovered about Mary's lawyer, the evangelical John Smyth.[33] It solved the question of why he had pulled out of the *Romans in Britain* trial at the last moment. Mary's solicitor had told me that Smyth had a religious conversion (he hardly needed one) and had been called by God to be a missionary in darkest Africa. But now it was alleged that after *Gay News*, he had offered his services to a famous boys' school near his country home. He would select the most attractive boys, take them to his potting shed and convince them that God wanted them punished for masturbating. They said he would take out a cane and beat them until their buttocks bled, causing them extreme pain in the short term and long-term psychological damage. There was a report which gave some credence to their complaints and the headmaster admitted he was informed of it. He said he called Smyth in and agreed not to report him to the police if he never came back to the school again. Smyth was advised to leave the country, and moved to Africa. Mary Whitehouse must have known, but she took him on a barnstorming tour of Australia in 1985 to present the case for 'Muscular Christianity'. (Smyth has described the so widely published allegations as 'nonsense'; a police report is, at time of writing, with the DPP.)

The role of Mary Whitehouse in gay liberation was significant: through her courtroom crusades against homosexuality, she actually provoked more and more of the LGBT community to come out of the closet and fight back, to get themselves elected to Parliament, appointed to the judiciary and to remind business and politics that they were a force to be reckoned with. I am proud to have been part of their struggle for pride in the love that now dares to speak its name.

Chapter Eight

Family and Friends

M y choice of career had brought me to a country with whose culture, comedy, literature and politics I had bonded since childhood, but in which I had not a single living relative and indeed not even a dead one since the famine in Skye in 1837. The Heath government introduced a 'patriality' test for immigration in order to disqualify entrants from the black Commonwealth, but its requirement of a paternal link to the UK excluded many Australians like me, and even 'non-patrials' who planned to marry an English partner. I took my plight up with Ted Heath himself, whom I met at a Young Conservative conference (I had been invited there to debate Mary Whitehouse). I had an English girlfriend, I explained: why should I not stay if I married her? 'Ho ho ho,' he replied (Heath laughed like Santa Claus). 'Why can't she join you in Australia?' Instead of proposing to Jane Turnbull, I tried another tack: I wrote a book, and my literary agent, Deborah Rogers, told the Home Office over-optimistically that I would be able to maintain myself royally on royalties. That did the trick, and my grant of 'permanent residence' came in 1976 in the same month as the book's publication.

This was despite the fact that *Reluctant Judas* was severely critical of MI5 and secret policing of Irish Republicans ('a book that knocks the wigged stuffing out of British Justice' said the review in the *Irish Times*).[34] So the really nice thing about my welcome to residency – perhaps one reason I have stayed for so long – was that I was the beneficiary of a tolerance that few other countries would extend to their critics, particularly to critics of their security services. I forbore for some years from taking the formal step of becoming a citizen, which would provide me with a British passport but mean automatic loss of my Australian citizenship. This became an inconvenience: at one point Australia fell out with France and diplomatic pressure had to be exerted to allow me to enter Strasbourg to argue a case in the European Court of Human Rights. Eventually, in 2003, Australia allowed dual citizenship, and I acquired my UK passport.

Nonetheless, I still had no relatives in Britain, and nor did my wife. But I had, since the *Oz* trial, been adopted into the large and loving family of John Mortimer, centred on the small house with a large garden in the Chiltern Hills, the setting for his play *A Voyage Round My Father*. At weekends it was the most joyous place of laughter and gossip and gumboots and children – eventually our children as well – enjoying lazy Sunday lunches warmed by a roaring fire in winter and bluebell picnics in the woods each spring. It was a privilege (although John and Penny never made us feel we were privileged) to be part of this quintessentially English family. Guests came from film and television – I was seated at my first lunch beside David Niven, a man as charming and fastidious as his screen persona. For all his fame, he was self-deprecating in his stories, telling how he had been lured into doing his first television commercial, for a brand of Japanese camera, but to save embarrassment had insisted it should be shown only in Japan. To his horror he was now being followed around London by Japanese tourists, brandishing the camera and imitating, with loud squeals of laughter, his actions in the advertisement. 'There is no hiding place,' he said with resignation.

In summer, the Mortimer caravanserai moved to what he dubbed 'Chiantishire' – a Tuscan villa outside Siena. With friends Jeremy Irons and Sinéad Cusack, Neil and Glenys Kinnock and others, we would spend days in the pool looking over the olive trees, visiting places where Shelley was shipwrecked and *Frankenstein* was written. There were nights at the opera – Verdi, invariably, with passionate Italian singers – although the Romanian Angela Gheorghiu, her voice carrying over the main square in Siena as she died in *La Traviata*, remains a memory. It was a night our young Georgie shared the unisex toilet at the interval with Jerry Springer and rushed back to our box to report: 'Jerry Springer doesn't wash his hands.' ('Well, darling, that's his job…') Tuscany in summer was full of the same literati we saw in Hampstead in winter – they took the same BA flights to Pisa, to drink excellent reds from the same chateau and villa-hop to each other's parties to talk about their latest BBC dramas. John would become bored with sleep at 4 a.m., spend the morning writing another Rumpole adventure and then join us for a late lunch by the pool and the evening excursion. He was forever genial and generous – non-judgemental but sharp in observing the vanities of the world through the blur of diminishing eyesight. He taught me, as his junior, the trade, and enjoyed in retirement sitting by the fire in his carpet slippers listening to the news I brought back from the Old Bailey.

In due course I became a man of property – mortgaged property in the form of a small two-bedroom bachelor flat in Notting Hill Gate. It was located in Pembridge Crescent, an address which features in English literature only in a Clive James poem ('Peregrine Prykke's Pilgrimage'), where it is used, somewhat ham-fistedly, to rhyme with 'dined on pheasant'. Notting Hill was a congenial place to live in the '70s, not unlike the Hugh Grant film, with Portobello Market, a good range of restaurants and reasonable proximity to Heathrow. After some years I bought a real house in Islington, a borough at the bottom of the Monopoly Board but gaining in value by then because of its proximity to the City. It was called the 'People's Republic of Islington' because of the progressive policies of its council, which had taken feminism to extremes by offering to provide a women-only cemetery for ladies who did not want to lie in proximity to abusive (but dead) males.

London was a perfect place to indulge my love of opera. I began as a poor student, standing in the gods of the Royal Opera House in Covent Garden watching Tito Gobbi's unforgettable entry as Scarpia in the Zeffirelli *Tosca*. From there I descried the two seats in the middle of the front row, discounted in price because the conductor might obscure the view. I usually obtained them – head-twisting when the conductor was the towering Colin Davis (who also had the irritating habit of humming loudly along with the orchestra) but a great bargain when it was the tiny Charles

Mackerras. Fortunately, I was seated well back in the stalls when 'our Joan' made her final appearance in her signature piece, *Lucia di Lammermoor*. From my vantage point, she pulled off an optical illusion with her voice: this large middle-aged soprano became in the mad scene a slim, love-crazed sixteen-year-old. *La Stupenda* indeed – I have never seen so many flowers as were thrown towards her that night.

Not far from Covent Garden was the Coliseum, where the English National Opera strove to achieve the socialist aim of its founder, Lilian Baylis, to provide opera in English that workers could afford. It did have some great successes – *Orpheus in the Underworld* was the comic one – and under the magisterial baton of Reginald Goodall it introduced me to Wagner's *Ring Cycle*, with the immolation of the great Rita Hunter (who later joined Opera Australia but could never do her magical Brünnhilde there – the Sydney Opera House stage was too small).

John Mortimer always said that he was glad he did not discover Wagner until he was sixty, otherwise he would have spent months of his life Ring-cycling (it would have been his only exercise). I discovered Wagner when I was thirty and must have spent months absorbing his leitmotifs (the length of attendance at the *Ring* compares with a flight to Australia). Degas's drawings excepted, I can't help but find ballet silly and I do not have the patience to sit through orchestral concerts. I cannot actually sit still in a living room on a wet Sunday afternoon and listen to or watch an opera: I need the expensive thrill of a live performance. After a long wait in the queue I have become a member of Glyndebourne, a special treat in Britain's most beautiful countryside. We took my brother Tim and his mother-in-law, who looked out from our picnic on the sun-drenched lawn during the interval and announced, 'This is the most wonderful day of my life.' Sadly, it was also the last, but it was a consolation after her heart attack the next day to know that she died happy.

There has been other music, of course. The sounds of the '60s are stored in a special compartment of my generation's brain and replay themselves constantly. When battling the police in cases at the Old Bailey, I would drive to court in a souped-up little pink Renault playing Dylan and, later, Springsteen to rev myself up for the fight. Driving home, however, would be the time for one of my favourite '50s Broadway musicals, to which I would tunelessly sing along. I did go through an early folk music period and actually wrote a play (unperformed) about Phil Ochs, the American troubadour of the anti-Vietnam movement. Ochs was hailed (mistakenly) as the successor to Dylan after the latter 'went electric' at the 1965 Newport Folk Festival, and he wrote my favourite put-down of people like me, 'Love me, I'm a Liberal'. (We need a revival of the caustic humour of the late-1960s folk movement to deal with the advent of Donald Trump.) My guilty pleasure, which I indulge whenever I come home from a visit to Sierra Leone or death rows, is Ivor Novello. After supping full of the horrors of the world, I think I am entitled to a short stay in Ruritania.

Theatre is my first and main love: in London the National, and in Stratford the Royal Shakespeare Company are delights that may keep me returning to Britain after Brexit. My own performances tend to be confined to lecture rooms, although I did tour a one-man show, *Dreaming Too Loud*, around Australia in 2015. It was nerve-racking at first to face theatre audiences of up to 2,000. Although I was initially rehearsed in London by a director who was taking time out from *Jesus Christ Superstar*, I owe what stagecraft I displayed to the great Australian theatre director Gale Edwards. I needed it – the opening scene had me blowing fake dust off an old law book, and on opening night I blew it right into my eye, half-blinding myself for the first act. John Mortimer, of course, also performed his own show – *Mortimer's Miscellany*. His doctors warned him that it might bring on a heart attack, but he was delighted at the prospect of dying on the stage like Molière. John's shows were popular, although he had the advantage of pulchritudinous props – two actresses who read his favourite poems. Much as I would have liked to have Amal Clooney and Jen Robinson read extracts from my legal opinions, the language would not be quite so poetic.

I have always empathised with actors – there is a ham in every barrister. I was first introduced to Cate Blanchett by Emily Mortimer, who was playing her serving maid in *Elizabeth I*, and I was struck by her intelligence and compassion. My favourite memory of Nicole Kidman is not from her films – not even from Kubrick's *Eyes Wide Shut*. It is from a New

Year's Eve party on Sydney Harbour. We were discussing a common trope among successful artists – the danger of crooked accountants (they need to have two, one to keep an eye on the other) – when Nicole suddenly leant forward and kissed me, and I really thought I saw stars. I did – behind us on the Harbour. I had not noticed, as she had, that it was midnight, the moment when the fireworks explode over the bridge and opera house.

Working through the years as what someone described as a 'cause célèbre' lawyer brought meetings with individuals whose notoriety outlived them. Myra Hindley, the Moors murderer, sought my help to get out of jail thirty years after her unspeakable crimes: she sat beside me like an old maiden aunt, plucking threads from her cardigan. A different person, of course, from the vile young sadist who tortured small children, but by now so frail and institutionalised that it would actually have been cruel to release her. There was, at the opposite extreme, Linda Lovelace, whose exertions I had defended at the Old Bailey. I was taken to dinner with her in Soho by a film producer who had bought the rights to *Deep Throat* – a deal I had to advise him would not stand up in English equity courts, which apply the principle that 'he who comes to equity must come with clean hands'. Ms Lovelace struck me as naïve, continually repeating that her performances were helping lots of marriages. 'You should see my post-bag,' she said, although in later years *Ordeal*, the book and movie, told a different story.

*   *   *

In due course my bank manager's faith in my financial future was justified, although, as the Beatles put it, I never cared much for money. When *Tatler* published a list of the remuneration of the 'top silks', I was charging the least – so little, indeed, that the others said I was letting the side down and demanded I increase my fees. Barristers pretend to have nothing to do with filthy lucre – they let their clerks 'negotiate' their large emoluments. I could never accept this subterfuge and often negotiated fees myself – invariably, I was a soft touch, offering discounts and often acting for no fee at all in cases which concerned human rights. I can understand the satisfaction that comes from an hourly rate which shows the labourer is worth his hire, and it must be said that my fees from wealthy American media corporations, ranging from the *Wall Street Journal* to *Penthouse*, subsidised all the *pro bono* work I did on death sentences and the like and allowed me to take time off to write books, which do not make money because they are about law. The Bar is a ridiculous profession in financial terms: solicitors pay themselves millions as partners, have big offices lined with fine art, and retire with large bonuses. For barristers, retirement does not even bring a gold watch – we are independent of our colleagues and our chambers, and can accept no perks. Independence is worth it, of course, despite the loneliness and lack of resources, but if you want money, become an estate agent or a hedge-fund trader or property developer.

In 1993, when as a newly established silk I should – or could – have been earning the large sums that would cushion a retirement (or a retirement to the bench), instead, for six months I was working for free, fourteen hours a day in my basement study, on a death penalty test case, *Pratt v Attorney General of Jamaica.*[35] My son had just been diagnosed with autism, and my wife had to bear the brunt of his behaviour during this period. The result of my work was that hundreds of men – most of them, I suppose, guilty of murder – were saved from the gallows after a month-long hearing in the Privy Council, but was it necessary for me to devote so much time to saving them, at the expense of my family? At the time, I guess I was driven by a sort of ambition (although success in such cases never brings material reward or popular applause, other than in the cells of the condemned) and by a fear of failure – a bug that sits deep in my stomach and has always driven me to succeed. Or at least to 'strive to achieve', and I wonder whether my insecurity may stem from those lowly school origins (would it have been different had I gone to Eton?). These are thoughts that come only on a psychiatrist's couch (or when writing an autobiography) and I have never felt the need to be shrink-wrapped.

I am still, in principle, a Gladstonian liberal, and in practice a Cromwellian puritan. My credo is human rights, interpreted commonsensically in the secular way I have argued in my books, although I have never denied (and sometimes proclaimed) the influence of Jesus Christ's parable of the

Good Samaritan. Christians irritate me only when they are cruel, as they sometimes are, and so do Muslims when they want to impose sexist customs like Sharia law, and likewise Jewish people who believe Israel can do no wrong. I love the Enlightenment because of its preference for rationality over dogma. As a puritan, I regard relief of the poor as an overwhelming imperative. Whether it fast-tracks you to heaven or not, it is the standard by which all politicians should be judged in their obituaries. Inequality is the gravest problem of our society and we should begin to address it in advanced countries by, for example, reforming the tax system, by publishing everyone's tax returns and ending overseas trusts and by imposing statutory caps on executive salaries. My main concern has not been for those workers who have trade union protection but for those who are out of regular work or otherwise disadvantaged – those who fall through the cracks of a well-resourced society. I would like to see a war on greed. I generally prefer Labour because it promises more for the poor, but governments of any political stripe can become calcified and corrupt if in power for too long. Labels like 'left' and 'right' are pinned by lazy journalists: what matters is a government that can provide the greatest happiness for the greatest number and the least misery for the rest of us.

Occasionally I come across blogs which accuse me of being a 'liberal interventionist' who was in favour of the disastrous and illegal 2003 Bush–Blair invasion of Iraq. This is at worst a lie and at best a mistake – the Gulf War that I favoured was the first, under George Bush Sr in 1990–91, which pushed Saddam out of Kuwait, a country that he had illegally invaded. Rightly, *his* 'coalition of the willing' did not go on to invade Baghdad.

Another criticism I notice when I make the mistake of reading comments attached to my articles on newspaper websites is that I supported the dropping of the atom bomb in 1945. I was not alive at the time, but this opinion is singled out on Wikipedia by I don't know whom and has been seized upon to accuse me of being a militarist. In fact, my historical research leaves no doubt that Truman was justified in dropping the bomb on Hiroshima (but not the second on Nagasaki) because it terminated a war that would otherwise have had to end with the invasion of Tokyo, in which hundreds of thousands of Japanese as well as Allied soldiers and airmen would have died, perhaps including my father. I have written a book (*Mullahs Without Mercy: Human Rights and Nuclear Weapons*) about how the scramble for nukes by brutal or unstable regimes poses the clearest present danger to the peace and the climate of the world, and suggested ways in which international law might assist the elimination of a weapon with the power to destroy us all.[36]

* * *

I did not meet my wife until I was forty-one; before then, I was fortunate in lovers and friends who still remain (in the words of Lennon and McCartney). One is Jane Mills, whom I met in my early days as an Old Bailey defender. She had been a researcher for Harold Wilson, and then a producer at *World in Action*. We had some fine times – in Cyprus, where we narrowly escaped the invasion by fascist Greek colonels, and in other parts of the Mediterranean. I took her away for some solitude because she had been nursing her dying parents; it was somewhere in the Aegean Sea that the ferry tannoy crackled with a call that her mother had died. We realised, as we saw the British consul waiting at the wharf, that there really is no hiding place.

With Jane, I embarked on probably the silliest adventure of my life, in a boat we hired in Corfu at a time when it was dangerous to sail close to communist Albania, a dark presence across the channel, with gunboats that intercepted trespassing tourists, who would be flung into jail. With some Australian friends, including Richard Neville and Julian Disney, we set out in a hired motor launch, curious to look at the forbidden land, having taken aboard too many bottles of Metaxa, the Greek brandy that is much more potent than ouzo. Jane had brought, in her bluestocking way, the latest copy of the *New Left Review*. This sparked an argument with Richard, which ended with him flinging the magazine into the water and Jane jumping in to retrieve it. By the time we had cut the engine and fished her out, the boat was dangerously close to the Albanian shore, and drifting closer because the engine would not start. Suddenly, from a hidden harbour, there appeared an Albanian gunboat. I was still sober enough to be terrified, although Richard, roaring drunk, seemed to think that a few nights in an Albanian prison would be worth writing about (fortunately, he then passed out). The gunboat was getting closer – they could see the bloodshot in our eyes – when I took command and broke out the oars. We had two Oxford scullers – Rhodes scullers, no less – and with Jane as coxswain, Julian and I rowed for our lives back towards the Greek shore. It was a superhuman effort – the gunboat followed for a bit, but then turned back. At the wharf, the watching fishermen had been highly entertained by our drunken adventure. 'Ouzo?' they shouted. 'No,' we called back, 'Metaxa.' The rest of our crew staggered off to bed, as Jane and I made for a tavern and ordered Amaretto and whisky, so we could feel grown up.

I did one great thing for Jane – I took her to Australia. First, to acclimatise her to local culture, we went to see Bruce Beresford's latest film, *Puberty Blues*. The co-author of the book, one Kathy Lette, was by this time (1983) an *enfant terrible* babysitting for mutual friends who thought her too *enfant* to take to dinner with me, and so we did not meet until 1988. Jane and I spent happy days at 'Happy Daze', Richard Neville's property in the Blue Mountains. He had married Julie Clarke there, under a waterfall, the previous year – an event the artist Martin Sharp (my passenger that day) and I had almost missed when my Mercedes, borrowed from my father, exploded in a cloud of smoke, and we had to hitch to the nuptials. Jane was so entranced by my country that she applied for the next available post at the Australian Film, Television and Radio School, and reckons her naturalisation ceremony was the most exciting moment of her life, other than her almost-trip to Albania. She now lives in Bondi with her partner and is a professor of film studies at UNSW – and I still take her to the opera.

Jane was followed in my affections by Bel Mooney, a *New Statesman* journalist (the first to be described as a 'busty hackette' in *Private Eye*), who was married at the time to Jonathan Dimbleby. She too came to Australia, to swim with me at Balmoral Beach and to gaze like a burnished goddess (at least in sunset photographs) on rocks at Hayman Island. It was an exquisitely romantic albeit difficult relationship: Jonathan and I got on well, but they had two young children and love did not find a way. Bel is now the agony aunt for the *Daily Mail*, dispensing wisdom, some of which may have come from our youthful entanglement.

Another love traveller to Sydney was Jeananne Crowley, an effervescent Irish actress who may still be seen tending to the Singapore wounded in box sets of *Tenko*, being seduced by Sam Neill in *Reilly, Ace of Spies*, and playing Michael Caine's long-suffering wife in *Educating Rita*. She was feisty and funny and we had good times, especially with her writer and artist friends in Dublin, but eventually she found me beyond domestication.

Nigella Lawson, of course, is as wonderful as she appears on television. We were introduced by the novelist Jill Neville, Richard's sister, who assured me Nigella would make a terrific wife – which I am sure she would have done. Jill's intuition was right, up to a point – we were instantly attracted, and I loved Nigella's intelligence and her wise insights into the literary and political by-ways of London establishments. She was a restaurant reviewer when we met and she began to cook after we parted (although if she had started earlier, who knows?). She became a literary editor at the *Sunday Times* and said to me at one point 'the *on dit* is that there is a remarkable Australian novelist soon to be published here – Kathy Lette.' I had heard the name, of course, as an author of *Puberty Blues*.

Nigella was used to invasions of privacy, but they affected me and still do – celebrities may be fair game, but the intrusive gossip columnist is the British nation's nastiest trade, and they dogged our relationship. Nigella effortlessly negotiated intellectual society – when I took her to meet Zelman Cowen at Oxford, it transpired she was on first-name terms with all its great philosophers (her mother had been the third wife of A. J. Ayer) – and she attracted politicians and journalists from all sides of politics, but lacked the confidence which she later found to recognise her own great talents. What most appealed to me – and it is not evident from coverage of her career – was her empathy with those who were sick or suffering; she devoted much of her time to consoling friends in need.

Nigella was my partner when I became a QC and finally made it into *Who's Who* ('Never make jokes in *Who's Who*,' she cautioned, much as Michael Kirby had warned against jokes in court). It was strange to be with someone who was already so well known. She did not share her father's politics and nor did I, but our relationship was a gift to the gossip columns. The very first party we attended – and left – together gave rise to instant comment in every tabloid, and soon to invented stories that we were engaged and that Mrs Thatcher's Chancellor of the Exchequer disapproved.

I was close enough to Nigella to decide that she should meet my parents. Providentially, I had arranged for them to travel around the Med on a Swan Hellenic cruise – a rather upper-class experience on a ship with Oxbridge professors describing the ancient history of the stopping places. When it docked in Corfu, Nigella and I, who were holidaying there, went to meet Frank and Joy, and had lunch with them on the ship. 'How are you getting on with the other passengers?' I asked.

'Well, of course, they are English,' my mother replied, 'and so they look down on us a bit. We are seated furthest from the captain's table.' They were enjoying the cruise, however, and I thought nothing more of their remarks until I spoke to them again afterwards. 'Oh, things changed quite dramatically after you visited,' said my father. 'The passengers became far more interested in us and we were put on the captain's table for the rest of the cruise.'

'Yes,' added my mother. 'Someone had recognised Nigella.'

*　　*　　*

My personal life changed dramatically in August 1988, when I was asked to do one of my Australian *Hypotheticals* TV shows on the subject of child abuse, at Brisbane Town Hall.[37] There were to be 2,000 people in the audience for this charity event. If it was Queensland, it must include Joh Bjelke-Petersen, its rabidly right-wing premier. Who would I seat next to him? I liked to surprise with juxtapositions, so I asked my producer to find someone the very opposite of Joh – young and attractive and uncorrupt. Kylie Minogue was first choice. She accepted at first, but just before I left for Heathrow, a telegram – yes, we used telegrams in those days – came from my producer: 'Kylie suddenly unavailable. You will have to make do with Kathy Lette.' For three hours, I thought, not thirty years.

Our first meeting was recorded thus: the panellists were at a Sunday school picnic in Melanoma, and I asked Kathy whether she would breast-feed her baby in front of Joh. Of course she said she would, and the startled premier pretended to be unconcerned at the hypothetical sight of her tit.

Afterwards, Kathy and I talked, and did not stop talking. We arranged to meet back in Sydney, where I took her to the opera, and we happened to be seated behind Gough and Margaret Whitlam. Kathy leant forward teasingly to Gough: 'What's the goss?' He turned around, looked at us both, and expostulated, 'You are!'

By this point, we were both in love, 'whatever "in love" means', as Prince Charles had unhelpfully put it. We certainly knew, in August 1988, that it meant making mischief together for an unforeseeable future. I was forty-one, Kathy twenty-nine: I think we both felt the urgings of our unborn children to get on with it. Kathy quickly checked me out with her friends, but most of them thought I was gay. One rather ungraciously observed that marrying me would be 'a good career move'. I checked her out with my friends – 'I'm thinking of marrying Kathy Lette,' I confided in Julian Disney. 'Well, I've never thought you really wanted to be a High Court judge' was his elliptical reply. My mother was delighted – that I was marry-ing anyone – although my father was, I think, disappointed that he would not have the opportunity to advise the Chancellor of the Exchequer.

Meanwhile, Kathy was determined to keep her promise to abandon her husband, home and hemisphere. I bought her a Qantas ticket (how em-barrassing to remember that I booked her economy, but she was only small in stature) for a flight to arrive shortly before Christmas. Her arrival made me apprehensive – how could I welcome her in a way that would show she had made the right decision, that we were true soulmates? My greetings with other girlfriends hot off QF1 had not been markedly successful – I met one of them, I seem to recall, in midwinter with a car that broke down on the motorway and a house where the heating had failed. I racked my brains: how could I possibly give Kathy a welcome that became her? The day before her arrival, I had a brainwave: I would take her to the toilet.

Not just any toilet, *the* toilet. The toilet that had been on the front page of every Australian paper for a week – the toilet where Alan Jones, the country's most reactionary shock jock, had been arrested and charged with gross indecency. I had no axe to grind with him – I had never heard his show – but I was aware of how much he was loathed by Kathy's Sydney circle, at a time when Sydney really was 'Jonestown' and his influence on behalf of the conservative cause was massive. And so it was that I collected Kathy in a car freshly oiled and greased, and headed from Heathrow to Soho's Broadwick Street public convenience, which is directly opposite (Alan, how could you have been so blind?) a police station. There we met his arresting officer, who chatted to us about the case (which was later dropped) and took the picture of the youngish lovers, beginning life together at the Alan Jones Memorial Toilet.

We repaired to my home in Islington and, after an unpleasant time with certain journalists, who thought I had committed treason by parting with Nigella (I was described, with alliterative waspishness, as the 'legal Lothario'), we settled down and married. Our marriage came to many as a surprise, although not to an uncle of mine, a Wollongong bus driver who knew my love of comedy and said with a grin, 'I know why you married her, you lucky bastard. You will spend the rest of your life laughing.' It didn't quite work out like that, but undoubtedly our love of wordplay and the endless possibilities of contorting the English language had played its part in our attraction.

Our house overlooked a church, which would have been convenient had the vicar not been Church of England and bound by its rules, which forbade it being used to marry a divorcée. In what was probably a spirit of ecumenicalism, he had allowed his building to be used by a voodoo cult, whose blood-curdling screams shattered our peace on Sunday afternoons, but our marriage was a bridge too far. In vain I pointed out that his church owed its existence to Henry VIII's desire for one divorce after another. In the end, we settled on Islington Register Office, where a gay registrar with a ring in his ear did the honours. I arrived late from court, still in my Ede & Ravenscroft, to meet my best woman (Jane Mills) and Kathy's literary bridesmaids – publisher Robert McCrum, playwright Dusty Hughes and poet (later Poet Laureate) Andrew Motion. The congregation quietly gambled on my middle name – the smart money was on Lochinvar – and when it turned out to be Ronald there were hoots of derision (Reagan has much to answer for). We held a party in the magnificent rooms at the Institute of Contemporary Arts, designed by Thomas Nash – I was a director of the ICA, and the setting was both bohemian and high establishment. Our son Jules was present, *in utero*.

Kathy and I were an unusual combination – Douglas Adams joked that my reputation for jurisprudential depth came to the surface after meeting my wife. My old friends were first to extend her a welcome to Britain – John and Penny Mortimer befriended her for life, Jeremy Hutchinson and Michael Foot bonded with her immediately. Of my own generation, Bernard Simons, the wonderful gay solicitor who advised the Terrence Higgins Trust for HIV/AIDS victims, was first to give his seal of approval – he owned a large house in Highgate which was shared, in various combinations, by Christopher Hitchens, Alan Rusbridger, Jeananne Crowley, Judy Daish, Duncan Kenworthy and other creative achievers. I would be there late on some Saturday nights, in Bernie's kitchen-cum-lounge room, comforting MPs whose depredations had just been disclosed in the early edition of *News of the World*. After Bernie's early death, his role in our life was taken by Mark Stephens, a mercurial litigator who shared our sense of mischief (although never at his client's expense). As with Bernie, I entrusted American and Australian clients to him, in the belief they would be better (and less expensively) served than by stuffed-shirt solicitors in the big City firms.

Kathy and I were, nonetheless, regarded as an odd couple, at least by the gossip columnists, and news of our dinner parties was routinely telegraphed. I suppose the ultimate north London gathering was one we held for Tony and Cherie Blair to meet some of our friends – John Mortimer, Salman Rushdie, Billy Connolly, Pamela Stephenson and Ronnie Dworkin, the Oxford Professor of Jurisprudence, whose wife Betsy (a lecturer in social policy) was the only one who knew how to make a hollandaise sauce for the salmon. When we moved to Swiss Cottage, at dinners I played the role of wine waiter, despite my experience at a party thrown by Nicole Kidman of taking a glass of champagne proffered by a small chap who I assumed was a hired waiter – I just did not recognise Tom Cruise. I confess to the occasional faux pas of this kind – after a dinner party *chez*

Michael Hutchence and Paula Yates (who were too spaced out to bother with *placements*), I said to my wife that I liked the saturnine fellow seated on my right – was he an Australian backpacker? 'That was Nick Cave.' 'And there was a pleasant young man on my left who looked like the young John Lennon?' 'That is because he is Julian Lennon.'

There was one occasion on which my mind proved a real liability. The makers of a movie based on *The Importance of Being Earnest* decided to invite the smartest people they could find in London to a party in the French Champagne region, in which we would show off our Wildean witticisms. It was pretty much a second XI by the time we climbed aboard the private jet to Reims, for lunch with Monsieur Krug (yes, the real Monsieur Krug), who presided over the table without much understanding of the English aphorisms that volleyed across it. To make him feel – well, proud – I said how happy I was to be drinking Krug rather than Taittinger, whose *patron* had been convicted of collaborating with the Nazis. As I dramatically expatiated on Monsieur Taittinger's crimes, I felt the satisfaction of a speaker whose words are having an impact on his listeners, notwithstanding kicks to my shin from underneath the table. Monsieur Krug started to splutter into his own vintage, all too well aware – as I was not – that all the great champagne families had collaborated: Taittinger was jailed because they needed a scapegoat. Much as I admire Russell Brand for refusing to brand himself by wearing Hugo Boss (who made prison uniforms for concentration camps), I now doubt whether historical awareness need extend to champagne. It flowed less freely after my well-intentioned interjection.

Only one of our dinner parties was designed to leak. Our friend Gordon Brown – a man even more serious than me – had become Prime Minister and was enduring a bad press, pretty much on the basis that he lacked the common touch. In the simplistic world of tabloid spin, this was easy to refute – by inviting him to dinner with Kylie Minogue. Their meeting became a subject for discussion in Parliament – even his enemies (or those with a sense of humour) celebrated his discovery of a lighter side. With Ed Miliband, we matched George and Amal Clooney, although sadly the stardust did not sprinkle. I have to say that George truly is one of the most decent, charming, intelligent and humble men I have ever met, and if the Democrats select him as their presidential candidate I shall give up the day job to work for him *pro bono*. Good guys do get corrupted by power (see Aung San Suu Kyi) but I do think that George could lead us to a better world – and, which may amount to the same thing, could beat Donald Trump. As for the latest Labour leader, Jeremy Corbyn, we have not offered a dinner party (he is verging on veganism) but have given him something infinitely more valuable – our daughter, who works for him.

Our dinners put together some interesting people from disparate worlds of law, theatre and politics – a nice night's entertainment, as Dame Edna, who sometimes attended, would say. Only once was there a hidden agenda, the result of a friendly fight between Kathy and the actress Maureen Lipman in St John's Wood High Street. Kathy had gone to buy a cake for our party that night and left her purse behind. She bumped into Maureen, one of the invited guests, who insisted on lending her £20, then refused to accept repayment. She was at the time playing Aunt Eller in the National Theatre's production of *Oklahoma!*: the curtain went up as she churned butter and heard the strains of 'Oh, What a Beautiful Morning' from Curly, played by a then-unknown Australian named Hugh Jackman. They both attended a party at our place after the show, but still Maureen refused to accept repayment. There was a whispered conversation between Hugh and Kathy: the next night, by the butter churn, Curly was seen to place something in Aunt Eller's hand: a £20 note.

*   *   *

Our son Julius was a beautiful baby – 'Baby Jesus must have looked like that,' exclaimed Jill Neville, I suppose accurately. He passed all his milestones with ease and at fifteen months had many words, until suddenly he shut down and lost them all. It was an anxious time – I could make him smile, at least, by singing Bob Dylan as badly as Bob Dylan – until after his third birthday, when he pointed at a shoe-rack in my old room in Longueville and said 'shoe'. But he could not recapture that early quick spirit, and we went to doctors all over Britain and Australia for a diagnosis, eventually of Asperger's, somewhere (no one is very sure) on the high-functioning end of the autism spectrum. He was not an FLK (social worker jargon for 'funny-looking kid') and was loving to his parents and charming to our friends, but there was something unusual – a crossed wire in the brain. He could do amazing things – memorise *Hamlet* – but could not add up or read a book.

It's hard on parents raising an autistic child – the divorce rate is extremely high. My only advice would be to have another as quickly as possible. Our daughter, Georgie, was born in the Lindo Wing two years later and delivered by no less than the royal gynaecologist (I will spare readers my wife's jokes about where his hands had been). She was a great kid – I can remember her at about age three advancing on children twice her size and age who were picking on her brother, and beating them up. She had something of her mother's jollity and her father's love of history. By age fifteen she was brilliant and beautiful, but her political beliefs had not crystallised, so she went along with her mother's tongue-in-chic arrangement to make her debut in Paris at *le Bal* (usually known as the Crillon Ball, after the hotel where it is held). This is a famous event, apparently, where the daughters of the crowned heads of Europe traditionally 'come out', although by 2009 the blue-blood test for aristocracy had changed. As well as Lady Kitty Spencer and the daughters of long-overthrown European royals, we had Hong Kong royalty (the daughter of a billionaire) and Hollywood royalty (the daughters of Forest Whitaker and Clint Eastwood). How did Georgie qualify as Australian royalty? Kathy claimed it was because of her own pure convict blood, dating back to the First Fleet, but maybe the organisers had been told of my relationship with the Kaiser. To dance with my daughter without trampling her, I needed a refresher course – the June Winter Academy days were long past. I booked some lessons at London's Pineapple Studios, but my footwork had not improved. Georgie was stunning, in a dress made without charge by our friend Collette Dinnigan, and money was raised for charity. I took Georgie outside the Hotel Crillon to show her the place where the aristocrats had been guillotined, and did notice the glint that came into her eyes.

I watched with fascination thereafter my daughter's ideological progress. Later, at school, under the influence of an inspiring politics teacher, she began to reckon that all should have access to the opportunities provided to her. At London University she achieved first-class honours in English and History and looked back on *le Bal* with irritation as an arcane survival of an elitist marriage market. She followed in my footsteps to the extent of being elected as a student president at SOAS,[38] although there were differences: she campaigned for justice for the cleaning staff, who did not cross our minds at the SRC in the Vietnam-dominated '60s. After a stint with Amnesty, she now works to bring about political change as an official in the Labour Party. This excites the *Daily Mail*, which got hold of pictures of her at *le Bal*, and when she was selected as a Labour candidate for a local council it could not wait to publish them (four times in four weeks!), falsely reporting that the dress cost £6,000 and implying that Labour's war on privilege cannot be waged other than by the underprivileged. At least this petty political propaganda serves to show off the talent of Collette.

When they were younger, we kept the children in touch with their grandparents and their increasing number of cousins through regular visits to Sydney, at Easter if possible and for a month over Christmas. Every Boxing Day we took a large room at a beachside restaurant, where Jules would make a speech toasting his grandfather (whose birthday it was) for his efforts in combating old age (one feature of autism is unremitting truth-telling). The gathering of Clan Robertson came together in all shapes, sizes and races. My international businessman brother Graeme's first marriage was to an Indonesian, his second to a Chinese woman. One of his daughters is an accountant married to a Mauritian businessman. My other brother, Tim, by now a Senior Counsel, has a daughter, Venetia, who took the Sydney University medal (in Theology) and then a PhD – she is a world expert on religious cults. It was a reunion that continued for forty years, and helped to make up for the loss of family time we have endured for the sake of our international aspirations. How could we go back to the London winter was the annual and aching question.

Schooling Jules proceeded, with difficulty, although it was heartening to sit in meetings in his state school with five or six different experts concentrated on his problems. This was the mark of a caring state. In time, however, he had to go to special schools – well, he was special – and then we heard from Tina Brown of a college in Cape Cod which could help those with his challenges. He attended for two years, and I crossed the pond to be with him every month or so, but it could not conquer the devastating loneliness of a boy craving friends his own age yet too wracked with anxiety ever to cultivate them. Those with experience of the condition will know the problems – as an acquaintance said to me when I mentioned that our son was autistic, 'I thought you and Kathy had the most marvellous life, from reading about you in the social pages. Now I realise the heartache…' Precisely.

I taught Jules tennis, which he loved and excelled at, to such an extent that I took him to be coached at the Bollettieri tennis ranch in Sarasota, Florida, where the CIA once had me sleeping with Pee-Wee Herman. Jules was given to writing pages of what we thought were random numbers, but when they were fed through a computer it was discovered they were the exact scores of every quarter, semi and final played at Wimbledon since the war. Our son is a genius receptor of useless knowledge, although it does startle the famous tennis players we meet when he reels off the score in matches they had long forgotten. I was quartered, for those Sarasota weeks, in the crummy hotel attached to the tennis ranch, reading my papers from the UN court in Sierra Leone, where I was a judge – a dismal business until Jules called with the message 'Sharapova on court', which brought me running, a relief from war crimes.

Jules also has an obsession with movies – he would amaze our actor friends by recalling their lines (including voiceovers) as a party trick. He wanted to be an actor – who doesn't? – but we doubted that he could put the artistic into autistic. He did an acting course, which he enjoyed, and then won a scholarship to an intensive course for differently abled actors. The catch was that it started in the first week of January, so he had to forgo his time on the beach with his family. So did I – the lot fell to me to take him back to England after Christmas. In the middle of Sydney Airport he decided to run away, and I had to sprint to catch him. I thought my life had reached its nadir: here I was, at age sixty-eight, chasing my 24-year-old autistic boy.

I am glad I caught him, because later in the year, a tiny miracle happened.

It was hell getting him through the course, but eventually he passed and was invited to an audition for a role in *Holby City* – the BBC's weekly hour-long medical drama with a viewing audience of around four million. He got the part of a character named Jason, and he thrived as the first autistic actor cast to play a character with autism. Soon people would stop him in the street and ask him for selfies and autographs. I almost cried with joy the first day I went with him to Elstree Studios, seeing how transformed he was: playing his character, he was happy at last – genuinely happy. I was happy too – and proud. Once, you had to use an actor as good as Dustin Hoffman to play the Rain Man – now, an autistic actor will play the part authentically if they ever make *Rain Man II*. Jules wants eventually to play Hamlet, who is obviously autistic (all that anxious equivocation, paternal obsession and misreading of social situations), and we are planning the movie – Hugh Jackman has been cast as Claudius, Jemma Redgrave (his co-star on *Holby*) as Gertrude, and Stephen Fry has volunteered to be the First Gravedigger ('Alas, poor Yorick!'). We are still looking for an Ophelia (so is Jules). I, of course, shall be the ghost.

For the past two decades, our family inhabited a home in Swiss Cottage, a half-mile north of St John's Wood (where it would be worth twice as much) and a half-mile south of Hampstead (where its price would triple). It's a quiet, middle-class suburb, full of psychiatrists and mistresses of faded rock stars, with some high-rise council housing – a genial place, which did not vote for Brexit. Not far away there was Hampstead Heath to walk on and Regent's Park to row boats and smell the profuse roses. Nearby is Lord's Cricket Ground, where the Ashes are displayed in an eggcup, although I prefer to watch my cricket from a couch in front of a television screen with beer in hand (the last time I was invited to a box at Lord's, I had Jeffrey Archer with his bad breath on one side and Cardinal George Pell with his bad conscience – he was meant to be at the Australian Royal Commission answering allegations that he had abused children – on the other). Just down the street and round the corner are the Abbey Road studios, with a traffic jam of tourists photographing each other on the crossing where the Fab Four once posed for the eponymous album. Over in Richmond, my old friend Gael Boglione is chatelaine of London's historic Petersham House, and lures us to lunches at its restaurant (made famous by Skye Gyngell) and to postprandial walks along the riverbank that leads to Runnymede.

What do I miss about Australia? Well, swimming for a start – there are plenty of pools at gyms in London, full of what Kathy describes as 'chlorinated phlegm', but oh, for the beach at Balmoral or the swim to the shark nets at Nielsen Park to watch the waves sparkle in the wake of the ferries to Manly. Although the Swiss Cottage house had a garden that came alive with colour in spring, and urban foxes that devoured the squirrels, who give a blood-curdling death yelp in the middle of the night, how I miss the wildflowers in my parents' garden in Sydney and the flash on the veranda of colourful parrots in the evening, and the tinkling of the masts on the bay.

My mother always said that I was not cut out for marriage. In Los Angeles once, a celebrated soothsayer inspected my palms and other visible parts of my body and declared with certitude that in a previous life I had been a monk. This kind of rang true. But mischief-making with someone you love is a good way of spending most of your allotted span. Kathy has occasionally tried the Christina Stead lament (leaving home and hearth for a man, etc.) but in truth she has not left the Australian persona which she inhabits and in which she writes, and I deserve some sort of award (although Sir Humphrey would veto it) for unleashing her on Britain to add to the gaiety of the nation. Gossip columns have found it funny to juxtapose her comments on men and sex with the fact that she is married to a 'serious-minded QC'. The joke wears thin. Kathy became a noted writer. She created in *Girl's Night Out* the perfect revenge on the two-timing male – prawns left in the curtain rails by his departing lover – which soon became an urban legend. In quick succession, her chick-lit classics, *Foetal Attraction*, *Mad Cows* and *How to Kill Your Husband and Other Handy Household Hints*, were all listed in the top ten of the bestseller charts. Some film rights were sold to Hollywood and we waited anxiously for the cameras to start rolling, but they never did – except in the case of *Mad Cows*, which was sold to a UK company and made into a movie, in which I played a scene with Anna Friel on a bus. I am listed in the credits as 'Man on the Clapham omnibus' (lawyers will get the joke). It is occasionally entered in competitions for the worst movie ever made. Sometimes, it wins.

*   *   *

As for my first love, it was always a joy to open the front door of our little house in Longueville after the taxi ride from the airport to kiss my mother's greying head. When I appear on radio programmes on which you choose music that means something to you, I begin with the judge's song from *Trial by Jury*, end with Isolde's ecstatic lament at the end of *Tristan und Isolde*, and include somewhere Verdi's 'Dio, che nell'alma infondere' from *Don Carlo*, a duet between two doomed young men determined to fight for human rights against the Inquisition. And I always dedicate the Judy Collins version of Lennon and McCartney's 'In My Life' to my mother. She would sit every morning in a shaft of sunlight in the lounge, reading every word of the *Sydney Morning Herald*, cutting out for me the mentions of my old friends and chuckling over my detractors. She had no liking for what she called 'the limelight' and would never appear on television programmes – not even on *Who Do You Think You Are?*, which was about her ancestors. Only once did she allow me to mention her in print, and that was because the proceeds from the book went to the Blind Society. It was called *Mum's the Word* and contained recollections by what it termed 'celebrated Australians' – Alan Jones, Hazel Hawke, Rolf Harris and other names of 1988.[39] Here is what I wrote then, and I did not alter a word when I read it at her funeral almost thirty years later:

> My first serious thoughts about Mum came when I had to list her occupation on a school form. 'Put down "Domestic Duties",' she said. I had a first, childish twinge of male guilt: is that how society really regards mothers? In those days, of course, it was.
>
> I can't help drawing inspiration from my mother, because I experienced at first-hand her humble strength and unfussy decency. She never preaches – just teaches by quiet example – how happiness comes from giving to others,

how to obtain pleasure from doing inconvenient duties, how to accept good fortune with humility, and bad luck with the determination to fight another day. She has no time for riches or vanity nor what she dismissively terms 'the limelight'. But although she's self-effacing and sometimes in fragile health, whenever I'm with her I feel as secure as a cub protected by its lioness. And when I hear that haunting song 'In My Life' ('There is no one compares with you…') it always seems to sum up my feelings about her exactly.

Of course, mums can't be held responsible for their children. Even Hitler had a mother, who doubtless encouraged little Adolf in his ambitions. Mine always says she just wants me to be happy – but whenever I am asked to do something which I feel to be morally right, although difficult publicly or damaging for my career, it's my mother's principles which give me the strength to do it. If I were a guest on my own *Hypotheticals*, and were asked where I drew the ethical line, I would have to admit that I could never do anything of which my mother would disapprove.

Chapter Nine

Hypotheticals

In the late 1970s I adjusted my name. In Australia it had always been 'Geoff'. 'Geoffrey' seemed to add an unnecessary syllable (Kathy jokes that in Australia it's too hot to say words of more than one). It was as 'Geoff Robertson' that I wrote articles in *The Guardian* and authored my first book, *Reluctant Judas*. My second, however, was a lengthy treatise on censorship law, published in 1979 by Messrs Weidenfeld & Nicolson under what the editor described as a 'cool' title, *Obscenity*. For some reason this venture into serious legal publishing drove me to consult my mother: under which version of her son's name would she like to see him make his academic debut? Her short answer left me in no doubt: 'Well, we named you Geoffrey.' As I have explained, I could never go against my mother's wishes, even when I thought them mistaken, so I wimpishly reverted to the name on my birth certificate. A few years later came the Australian television series *Geoffrey Robertson's Hypotheticals*.

The programmes came about, initially, through an attachment to university life. Sometimes I rather fancied becoming a professor, with a large office overlooking a leafy quadrangle, where my textbooks could be researched and footnoted by a squad of eager postgraduate students. Instead they were written by a one-man band, toiling over footnotes that have sometimes betrayed a need for researchers. My career as a barrister did not permit acceptance of full-time lecturing offers, but in 1981 I did manage a six-month visiting professorship at Warwick University, with a lecture schedule occasionally disrupted by recalls to the Old Bailey. My main innovation there was to adopt the case-study technique developed at Harvard, in the hope that my role-playing classes were amusing and challenging as well as didactic, and so would live in student memory longer than the classroom dictation I had endured at Sydney and Oxford Universities. While at Warwick, a talent scout from Granada Television found me. He had come looking for an English academic to join a trio of Harvard law professors to ringmaster hypothetical case studies for a US (CBS) and UK television series.

Our US producer, whose idea it had been to lift the Socratic method from the classroom and adapt it for television, was the legendary Fred Friendly. He had been Ed Murrow's producer for his wartime broadcasts and his CBS programme which destroyed red-baiting Senator McCarthy (in the film *Good Night, and Good Luck*, Friendly is played by George Clooney). He was a big, amiable American carrying the weight of history lightly on his shoulders and was happy enough to let me take the action in the shows wherever I liked. But there were limits – we were recording for a US audience as well. I did one programme about the media in war, with CBS journalist Morley Safer, *New York Times* correspondent Johnny Apple, Alexander Haig and James Schlesinger from America, and British politicians and journalists, including Harold Evans and Jonathan Dimbleby. Fred made a visit to my hotel room late on the evening before the show was to be recorded. He settled down with a whisky and asked, 'How are you going to end it?' I said that I would probably have Safer or Apple taken hostage and killed after a botched rescue mission. He shook his large, owlish head. 'That won't work on CBS – killing an American. Think of another ending.' It was late, but I tried. 'OK, I'll kill a Brit. Jonathan Dimbleby, perhaps?' Fred smiled: 'That would be entirely appropriate.' In all the shows that I made for CBS/Granada, this was his only editorial interference.

Under the guidance of Fred and the brilliant English producer, Brian Lapping, I spent excitable hours in Granada TV studios during the '80s offering bribes to businessman, dispatching policemen into massage parlours to arrest judges, encouraging American generals to invade Caribbean islands (they actually invaded Grenada a few months later), arranging deals between journalists and terrorists, and becoming the world's first pregnant man, all in the service of imaginary stories which might – and sometimes did – come true before the programme went to air.

One show caused an international stir – and still does, decades later. It was about the consequences of the fatwa imposed on Salman Rushdie in 1989 by the Ayatollah Khomeini – the first notable example of Islamic extremism. Among the panellists was the singer Cat Stevens, in his born-again persona of Yusuf Islam. He found himself dining in a restaurant and, on noticing Salman at a nearby table, evinced a willingness in some circumstances to execute him. It was a frighteningly real moment, but it does show how the format can elicit honest responses which would not be ventured on any other kind of programme.

The English editions were classed as 'educational' – copies were sent to universities – but they were not screened in prime time and they were performed before small, selected audiences who were not encouraged to laugh. I always felt these programmes had the potential to be less earnest and more entertaining, as I mentioned over a tennis game with the producer of Channel 9's Sunday programme, who became enthused at the prospect of an Australian *Hypothetical*. It was the beginning of a television career that I had not anticipated, which required me to boomerang back to my native land every few months.

I called myself a 'moderator', although moderation is probably not the characteristic I mainly displayed, as a Keystone traffic cop with ants in my pinstripe pants, directing intellectual pile-ups between sixteen opinionated participants on subjects that are deathly serious (child abuse, the right to die, race relations) or in most contexts deathly boring (multicultur-alism, the Australian constitution). Always at the back of my mind was a challenging statistic: viewers cannot absorb more than three minutes of a 'talking head'. And I had to make sixteen talking heads, positioned around a horseshoe table, interesting television for sixty to ninety minutes.

Historically, the first hypothetical moderator was Socrates, who walked around the ancient agora postulating imaginary situations and asking Athenians how – and more importantly, why – they would react. His im-agination was mischievous, his dilemmas disturbing to a small society – so much so that it decreed his death because he asked too many unsettling questions. The Socratic method aims to tease out the rationale behind a decision, and then examine whether that rationale can serve as a general principle by applying it to other, similar cases. If not, the original decision is exposed as opportunistic or wrong. The Socratic method, properly applied, uses the hypothetical to draw out ethical rules and test their value by seeing how they apply to hard cases.

That's the theory. My practice is to choose a subject which on closer examination comes bristling with unforeseen ethical dilemmas – medicine, the law, politics and business are all grist to the mill. Then comes the selection of sixteen participants. All are allotted roles they play or have played or might well play, and they comprise men and women in public life as well as journalists, police officers, accountants and actors. There has to be a political and ideological balance (some do not understand this and want me to choose exclusively panellists with nice progressive views, but many of the highlights of the show occur when the logic of the storyline induces a reactionary to act like a liberal, or vice versa). The event itself must be unscripted and unrehearsed: the show's secret is its spontaneity. I meet the sixteen panellists briefly after make-up, to try to memorise any faces I don't already know, and tell them not to make long speeches. I give no inkling of the questions they will be asked. I am never sure of them myself, because it is through the responses, which can be unpredictable, that the storyline has to be developed. I ask the participants to imagine themselves in a movie in which they are playing themselves.

On the set, of course, we have the cast. But every good story needs some bad people to advance the plot. I keep up my sleeve some colourful characters: General Buldoza, the all-purpose dictator, and Colonel Bazooka, the aggressive military chief; Amanda Autocue, a not over-bright journalist; Senator Gladhand, a corrupt politician; Inspector Scarpia (a police chief); Phil Fickle (an informer); Katie Bombshell (an actress); Judge Knott and Dr Jekyll (a mad scientist from the University of Wollongong) and so on. I play these people, to tempt and cajole the panellists and to advance whatever plot will throw up ethical dilemmas, in imaginary states such as 'Amnesia' or 'Uforia'.

As we know, conventional wisdom holds that talking heads make boring television. 'If it's not visual, it's not a story' is a common adage among television folk. But the important decisions that are made in the real world are seldom set against glorious sunsets. They are made by people (usually men in grey suits) sitting around a table in a nondescript room. There may be a few notepads, a potted plant and a picture of the incumbent President, but the momentousness of the decision generally bears an inverse relationship to the splendour of the surroundings. Hence the bare *Hypothetical* stage, and the object of showing how important decisions are actually made, something more than can be revealed amid the pleasantries of a studio chat show or the rituals of a press conference or a television interview, where development of ideas can be diffused by ego-driven presenters and rehearsed responses from cagey politicians.

That said, a *Hypothetical* is just another television programme – an insubstantial pageant that fades after the last repeat. It is not designed to reach a particular conclusion or to solve an intractable problem or to convey a subliminal message. All that can be claimed for the format is that it sometimes makes viewers sit up and think, and distinguish in their own minds between good arguments and better arguments.

The format can elicit uncomfortable truths from practised equivocators. The very atmosphere conduces to candour, as a decision-maker is surrounded by experts who know how he or she has acted in similar situations. They cannot dodge a difficult question by saying, 'I'd call my lawyer' or 'I'd need to consult my advisers' – the lawyer or adviser is on the panel, to be called or consulted immediately, after which the decision must still be taken. The viewer is invited to become a fly on the wall, a witness to scenes that television cameras normally cannot capture because they do not penetrate the closed doors of boardrooms or lawyers' offices or doctors' surgeries. The fact that the scenarios are imaginary makes the *Hypothetical* a libel-free zone – truths may be told without the constraints of betraying confidences or embarrassing colleagues or creating a political kerfuffle.

At least, that is the theory. But one show I did on media ethics for Kerry Packer's Channel 9 in Australia in 1984 became a major censorship scandal.[40] Packer, together with Murdoch and Fairfax, controlled the Australian media, and you couldn't do a show about media ethics without a media mogul. I confided to the producer that I thought my choice of name – Sir Rupert Fairpacker – was too long. 'Why don't you call him "Kerry Murfax",' he said brightly. Great idea, and Kerry Murfax was born. Had I stuck with Sir Rupert, the proprietor of Channel 9 may not have assumed the moniker referred to him.

My opening was short:

> Welcome, ladies and gentlemen, to a land where press is free, trial is fair and news is plentiful. Much of that news is provided by you, employees of the Murfax organisation – a media octopus whose newspapers, radio and television stations are dedicated, at the insistence of your proprietor Kerry Murfax, to the proposition that the public have a right to know.

The first question was easy – would they expose Mr Justice Benchmark if they learnt he was an occasional cocaine sniffer? Trevor Kennedy, editor of the Packer-owned *Bulletin*, a news magazine, spoke for them all.

> KENNEDY: I think it's a very important story. Cocaine is a drug that supports a rather unpleasant infrastructure of organised crime and all other sorts of things. By using cocaine the judge supports that.
> MODERATOR: You're part of the law enforcement network? You're going to enforce the law of cocaine against this judge?
> KENNEDY: We're part of the information network, which simply exposes the truth about as many things as we're able to.
> MODERATOR: But what's the public interest in this particular truth?
> KENNEDY: Well, the public interest is simply in knowing what big and important people do.

More difficult was whether to expose Australia's top fast bowler for the same offence, in the middle of a finely balanced Test against England. 'If we look like winning, I think probably not,' decided the editor of *The Age*. Otherwise, they all nodded sagely at the philosophy offered by a Packer editor: 'I know that journalism can create a lot of harm, but I also think in the long run it does more good by publishing the truth.'

That is, until the next client of my cocaine dealer was brought to their attention – none other than Kerry Murfax, heard in a tapped telephone call ordering several grams of the drug. I asked the question of Kennedy, who went ashen and seemed to slide under the table, as did the Channel 9 lawyer. Politicians around the table particularly enjoyed watching the journalists squirm, but we had to move on, to issues about publishing secret government documents, protecting sources and invading privacy. One editor even said, 'I have to live with my conscience,' which I thought was the best line in the show.

After a few more murders and privacy invasions, it was back to the case against Kerry Murfax. Trevor Kennedy finally summoned up the courage to confront him with the wire-tap evidence that he had ordered cocaine. Kerry, as played by me, gave a long and loud proprietorial laugh and explained that he was acting as a decoy, pretending to buy it at the request of the police. The cocaine dealer had contacted him earlier and, like the good citizen he was, Kerry had reported the offer and helped to trap the criminal. 'I wouldn't break the law, because I would lose my television licence and you would all be out of work.' The laughter – somewhat relieved – at the last line gave me a moment to face the audience as Geoffrey Robertson and deliver a message that I had often tried to convey to Old Bailey juries: 'Where there's smoke, ladies and gentlemen, there's usually fire. But sometimes, there's only a smoke machine.'

So Kerry came up roses in the end. But perhaps Kerry Packer and his lawyer Malcolm Turnbull did not watch until the end. The tapes of the show mysteriously disappeared – possibly deep-sixed in the ocean off the Packer residence at Palm Beach. The producer waited and waited – the tapes had simply evaporated. Of course, the editors and journalists on the panel, and their guests in the audience, became curious: when would the 'media *Hypothetical*', titled 'We Name the Guilty Men', be put to air? The Channel 9 press office provided a stock answer, for over a year, that it was 'still being edited'. One of the participants then blew the story in his column in the *Herald*, acidly remarking that this would be the most exquisitely edited programme ever to grace Australian television. Given that I had battled against censorship since a schoolboy, it was ironic to be caught up in a controversy over a ban on my own show.

It was nervousness over a drugs trafficking inquiry into Kerry Packer that caused him to destroy the show about the proprietor he thought was his namesake, but Kerry Murfax's innocence was also prophetic. A Royal Commission was following some claims about drugs secreted in stumps brought from Pakistan by the Packer cricket team, but this and other allegations turned out to be smoke without fire – another smoke machine. Banning the show was entirely unnecessary, but it did have one good result – a telegram from the chairman of the national broadcaster, saying that *Hypotheticals* were obviously too difficult for commercial television – could I do them for the ABC? I could, and looked forward to having them screened without commercials. But it was not the last I heard from Mr Packer.

A year or so later, in London, I received a brief from Malcolm Turnbull to advise a 'Mr Bullmore', an Australian media mogul in trouble with the tax department over investment in a questionable film scheme. I duly provided an opinion, as did several silks. I had pronounced Mr Bullmore innocent, at least on the evidence the department had collected, and was invited to meet the man himself at the Packer hospitality tent at Wimbledon.

Let me make clear that I would accept an invitation to Saddam Hussein's hospitality tent at Wimbledon, if it came with good tickets to Centre Court in the final week. In the case of Kerry Packer, it became a fixture. On one occasion I was there when Alan Bond was negotiating to buy Channel 9 for $1 billion. ('You only get one Alan Bond in a lifetime,' said Kerry later.) Bond emerged from the meeting looking depleted, as well he might, so I took him off to watch the girls' doubles final in an attempt to cheer him up.

Kerry was famously generous to friends and advisers. His generosity was distributed by his secretary, at the door to his suite at the Savoy: she asked as you went in (with piles of cash in front of her) how much you would like. Despite the temptation, I really did have to be prim and proper with my tax and said I would be sending a fee note. At a social meeting at the Savoy, after he'd returned from an extremely painful kidney dialysis, Kerry presented me with a dilemma worthy of *Hypotheticals*. He asked me to join him in a quiet bedroom, and – in obvious pain – vented his fury at the delay in the decision on whether to prosecute him over the film scheme. The decision would be made by the Australian DPP Ian Temby QC, whom I knew. Kerry worked himself up to a lather of anger, saying – twice – 'If that Temby decides to prosecute me, I will have him killed.' 'Oh no, you won't,' I replied, and did my best over the next half-hour to reason him into a less murderous state of mind (I thought, successfully). Still, the threat had been made. Should I report it to the federal police, to the Attorney General, to Temby himself?

If this had been a professional engagement, it would have been covered by legal confidentiality, which can only be broken to reveal what is quaintly termed 'iniquity' – though iniquity would, of course, include a threat to murder. Some guidance at the time came from a famous case in California (*Tarasoff v Regents of the University of California*), where a psychologist, Dr Lawrence Moore, was sued by the parents of Tatiana Tarasoff, who was murdered by Moore's client, after this man had threatened to kill her in the course of a confidential conversation with Moore. The court held that Moore had a public interest duty to tell the victim and her family of the threat. That case turned on the credibility of the threat: in my situation, Packer was sick, and lashing out at his demons; I did not judge his threat to be credible – he would never, when he calmed down, arrange to implement it. But the dilemma was disturbing, and I was relieved a few days later when the Attorney General announced that on Temby's advice Mr Packer would not be prosecuted.

A few years later, I was to create some English law on this difficult subject, acting for a prisoner who had been convicted of three murders while suffering mental illness. He had been placed in a secure hospital indefinitely. He wanted to apply for parole on the grounds that he was no longer a danger to the public, and his solicitors retained a psychiatrist to report on his current mental state. To their surprise, he reported that the man was, in his opinion, still very dangerous. Understandably, they withdrew the application. The psychiatrist, on being told that his opinion would not be needed, sent a copy to the Home Office, in a blatant breach of his duty of confidentiality – or so I argued in the courts. The judges agreed, but found a public interest justification for the breach. They did not impose a duty on the psychiatrist to inform on his client, but allowed him a discretion to do so if, as a professional, he sincerely believed that lives were at stake.[41]

The problem is that professionals can have inflated opinions of their own ability to detect 'dangerousness'. In Kerry's case, I did not think there was any danger he would carry out his threat. If I had, my conscience – and, I reckon, my ethics – would have bound me to inform.

Back in Australia, in the '80s and '90s, my programme enjoyed high ratings, in large part because it had no difficulty attracting ministers – even Prime Ministers – and leading public figures. That had been Brian Lapping's difficulty with the UK shows: British politicians are reluctant to take the risk, except behind closed doors, that their American and Australian equivalents saw as a public duty, to expose their thinking to the public without the presence of their aides and advisers. It was enjoyable for me to find little-known people destined to go far; on one show, 'Send in the Clones', about the dawning wonders of *in vitro* fertilisation, I had Ian Temby QC (alive and well) and two brilliant Australians, of whom much more would be heard. One was Alan Trounson, a reproductive scientist who realised that anything he could do to an Australian sheep he could do to an Australian woman (although, on this show, he pioneered male pregnancy). The other was an unknown Melbourne ethicist named Peter Singer. It was obvious he would go far after his first exchange with the Anglican Dean of Sydney, Lance Shilton:

SHILTON: The Bible says there is a certain role for men and a certain role for women. Its teaching is very clear about that. There is no biblical evidence for confusing the roles.
SINGER: So far as what's not in the Bible, you could point out that the pop-up toaster is also not mentioned, but that doesn't mean we shouldn't have them.

And so we debated those unthinkable ideas that bioethics was beginning to throw up: the pregnant male has not quite eventuated, but most of the others have, protected by the impeccable logic of Peter Singer, now a Princeton philosopher, and those who think like him.

'What's Your Poison?' was a programme about drugs, with politicians, customs officers, federal police, psychologists and popstars. It attracted the attention of educators, and was the first *Hypothetical* to become part of a kit distributed to schools and universities. The storyline was prophetic, in that it envisaged almost exactly what was to happen, years later, to Australian drug mules when information which could have them executed was passed by the federal police to their opposite numbers in countries with the death penalty, like Indonesia and Malaysia. There were still calls for the reintroduction of capital punishment in Australia, most loudly from Gerry Peacocke, the MP for Dubbo:

MODERATOR: Xanadu, ladies and gentlemen, is a land of tinkling temple bells and genuflecting elephants, a romantic Qantas stopover where the heroin is pure and the massages are not. In Xanadu at midday today, President Kubla Khan has decreed that three drug traffickers will be tied to lampposts in the city square and shot. Gerry Peacocke, you're in Xanadu on a parliamentary study tour. Here's a chance to see something they don't do down in Dubbo. Perhaps they should. Are you in favour of executing drug pedlars?
GERRY PEACOCKE: Indeed I am.
MODERATOR: So you approve of the execution. Will you go and see it?
PEACOCKE: Absolutely. If you believe in the death penalty, I don't think you ought to be afraid to see it.
MODERATOR: It will be a fairly harrowing occasion. You might need a stiff drink or two before you go.
PEACOCKE: Before and after, probably.
MODERATOR: That's a pity. Xanadu is a Muslim country. The penalty for drinking is being stoned to death, like adultery. Xanadu is a dangerous place for Australian politicians.

'What's Your Poison?' was conducted in a brick hall in Sutherland Shire (the location for *Sylvania Waters*, one of the first reality TV shows) before an audience of 900 people who turned up on a weekday afternoon in response to a small announcement in the local paper, to sit through a long and circuitous interplay between the panellists on the problem of drug addiction. The ABC's response was to suggest that henceforth we should charge for admission! I thought it showed that 'people out there' wanted television to extend knowledge, to educate and inform as well as to entertain – which was the ABC's charter purpose, after all.

I make no great claims for *Hypotheticals* – I wonder if in some ways I did the show as a reason to come back and see Mum and Dad as they were growing older, to show them that the child they had nurtured at Eastwood had grown up to rule the world for a few hours in a spot-lit semicircle. I was the small boy who couldn't ride a bike, and this was his way of saying, 'Look, Mum, no hands.'

*   *   *

In Britain, *Hypotheticals* are remembered, if at all, as an emanation of the early '80s, a time when commercial television had to earn 'brownie points' from its regulator, the Independent Broadcasting Authority, by providing the public with what it was deemed to want – in this case, a 'high-quality' current affairs programme ring-mastered by authority figures – American professors and British barristers – from outside the familiar media milieu. As Thatcherism loosened regulation, the public was increasingly allowed what it really wanted, by way of 'reality television' – *Big Brother*, *I'm a Celebrity, Get Me Out of Here!* and, inevitably, *Love Island*. I am not complaining, so long as the BBC is left to cater for different, if less popular, tastes. For that purpose, it retained me some years later for the most bizarre *Hypothetical* I have ever conducted, in the middle of a game park in Zimbabwe, with a few panellists who were more ferocious than the lions patrolling outside our perimeter fence. There was General Gowon, author of Nigeria's genocide against the Igbo people; Valentine Strasser, who had led a bloody coup in Sierra Leone; and the President of Zimbabwe, the Reverend Dr Canaan Banana, before he was jailed for sexually abusing small boys.

The thesis, which I had to work into a storyline, was the artificiality of

Africa's colonial borders, fixed at places where, for example, an English missionary met a German explorer (or vice versa). It was a long afternoon, and as the sun was setting we had gone through war and plagues and army coups to an ending that was happy enough, although I cannot now remember it. The programme was visually stunning, and not only because of the wildlife – the panellists dressed ceremonially and I wore an Elton John cast-off jacket. It went out on BBC2, and for years afterwards people of African descent would come up to me to express their amazement that it had ever been made.

The media is always trying to find ways of making worthy subjects interesting for general audiences (they call it 'infotainment'), and courtroom formats – with live barristers – come in useful. For some years I chaired a Radio 4 programme called *You the Jury*, in which public figures would propose and oppose a motion (three minutes), call two witnesses each (two minutes, three for cross-examination), make a closing speech (three minutes) and then be told what the audience voted at the end, with the revelation of how it voted before the debate started. With my opening remarks, interventions and conclusions, we managed to bring the programme in at forty-five minutes. It was fast-paced and furious and we had some excellent performers – the powerful Methodist preacher Lord Soper and miner's leader Arthur Scargill were audience favourites – and the results were sometimes quoted in public discussion. But the attention-grabber, namely how the original vote had been changed as a result of the debate – always struck me as a bit of a con: those of strong views will vote against them at the outset, to help the pretence that the debate has caused a 'swing' in their favour. The BBC did its best to find a fairly honest panel of about 100 regular 'jurors', but the danger is always there, whenever the format is used (as it is in Intelligence Squared debates and the like). Years later I would occasionally join in a successor programme called *The Moral Maze*, with a similar format but without the expense of a jury or the spontaneity that comes from a 'live' audience. I could never master the art of a two-minute cross-examination and was always outclassed in rudeness by David Starkey.

I can't help thinking that these formats make complex issues simplistic rather than simple, and I do not greatly enjoy debate by sound bite. The only time I felt that it had an impact was in a *You the Jury*-style *Newsnight* debate in front of a live audience at the start of the controversy over the arrest of General Pinochet, when most people had not made up their minds about this surprising turn of events. I was all for it, of course, and was perhaps fortunate in my opponent, the 'artificial silk' David Mellor. It was a measure of his own realisation that he had lost the debate that he ended it by leering at me, 'You're very left-wing,' which (a) I wasn't and (b) was not relevant to the question of whether visiting torturers should be arrested.

The show that I most enjoyed chairing was a Sunday morning pro-gramme – *The World This Weekend* on the newly opened Channel 4. Under its dynamic management duo, Jeremy Isaacs and Liz Forgan, it was out to break the mould of news coverage, and vouchsafed me an hour – albeit an early hour – to probe international flashpoints, sitting around a table with two or three statespeople who had contributed to them. I prepared as for a cross-examination, and crossed swords with political friends – Benazir Bhutto, Bill Hayden, Abba Eban, Tariq Ali – and foes (the early neo-con Richard Pipes, and General Vernon Walters, Reagan's ambassador at large, who defended US support for tyrannies because 'only a third of the coun-tries in the world are democracies', as was in fact the case in the 1980s).

Working with Channel 4 led me to proffer Jeremy and Liz some advice about a new way of covering the courts. I had always been in favour of televising trials – the barristers would be better prepared, the judges better behaved and the public better informed. Leaders of the British legal pro-fession at the time would not countenance it, but having recreated the *Oz* trial for the RSC, I saw no reason why the day's play at the Old Bailey, in important trials, could not be replicated that evening on television by actors reading the transcript. There was a very important trial coming up – that of Clive Ponting, a civil servant in the Ministry of Defence, who was accused of breaching the Official Secrets Act by leaking documents which showed that Mrs Thatcher's decision to sink the Argentinian battlecruiser *Belgrano* ('Gotcha', as *The Sun* had said) was in fact a war crime (the ship had been steaming at full speed away from the conflict) causing the deaths of 323 Argentinian sailors. Channel 4 agreed to hire actors to play the parts of the lawyers, judge and witnesses (not, of course, the jury) and stenographers would produce a running transcript to be quickly edited for a live broadcast at 10.30 every evening of the trial.

Of course, the government got wind of it, and the judge would not hear of it after he had hauled us into court to explain. Quite wrongly, in my view (there was no law against it), he injuncted Channel 4, using the excuse that if he and the witnesses were played by actors, they might over-act and give jurors who watched Channel 4 the wrong impression of what they had already heard that day in court. To underline his pettifogging point, he said that actors were not like newsreaders, trained to keep a straight face. This comment gave us a cue he had not intended: Channel 4 laid off the actors and hired retired newsreaders. They returned to the screen with relish and, of course, over-acted (the judge did not understand that professional actors, unlike newsreaders, can be directed to portray protagonists neutrally). In any event, the show went ahead, with remarkably high audience ratings (over half a million tuned in every evening). Its seasoned presenter, Godfrey Hodgson, showed a flicker of emotion only once – when announcing Ponting's acquittal.

We had, to this extent, circumvented government censorship, but I wanted to go further. Our argument for the original programme had been rejected by the judge – wrongly, I believed – but there was no right to appeal. This was a serious anomaly: idiosyncratic trial judges were stopping newspapers from reporting evidence, or names of defendants, and the press had no right to have their decisions reversed by a higher court. Britain's lazy media (or its media's lazy lawyers) had put up with this passively, despite the fact that as long ago as 1966, Gerald Gardiner had allowed individuals and companies to petition the European Court of Human Rights in Strasbourg to force the government to provide them with an effective remedy for any breach of their rights. Jeremy and Liz agreed that I should take the case to the European Court (the BBC would never have done so – its executives were reluctant to challenge the government in the interests of free speech), so I took what Barbara Castle called 'the little Fokker' to Strasbourg. The government struggled – it had to concede that UK law allowed the media no right to challenge gag orders imposed by judges – and Strasbourg ruled in our favour: we had no effective remedy and the government was bound to provide one.[42] Not only did we receive our costs (Jeremy patriotically wondered whether he should accept them, but I think I convinced him to do so; for barristers, having their costs paid by the government is a sweet symbol of success), we also participated in the settlement negotiations which produced Section 159 of the Criminal Justice Act 1988, now regularly used by the media to appeal against gag orders to the Court of Appeal. It had been my first first-hand experience of advocacy in Strasbourg, and I was knocked out by the result – a new law to expand free speech, the terms of which the government had first to negotiate with you and then require Parliament to pass. My reaction? Give me more of it!

An Intelligence Squared exercise I did enjoy – especially because it partnered me with the legendary John Julius Norwich – was to prove that Pius XII was 'Hitler's Pope' because of his silence during the Holocaust, even as Jewish people were being arrested under his own Vatican window. By the time a later Pope came to town, in 2009, the BBC disgracefully refused to give a platform to those of us who deplored the blind eye Benedict had turned to child abuse, and it covered his visit uncritically for four days. I had by then written a book to demonstrate that Vatican connivance at priestly paedophilia amounted to a crime against humanity, and was invited to the only contrarian platform available – to speak with Richard Dawkins and abuse survivors from the back of a lorry, to protesters massed opposite Downing Street. The BBC refused to cover it and I almost passed out from the carbon monoxide from the truck's exhaust. I vowed not to rabble-rouse from the back of a truck again, but a crisis in legal aid funding and a fool (Chris Grayling) as Lord Chancellor brought me back to the top of a truck outside the Ministry of Justice to rally the troops. Some of the protesting barristers wore their wigs and gowns, so the police hesitated to arrest us for blocking the highway.

The last occasion on which I took the media role of advocate was for a Google Intelligence Squared debate on the legalisation of cannabis, genially opposed by Eliot Spitzer, the corruption-busting Attorney General of New York State, touted as a Democratic presidential candidate until he was exposed as a client of one of the escort agencies he had been trying to close down. I had a good team, ranging from Richard Branson to Russell Brand, with Bernard Kouchner (former French Foreign Minister) and former Presidents of Mexico and Colombia as supporting witnesses. The other side made the mistake of including Peter Hitchens, the *Daily Mail* columnist, who performed poorly (he was outwitted by Russell Brand). It was professionally chaired by Emily Maitlis, but that did not stop Hitchens from complaining in his next column.[43]

There was only one time when I was tempted to become an entertainer – or at least a version of Michael Parkinson. The BBC invited me to host several editions of *Friday Night, Saturday Morning*, the variety-cum-chat-show which went out in the late 1970s at 11.30 p.m. on Fridays. My shows introduced to television Rik Mayall and Ade Edmondson, and I interviewed Clive James, several actresses, the controversial human rights luminary Seán MacBride, and Jill Foot, known as Michael's wife but forgotten as a writer of important movies. It was a pleasant experience, but when the BBC asked if I wanted to pursue the prospect of becoming a 'celebrity', I demurred: I lack charm, and the other qualities which make Graham Norton such a success. The crunch came shortly afterwards, in the Old Bailey lifts, when a juror complimented me on a television appearance and I had to ask, 'Which one?' It was time, I realised, for the cobbler to return to his last.

Chapter Ten

Hard Cases

———————

'Hard cases make bad law' is a saying generally related to decisions which err on the side of sympathy, or which seem to bend legal doctrines to exonerate people who have acted reasonably. It is not heard much these days in Britain, where a Human Rights Act permits judges to interpret the law with due regard to humanity and civil liberty. Before that reform in 1998, I did find a number of cases 'hard' in other ways. The first marked the only occasion in my career when I have been criticised by an appellate court – for doing something in defence of a madam that it was said no 'experienced' counsel would have done, other than Rumpole, who would have gotten away with it. But the hardest cases, in terms of the toll they took on defenders of the sometimes innocent, were the 'terrorist trials' of Irish men and women suspected of IRA atrocities. Then there is a story about the perennial dilemma of what Americans call 'the fruit of the poison tree' – whether to proceed against citizens whom agents of the state have tempted to commit crime. And then the case on my conscience, where I failed to convince a jury (although I convinced half of them) that my client was not guilty of murder. Finally, my own case, when I was hauled before a disciplinary committee to face an allegation from a powerful newspaper.

*   *   *

I started as a barrister by grubbing around magistrates' courts and mitigating after 'guilty' pleas at the Bailey. The brief to plead for Cynthia Payne,

RATHER HIS OWN MAN

when it arrived on my desk, seemed unexceptional and uninteresting. She was a middle-aged madam, charged with 'keeping a disorderly house' in the genteel south London suburb of Streatham. It had been surveilled over the months by a team of fifty local police, who noted descriptive details about her male customers caught *in flagrante* (and allowed to leave) when they raided the house to arrest Cynthia. She had all sorts of medical problems but had drawn a severe judge, and I would have to extricate whatever mitigating features I could find in the facts, and make a final speech that might induce him to mercy. The facts suggested only one line of mitigation – her clients were all middle-aged and upper-middle class. The police had observed them:

Man in dark suit, 45–50
Man, 60, bald, blue blazer
Middle-aged man, black suit, white shirt and tie
Very smart elderly man
Man, 50, white Rover car
Man in trilby hat, briefcase
Man in smart-looking suit, smoking pipe

Clearly, they all knew what they were getting up to. And the house (as the prosecutor had to admit) was anything but disorderly: 'It was a large and well-run house, run by an experienced and able brothel-keeper.' She shared it with a former RAF Spitfire pilot, decorated for his war service, who lived there in return for being allowed to work as her 'slave'. They held party nights, on which men who paid £25 were given a luncheon voucher that entitled them to mount the stairs and the ladies waiting in the bedrooms. Surely, I thought, with my law school criminology course fairly fresh in my mind, this was not a crime that merited imprisonment for Cynthia? The women were not all in it for the money – there was a sub-postmistress from Glamorgan, for example, who said she came to Cynthia's parties for fun. As the prosecutor explained, 'I emphasise that there was no question of any of the girls being forced or coerced into prostitution ... they could, without being facetious, be described as amateurs taking part to raise money for Christmas.'

The day before the hearing I was visited by Cynthia and some leaders of her trade union – the English Collective of Prostitutes. They explained that Cynthia's services were not only to middle-aged and elderly men, but to the women, by providing them with a safe place to work, with classy clients and an ex-squadron leader to keep order. The English law on prostitution forced women in that profession to work without male company (or else that male would be guilty of 'living off immoral earnings') and alone, in cramped, unattractive flats, where they were prey to abusive, drunken or violent customers. The alternative was to work on the streets, which was worse, because it was even more probable they would be assaulted, and easier for police to accost and blackmail them.

I had no experience of English (or Australian) prostitutes, but the law certainly seemed an ass, at least for sex workers. The men, who had instigated the crime, were always allowed to walk away. I wondered who they were. The police had at least taken their occupations, so the next morning before court I had a whispered conversation with the superintendent in charge of the case. When he gave evidence, I asked some questions:

Q: As far as the clients were concerned, the fifty-three men, I think, who were found in the house at Ambleside Avenue when you raided it, they were broadly speaking middle-aged and elderly men?
A: There was a general cross-section, but principally middle-aged and elderly. ['If Mr Robertson had stopped there, he might have done his client some good,' the Court of Appeal was later acidly to observe. 'But he went on...']
Q: Of that cross-section, you had businessmen, managing directors, accountants...?
A: Yes.
Q: You had barristers?
A: Yes, sir.
Q: And solicitors?
A: Yes.
Q: Among those fifty-three men you had a Member of Parliament from Ireland?
A: Yes.

Q: You had a member of the House of Lords?

A: That is correct.

Q: You had several vicars.

A: Yes.

The press reporters scribbled furiously, and one or two left to phone in their copy for the evening papers. I made my mitigation pitch to the judge, with words that I naïvely thought might move him to mercy:

> Your Honour, by the plea of 'guilty' to these offences, Cynthia Payne recognises that the party is over and she, and she alone, is picking up the tab. The fifty men who flocked to Ambleside Avenue have escaped punishment, as men always do in this class of offence. The Wolfenden Committee, reporting in 1957, pointed out that if there were no customers, there would be no prostitutes. That is true today and has always been true.
>
> Cynthia Payne was called upon to provide those men with good times ... endless parades of suburban male respectability beating a path to the door, queuing on the stairs, waiting for a vacant room. Had the police not raided, the men would have donned their trilbies, picked up their briefcases, adjusted their ties and gone off to their otherwise respectable lives. Now their hostess is in peril of imprisonment. They took their pleasures and departed, and she stands alone in the dock.
>
> ... It is easy for barristers to condemn frailty and wish that people were better behaved. In view of the evidence in this case, that would sound rather smug. All I can ask is that Cynthia Payne receive a measure of mercy for her misbehaviour, frivolity and immaturity, and some understanding of the pressure on her from her own social circle and the eager demands of her male customers, recognising ultimately that without those customers there would be no prostitutes.

This was a speech that produced aggravation rather than mitigation. It inflamed the judge, who gave Cynthia eighteen months in prison, as well as a massive fine. How dare I, an upstart Australian barrister, use the disposal of a brothel-keeper to expose British hypocrisy? Much of the fury I encountered from the three judges in a hastily summoned Court of Appeal was provoked by the fact that the story had been on the front page of all the newspapers – the luncheon-voucher brothel where the upper classes (and 'several vicars' – how the press loved that) took their pleasures, while the woman who provided them went to prison. The story flew around the world. There was a full-page essay on the case in *Time* magazine, taking as its text King Lear's indictment of sexual hypocrisy: 'Thou rascal beadle, hold thy bloody hand. Why dost thou lash that whore? Strip thine own back. Thy blood hotly lusts to use her in that kind for which thou whipst her.' My mother telephoned from Sydney, having been alerted by a neighbour: 'You have made it to the front page of Mr Murdoch's *Mirror*, dear. Fortunately, they spelled your name wrongly.'

The legal establishment had never been more humiliated, and it had to act. Appeals usually took a year but something had to be done quickly – women had started to demonstrate outside courts, with awkward demands such as 'Where are our women judges?' (At the time, there was only one in the UK.) The Court of Appeal convened in record time – just two weeks. It was presided over by Fred Lawton, who had been a prominent fascist in the '30s, marching through the Temple in his brown shirt as one of Oswald Mosley's officers. As if to atone, he had become the most moralising of judges, and now he was apoplectic, my questions to the police officer being the object of his anger. 'If you hadn't asked these question, this case would have been reported in four lines in the *Streatham Gazette*!'

But if I had not asked them, my client would not be having her appeal heard only two weeks after her eighteen-month sentence was pronounced, and would certainly not be having that sentence cut by a year. That was the answer which went through my mind, in a Rumpole-like voiceover, but I did not dare to give it. I did not dare say anything, as another judge continued: 'And there would have been no cartoons.'

'Ahh – those cartoons,' groaned Lawton, wincing visibly at the memory. The wittiest was on the front page of *The Guardian*. It showed a vicar in bed with a prostitute, confronted by a perplexed police officer. 'I demand to see my solicitor,' says the vicar, 'who is in the next bedroom.'

Having remarked that the revelatory questions would not have been asked 'by a counsel with more experience' (in which case his client would have been disposed of without publicity or appeal), they reduced her sentence, and in a couple of months she was set free. Cynthia left prison in a Rolls-Royce, the toast of the tabloids, and was taken directly to the BBC, where she was interviewed on *Newsnight*. She was solemnly asked why she had refused to allow me to identify her famous clients. She paused, in deep thought. 'Well,' she eventually answered. 'Me morals may be low, but me ethics is high.' She had found a distinction that had eluded philosophers for centuries. Her future on the chat-show circuit was assured.

Some years later, after the inevitable book (*An English Madam* by Paul Bailey) came the inevitable film, *Personal Services*. Terry Jones, its ex-Monty Python producer, wanted it to end with Cynthia's sentence being delivered by a judge whom we recognise, in the last frame, as her first client. I was asked to advise on the libel risks, and pronounced them obvious and enormous (although every prostitute I ever defended boasted of having had judges for clients – usually, I suspect, mistaking solicitors' clerks for their more esteemed colleagues). Terry solved the libel problem creatively, with a last scene in which the camera panned around the court to reveal every male in it – judge, barristers, solicitors, clerks and ushers – as her former clients.

Too much public time and money was spent in those days on 'vice' in the courts, prosecuting and condemning it. 'It', as Elinor Glyn apostrophised, undoubtedly corrupted – the laws, and the police who corruptly enforced them. There is no solution to the problem of prostitution and pornography short of decriminalising the trade and treating those who ply it, like Cynthia Payne, as workers in a sex industry which should be regulated for everyone's health and safety. The alternative is to prosecute the clients for the crime of paying for sex – a law that has now been introduced, with mixed results, in Sweden. The most piquant comment on Cynthia's crime of 'running a disorderly house' came from her neighbour in Ambleside Avenue, the composer Carl Davis, who said that he had never heard any noise from next door. The old men queuing on her stairs clutching their luncheon vouchers were both sad and comic, but they did not spill out into the street to frighten the musicians.

* * *

There were much more serious, much harder cases. My early days at the Bar coincided with the resurgence of mainland violence by the IRA, which began with the bombing of the Old Bailey in 1973 and continued the following year with explosions in two Birmingham pubs that took twenty-one innocent lives. These atrocities put pressure on police to produce results. They did so by recording false confessions from suspects – the alleged perpetrators of the two pub bombings, who became known as the Birmingham Six, for example, served seventeen years in prison before the advance of science proved that police notes of their alleged admissions had been fabricated.

My concern was that pressure on prosecutors was also leading to rigged trials, and my first book, *Reluctant Judas*, told the story of Kenneth Lennon, a Sinn Féin supporter turned MI5 informant on the IRA. He had been caught with an IRA member surveying a prison that held three other members and was put on trial, together with his partner, charged with conspiring to break them out of jail. To preserve his cover, the evidence was rigged (with the approval of the DPP) to ensure his acquittal, while his partner was convicted. But the IRA saw through the ruse – why would the police give false but favourable evidence against an Irishman? Why would they tell the jury he had no Sinn Féin literature in his house, for example, when locals knew it was full of Republican pamphlets? A 'hit squad' from Ireland picked him up, convicted him after a private trial and executed him, dumping his body by a motorway leading to Gatwick Airport before making their escape to Dublin.

I held no brief for the IRA – they were murderous thugs – but I wanted to expose the way the authorities were bending the rules in this war on terror. *Reluctant Judas* was welcomed in Ireland and its message had cautious support from *The Economist* – 'It would be intolerable if Mr Lennon had been urged to egg on others to commit crimes for which they are now serving long prison sentences if the police can, in fact, fix a trial by a jury, so that their informer is acquitted and his partner convicted.' That was exactly what they had done, yet few did see it as intolerable. 'It is absurd and dangerous to apply the Queensbury rules to measures taken by the authorities. In this context there is no "right" or "wrong" – all that matters is success,' countered the voice of the establishment, the *Daily Express*.

Soon, I was appearing for IRA suspects, doing the 'bomb cases' that I had been warned would damage my career. Miscarriages of justice did occur, but mainly through the mouths of expert witnesses – so-called forensic scientists who would speculate loosely on links between my clients and the parts of the bombs that had been recovered. It was not easy – I had to become an expert on the wiring of circuit boards. And a critical problem with these trials, which have conduced to so many wrongful convictions, was that they were labelled 'terrorist' trials, which of itself prejudged the guilt of Irish (especially Irish Republican) defendants. The atmosphere – which jurors picked up – was intimidating and redolent of guilt: there were police sharpshooters on the court roof, police Alsatians prowling the court's yard and a security helicopter hovering over the Old Bailey, narrowly avoiding collision with the raised sword of Lady Justice. Intense body searches were inflicted on all who entered, including the jurors. For counsel, there was maximum security before you reached your client's cramped cell, thick with body odour and bad breath and the smell of boiled cabbage and urine. I did notice, however, that the prison officers made one concession to class – they never made us take off our wigs, though we could have smuggled in guns or drugs underneath them.

The ethical problems of giving terrorist suspects a full-blooded defence, as was their right, could be agonising. The most difficult – which I have replayed in *Hypotheticals*, where it never receives a satisfactory answer – happened to a QC friend. We were co-defending a group of Irish suspects accused of planning terrible atrocities – bombings of summer resort hotels around Britain. There was no evidence against the QC's client, other than that he had turned up at the door of the 'safe house' just before the police arrived. Everyone expected his case to be thrown out by the judge. But this barrister was punctilious, and insisted on going to Scotland Yard to inspect his client's clothes and property, which had been confiscated by the police on his arrest. They were arrayed on the table by a police officer, who then sat back in a chair reading a copy of *The Sun*. The QC examined them, finding a Catholic medallion that his apparently devout client had worn around his neck. He held it up and tapped it, and out popped a piece of tissue paper – on which the targets and explosive recipes were minutely written.

In the few seconds before the police officer looked up, the barrister had to decide what to do. He could slide the tissue back into the medallion and hope for his client's sake that it would not be found. He could say to the cop, 'Here is the evidence you have been looking for – evidence that my client is guilty.' Or he could eat the paper, ensuring his client's acquittal. That is what his solicitor later suggested that his duty to his client required him to do. Unfortunately, or fortunately (depending on your solution to the dilemma), the solicitor had sent an articled clerk, who asked my friend loudly, 'What's that? It looks interesting.' The police officer looked up from his newspaper and took possession of the tissue paper. It became the evidence upon which the client was sentenced to twenty-seven years in prison.

Well, what would you do? Destroying evidence is a crime which counsel has a duty not to commit (so much for the third option). Although every citizen should assist the police, that does not extend to barristers incriminating their own clients (although many think it should), so professional duty rules out the second solution. Faced with that dilemma, I would have shoved the paper back in the medallion and told the client to pray to the Virgin imprinted on it that the secret would stay there, and advised him to find another barrister (because we cannot set up fake stories for clients we know are guilty).

One case that entered the law books involved three young Irish people of good character and university background who had been found by police camping on a hillock with binoculars and poetry books. Their location gave a clear view over the country home and driveway of the Secretary of State for Northern Ireland, and they had noted down the number plates of some of his police protection vehicles. They had no guns, no explosives and no assault rifles, yet they were charged with conspiracy to murder the Cabinet minister. They had well-placed connections in Dublin, where many Republican sympathisers believed that the charge was over-egged. Before the trial, my instructing solicitor asked to see me privately. She opened with an observation. 'I see that your junior is engaged to the daughter of Hugh Fraser?' (Fraser was a Tory MP who had been the target of an IRA bomb which had killed someone else.)

'Yes, that's right. Ed [Fitzgerald] is a very good junior.'

'And I'm told that gossip columns say you're going to marry Nigella Lawson?' (Nigel, Mrs Thatcher's Chancellor of the Exchequer, was another IRA target.)

'Yes, I am told the gossip columns are saying that.'

There was a long silence. 'Well, how do you think this will look in Dublin?'

'I think it will look good. Here we are, reportedly about to be married into the establishment, yet prepared to defend the people accused of plotting to kill a Tory minister.'

She slowly shook her head.

'Come on, do you suggest that the privilege of defending your client requires my junior and me to abandon our intended wives?' From her steely look, that is exactly what she thought we should do.

The case went ahead and the police had no more evidence. Perhaps they had been bird-watching, we suggested, or collecting evidence for a journalistic exposé of the Northern Ireland Secretary, notorious among Special Branch protection officers for making them labour on his farm. The defendants offered no evidence, as was their right, and my final speech shredded the prosecution speculation – there were lots of reasonable doubts and the jury seemed willing to acquit on the charge that these defendants were definitely planning the murder of a Cabinet minister.

I was driving home – I was booked to fly to Singapore the next day to defend some of Lee Kuan Yew's detainees – when I heard the six o'clock BBC news. The Northern Ireland Secretary, the alleged target himself, had proposed to abolish the right of silence (i.e. the right that the defendants had just exercised, to say nothing and to have no inference of guilt drawn from their silence) because IRA terrorists were using it to get themselves acquitted. Then on came the loquacious Lord Denning, even more a menace since he had been forced to retire, explaining that every defendant in an IRA trial who claimed the right to silence must for that reason be guilty. The media the next day was so massively prejudicial that I cancelled my flight and returned to court, demanding the right to re-address the jury. Permission was granted, but it was an uphill task to explain to them that Lord Denning knew nothing about criminal law (which was in fact the case – he was a great civil lawyer). The three were convicted and jailed for twenty-five years. It was heartening, however, that when we took the case to the Court of Appeal, it recognised how prejudicial the publicity had been and quashed the convictions (no doubt Dublin was satisfied).[44]

That might have been why I was instructed to defend Dessie Ellis. His fingerprints were all over the circuit boards of the bombs that had caused civilian casualties in England and killed many soldiers and policemen in Northern Ireland. So dire had been the consequences of his conduct that the Irish Republic had given him up – the first Irishman ever extradited to face 'British justice' – a phrase which, since the trial of Roger Casement, had been regarded by Republicans as a contradiction in terms. I did not at first see how Ellis could be defended – the evidence against him was overwhelming, the right to silence would do him no good, and I did not fancy a long Old Bailey trial challenging what in this case seemed accurate scientific evidence. But I usually tell clients that 'the truth will set you free', and Ellis told the truth. He had indeed made many of the IRA bombs. He had done so in a remote part of the Republic, where he was told – and believed, otherwise he would not have made them – that they would be used to kill only policemen and British soldiers in Northern Ireland. In other words, he had no intention to kill anyone in England, and he believed his bombs would not be used there. This was a defence in law, but how to put it before an English jury unlikely to credit the distinction, or to believe it should avail a man causally responsible for many deaths?

I called the defendant into the box to give his truthful evidence. I called Bernadette McAliskey, who as Bernadette Devlin had won worldwide fame for leading Catholic protests in the North: she explained to the jury the mindset of Republicans like Dessie Ellis. They saw themselves as soldiers in a war of liberation, entitled in that war to kill their enemies, i.e. British soldiers and Protestant police. Civilians, other than informers, they regarded as off-limits, and they were opposed to extending the war to the English mainland. That was Ellis's belief (although not shared by other factions in the IRA) and it supported his testimony. For complicated jurisdictional reasons concerned with his extradition, he could not be tried for those Northern Ireland killings, although the jury must have hated him for it. All they were called upon to consider was whether he intended or knew that other IRA factions would use his bombs for explosions in England, in which case he would be jailed for life.

All I can say is that the jury found him 'not guilty' – the most extraordinary acquittal, given all the prejudice against him, even in his own country. He had been acquitted because he did not have the criminal intention that the prosecution had alleged, namely to kill people in England. The verdict must have astonished those 'people in Dublin' who were shadowy paymasters of the IRA. It would be too much to suggest that it restored their faith in British justice, since they had never had any faith in the first place, but it did show others in the Republic that the traditional enemy could at last give them a fair trial.

* * *

Dr Samuel Johnson – the chambers I shared with John Mortimer were named after him – had a pretty good grasp of human nature. 'There is', he asserted, 'a proof to which you have no right to put a man. You know, humanly speaking, there is a certain degree of temptation, which will overcome any virtue.' This problem has exercised every criminal justice system since Adam was arraigned in the Garden of Eden: whether to punish a person who has been talked into committing an offence. Eve was not framed, as my dear friend Helena Kennedy contends: she was the first dupe of the state serpent. It lost its power to stand upright as punishment for using her as a honey trap, inveigling Adam into crime.

Police in London rarely 'solved' crimes by detection work, but in their 'war on drugs' they had no hesitation in using agents provocateurs to set up defendants in sting operations, tempting them to break the law. This power could be abused for corrupt purposes, by police who had a hold over informants who were also drug dealers – they sold the drugs on behalf of police, who took their share of the profits. The police even supplied them with drugs to sell, taken from those seized in other busts. This is an account of an Old Bailey trial which exposed the racket and pushed the law about unfair provocation a little further in favour of the wisdom of Dr Johnson.

Let me set the scene: two young men are playing frisbee on the green in front of Holland House in wealthy Kensington. Rafi, a fly Indian, has not a care in the world: he has a wealthy girlfriend, and does bits of import/export when he needs to boost his self-esteem. His friend is working class, from Newcastle upon Tyne, hip and generous – in fact, he has provided the line of cocaine they have just sniffed to put them in a mood for the game. Rafi has been easily charmed by this new acquaintance, Cornelius Buckley, and calls him, affectionately, 'Con'. This nickname is appropriate in a way Rafi does not suspect, for Con works with a police team in Notting Hill, conning new acquaintances into drug deals, in the course of which they get nicked. Con is rewarded for his efforts – officially, by a modest £150 per arrest from the Scotland Yard informants' fund. Unofficially, he receives a proportion of the cannabis seized at each bust, which he recycles in the streets and pubs of Notting Hill Gate, returning a share of his profits to the police. He has already notched up twenty-four arrests and today he is hoping to set up another. So after the game he tells Rafi that he has a friend who owns nightclubs in Birmingham, who 'has a lot of bread' (money, for younger readers) and is desperate to obtain 20 kilograms of hash.

Rafi is at first unwilling to help, but over the next few weeks Con works upon him, inveigling him into the joint enterprise out of friendship and the promise of easy profit (the purchasers are offering £14,000, a lot of money in 1976). Rafi is not, and never has been, a drug dealer: he smokes pot, enough to think the law an ass and to make him less worried about breaking it. After several weeks of dangling conversation, Rafi succumbs and approaches a supplier, who is willing to obtain this large amount of cannabis so long as Rafi will take the risk of delivering it to the buyer. Rafi has been persuaded by Con that there is no risk at all – the nightclub owner is a close and trusted friend.

This was how Rafi and the supplier came to drive with a suitcase containing 20 kilograms of hashish to meet Con and his trusted friend in room 7068 of the Kensington Hilton, just off the Shepherd's Bush round-about, regularly used by resting or adulterous aircrew after long flights to Heathrow. The supplier waited with the suitcase in the car while Rafi went up to the appointed room. Con opened the door and introduced two big men, who swore loudly and behaved as coarsely as Birmingham nightclub owners might be expected to behave. They placed a large bag crammed with bundles of £20 notes on the table, withdrawn that morning from Scotland Yard's special vault for used banknotes, in the sum of £14,000, and invited Rafi to count the money. Having quickly done so, he returned to the car, collected the suitcase and brought it to the room so the night-club owners could inspect the 100 cannabis bricks inside it, each in a linen wrapping, stamped with a special blue-ink seal in Arabic lettering to indi-cate the batch and date. (These seals were used by Middle East producers to denote the origin of commercially grown cannabis, for an international black market which had become brazen enough to label its product like wine.) At this point, the police officers dropped their pose and handcuffed Rafi, while Con slipped away into the bathroom, scooping up a dozen slabs of cannabis as he went. It was only later, when Rafi was formally charged with being in possession of only 14 kilograms of cannabis, that he realised he'd been set up.

What he did not volunteer, understandably, was how many kilos of the drug had actually been in his possession. People rarely do volunteer the fact that they are more guilty than charged. That was the beauty of these sting operations. The victims were caught red-handed and were happy to plead guilty to the lesser amount, in the hope of a reduced prison sentence. The missing slabs, their labels intact, would stay in Con's shoulder bag until he sold them on the street, at street prices, and handed the proceeds to the detectives. Everyone profited and no one complained. And the best thing was that the actual evidence went up in smoke. All except for the Arabic seals, which Con, as a cannabis connoisseur, kept, in the way others collected stamps. His role as an informant who participated in the offence would never be disclosed, because judges in this period routinely refused to order the identification of police informants, believing that this was 'not in the public interest'. Indeed, no trials were ever expected to take place:

LEFT 'Way to go, Dad!'
How to land your
plane on a roof, 1943

FAR LEFT Flying Officer
Frank Robertson, 75
Kittyhawk Squadron, 1944

LEFT Corporal Joy Beattie,
Townsville, 1942

FAR LEFT Backyard
Eastwood Blues,
with Davy Crockett
(brother Graeme), 1954

LEFT That weak backhand
grip! (1958)

Mata Hari: Jane Turnbull and the Dreaming Spires, 1972

Agony aunt in her youth: Bel Mooney,
Hayman Island, 1979

Tenko survivor Jeananne Crowley, 1982

ABOVE Wizards of *Oz*: Felix Dennis (*giving the V sign*) with (*to the right*) Richard Neville, James Anderson and long-haired lawyer, outside Wormwood Scrubs Prison, 1971

ABOVE LEFT *Hypotheticals*, 'Sign or We'll Shoot', 1986, with aboriginal activist Michael Mansell (*left*) and Sir John Kerr (*right*) (Photo courtesy of ABC TV)

ABOVE Taking silk – with Nigella, 1988

LEFT Outside the Old Bailey, 1999

FAR LEFT Youngish love, at the Alan Jones Memorial Toilet, Soho (Photo by Mr Jones's arresting officer)

LEFT George Harrison teaches Jules, aged four, to play

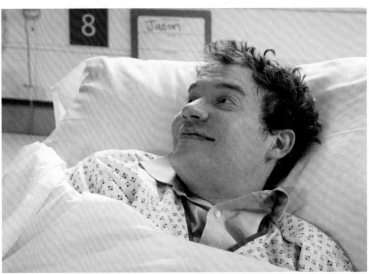

LEFT Jules as Jason in *Holby City* (Photo courtesy of BBC TV)

FAR LEFT Treading on Georgie's toes at *le Bal*, 2009

LEFT Georgie rallies her troops to protest arrests of students, 2014

Sailing on Sydney Harbour with John Mortimer, 2008 (Photo by Joe Skrzynski)

Home entertainment: (*left to right*) Netti Mason, Stephen Fry, Billy Connolly, Kylie and Dannii Minogue, Kathy and Jules

Founding Doughty Street Chambers, 1990, with (*left to right*) Gavin Millar, Chris Sallon, Helena Kennedy, Peter Thornton and Louis Blom-Cooper

Flowers from refugees, at Court of Penultimate Appeal, Hong Kong (Photo courtesy of the *South China Morning Post*)

My UN war crimes court, Sierra Leone, 2003

Kathy amuses the Queen (but note frown on the left) (Photo by John Stillwell/PA Archive/PA Images)

Team Assange: Amal Clooney (obscured, for once), Mark Stephens, Julian Assange, John Jones and Jen Robinson, 2011 (Photo by Yui Mok/ PA Images)

With Andrew Lloyd Webber and Mandy Rice-Davies at the launch of *Stephen Ward Was Innocent, OK*, 2013 (Photo by John Stillwell/PA Images via Getty Images)

With Amal, in our Ede & Ravenscroft, at the European Court of Human Rights, 2015 (Photo by AP/Christian Lutz)

Protesting Legal Aid austerity cuts at the Ministry of Justice, 2013 (Photo by Pete Riches)

Celebrating Mum's ninetieth birthday, with Dad, 2013 (Photo by John Fairley)

men like Rafi would all plead guilty, make their excuses and go to prison. Being conned by an agent provocateur was not a defence in English law.

In the US, if defendants admit that they committed a crime but satisfy the court that they would not have done so without the 'creative activity' of the police or their agents, they are entitled to acquittal. In the words of American Supreme Court Justice Felix Frankfurter:

> The power of government is abused and directed to an end for which it was not constituted when employed to promote rather than to detect crime and to bring about the downfall of those who, left to themselves, might well have obeyed the law. Human nature is weak enough and sufficiently beset by temptations without government adding to them and generating crime.

'Entrapment', as it is called, is not an easy defence to run, because the court will draw a line between the trap for the unwary innocent and the trap for the unwary criminal, and will readily infer that far from being a lamb led to the slaughter, the defendant is a wolf snared on the prowl. Nonetheless, an entrapment defence would have succeeded for Rafi, who was not a drug trafficker and would not have become involved in a big drugs deal had it not been for Con's persistent persuasion and the temptation of a promised suitcase full of cash.

But we were not in the US; we were in the Old Bailey. Rafi and this supplier's choice of counsel, however, led to a remarkable coincidence, which gave the makings of a possible acquittal. I happened to have been briefed not only for Rafi but for a defendant in another drug bust carried out by the team of police officers who were using the services of 'Con'. My instructions mentioned, in passing, that the charges seemed to relate to less cannabis than the defendant had actually supplied. 'How interesting,' said Mike Mansfield, the barrister who was acting for the supplier, Rafi's co-defendant. 'I've just had a brief in another case where exactly the same thing has happened – same informer, same mysterious shrinking cannabis.'

There might not have been an entrapment defence, but there was a thin but discernible line of legal authority to the effect that every trial judge has an inherent power to exclude evidence 'obtained by conduct of which the Crown ought not to take advantage, even though tendered for the suppression of crime'. The moral imperative – 'ought' – seemed to open the window, at least a crack, to the full blast of an argument about the immorality of the state itself creating the crimes it was meant to be prohibiting. It would not be a 'defence' which could be laid before a jury, but we might just prevail upon a fair-minded judge, before the trial commenced, to throw out evidence obtained by a flagrant agent provocateur, and the prosecution would have to be withdrawn. Nonetheless, no one would regard our suspicions, although based on similarities in four different cases, as proof of anything. We needed Con. Not the smooth-talking Con who had duped all these dopes, but a reformed and repentant Con, willing to tell the truth under oath in the witness box.

'Turning' Con to this extent – 180 degrees – was beyond the power of any defence solicitor, who would first have to find him somewhere in the basements of Notting Hill. 'And I don't like the media,' said Mike (who has changed in this respect). But I thought it was our only hope. The *Sunday Times*, under my friend Harold Evans, was a newspaper with the resources to uncover injustice, and its 'Insight' team had recently hired David May, the former editor of *Time Out*, who did not need a compass to find his way around Notting Hill basements. David tracked Con down just as the trial was about to start, and demanded an interview. Con ran for his life. But the next day he turned up at the *Sunday Times* with an unusual request. He wanted protection, not from all the people on whom he had informed, but from the police officers who controlled him with their threats to put him behind bars if he didn't hand over the profits from selling 'their' drugs. David was careful not to offer Con money: he wanted the truth, on tape. It was the only way, he explained to Con, that he could free himself from the clutches of Scotland Yard. Con said he would think the matter over.

Meanwhile, in the courtroom, the crunch had almost come. I had persuaded the judge to hold an inquiry, before a jury was sworn, into whether the evidence – seventy-seven slabs of cannabis, piled high on the exhibits table – had been obtained so unconscionably that the prosecution ought not to take advantage of it. The police officers were outraged by the suggestion. Con was a reliable and trusted informer, they swore, whose behaviour gave them no reason to suspect that he was acting as an agent provocateur. They knew nothing about any missing cannabis, and treated my cross-examination with practised derision. The senior officer turned to the judge: 'I have no idea what counsel is talking about.' The judge nodded grimly, as if to indicate that his patience was wearing thin. I put Rafi into the witness box to explain how he had been persuaded to commit a crime he would otherwise never have contemplated, but the judge seemed unconvinced.

I told David May we had run out of time: unless Con told the truth that evening, Rafi would have to plead guilty. At 2.40 a.m., David woke me with a call to say that Con had just confessed, on tape, to everything we had suspected. I subpoenaed him to repeat his taped confession in court. Unless prosecuting counsel could shake him, this case would die of shame.

He came to the Old Bailey nervous and subdued, casting frightened glances at the police officers he was about to accuse. He told a disconsolate story, of drifting to London and becoming a persistent if minor criminal in the Notting Hill area. He was terrified of prison: his petty-criminal father had hanged himself rather than face a custodial sentence. So the police team had a strong hold on him. 'You will go away for a very long time,' he was told, unless he did them some favours. That meant informing on accomplices and providing regular 'drinks' for the police out of his reward money and earnings from drug deals. So he went to work, specialising in drug busts. He had pursued Rafi tenaciously because he saw the possibility of a lucky break – a big deal, from which he could make a lot of money. 'Rafi wanted to back out of the deal, he was trying to lose me, but I was holding on. He trusted me. The police told me to encourage him, so I tried to make him feel at ease – I tried every trick in the book.' At the time of the bust in the Hilton, he had snatched some cannabis bricks before he was pushed into the bathroom, where, he said, the police officer met him afterwards to put 'a little present' – more cannabis bricks – in his shoulder bag. The police would want their share of the proceeds: 'Where's my drinks money?' was their routine greeting. Why had he finally agreed to tell his story to the *Sunday Times*? 'An innocent man is in the dock because of me.' The remorse in his voice sounded genuine.

The prosecutor (Allan Green, later the DPP) had prepared his first question carefully. 'I put it to you, Mr Buckley,' he said confidently, 'that you have not one scrap of evidence, not one scrap, to support the story you have been telling us.'

There was a long silence, Con's face crinkling with the effort of some internal memory scan. 'We-ell,' he said eventually, 'as a matter of fact, I do.'

It was not the answer the prosecutor had expected. 'And where is this evidence, Mr Buckley?'

'It's in me mum's flat up in Stoke-on-Trent. It's under me bed, actually, in an old shoebox.'

The stout barrister valiantly tried to avoid collapse. 'And, Mr Buckley, what evidence would we find in this shoebox to support your story?'

'It's me box of cannabis seals. I've kept them all, you see. The labels of the cannabis I was given to sell. I'm sure some of the seals from this load are there.'

The judge called an early adjournment: arrangements would be made to retrieve the shoebox and bring it, unopened, down to the Old Bailey on the morrow.

The next morning, while we awaited the dispatch rider, Con was invited to inspect the seventy-seven slabs of cannabis – that part of the load at the Hilton which had made it into police custody. 'Just tell us, Mr Buckley, which of these ink seals do you have in your shoebox?' As the coverings of the bricks were handed to him, Con's eyes lit up. He sniffed them as if they were the corks of vintage wine. Finally he selected eight different seals, which he said would match eight of those from his bedroom collection.

The shoebox duly arrived and was solemnly handed to Con as he stood in the witness box. Eight seals from the Hilton haul were laid out like playing cards on the desk in front of him. He opened his shoebox and produced one matching label, then another. 'Snap' – eight times. It was a wholly convincing performance. His hobby had produced the evidence which proved that Con had been in possession of blocks from the same shipment as the Hilton cannabis: the only reasonable deduction was that they had come from the same bust. How, now, were the police to explain this?

They were forced to troop back into the witness box to deny, unconvincingly, Con's allegations. How had Con come into possession of the ink seals which matched those on the wrappings of the cannabis slabs seized in room 7068 at the Kensington Hilton? 'It's a mystery to me, sir,' was the reply from a rather more respectful police inspector. All vigorously denied the allegations that they had 'licensed' Con to deal in drugs and had taken their cut from his reward money, but in order to do so their confident assertions, made the previous week, about Con's reliability as an informer had to be jettisoned. It was not long before we had some new police officers sitting in the back of the court. They were from A10, Scotland Yard's special squad which investigated allegations of corruption against police officers.

In the end, the judge had no doubt that the prosecution evidence should be excluded. Buckley, he held, was plainly an agent provocateur; Rafi was not dealing in cannabis and would not have done so without Con's persuasion. Although informers were vital to detection work, it would be 'unfair and ignoble' to allow a prosecution based on the work of this informer to proceed. He directed that the evidence against the police should be sent to the DPP. Rafi was released from the cells below the Old Bailey, to stumble blinking into the summer sunshine. He had obtained a large amount of cannabis and had tried to sell it, and yet now he was free. Buckley-related drugs cases awaiting trial were abandoned, which meant that twenty-four prisoners convicted by the team had to be released. The full story was recorded on the front page of the *Sunday Times*, telling the tale of 'Cornelius and the Case of the Vanishing Drugs'.[45]

These were remarkable results, and many law enforcers did not like them. They believed that lawyers should not examine the methods by which criminals were brought to book, or argue that evidence of their guilt had been unfairly obtained. It was no business of the courts, in other words, to set standards for the police. It would have been better, said these officials (and some judges agreed with them), had Rafi pleaded guilty and gone to prison for six years, rather than having a trial which provided an opportunity for barristers to make public accusations against Scotland Yard.

The problem with this argument is that misconduct by police or by their agents will rarely be revealed unless there is an opportunity to do so in a court. The very reason police are tempted to conspire with criminals is because they know they will not be informed on by colleagues, nor called to account through internal disciplinary systems. What gives pause to the corrupt policeman is that wild card, the defence barrister, who may just nail him in open court.

*　　*　　*

Most barristers will, by the end of their career, have a case that still haunts them – lost because they overlooked a winning argument, or failed to ask a crucial question, or asked one question too many. The case on my conscience is one in which I failed to persuade enough members of a jury – although I persuaded some of them – that my client, a Chinese refugee named Wang Yam, was not guilty of murder. He was later convicted by a majority verdict at a retrial after being defended by another QC, and jailed for life. Wrongly convicted, I believe, in the sense that his guilt could not be proved beyond reasonable doubt, either at the time of his first trial or at his second – and certainly not today, as new evidence came forward after he had spent eight years in prison. The case has become quite notorious: a book has been published disputing the verdict,[46] it has had some sensational newspaper coverage and has been taken to the Supreme Court and beyond, i.e. to Strasbourg, where it is pending. It remains a mystery, shrouded in secrecy said to be required by national security.

The murder, in 2006, of 86-year-old Allan Chappelow, seemed particularly brutal. It took place in his house in Downshire Hill, Hampstead – one of London's most desirable addresses, leading to Hampstead Heath. He was an author, who in the 1960s had written a learned and lengthy biography of George Bernard Shaw and had stored in his large, part-derelict house several tons of the old page proofs. It was under them that his body was finally found by police several weeks after his death. His body was badly decomposed, but forensic evidence suggested that hot wax had been dripped on him, he had been tied up and possibly tortured and had suffered severe blows to the head. There was no clue to point to his killer, other than DNA found on the butts of seven cigarettes in an ashtray, smoked (so I assumed) while the torturer watched his sufferings and waited for him to spill whatever beans he happened to possess.

Soon after finding the body, the police identified their prime and only suspect. He was a Chinese refugee named Wang Yam. They had evidence to show that after the murder he had been busy trying to steal Chappelow's identity by passing himself off as the dead man in calls to his banks and credit card providers, using information gleaned from stealing his mail. The prosecution theory about the murder (to account for the fact that his passport and other identity documents found in the house had not been taken by the murderer) was that Chappelow had found him on the doorstep in the act of stealing his mail: they had fought and Wang Yam had killed him and buried his body under 560kg of book proofs then quickly made his escape. This theory did not account for the hot wax or the cigarettes – Chappelow was not a smoker, and it was not his DNA on the butts.

Wang Yam, a few weeks after the murder, had travelled to Switzerland. There he was arrested and sent back in custody: his first words to the British police were to request that they dial a telephone number which he said would explain everything. What happened next was the subject of secret hearings; when *The Times* speculated about them, the paper was prosecuted for contempt, although the case was abandoned after a former Law Lord, writing an article on 'open justice' for the *London Review of Books*, made similar conjectures. Thanks to a court order, even eleven years after the first trial I cannot comment on evidence that was heard in secret, and the European Court of Human Rights cannot be provided with any information about it to assess whether his trial was fair.

Nonetheless, it can be said that Wang Yam's defence hinged on his claim that he was infiltrating a gang of serious criminals and maintaining his cover by participating in an identity theft they had arranged. The first days of the trial were spent arguing over whether the evidence of Wang Yam's motivation for becoming involved with this gang could be heard in open court. The judge (and then the Court of Appeal) decided that national security would be imperilled if it was, so *R v Wang Yam* became the first murder trial in modern English history to have a substantial part of its evidence heard behind closed doors. I argued the case for open justice unsuccessfully and simply note that one of my arguments was that if the evidence was heard in open court, the case would attract a great deal of publicity, which might encourage defence witnesses to come forward. Exactly the sort of witnesses who, eight years later, emerged to cast questions over Wang Yam's guilt.

Our forensic problem at the trial was that the jury would undoubtedly find that Wang Yam was guilty of theft, or at least handling, of Chappelow's bank statements and credit cards a week or so after his murder. There was no evidence to connect him to the murder itself, but *post hoc ergo propter hoc* is a common fallacy. So is over-reliance on circumstantial evidence. This all pointed to Wang Yam – the only man apparently seeking to profit from the death. Jurors were likely to convict him of murder, unless we (I was doing the case with Kirsty Brimelow, a top defender on the verge of taking silk) could come up with another possible suspect. Wang Yam provided the nicknames of three gang members, but they could not be traced. No associates of Chappelow could be brought into the frame. He was presented as a recluse, who seemed to live among his rubble, venturing only to the local library every morning to read *The Times*. Police made few enquiries among his neighbours – the cops were not really interested, because they thought they had their man.

Legal aid did not extend to provide my over-stretched solicitor with an enquiry agent. I was left to do my own research, and contacted a friend who lived nearby – West Hampstead is full of QCs and Law Lords. I was told that the neighbours had clubbed together to pay for a security company to keep an eye on their properties, but this had made them feel less secure because it was staffed by unfriendly Albanians. I called some evidence about this, but it went nowhere. Nor did my suggestion that Chappelow may have met his murderer on Hampstead Heath, which was well known to be a gay pick-up area at night. I suspected, from going through his possessions and hundreds of his photographs, that he probably was gay, but that was not relevant – unless it could be shown that he was given to assignations at the pick-up places on the Heath. I made such speculative suggestions in my final speech to the jury, but they lacked force – my best point was the lack of any evidence to place Wang Yam inside the house or any incriminating forensics from his flat or his possessions (this murderer would have been splattered with blood). Then there was the mysterious DNA on the cigarette butts of the presumed torturer, waiting (or so it seemed) for Chappelow to disclose the combination of his safe or some other secret while hot wax was dripped on him. At this first trial, the jury could not agree.

Wang Yam was gentle, weak and voluble in a way that psychiatrists would identify as having 'flight of ideas'. When called to the witness box he wailed inconsolably for five minutes before I could ask him a question. I could not see him as a brutal killer. He was, interestingly enough, Chinese royalty – his grandfather had been Mao's third in command during the Long March, and was venerated by the Communist Party as a hero – this fact probably saved him from retribution when he turned against it and joined the student revolt in Tiananmen Square. Afterwards, he had been permitted to travel to Britain, where he was admitted as a refugee and involved himself in some anti-Beijing activity. Whether or not his use of Chappelow's stolen credit cards could be connected with work to infiltrate a criminal gang was the subject of evidence in closed court, and of closed portions of our final speeches to the jury on the charge of murdering Chappelow. Wang Yam was out to profit from Chappelow's finances, but did he know of the murder, and more importantly did he commit it? The jury could not agree, although it was out deliberating for three days.

At his retrial, the new jury found him guilty. I could not defend him because I had other professional commitments which clashed with the date the court insisted the retrial must take place, but he asked me to return as his counsel for the appeal. The retrial had, however, been fair, and no fresh evidence was available: the jury verdict was allowed to stand.

And stand it did, for eight long years, until his case engaged the attention of the CCRC – the Criminal Cases Review Commission, a body charged with reviewing questionable convictions after all appeals against them have been exhausted, and bringing really doubtful verdicts back to the Court of Appeal, where judges can decide if they should be quashed. The reason for reviewing Wang Yam's case was that *Guardian* journalist Duncan Campbell had uncovered three new witnesses. Two of them were not really new – disgracefully, their evidence was known to police even before the first trial but was not passed on to the defence. There was a witness who had reported a mailbox theft near Downshire Hill by violent men, and it had uncanny parallels with the modus operandi allegedly used

by Wang Yam. He could not have done it, because he was in prison awaiting trial. The police report – which raised the possibility that these robbers
killed Mr Chappelow – was never passed on to the prosecutor, who would
have passed it to me. It would have gone before the jury as important
evidence for the existence of another suspect.

They would have hesitated to convict had they heard from another 'new'
witness, an elderly man living nearby who had seen and spoken to a man –
white, aged about fifty, with an Irish accent – entering Chappelow's home
just after his death. Although the witness went to the police with this obviously important evidence, a policewoman told him it was irrelevant and
sent him on his way. Whether she was irresponsible, or had imbibed the cer-
tainty among her team that their suspect, Wang Yam, was guilty, is not clear.
Suffice to say this vital witness never came to the knowledge of prosecutor
or defence counsel. Had either or both witnesses testified, the impact on the
jury would have been such that Wang Yam could well have been acquitted.

It was the third new witness, however, whose testimony would in my
view have assured a 'not guilty' verdict, although it cast a very different light
on the killing. It was delivered precisely and with deadly seriousness by a
local government official who seemed to be addressing his own demons as
well as the court. He was, late at night on the Heath, a sadomasochist of
somewhat extreme bent, prowling for partners of the same predilection,
whom he would handcuff, place over what he termed 'the spanking bench'
and beat unmercifully. He brought the handcuffs – 'They were not for pleasure,' he told the judges, elliptically. The man whom he often met, between
the hours of 11 p.m. and 3 a.m., and who joined him in these exercises was
named Allan, whom he identified as Chappelow. They did not have sex –
just shared pain, in this *Walpurgisnacht* that took place between consenting
males three or four times a week, around a bench in a clearing in the woods.
Allan had asked him back to his nearby home, but he declined out of concern that the old man wanted sex. 'I am not into necrophilia,' he explained,
rather cruelly, I thought. But on two occasions he had seen 'Allan' leave the
scene with another man, possibly headed to the house in Downshire Hill.

The testimony was shocking – in the large, half-empty appeal court where
I heard it, shivers ran up spines. It conjured up an entirely different but

tantalisingly credible scenario: Chappelow, the distinguished author, transforming at night to the masochist on the Heath, tied up and tortured by volunteers from a semicircle of men clad in black. From this dark spectacle the imagination leapt to the pathologist's picture of a body tied up and beaten, tortured by hot wax and perhaps burned by cigarettes which were then stubbed out, leaving the DNA of a passing sadist. I had speculated to the jury that the killing might have been by someone he had met on the Heath, but I did not envisage the possibility that Chappelow might have been a willing 'victim' in a sadomasochist ritual gone wrong. The pathology could have been interpreted to match this scenario, in which case it would have been unlikely that a jury would find Wang Yam guilty 'beyond reasonable doubt'.

That was the view of the CCRC, which investigated with great thoroughness and was convinced Wang Yam's conviction had been a miscarriage of justice. The case against him of murder was circumstantial, and the fresh evidence, it said, must have raised jury doubts. In 2017 it used its power to refer the case back to the Court of Appeal, where I listened to the fresh evidence (I was in court as an interested observer, not as counsel). The appeal judges found the new witnesses credible, but relied on the circumstantial evidence to uphold his conviction. The case serves as a reminder of the fallibility of human justice here – as well as there and everywhere.

*   *   *

When the farcical trial was over, Mr Geoffrey Robertson QC crowed 'Mr Scargill is as innocent as a newborn lamb.' If he believes that, he'll believe anything … MR SCARGILL IS NO LAMB, MR ROBERTSON. NOR WAS HE BORN YESTERDAY.

The *Daily Mirror* editorial was understandably bitter. The newspaper had spent a fortune on investigating and condemning miners' leader Arthur Scargill and the National Union of Mineworkers over their desperate attempts during the 1984–85 miners' strike to combat the Thatcher government, which was determined to close the pits. There had been trusts created, bank accounts opened, donations put in and taken out, and the

Daily Mirror had made these transactions sound deeply dodgy. They had been undertaken, after all, on behalf of miners, men who work with their hands for modest wages. It was outrageous – possibly even criminal – for such people to have trusts in their favour, operated through overseas bank accounts: who did they think they were, Robert Maxwell?

I had encountered the *Mirror's* proprietor only once before, when invited to a lunch in his boardroom to unveil his plans for a new, Labour-friendly London evening paper. I was there with other potentially supportive figures – the super-bright Tessa Blackstone (now earning the gratitude of the Bar as head of its Standards Board) and Ken Livingstone, sane and sarcastic (in the days before he went a bit loopy over Hitler). Maxwell, an enormous man with permanent perspiration on his brows, clapped his hands for silence and turned to his features editor, the experienced journalist Yvonne Roberts. 'Now, show them how our progressive paper will deal with the important issues of the day.' One important issue of that day concerned Prince Edward, who had just announced his decision to break centuries of royal tradition and not enlist in the armed forces – he had been condemned as 'the royal wimp' in most papers. 'Instead, we shall salute him,' announced Yvonne confidently. 'We shall congratulate him for rejecting the military tradition of the royal family, we shall...' 'We shall do no such thing,' Maxwell erupted. 'We shall condemn this royal wimp...' He went on, crushing his senior employee, and showing his real character as a bully. When he asked for ideas for the paper, I suggested an ombudsperson, to correct its mistakes, an idea he rather liked and offered me the job. I declined – his face contorted in amazement (nobody refused Robert Maxwell) until I explained that I would in that event be unable to accept briefs to sue his paper. A motive based on money he could understand, and as we broke up he offered me a place on one of his advisory boards. He rattled off a list of politicians he paid to have on his 'advisory boards', and doubtless in his pocket. As we left, we noticed the former British ambassador to the US, now his employee, in a glass office framed by golden strips. 'The gilded cage,' I whispered to Tessa, or she to me. It was sad that the Labour Party, under the principled Michael Foot, should have to depend on characters like 'Capt'n Bob'.

Encouraged by 'Capt'n Bob' – who was still, at this point, larger than life, his massive theft of his own workers' pension fund as yet unexposed – a team of rather dim-witted journalists at his *Daily Mirror* had gone about the business of destroying Arthur Scargill. They had paid £50,000 to his driver, and £80,000 to one of his officials, for information and documentation. They had published the result of their investigations under banner headlines which ran for four days calling Scargill a crook. The miners' union set up an independent inquiry conducted by a former judge, which exonerated Scargill from all the serious accusations. It did, however, raise a number of criticisms and questions relating to trust law and accounting practice, and it was read with interest by an obscure and hitherto inactive government official called the Certification Officer for Trade Unions. It struck him that the union had not disclosed any trust funds in its 1984 report, and there was an argument in law that it had a duty to do so. There was also an argument in law that it had no duty at all to do so. Instead of asking Parliament to clarify the law, or telling unions that in future funds of this type would need to be notified, the Certification Officer embarked in 1991 on a very belated criminal prosecution for 'wilful neglect' to notify his office of the existence of trusts which (although outside the union's control) were designed to benefit its striking members. The maximum fine was only £400, although the vast number of journalists who congregated in and around the court might have suggested that Arthur Scargill – at the time, Mrs Thatcher's main enemy – was up for serial killing.

It fell to me to open the defence and to urge the judge to dismiss the charges on the grounds that there was no admissible evidence to support them. I explained how the matter originated in allegations of corruption against the defendants made 'in a national newspaper as a result of very extensive bribes, not disclosed to its readers, which have obviously tainted the evidence of the prosecution witnesses who received them'. For this attack on its behaviour (and, more importantly, I suspect, for getting Arthur Scargill off the charge), the *Mirror* editorially condemned me. I could wear that – all in a day's work when you defend unpopular people who happen not to be guilty of the charges brought against them. But the editor of the *Daily Mirror*, one Richard Stott, was not content to attack me in his editorial. For the first and last time in my career, I was made the subject of a complaint to the Professional Conduct Committee of the Bar Council that seemed plausible enough for this disciplinary committee to investigate. My misconduct, in Stott's eyes, was to subject his precious newspaper to gratuitous criticism by falsely accusing it of 'bribing' its informers by paying them large amounts of money.

Any complaint against a barrister by the editor of a national newspaper (the *Mirror* had a circulation of three million in those days) had to be taken seriously. It was, and I was called upon to explain my conduct. I was confident that the offending words had been relevant to our defence, and not inaccurate in relation to the conduct of the *Mirror*, which had rewarded potential witnesses with large sums of money for breaking the confidences of their ex-employer. But any lawyer who defends himself has a fool for a client. So I consulted Richard Du Cann QC, a former head of the Professional Conduct Committee and the advocate whose views on ethical matters I most respected. I found myself, at the close of our discussion of the case, feeling that sense of dread which so many clients must feel as they come to the crunch with their counsellor: 'Do you think I have anything to worry about?' Dick was too fond of teasing not to let several miserable beats go by before expostulating, 'No!'

The Professional Conduct Committee gave long and careful consideration to Stott's complaint, and dismissed it after a spirited discussion. They had studied transcripts of the trial, obtained responses from all the other participants, and could find no basis for criticising me. Any professional disciplinary body which sits in secret and dismisses an unjustified complaint is an easy target for criticism, however, and I would have preferred the matter to have been dealt with publicly. I doubt whether Stott would have relished the publicity his rivals would have given to the nice question of whether the *Mirror*'s 'chequebook journalism' amounted to 'bribery' when it amounted to £130,000, but he worked himself into a high lather of indignation for one last abusive letter to the Bar Council about its verdict, which he ungraciously copied to me.

Thank you for your letter regarding the 'investigation' into the conduct of Mr Geoffrey Robertson QC. Once again you have fully vindicated the reputation of your Council for justice not only not being done, but not being seen to be done.

Fiat justitia! I suppose there is somebody still at the Bar who understands Latin. Incidentally, I know you are not over-fastidious about accuracy but the name is Stott, not Scott.

This masterpiece of injured dignity (he had been addressed as Richard Scott) was dated 13 September 1991, a few weeks before Robert Maxwell, unable to face an investigation of his criminality in looting the *Mirror*'s pension fund, committed suicide by jumping off his boat in the middle of the night in the middle of the Mediterranean. The absurd Stott first wrote hagiographic obituaries ('The man who saved the *Mirror*') and then, at long last and only when it was safe to do so, the truth ('Maxwell was a crook'). Although he had failed to uncover the massive criminality taking place under his own nose, he was said to be a good editor, and in defending his staff he was doubtless doing what he thought was his duty; I was sorry he could not see that I was doing mine in defending Arthur Scargill.

Chapter Eleven

In the Privy

There was another court which I had as a teenager dreamed of one day addressing – the Privy Council. On the staircase of its building in Downing Street, a few doors from the home of the Prime Minister, hung portraits of long-dead Law Lords who had once decided the meaning of constitutions of all fifty-two Commonwealth countries. Their successors, still with quite a few of these constitutions in their keeping, sat at a horse-shoe-shaped table facing counsel, who stood to address them from a big polished lectern. Through the high windows on your right you could see Big Ben and Whitehall – the parade of black taxis and red double-decker buses reminding you that this was once at the epicentre of the British Empire, a court that jurisprudentially orbited in space, landing one day in Antigua, another in Brunei, another in Mauritius. The concentrated legal minds in the chamber had to imagine they were in the slums of Kingston or the tenements of Hong Kong or the sheep-filled meadows of New Zealand, depending on the nature of the case and the country from which it arose.

The proceedings were sedate – there was none of the bustle and drama of the Old Bailey – but they could be of great political importance to member states of the Commonwealth. The high walls of the main chamber were lined with law reports, and nearby was a library with laws of every country within the Privy Council's jurisdiction. I loved the atmosphere of this place and its ghosts from colonial history. When the Privy Council was moved, in 2009, to the Supreme Court building down the road in

Parliament Square, I begged various High Commissions to purchase the building and turn it into a museum of Empire legal history. None was interested; the Commonwealth is not now a force to be reckoned with in the world.

It was as a death row lawyer that I first climbed those stairs, to what I hoped would be justice for men in the Caribbean who were facing execution. Their petitions were heard every Tuesday morning, when the Law Lords who sat 'on the Privy' would interrupt their hearings of cases they thought were much more important – about gas pipelines in Brunei or bridge collapses in New Zealand – and listen to my last-ditch appeals.

The real problem for death row lawyers is that you can never abolish the death penalty; you can only make it harder to carry out. If people in a democracy vote to support it, there is nothing the courts can do to strike it down, because that would be to defy the will of Parliament. It's no use calling evidence to prove that death is no deterrent to crime. (Though, since 1990, states in the US without the death penalty have had consistently lower murder rates.)[47] Rational argument gets you nowhere – the courts simply have no power to stop hangings, or lethal injections, or the operatic barbarity of death by firing squads, or Stalin's favourite procedure (and actually the least agonising of all): an unexpected bullet in the back of the head while being walked down a dark corridor.

We can, of course, find errors in the legal process, and I would spend weeks scouring dog-eared trial transcripts for such errors. But the death penalty itself was untouchable. The most ironic thing was to see black politicians in the Caribbean following their colonial masters and keeping all the sadistic rituals of the gallows: reading the death warrant outside the cell of the condemned man; weighing and measuring him for the drop; the execution always at dawn, witnessed by an official party who would sit down to a cooked breakfast while the body twisted in front of them for the regulation sixty minutes. The body was never returned to the relatives, so that they did not see the 'giraffe effect' – hanging elongates the neck. In Jamaica's prison, they buried the corpses in the kitchen garden – and produced the best vegetables in the country.

I would visit these death rows, in Trinidad and Jamaica, where men waited years to be executed – governments changed, appeals took a long time, nobody was hanged until the public demanded vengeance after a nasty murder. And of course, ten years later the state is not killing the same man who has committed the crime. Some of the men I defended were reformed individuals. Some had become mentally ill. And some had always been innocent – the very fallibility of criminal justice is another strong objection to the death penalty.

The argument that has now virtually stopped executions in the Caribbean and East Africa came to me when I visited Michael X. His real name was Michael de Freitas, and he had been a black power leader in Britain in the '60s and a friend of John Lennon. His name arose from a mistake by a hotel receptionist in Birmingham, when Michael was escorting the American black power figure Malcolm X, who had asked for 'a bed for the night, and another for my brother, Michael'. The receptionist simply assumed (well, you would, wouldn't you) that the name of Malcolm X's brother Michael was Michael X. When he saw it in the hotel register, De Freitas liked it so much he adopted it.

In the early 1970s, Michael X left London and went home to Trinidad, where he founded a commune. A double murder (of Gale Benson, daughter of a Tory MP, and Joseph Skerritt, a local barber, both followers of Michael X) was committed there, and in due course he was convicted of Skerritt's murder and sentenced to death.[48] I met him when he was one of the living dead, on death row at the Royal Gaol in Port of Spain, with thirty other men, each in monkey cages that measured 8 by 6 feet, with a mattress and a slop bucket, kept there twenty-three hours a day in sweltering heat, subjected to a cacophony of screeching and screaming from other inmates.

As I sat with Michael, for several hours on several days, I began to appreciate what I later termed 'the death row phenomenon', a form of mental torture caused by alternating hope and despair. Listening to the reading of the other men's death warrants and the sound of the trapdoor opening in the execution room next door induces mental derangement in doomed men who do not have a kill-by date, but it gave me an idea. I said to him, 'Michael, this is actually a place of mental torture – maybe we should argue that a long stay on death row amounts to torture, which is banned by the constitution.'

I'll never forget – Michael smiled, for the only time during my visits, and put his finger to his lips. 'Shhh,' he said. 'Listen. This place is always full of noise.' Now, there was total silence. Every man on that block was pressing against the bars of his cage, leaning towards us and straining to hear. 'You must realise that for them, you represent hope,' he said. 'Their only hope. Promise me that one day you will make this argument, for their sake, not mine. They will hang me, no matter what.'

And they did. We took the argument – that a protracted period on death row amounted to torture – to the Privy Council, but Lord Diplock derided it; he said the delay was Michael's own fault for appealing. I was about to file for an injunction to argue another point when the Trinidadian government rushed Michael to the gallows, at midnight, without telling us, so we could not get a judge to stay his execution.

I had made a promise to him that day on death row, when silence fell, and twenty years later I was able to fulfil it when my argument finally succeeded. A prolonged stay on death row, the Privy Council ruled in 1993, amounts to torture, and means the death sentence has to be commuted. This case, *Pratt & Morgan v the Attorney General of Jamaica*, has by now led to the commutation of death sentences in over 1,000 cases in the Caribbean and throughout East Africa. It is the case I look back on with most pride – it took six months to prepare, *pro bono*, and I led a team of barristers from my newly established chambers in Doughty Street. It reversed the ruling in Michael's case and demonstrated the importance of upholding international humanitarian standards for prisoners, even for convicted murderers.[49]

Another case that illustrated the danger of the death penalty – and the difficulty of oral advocacy in America – was that of Krishna Maharaj, whom I met on death row in Florida and represented before the state's Supreme Court. He had been convicted of a brutal double murder, of a father and his son, and was sentenced to die in 'Old Sparky' – the electric chair in Florida State Prison. I was not surprised that the jury had convicted him: although he had seemingly credible alibi witnesses, the prosecution had evidence of a grudge against the victims, his fingerprint in the hotel room where they were murdered, and even an eyewitness – flaky, but the jury believed him. The task was to have his death sentence commuted; because he was British, several hundred MPs had jointly instructed me to make the argument on his behalf, and I was specially admitted to the Florida Bar to do so. It was an unnerving experience addressing its state Supreme Court: I was allocated only twenty minutes to distil my written submissions (even in the US federal Supreme Court, advocates are allowed only half an hour). There was a green light on the lectern which flashed red when you had two minutes left and stayed red when your time was up – take any extra time and you can be punished for contempt of court.

The advocate's art in these circumstances is to concentrate on the best point and to answer questions from the judges as quickly and crisply as possible. We succeeded, to a degree: the death sentence was vacated, but not the double murder conviction. Kris would spend the rest of his life in jail. He was stoic when I saw him later, in one of those orange boiler suits now familiar from Guantanamo Bay, determined to fight on to prove his innocence. Notwithstanding the strength of the prosecution evidence, I really could not believe he had gunned down the victims. And fifteen years later a brilliant death row lawyer, Clive Stafford Smith, proved that he hadn't: Clive collected compelling evidence that the assassination had been ordered by Medellín cartel boss Pablo Escobar, and carried out by one of his hitmen. The victims were drug couriers who had sold his cocaine but failed to hand over the proceeds. In 2017, a federal judge ordered a full rehearing of his case, which we hope will be the cue for Kris's release after thirty years of wrongful imprisonment – the first ten of them on death row.[50]

But you cannot count on ending capital punishment in the US, where those who are most pro-life when it comes to depriving women of their right to an elective abortion are most pro-death when it comes to killing convicts. In 1976 I was part of the defence team for the boxer Rubin 'Hurricane' Carter, who had already spent nine years on death row, having been convicted in 1966 for a triple murder which it was, by the time of his retrial, fairly clear he had not committed. Bob Dylan's song 'Hurricane' tells it like it was – the man who could've been middleweight champion of the world, had it not been for perjury and race hate. Norman Jewison's movie, starring Denzel Washington, was pretty accurate as well.

The case took me to the mean streets of Paterson, New Jersey, where I encountered vicious looks from white passers-by because I was with 'The Hurricane' while he was briefly on bail. It was obvious he would be re-convicted by a local jury. Rubin himself knew he had no chance, even though – in fact, because – he had become a national celebrity. 'See how they hate me? They're gonna convict me.' With sadness, I had to agree. Eventually, in November 1985, he was released, and set up an organisation that uncovered more than seventy wrongful convictions of men on death rows in the United States.

It was the Privy Council which finally decided my most dramatic and difficult death penalty case, defending 114 Islamic militants who had attempted a coup in Trinidad in 1990. The government had been trying to close their mosque, but that did not excuse their response – an armed overthrow of the government. Led by their imam, Yasin Abu Bakr, these members of the Jamaat al Muslimeen took control of the country's only television station, from which Abu Bakr made some incoherent broadcasts while his followers, armed to the teeth, took over the Parliament building (the 'Red House') with the Prime Minister, Cabinet and a number of MPs (including two opposition MPs) still inside it. They killed eight policemen and caused millions of dollars' worth of damage in the process. There followed the kind of scenario that can normally only occur in a *Hypothetical*: the Prime Minister and his entire government held hostage in Parliament, and the head of state – the President – safe under the protection of the army, some distance away.

What happened then was later subjected to minute analysis in the courts. The President was at his crisis centre with the army chiefs, who advised that they could not storm the Red House to release the hostages because they would be killed by the time the soldiers managed to overcome the terrorists. The Muslimeen could possibly be starved out, but that had problems, notably for the Prime Minister, who was a sick man and without his medicines.

Then arose what seemed to be a brilliant idea. I described it in court as having come from a 'bush lawyer', for which Australian phrase I had to apologise when it transpired that it had come from the next Chief Justice. It was this: the President had the constitutional power to pardon, so why not offer the insurgents a way out? They would be offered a presidential pardon if they released the hostages and surrendered. The seeming brilliance of the idea was that the pardon, the President was assured, would actually be legally invalid because it would have been granted under duress. It seemed the perfect trick: after the pardon had induced their surrender, all 114 terrorists would be prosecuted for treason, and hanged. What was so wrong about this advice was that the President himself was under no duress at all – he was safe in the arms of the army. No one was holding a gun at his head – the guns were being held at the head of the Prime Minister and Cabinet some distance away in Parliament. A pardon granted by the President, by his own deliberate act, would in these circumstances in fact be valid. However, having been assured by his lawyers that it would not be worth the paper on which it was written, the President wrote it. The only problem now was how to bait the trap by getting the document to the terrorists. All telephone communication with the Red House had been cut, it was before the era of emails and mobiles, there was no Trojan horse, and carrier pigeons were unavailable.

The solution took the form of an Anglican priest – and priests really are useful in this kind of situation. He was a man of some courage, and was known to the Muslimeen through ecumenical connections. Under a white flag he ventured into the Red House to deliver the document. The terrorists were tempted, but were concerned that they'd had no legal advice, until they realised the Attorney General himself was their captive. He consulted the constitution and showed them the section vesting the power of amnesty in the President – this pardon document, he was happy to advise them, would save everyone's life. One of the hostages – an opposition MP – asked to see it and then did something that would save 114 lives: he photocopied it, and kept the photocopy.

Meanwhile, the terrorists sent the priest back and forth for three days to seek more conditions and assurances concerning the Muslimeen mosque (as an indication of good faith, they had allowed the ailing Prime

Minister to leave), until they were satisfied. Then the hostages were released and the 114 hostage-takers came out smiling, handed over their weapons to the police and took their seats in the army buses that they had been told would deliver them to their mosque. Instead, it took them to the Royal Gaol, where their belongings were confiscated and they were charged with treason, a hanging offence.

'What about our pardon?' they asked.

'What pardon?' was the response. The original document had been taken from their leader and was never seen again. There was no pardon, the government assured the court, which denied the men bail. Even if there had been a pardon, the government lawyer added, it would have been invalid for duress.

The government had to come clean once the photocopy was produced, but it was determined to hang the Muslimeen nonetheless and an English QC was hired to tighten the noose. I had been retained to save the necks of the insurgents; indeed, to have them set free on the strength of the pardon, so I made an application for *habeas corpus*, requiring the state to prove that their detention was lawful. The government claimed that I could not derail its treason trial with this tactic, and we fought it all the way to the Privy Council. There, we examined every pardon ever proffered, most notably those given by President Lincoln to Confederate forces after the civil war. To dishonour them, he had said, would be 'a cruel and astounding breach of faith'. The Privy Council agreed with my argument that *habeas corpus* before trial was the correct way to test the issue of whether the pardon was valid.[51] So back to Trinidad we went, having won this first skirmish, to test it.

The case was heard in a large hall with a vast dock specially built to house my 114 clients, below a gallery which accommodated several hundred of their relatives. They were understandably anxious and on the first day pandemonium broke out – I found myself standing on the Bar table, my back to the softly spoken judge, making a loud speech beseeching everyone to keep quiet and have faith in justice. The judge possessed that wonderful quality of independence, not always found in the Caribbean judiciary, and he ruled that the pardon was valid.

Before my clients could be released, the government appealed. It lost 2–1 in the Court of Appeal, whereupon it immediately appealed again to the Privy Council. The Court of Appeal had not only granted *habeas corpus* but had awarded substantial damages to the Muslimeen for wrongful detention – by now they had been in prison for two years. Understandably, this had incensed the public: why should their taxes compensate terrorists who had killed eight policemen in cold blood and whose rampage had cost millions to repair? It was obviously an unjust result, although it logically followed from the validity of the pardon that they should not have been put in prison and should now be compensated for that loss of freedom.

All eyes turned to the Privy Council: we argued the case for many weeks and awaited the judgment. The Law Lords ruled that the pardon had been valid when granted – it had not been vitiated by duress. If the Muslimeen had surrendered their hostages when it was first delivered, it would have entitled them to liberty. But they kept negotiating for better terms over the following three days, and that invalidated the offer – the pardon, the Law Lords decided, carried an implicit condition that it should be accepted forthwith. By this clever, if somewhat specious, reasoning, the court concluded that the pardon had become invalid by the time they were arrested, so they could not get damages for wrongful imprisonment. But this did not mean they must hang: by offering the pardon in the first place, the government had given them a 'legitimate expectation' to believe that they would not be put on trial for their crimes, and it would be an abuse of process for the prosecution to continue to their conviction and execution.[52] This was truly a Solomonic solution – neither strictly legal nor strictly logical – but as fair as possible in the circumstances. It spared the Muslims their lives, but they would not receive a dollar in damages. The public were overjoyed, and as a result of the case Trinidadians still demonstrate in favour of keeping the Privy Council whenever any patriotic politician suggests that this colonial relic should be abolished.

Why, my wife frequently asked, did you devote so much of your time and energy to saving the lives of worthless murderers? It was a fair question, given the absence from family and from remuneration that my death penalty practice entailed, not to mention that most of my clients were probably guilty. I met a few who were not – Kris Maharaj, for example – but even Michael X, in the murky circumstances of the killings in Trinidad, probably deserved a lengthy sentence for manslaughter. The Trinidad Muslimeen had behaved like terrorists, and most of the men I defended, or who benefited from the success of my argument in the Pratt & Morgan case, were serious criminals. So why spend months – years, in fact – cudgelling my brains to find ways to outwit states that wanted to string them up? I have no religious or philosophical belief in the sanctity of life – there are clear cases when taking it is in the public good. Intellectually, of course, I believe the arguments against capital punishment, but my wife's point was 'Why not leave them, sometimes, for others to make?' That was not an option when I made my promise to Michael X or when I accepted instructions to try to save the lives of the Muslimeen. But why summon up passion – and I was and still am passionate – to stop the executions of murderers and drug traffickers? I guess because I believe quite simply that law is there to protect life, not to take it, for the reason given by the prison reformer John Bright as long ago as 1850, when the gallows in England were in full swing: 'If you wish to teach the people to reverence human life, you must first show that you reverence it yourself.'

*　　*　　*

The Privy Council is indeed a colonial relic, and it has presented the not entirely satisfactory spectacle of white male judges (sometimes joined by a Caribbean colleague) striking down the decisions of local courts in small but independent Commonwealth nations. My justification for its continued existence is twofold. First, it is no bad thing for any country, no matter how advanced, to have an independent arbiter, especially on human rights issues. The forty-seven countries of Europe – including such proud nations as Germany, France and the UK, and even (most of the time) Russia, accept the rulings of the European Court of Human Rights, while others such as Canada and Australia defer to decisions by the UN's Human Rights Committee. Their laws are in consequence improved and moved in a more humane direction. The Privy Council, itself increasingly influenced by international human rights law, has performed that function well in recent times, and there is no longer any whiff of colonialism in its rulings. Its operations – which are not inexpensive – are free to applicants and their states and the cost should be paid from the UK's overseas aid budget.

Secondly, in small communities, judges come under local pressure and expectations, especially in cases against the government, and are frequently conflicted if not 'got at' by the island's political masters. The most preposterous decision I have ever received was in Antigua, where a judge held, by distorting the law, that our Royal Commission into gun-running could not obtain evidence outside the island's twelve-mile limit. This was nonsense, since we had been set up to investigate arms trafficking, via Antigua, from Israel to Colombia.[53] But the evidence sought was against the son of the Prime Minister, who had been corruptly dealing with the Medellín cartel. I assumed this judge had been bribed, but was later told that he was at the end of his tenure and needed to win the Prime Minister's favour in order to be appointed to lucrative post-retirement positions.

For an example of how the Privy Council can work to correct legal errors, a more recent case from Antigua is instructive. It concerned a local power company, awarded a contract to build a power station to secure the island's electricity. Halfway through its performance of the agreement, the government suddenly ordered it to stop and awarded the remainder of the contract to the Chinese. Any first-year law student could recognise this volte-face as a breach of contract, and probably much else besides. Yet when I brought the case in Antigua with Kim Franklin (once a student of mine and now a very good contract lawyer), the judge at first instance held for the government, for no good legal reason. The Court of Appeal for the Eastern Caribbean seemed, at the appeal hearing, to recognise the mistake, but its judgment was mysteriously delayed for twenty-two months, until the Chinese power station had been built. When finally delivered, turning down our appeal, it was plainly wrong in law, as the Privy Council immediately detected and put right, decreeing that damages and costs must be awarded to the plaintiff. For good measure, it held the Prime Minister guilty of abuse of power for ordering the police to enforce the breach of contract. *Antigua Power v Baldwin Spencer & Others* should be studied by anyone who thinks that justice can always be done without resort to the Privy Council.[54] Of course it would be better if the Privy were re-constituted as a Commonwealth human rights court, with judges selected from a range of member nations, but this is not likely in the foreseeable future, and the Privy Council arrangements do at present serve to rectify injustices in its dozen remaining client countries and to limit the use of the death penalty.

*   *   *

The Privy Council was permitted by Lee Kuan Yew to rule in Singapore – he found it helpful in reassuring English investors – until it condemned the injustice he and his loyal judges had visited upon his opponent, Workers' Party leader Joshua Benjamin Jeyaretnam. Ben was the most congenial of politicians, with his mutton-chop whiskers and belief in democracy, and his party only ever won one seat – his own – in the national Parliament. But that was enough for Lee, a malicious man, to humiliate and destroy him. Heavy libel damages were awarded against Ben for mild criticisms of Prime Minister Lee, and the compliant judges humiliated Ben further by removing him from membership of the legal profession. The Privy Council declared that Ben was innocent, and condemned the judges. For that reason, Lee decided to abolish any further appeals from Singapore to the Privy Council.

It was a strange experience to cross swords with Lee in court. During libel actions he would bring against my American newspaper clients for any mild criticism of his governance, Singaporeans would queue every morning for seats in the gallery to hear his cross-examination, because it was the only place where they could safely laugh at their authoritarian Prime Minister. In one case the judge announced that he was awarding additional damages because my questions had 'hurt Mr Lee's feelings'. The Malaysian Bar Council put out a press statement: 'This is the first evidence that Mr Lee has any feelings.'

In Singapore, I came across people of great principle, people it was a joy to defend. They comprised the young Catholic social workers who had been inspired by liberation theology and had begun to be critical of the government. For this, they were detained in prison for several years, where they were subjected to the secret police speciality – the torture that leaves no marks because it takes the form of being required to sit naked and suffer sub-zero blasts from souped-up air conditioners. There were two female playwrights as well, accused of writing plays that 'exaggerated the problems of the poor'. And I won a great victory – the first victory ever, and the last – against Lee Kuan Yew's government, in courts where judges were instinctively biased in his favour. The Court of Appeal was forced to grant *habeas corpus*, because the detention orders had not been signed by the Minister of National Security, as the law explicitly required, but by his head of department. On such legal technicalities does liberty often hang.

There was great excitement the morning this judgment was handed down. The prisoners' relatives were overjoyed: they could not believe we had won, and rushed from court straight to the gates of the prison and waited outside for their children to be released. The detainees were given suitcases in which to pack their clothes and told to take their pictures down from the walls of their cells. They were ushered onto a bus, which drove through the gates towards their relatives, who were laughing and cheering, onto the main road. Then it turned and drove back through the gates to the prison. There, they were presented with fresh detention warrants – signed by the Minister for National Security. In Lee Kuan Yew's Singapore, you always lost. Even when you won, you lost. And just to make sure you never won again, Lee passed a law – the Internal Security (Amendment) Act – which provided that 'there should be no judicial review in any court of any act done or decision made by a minister'. Goodbye, *habeas corpus*. Goodbye, Privy Council.

Hong Kong, too, suffered from the loss of the Privy Council when it reverted to China. Before then, I appeared in cases where the Privy required Hong Kong to accept persecuted Chinese fleeing from Vietnam as refugees. But its successor – the 'Court of Final Appeal' – had its judgments subjected to the approval of the Chinese government. It was a good enough court, with a Commonwealth member – for a time, Sir Anthony Mason, the former Australian Chief Justice – sitting as one of its judges. When a case about these refugees came up, the Court of Final Appeal decided they could stay in China. No, they could not, said the Communist Party in Beijing, and negated the decision. I tried again, arguing that the first decision had created a 'legitimate expectation' that the refugees could stay. 'Otherwise,' I said, looking straight at Sir Anthony, 'you are not the Court of Final Appeal, you are the Court of Penultimate Appeal.' He winced, but had to turn us down. It was a hard case, made harder by the refugees themselves, who turned up at the court door every morning to present their advocate with bunches of flowers. The case did arouse a lot of anger, however, so much so that the local police did not have the heart to arrest settled families. Beijing has not used its constitutional blackball since, although there are signs that the newly emboldened Xi Jinping regime will do so, should the Court of Penultimate Appeal ever decide to acquit pro-democracy demonstrators.

In Commonwealth countries in Africa, subverting democracy was often done more openly once the 'Big Men' emerged. Independence leaders like Jomo Kenyatta in Kenya and Dr Hastings Banda in Malawi wanted themselves and their parties to lead for ever, just like Lee Kuan Yew. They abolished the Privy Council and imported some Marxist lawyers to rewrite their constitutions and turn their countries into one-party states. You could vote in elections, certainly, but only for candidates presented by the official party led by the Big Man. I was happy to play a part in trying to dismantle these anti-democratic constitutions, which ensconced one party (in Kenya, one tribe) and led to massive corruption. My friend Paul Muite, when head of the Law Society of Kenya, publicly asserted that the constitution could be interpreted as permitting the formation of opposition political parties so long as they did not put candidates up for election. The government prosecuted him for sedition for uttering this opinion, and Paul asked me to defend him. I was about to leave for Nairobi when the news came through that I had been banned from entering the country. It is strange – for all the inconveniences I have caused to governments, whether in communist states, in apartheid South Africa or in various mini-dictatorships, Kenya has been the only nation formally to forbid my presence.

It could not, however, forbid me from bringing a case against Kenya in the World Bank's arbitral tribunal, which sat in Paris. It arose at a time when corruption in Kenya was endemic: it started with the Big Man at the top, Daniel arap Moi (Kenyatta's successor), and the poison trickled down into every public official and most local judges. Abolition of the Privy Council made its exposure less likely, but the World Bank tribunal (ICSID) had independent adjudicators, available for investors to access if contracting with governments that were unreliable or whose judges were amenable to government pressure. My client was the proprietor of Kenya's duty-free stores, who complained to ICSID when they were expropriated by Arap Moi. He explained to the tribunal that to obtain the contract he had followed the normal procedure: he turned up at the presidential palace with half a million US dollars in cash in his briefcase. He was told to leave it in the waiting room while he met the Prime Minister. Arap Moi made small talk until he received a telephone message, whereupon he took his gold – solid gold – pen and signed the contract. My client picked up his bag as he left and was puzzled that it was much heavier than before. When he returned to his hotel, he opened it to find it full of corn – maize that was the local staple. This is how every contract with the Kenyan government was sealed during the Arap Moi years, and only because of ICSID's international arbitration could the corruption be exposed – an exposure that helped to end his rule.[55]

The Big Man I encountered face to face was Dr Hastings Banda, 'President for Life' of Malawi. He was in fact quite small, with a leathery visage that made him look like the movie alien E.T. He had been an independence leader in the 1960s – I have friends who remember, and regret, protesting on his behalf when he was detained by the British colonial authorities. After independence, he quickly dispensed with democracy and used the emergency law under which he had been detained to imprison anyone who criticised him. Television was banned and he controlled the only radio station and newspaper in this one-man, one-party state of nine million people, rated by the World Bank as one of the poorest countries in the world, despite its agricultural wealth. That was being harvested by an amoral corporation, Lonrho, which shared its tax-free profits with the President for Life.

By the time I met Banda he was over ninety, not that his age stopped him from pawing the female member of my delegation from the British

Bar and Law Society (we were there to discuss prison conditions, which we would have experienced first-hand had she slapped his face). He had a chief mistress, styled the 'official hostess' of the nation, Cecilia Kadzamira. Banda had made it a crime to possess any Simon & Garfunkel album featuring their song 'Cecilia' – 'Cecilia, I'm down on my knees, I'm begging you please…' were not words the President for Life wanted to be heard openly in his country.

Other actions were less comical. There were stories that he fed people he hated to crocodiles in the dark southern reaches of Lake Malawi. I was certain that he had ordered his chief inspector of police to arrange the deaths of four MPs who had criticised him in Parliament. A secret police unit had bashed their brains out and placed their bodies in a car, which they pushed over a cliff. The government announced that they had suffered a road accident while trying to flee the country.

After thirty years of despotic rule, aid donors and foreign governments (notably, the European Union) finally insisted on multi-party elections in Malawi, which Banda (financed massively by Lonrho) agreed to call only because he expected to win. The people, however, decided to be rid of him, and the new government set up an inquiry into the deaths of the four MPs. It decided that Banda had been responsible. He was put under house arrest and I was asked to return to assist his prosecution. We obtained gruesome confessions from the secret policemen who had committed the murders: they were all practising members of the Church of Scotland (the main religious group in the country, thanks to Scottish missionaries) and were happy to confess in return for a light sentence. They testified to being ordered to kill by the chief inspector of police. But he was dead (I suspect that Banda had him killed in order to shut him up). He had not left any document incriminating Banda, but he had left a wife, who vividly recalled how he had agonised with her for two days about carrying out the order to kill he had received personally from Banda, in fear that the tyrant would have him murdered if he disobeyed.

This was highly credible evidence: the only problem was that it was not admissible in court. It was what lawyers call 'hearsay' for the wife to describe what her husband had told her, and hearsay upon hearsay for the jury to hear what he had told her about what Banda had told him – i.e. to kill the MPs. I tried to find a way around this problem by charging Banda with conspiracy to murder, but the judge did not agree that the devastating evidence could be admitted through this device and Banda was eventually acquitted. He was dying, in any event, and at least a tyrant had fallen far enough to be put on trial for multiple murder – a trial that, unlike any conducted during his rule, had been open and fair.

Robert Mugabe was another Big Man who went bad in the absence of any restraint by the Privy Council. In 2002, I was summoned by *The Guardian* to help defend their correspondent, Andy Meldrum, who was facing prosecution for the novel crime of 'abusing journalistic privilege'.[56] It carried two years' imprisonment and was used exclusively to punish those who criticised Mugabe in print. For this reason, *The Guardian* had ceased to distribute copies in Zimbabwe; Andy's reports could be read by Zimbabweans only online. The keenest readers of *The Guardian's* website were secret policemen working in an underground room in the main police station in Harare, intercepting all internet stories they could find that were critical of Mugabe. This gave us (I was working with the courageous Zimbabwean lawyer Beatrice Mtetwa) a defence that the local court had no jurisdiction because the 'crime' had been committed on a website based in London.

But where was the evidence? We all trooped from court to the business centre of the Sheraton, where a police officer tried for hours to find it on the Guardian Online. The paper had, of course, taken it off after Andy was arrested, and the police had not worked out how to preserve it. The magistrate, correctly and courageously, acquitted. Reprisals soon came – his car was burned. Beatrice was assaulted; the bravery of lawyers in these places at these times is both heart-warming and heart-rending. As for Andy, when he walked from court a free man he was stopped by a cop and presented with an order for his deportation. As in Lee Kuan Yew's Singapore, so it was in Robert Mugabe's Zimbabwe – when you win, they make sure you lose.

*　　*　　*

The Seychelles, a collection of 115 island jewels set in the coral waters of the Indian Ocean, may well be the most beautiful place left in the world. Its people – 94,000 'Seychellois' – are descendants of African women slaves and tars of the British Navy, which freed them from slave ships in the early nineteenth century and brought them to the largest island, Mahé, for education and, as inevitably happened, copulation. The island received its independence from Britain in 1976, led by an exuberant barrister from Middle Temple, James Mancham, who invited dozens of bikini-clad Hollywood starlets to grace his inauguration. He made the mistake of going off to be photographed with the Queen at her Silver Jubilee celebrations and in his absence was deposed by the opposition leader, France-Albert René, a dour Marxist barrister from Lincoln's Inn.

René was clever and compromising: he realised that his undemocratic reign depended on the tolerance of the US, so he allowed it to keep its CIA monitoring station on the island, while at the same time permitting Russian 'fishing trawlers' to enter his territorial waters and monitor the monitors. Come *glasnost*, however, the trawlers withdrew and the US ambassador told him the game was up: America no longer needed the monitoring station (they had a better one at Diego Garcia, where they could waterboard as well) and the State Department wanted the Seychelles to become a real democracy. René knew when he was beaten, and in 1990 asked the Commonwealth secretariat to provide a lawyer to advise how to deconstruct and democratise the constitution. I was the fortunate recipient of the brief.

It was the most pleasant of jobs, drafting constitutional clauses between swims and snorkelling. René, like most Marxist leaders, had abolished appeals to the Privy Council (I could not persuade him to revive them) and confiscated the property of foreigners and opponents, and my new constitution had not only a Bill of Rights but a section which would enable those who had been expropriated to claim back their property, or else receive compensation. It was duly passed, and I left the Seychelles to its enjoyment of multi-party democracy.

Shortly afterwards, back in London at a birthday dinner for Billy Connolly, I found myself sitting next to George Harrison. He told me of his own love for the Seychelles – he had bought a property there, years before, with Peter Sellers, but it had been seized by the government. I looked at my watch. 'Well, George, you have eighteen hours to get it back' – that was when the time for claims to the new compensation tribunal ran out. George rushed through a claim and we returned together to a country delighted to have a Beatle back as a property owner. He met René, and there was some talk of making 'Here Comes the Sun' the country's national anthem. George is often depicted as curmudgeonly, but he was wickedly funny in private and his wife, Olivia, is always a delight. He would sit on the beach in the late afternoon, strumming a guitar, while elegantly dressed passers-by muttered disdainfully about allowing 'some old hippy' on their private beach. My wife had one moment of doubt, when she received a message from George's office asking her to take an unopened package to the Seychelles for him on her next trip: passing customs officials with a secret substance for a Beatle did give her pause, so she took a peek. It was hair dye.

Back in Britain, we would visit George and Olivia at their garden-fringed mansion, Friar Park, in Oxfordshire. It was an amazing museum of modern music, often with live exhibits. The elderly Indian gentleman nursing a sitar turned out to be Ravi Shankar; the small bald American inspecting the guitar collection was Paul Simon, and so on. George and Olivia were the kindest of hosts. George was particularly kind to Jules, teaching him how to pluck a guitar and putting up with his obsessive questions about the history of the band. Jules loved running around the amazing house – which is where tragedy soon struck.

The price of fame, sadly, is eternal vigilance, but George, an intensely private person, hated security – even after John Lennon's assassination. Inevitably, I suppose, there came a man – a very big man – who suffered from paranoid schizophrenia and whose voices had ordered him to save the world by killing a Beatle. He went to Liverpool to look for Paul (who had long since migrated to St John's Wood) and then heard that George lived somewhere near Marlow. He caught a train to this small, picturesque town on the Thames and made for the church to ask the vicar for directions. Although he must have looked wild and distracted, the vicar helpfully pointed him towards Friar Park. He broke in that night and savagely attacked George, causing serious injuries. Olivia, with a supreme strength endowed by love and courage, hit the intruder with a lamp and then a poker, rendering him unconscious. He was prosecuted, of course, and placed in a secure hospital, to be released only when Parole Board experts told the Home Secretary that he was no longer dangerous.

George and Olivia were concerned to be notified if that happened and I could understand George's worry – of course he should be warned when a man who had almost killed him through some mental compulsion would be back on the streets. They were not concerned necessarily to block the release, but wanted to be satisfied that his would-be killer was no longer a danger. But one defect in English law in 1999 was that it gave absolutely no rights to victims of crime – no right even to be represented in court when the assailant was being sentenced – so the release would be secret. That should change, I thought, and I stood up at the Bar table to address the judge before he passed sentence. Defending counsel tried to restrain me. 'Mr Robertson QC cannot be heard,' he shouted. 'It is immemorial tradition that victims have no role in sentencing.'

'Well, traditions are made to be broken, my Lord,' I countered, and the sentencing judge patiently listened to me break them – perhaps the first time that a lawyer for a victim has been allowed an address such as this. I did not want to influence the appropriate sentence; I merely wanted the judge to add a recommendation that George and Olivia should be notified before the Parole Board released the defendant. He was sympathetic but decided he had no power to make the recommendation. But journalists were there, in their dozens, and the argument was widely enough reported for the Home Secretary to state that he was minded to agree with it and to allow victims or their families to have their say in court and to be given warning of an assailant's release. Soon they were permitted to make 'victim impact statements', which would be read to the judge before sentence.

I suppose had 'victim impact statements' been on the cards when I was a young defence barrister at the Old Bailey, I would have vigorously opposed them. But now I really can't see any harm; in fact some good has come of them. So long as the statement is not too mawkish, or too vengeful, it helps the victim (if alive) and murder victims' family members to achieve some closure and to come to terms with their loss. And if it does serve to illuminate the harm and increase the sentence, so what? Those who kill or injure fellow humans cannot complain if their victims also receive justice.

The law's lack of concern for victims was a reflection of the inward-turning 'professionalisation' of penology: once the public phase of sentencing was over, all decisions about a prisoner would be made by experts, in utter secrecy, untroubled by emotional victims who might take angry feelings to tabloid newspapers, which would oppose the release of murderers or paedophiles. I had been instinctively approving of a system that allowed humane decisions to be taken in secret and which might not be taken at all if made in public, but I had never been friendly with a victim of serious crime until it happened to George – I could understand and sympathise with his concern to be told about the release of a man who had tried to kill him. In America, he pointed out, Yoko Ono had not only been told about plans to release John's killer but had been entitled to be represented at the parole hearing to cast doubt upon so-called expert prognosis as to his 'un-dangerousness'. In Britain, contrastingly, victims were treated by law-yers and officials as an embarrassment. In due course some changes were made, and victims were at least told about release dates, but Parole Board hearings remained secret and (quite absurdly) the reasons for its decisions could not be reported. It took legal action in 2018 by victims of the 'black cab rapist' John Worboys to uncover the secret reasons for the decision to release him – like so many decisions taken in secret, it turned out to be seriously flawed. When there is a case for humane treatment of serious offenders by returning them to society early, it must be good enough to withstand public scrutiny – those guilty of horrific crimes should have no automatic entitlement to secret absolution.

*　　*　　*

It always amuses me when friends are awarded their CBEs and OBEs: as a 'Commander of the British Empire', you command no more than half a dozen tax havens. That is, today, the main purpose of parts of the remaining Empire – Anguilla, Bermuda, Montserrat, the Cayman Islands and so on: to enable multinationals, and wealthy family trusts, to avoid tax. I once was taught that there was a difference between tax evasion and tax avoidance, but now I am less sure – they both enable the rich to shirk their duty to provide for the poor. It is a disgrace that this is how the UK operates on behalf of the wealthy of the world – in particular, American alcohol and pharmaceutical companies, who set up headquarters on coral-fringed 'treasure island' cays with low tax rates in order to defeat the US tax authorities. The only downside for them of such locations is that when disputes arise they must be fought in the local courts, virtually under a palm tree, and then on appeal to the Privy Council. Part of that downside, since American lawyers are not admitted to practise in UK dependencies, is that they must rely on English QCs to fight their legal battles.

It's a very scenic circuit, from Anguilla to Bermuda – the beaches are beautiful, the rum is the stuff of pirate legend and the judges can be dilatory. I travelled upon it to do a particularly exotic-sounding case – *Bacardi v Tequila*. It concerned the will of Martin Crowley, a Californian who had one great idea in his life. He realised that many American boomers would have had their first youthful bout of drunken sex after drinking cheap Mexican tequila. Now that they were getting old and wealthy, nostalgia (and Viagra) might drive them back to that drink – provided it could be beautifully refined and presented. So in 1989 he and a fellow entrepreneur, John Paul DeJoria (co-founder of the Paul Mitchell range of hair products), produced an exquisite tequila, decanted in handmade, numbered bottles, and called it Patrón. Sales at first were slow, but they started to pick up. Then, in 2003, Crowley died – a heart attack at his villa in Anguilla, where his drinks company was based for tax reasons. He had fallen out with his ex-wife, and they had no children of their own, so he left his estate – it was not at the time worth very much – to set up a trust called Windsong, to 'educate the poor children of the world'.

Soon the money from sales of Patrón started rolling in, and the share price rose high enough for his ex-wife to challenge the will. She failed, as did his father. DeJoria, however, had a contract which gave him the right to buy Crowley's shares on the latter's death. But for how much? Would the poor kids of the world get only US$5 million (the half value at the date of the contract) or US$150 million (the half value at the date of Crowley's death)? To complicate matters, the trustees did not have the money to fight DeJoria, so they did a deal with Bacardi (also based in the Caribbean for tax reasons) to fund their fight against him, in return for giving Bacardi the right to buy the shares for $200 million.

To complicate matters even further, the value of the shares just kept rising as more people started drinking Patrón. Actions were brought against the executors in Anguilla, but the Windsong Trust was based in California, where courts took a generous attitude towards their local charitable trusts. To cut a long legal story short, the poor kids of the world would receive much more money were the case heard in Los Angeles rather than in Anguilla, because the Privy Council (the island's final court of appeal) had judges who took a strict view of the English law of contracts and may well have decided to give only $5 million to educate the impoverished children.

So we embarked on that most aridly intellectual of all legal arguments – litigation over where to litigate. It is decided by applying rules described in Latin – *forum non conveniens*. I happened to be an expert on the subject, having appeared in many cases on behalf of American papers, which prefer to be sued for libel in New York (where they may win thanks to the First Amendment) rather than in London (where they will probably lose). It was for that arcane knowledge, rather than for my human rights experience, that the poor kids called me to Anguilla.

This lovely little island, named by Columbus because he thought it looked like an eel, is a footnote in British history. The UK did not want it, and tried to get rid of it by attaching it to another island, St Kitts, to which it was giving independence. But the Anguillans did not want independence and particularly did not want it with the St Kittians, whom they loathed. So they staged a kind of musical comedy revolution, confining the Governor General to his mansion and locking their British bobby in his police station. Harold Wilson, Prime Minister at the time, ordered an invasion – seventy SAS paratroopers were dropped on the beach, and to their bemusement greeted with hugs and flowers. The Anguillans all surrendered with great delight – now they could be dependent on Britain for ever! The island lives off its luxury hotels and luxury lawyers, who serve all the tax-avoiding companies based there. I was admitted to the Anguillan Bar and tried to move the case to California to win more money for the poor kids of the world – at least $250 million, because by this time Patrón's shares had doubled in value to $500 million.

The three parties claiming a share in this pie skirmished in Anguilla for a couple of years, as the pie grew meatier every month. Usually there was a judge on the island, although sometimes one had to be chased in a small plane around what stamp collectors know as the Leeward and Windward Islands. I would pack my wig and silk gown and take an eight-hour flight from London to Antigua, jump on a chartered single-engined Cessna for a dash across the sea to Anguilla, check in at a luxury beach hotel (there were no others) and prepare submissions for the next day. I never quite knew when the hearing would end: one sneaky opposing counsel found out the time of my flight back to London from Antigua and kept talking, hoping I would jettison my reply and run for the Cessna parked virtually outside. I certainly made my reply very quickly – it was probably all the better for concentrating on my best point – and then ran to the Cessna, its engines idling. We broke an airspeed record for small planes on the flight to the airport in Antigua, taxiing up to the big 747 just as they were about to remove the gangway. It was certainly more exciting than life on the Wales and Chester circuit.

In 2008, when the value of the shares reached $1 billion – Patrón really had taken off and my team (which included Californian lawyers and London's best litigation solicitor, Mark Stephens) was drinking it prolifically – all sides suddenly saw sense. Bacardi wanted to own the brand, DeJoria wanted money and hypothetically the poor kids wanted to be educated. Why not try mediation? We did, and our opponents did not do things by halves – the top floor of the Bellagio Hotel in Las Vegas was chosen as the venue where a New York mediator would attempt to bash our heads together. It worked, and the poor children of the world came away with US$550 million.[57] I promised to find some worthy kids to educate and suggested some schools in Palestine, although Windsong wants to work with the Prince's Trust so their choices may be less controversial. They did take up my suggestion to set up a tennis coaching club for Caribbean children in Anguilla, which is doing well despite the heat – roll on an Anguillan Davis Cup team.

*   *   *

My last appearance in the Caribbean, if only by telephone, was in 2016, in a curious case that led to the fall of the government of St Lucia. It was the result of the divorce of a beautiful American model by a fabulously wealthy Saudi Arabian sheikh. Christina Estrada had been a Pirelli calendar girl who had given up her modelling career to marry Dr Juffali, one of the world's wealthiest men (worth $20 billion, by some accounts). After eleven years he fell for a doe-eyed Lebanese television presenter and ended the marriage without telling his wife, simply by saying the Talaq ('I divorce thee') three times. The Talaq was recognised in the UK, but our family law, famously (or notoriously) favouring wives, applied to his assets – he had several homes in England, including a country estate, where he had lived for much of the time with Christina and their young daughter while amassing his fortune. He had a horror of English matrimonial law ever since he had divorced his first wife – a court in London had awarded her $10 million, a record at the time. Now, the tabloids predicted that the award to Christina was likely to be the highest in British history and he did not want to pay it.

Here's a question. If you are one of the richest men in the world, how do you evade an obligation that binds everyone else – the law about division of matrimonial assets in the land where you are living? You take advice from a good lawyer, obviously, and it may give you the idea of buying a large yacht and cruising the Caribbean. You moor at a small island state you may never have heard of, and have lunch with local people of influence (easy to find in St Lucia, with a population of only 178,000). In due course, but unknown to St Lucians, the government appoints you as St Lucia's ambassador to the Court of St James, a high diplomatic post which carries complete immunity to the law – including the divorce law – of the UK.

Thus it was that Dr Juffali became St Lucia's plenipotentiary to a little-known United Nations body in London, the International Maritime Organisation, although he had no connection to St Lucia and no knowledge of merchant shipping laws, or mercantile safety, or any other topic that this obscure organisation exists to consider. Although he never bothered to turn up to any of its meetings, his very appointment to this esteemed position guaranteed him diplomatic immunity from any action in the UK courts which would require him to support his ex-wife and child. When Christina made her application to the family court, after he refused to enter into an agreement to support her, the sheikh's solicitors pointed out, to her amazement, that he was a high diplomatic personage immune from any legal process. She seemed to be legally snookered.

That was when her wily solicitor, Negar Yazdani, sought my advice. I knew no matrimonial law, but I did know constitutions and I knew Sir Ivor Roberts, the editor of *Satow's Diplomatic Practice* (the diplomat's bible) and one of the UK's most distinguished former ambassadors. He explained just why the sheikh's acquisition of his immunity was unlawful, and would in any event bring the whole system of diplomatic immunity into disrepute.[58] I prepared a forceful judicial review claim against the St Lucian government, and found a plucky local lawyer to file it (not an easy task on a small island where most lawyers were connected with – often, related to – the government). My appointment to the St Lucian Bar was accomplished by a pleasant telephone call to the court of the local judge and I prepared by packing my swimming trunks beneath my wig and gown.

Once the case was filed, the scandal became public. The government had kept very quiet about the appointment, and the people of St Lucia had no idea that their country had been represented for the past two years by a billionaire sheikh. The government played the patriot card, claiming that we were part of a Western plot to undermine the independence of small islands (this did not wash with cynical St Lucians) and it tried to postpone the impending elections until the scandal had blown over.

Cases like this, for all their interest to lawyers, are usually won or lost by less formal means of combat. My most significant contribution was to meet with the foreign editor of Britain's *Daily Telegraph* – a paper that still cared about diplomatic niceties – to give him an exclusive on the story about our application in St Lucia to quash Juffali's appointment. The report caused flutters in diplomatic dovecotes – it coincided with concerns about Caribbean islands selling their passports to international criminals, and the UK Foreign Office began to wonder whether it had been right to accept without question the dubious credentials of Dr Juffali as St Lucia's ambassador to the Court of St James. The tabloids, of course, picked up the story of the ex-Pirelli calendar girl and her quest for what they described as the largest divorce settlement in history. The sheikh retained an expensive law firm and a big public relations agency in an attempt to fight Christina's action in England, but his Achilles heel was St Lucia, where a new government could simply revoke his appointment or else waive his immunity. I turned to an old friend, Sir Nick Lloyd, chairman of the imaginative international PR firm BLJ, to get to work on the opposition in St Lucia, encouraging them to fight the election over the appointment. The more the opposition attacked the government over its secret deal with the sheikh, the more their electoral prospects improved: their main promise, if elected, was to end Dr Juffali's immunity by revoking his appointment. They were elected.

This result was curtains for the sheikh and his immunity from the maintenance claim by his wife. His daring plan to evade British divorce law by donning the invisible cloak of immunity was shattered, and the English Court of Appeal found him a UK resident. Not long afterwards, sadly, he entered a clinic in Switzerland, where he died from cancer. I do not doubt that Dr Juffali was an ingenious and generous man, but after his divorce he could not divorce himself from a cultural mindset that insisted on keeping an ex-wife under his thumb, dependent on his handouts rather than receiving maintenance by right.

As for the law relating to diplomatic immunity, it certainly has its oddities (Julian Assange, on one view, has been a beneficiary) and it is open to serious abuse, as when guns and drugs are smuggled in the sacrosanct 'diplomatic pouch' and consular criminals are protected from prosecution for serious crimes. Its use should be limited as far as possible – the case of Dr Juffali has at least caused the Foreign Office to reconsider its automatic acceptance of diplomatic credentials (although not so far as to disqualify

all the Sir Les Pattersons). The most common abuse in London is the refusal of embassies to pay parking fines – diplomatic vehicles cause congestion
by parking wherever they like, and the Americans, who rack up over $1
million in fines every year, refuse to pay them. This is ironic, since it is
the US which solved the problem of unpaid embassy fines in New York
by deducting the amount from each country's aid budget, and the worst
offenders quickly stopped offending.

*   *   *

I log more air miles in a month than my father managed throughout the
war. I have only been in one emergency. Mine was on the way to Trinidad
on the government airline BWIA. It stood for British West Indian Airlines, although the local interpretation of the acronym was 'But Will It
Arrive?' It didn't when I flew on one of its planes with Lord Mackay, Mrs
Thatcher's Lord Chancellor, whose counsel I was for a Royal Commission
into the legal system of Trinidad and Tobago. The good lord was famously
religious – a member of the Free Presbyterian Church of Scotland (sometimes known as the Wee Wee Frees), the last outpost of sixteenth-century
Calvinism. He sat across the aisle, submerged in the latest John Grisham.
The old three-engined TriStar shook a bit when one engine shut down
halfway across the Atlantic, but he did not look up from his novel. Then
the second engine seemed to explode and the pilot told us that he would
have to make an emergency landing in the Azores. This was when I noticed
the royal commissioner had replaced his John Grisham with a copy of the
Bible. I wished his prayers well (Kathy and Julius were on board) as we
went bumping and grinding through the clouds to a clump of rock in the
middle of the ocean. We crash-landed bumpily and I made a dash to hire
the island's only taxi to get my family and Lord Mackay to the island's only
hotel. I called the Attorney General of Trinidad to assure him that we were
safe – the plane had been listed as missing. *The Times* ran the story the next
day, of how Kathy Lette and Lord Mackay were on board, and it produced
some speculation at the Bar about how they would survive if marooned
together on a desert island.

In all these cases, and many more, I have been privileged – by dint of being an English QC – to promote the values of free speech and fair trial in courts of the Commonwealth that have one thing in common: they are bound by constitutions that direct them to respect the rule of law. It often strikes me as regrettable that these fifty-three cricket-playing nations (well, leave out Canada) cannot set up a human rights court that encourages compliance with the basic rules of the justice game. But what the Commonwealth really needs, if it is to have any traction in the world, is inspirational and charismatic leadership. For some years it had a virtually invisible Indian diplomat as its Secretary General, who would not have known a human right had he fallen over one. His recent replacement, Patricia Scotland, has done her best to reform the secretariat, but is hamstrung by a tiny budget and fifty-three 'High Commissioners' – often retired politicans – who dote on the royal family and treasure their invitations to the palace. They were a pushover when the Queen insisted in 2018 that her successor as head of the Commonwealth – a position which is not hereditary – should go to her eldest son. Charles is not independent (this is not the British Commonwealth any longer) and is hardly inspirational. They might have chosen someone who is – Graça Machel, for example, Nelson Mandela's widow and a fine humanitarian. And since the only qualification for the job is to have a parent born in a Commonwealth country, they missed the opportunity to invite the perfect candidate, whose father was born in Kenya. A man both charismatic and competent, whose voice could combat the stupidities of Donald Trump; they lacked the imagination to crown Barack Obama as head of the Commonwealth.

Chapter Twelve

Doughty Street Chambers

The Temple is a part of London, between Fleet Street and the Thames, where legal and literary ghosts float into focus. Across from the gas lamps outside my rooms in Dr Johnson's Buildings, where tourist guides would imagine the good doctor at verbal play with Boswell, stands the Temple Church, built by the crusading order of monks, the Knights Templar. They lie there, with their effigies over their graves and broadswords resting on their chests of chain mail, featuring most recently in a scene in the movie *The Da Vinci Code*. The Pope closed down their order in the fourteenth century, partly because of allegations that they were abusing small boys – *plus ça change*.

In 1998 I was made a Master of the Middle Temple, which has its own by-laws – for example, it is an offence within its precincts not to address me as 'Master', a rule which upset my wife. I have a flat which overlooks the courtyard where *Twelfth Night* was first performed before Queen Elizabeth I in 1602. This apartment once belonged in Charles Dickens's imagination to Pip, the hero of *Great Expectations*: in Chapter 39, he hears clumping on the stairs and to his horror meets his real benefactor – the convict Magwitch, returned from Botany Bay. The bells of St Paul's ring in the distance, and just opposite is Middle Temple Hall (familiar from many movies), where the armour of barristers who went to war against King Charles I in the 1640s, arranged around its circumference, looks down on a large portrait of their royal enemy painted by Van Dyck. After grace, masters may dine on a table that served Sir Francis Drake aboard the *Golden Hinde*, and at the doors stand the two giant globes on which Sir Walter Raleigh planned his voyages. Cartographers in the time of Elizabeth I had no inkling of the Great South Land – I dine looking at a world without Australia.

It was here that I came across one important ghost that historians had overlooked, and I wrote a book about him. John Cooke was a brave and brilliant barrister. He was a plebeian from a poor share-cropping family, but he managed through Puritan connections to win a scholarship to Oxford, and later defended radicals. When Oliver Cromwell's weak-kneed lawyers refused to commit treason by arraigning Charles I – despite his responsibility for starting the civil war – Cooke took the brief and prosecuted him on the charge of tyranny, accusing him of torturing prisoners, burning civilian towns and ordering other actions which today would be described as crimes against humanity. He drafted Parliament's declaration of a republic and then its statute abolishing the House of Lords, and later served as a judge until the return of Charles II, who had him convicted at a rigged trial and disembowelled ('hanged, drawn and quartered') in front of a crowd of jeering royalists.

Cooke was a great visionary, whose writings first envisaged a national health service and a system for legal aid, as well as the abolition of Latin in courtrooms. He upset his profession by insisting that barristers should do at least 10 per cent of their work for free – an ethic I had in mind when I set up Doughty Street Chambers. He was first to work out a way to hold a head of state accountable for crimes against his own people – a way which was not explored again for centuries, until international criminal law began at Nuremberg and later came to grips with the likes of General Pinochet, Slobodan Milošević, Charles Taylor and Saddam Hussein. He was, some reviewers surmised, the barrister I would most like to have been.

I discovered John Cooke by happenstance, when my old monarchist friend Michael Kirby, elevated to Australia's High Court, was invited to the Inns of Court to lecture, on the 350th anniversary of the King's trial, about how unfair it all was. I was asked to deliver a response, and thinking that the occasion would be full of irreverent law students, I prepared to entertain them with ribald republican jests. I was unaware how far Michael's fame had spread: his lecture was graced by most of Her Majesty's judges, who were shocked by my efforts to celebrate her ancestor's beheading with antipodean *lèse-majesté*. But I had blown the dust off enough law books to realise that historians – and Michael – were wrong about the trial and negligent in ignoring John Cooke, and in *The Tyrannicide Brief* I tried to put the record straight.[59] David Williamson later turned it into a play, which had a much better reception from Her Majesty's judges when it was performed at Gray's Inn in 2012.

*   *   *

English barristers work from 'chambers' – a set of rooms and clerks servicing a collection of individual advocates operating in the same area of the law, who pool resources and have a somewhat feudal connection with the 'head', who gives the chambers its character and stature. Dr Johnson's Buildings earned its repute when it was home to Clifford Mortimer, who was blind and was immortalised for his forensic cunning in his son's play *A Voyage Round My Father*. During my tenancy, as I have described in Chapter Six, it was led by Emlyn Hooson QC, the Welsh Liberal MP who always gave me encouragement and support. He attracted others of his tribe, who were very congenial but somewhat infatuated with the pretensions of the Bar – our clerks would have to walk behind them, carrying their robes, up and down the Wales and Chester circuit.

It was not so much the Welsh Liberals as the mice in the skirting boards, woodworm in the walls and the erratic heating system, which seemed to have spluttered for several centuries, that inclined me to look elsewhere and to set up a chambers that would be different to the self-satisfied coteries of the English Bar, notorious for denying access to women and minorities. They were run by venal clerks on commission, who discriminated on grounds of sex, race and politics in allotting work. Male barristers, mostly from private schools and Oxbridge, tended to offer 'seats' to young men of similar pedigree, and the result of this cloning affected not only the profession but the judiciary recruited from it: upper-middle-class, white, male and complacent. Barristers had complete immunity from ever being sued for negligence: they were the incarnation of the Ogden Nash couplet:

Professional men, they have no cares,
Whatever happens, they get theirs.

Twenty colleagues from Dr Johnson's Buildings joined me with the aim of changing all this. We wanted to maintain the independence of the individual practitioner – which is the true glory of the Bar – but to work in a more consumer-friendly environment, using our intellectual strengths and pooled resources to run campaigns on behalf of our clients; to lobby for progressive law reform; to set up human rights charities; hold lectures and seminars; support the legal aid system; and generally to harness collegiate force to defend clients against the power of the state. Striking out from the protective traditions of the Temple was a gamble, but Lord Mackay, as Lord Chancellor, was urging deregulation and I had confidence in my colleagues – well justified in due course, when three were made High Court judges, one became the Chief Coroner and several more were appointed to judicial positions.

In 1990 we found some houses in Doughty Street, Bloomsbury, within walking distance of the High Court. The street came with its own history – it had been listed in the eleventh-century Domesday Book as 'a vineyard surrounding a wood for 100 pigs', which seemed an appropriate place for grubbing lawyers. Charles Dickens was still in evidence – he had lived next door, in a house that was now a museum with a pleasant coffee shop in its gardens, to which clients could repair and read *Bleak House*, a sobering story of how madness comes from the law's delays and complexities. Opposite was the former home of the essayist Sydney Smith, who had famously called the Society for the Suppression of Vice 'a Society for suppressing the vices of persons whose income does not exceed £500 per annum'. As many of my early battles were against Mary Whitehouse, I felt in good company.

We decided that for our post-modern Bar practice, in a dramatically changing society, we would need someone we called a 'practice manager' to promote our ethos that law should be for the many and not for the few, and foster our practices so that we made enough money to pay the rent – at home, and of chambers. There were no 'practice managers' at the

Bar in those days, but we drafted an advert and interviewed the applicants. The best had a Master's degree in Chinese and experience as a press officer at CND, so we took her – Christine Kings – on spec, as it were. She turned out to be just the ticket, terrific to work with and deserving of much of the credit for keeping us on an onward and upward trajectory in our first eighteen years (most Chambers now have a practice manager, and Christine is among the most respected). We also hired a female senior clerk – virtually unheard of in the Temple – and committed to diversity in hiring new members. I was the only QC when we started; a quarter of a century later, we have thirty-four silks, eleven of whom are women, as are fifty-one of our 110 junior counsel, and we keep winning awards for our dedication to diversity and gender equality.

I drafted a founding philosophy which stated our imperishable commitment to the legal aid system, always under attack from governments looking to make budget cuts (so much so that in 2014 barristers in England actually went on strike, protesting colourfully – they wore their wigs and gowns – while I made speeches from the back of a truck, like a trade union leader). Those cuts in legal aid put some rival chambers out of business, but the funding model I had established at the start saw us through. Our barristers divide 50/50 into criminal and civil practitioners. Half of our work is done at full commercial rate, while the other half is made up of legal aid (paid by the state at about one-third or less of the commercial rate) and cases done 'pro bono' – these, my wife said, are the Latin words she most wishes never to hear again, unless they mean I am acting for a wealthy Irish rock star.

Our founding philosophy also stated our dedication to the taxi-rank rule, whereby barristers undertake, subject to availability, to accept any client whose case comes within their field of practice. This is to ensure that access to justice is afforded to all, however obnoxious. We have acted for some obnoxious clients, ranging from Myra Hindley and Abu Hamza to Silvio Berlusconi and the UK Home Office, but have always given it our best – for a barrister, I think there is no point giving any less. We did make one exception: 'The only work we will refuse on principle involves the upholding of death sentences.' I did not think at the time that we were likely to be asked to uphold any, but of course times change and my solicitor friend from Trinidad, Ramesh Maharaj, once so keen to instruct me to save his clients on death row, became the Attorney General in a government pledged to bring back the death penalty. It came under great pressure from the US to rid the region of a gangster named Dole Chadee, allegedly the Caribbean's leading drug trafficker. Ramesh sent me the brief to prosecute Chadee and his gang for murder, which carried a mandatory death sentence. For that reason, I declined. Ramesh begged me to find a lawyer less bothered about the principle, so I nominated my friend Tim Cassel QC, insouciant about the consequence of his cases, and a rather good prosecutor. A week later came a call from Chadee's solicitor in Trinidad – would I accept a brief to save his client's neck? I agonised – not because the fee offered was astronomical, although it was (he was a very big drug trafficker), but I had opened the prosecution brief, and felt ethically conflicted about accepting instructions from the defence. Chadee and his gang were convicted, and Ramesh (well versed, as my one-time junior in the Privy, in death penalty jurisprudence) rushed them to the gallows before the rule in Pratt & Morgan could operate to commute their sentences.

A record survives of the Doughty Street launch party. We hired a jukebox and I stood on a packing crate to announce that we had moved out of a museum and into the real world: 'We want Doughty Street to become an engine room where barristers are stoked by solicitors instead of being stroked by solicitors; where law fuels fact in a spontaneous combustion of ideas and tactics; where the fire in the belly is tempered by the iron in the soul' and so on, through many mixed metaphors. I promised we would strive to abolish the 'pantomime flummery' of wigs and wing collars, and the unfair rule of barristers' immunity from actions for negligence. My most revolutionary promise was that we would have a crèche, in which our own and our solicitors' children and even our clients' children would be welcome. This is the only promise upon which we have not yet delivered.

We immediately initiated the Doughty Street lecture series, bringing over from New York the impassioned Professor Nadine Strossen, president of the American Civil Liberties Union, to explain just what a full-blooded commitment to civil liberties could mean. The most moving and influential Doughty Street lecture was given to a packed audience in St Martin-in-the-Fields on World Aids Day in 1995 by Michael Kirby. He unveiled a charter for compassionate reform of anti-LGBT laws, which was taken up by lawyers throughout the Commonwealth and is now a full-time project run by one of our outstanding gay barristers, Jonathan Cooper. We also began, at an early stage, to donate some of our earnings to causes and campaigns that promoted our beliefs about justice – one of the first was the Arthur Koestler Trust, to teach art to prisoners, while more recently we have expended considerable resources on campaigning against the UK government's inadequate response to the refugee crisis. We acquired more members – notably Kirsty Brimelow, chair of the Bar Human Rights Committee, and James Wood, an expert on righting wrongful convictions – of the Bridgewater Four and other victims of police mistakes.

As head of chambers, I became a member of that charmed circle of the legal establishment 'sounded' by the Lord Chancellor about judicial and silk appointments, and responsible for disciplining any of my members who got up a judicial nose. Helena Kennedy was the first 'Doughty Street irregular' to take silk, in 1991 (to the delight of her compatriot, Lord Mackay, who granted it). After a murder trial in which her clients were acquitted, I received a long, hand-written complaint from an elderly High Court judge, who wanted me to discipline her for speaking in a language he could not understand (she had a strong Glaswegian accent) and for wearing a collection of silver bangles which, he complained, had distracted – if not bewitched – the jury into a wrongful acquittal. I suggested that he make his complaint to Helena herself, but he lacked the gumption to do so. Helena – now a baroness advancing law reform as Chair of Justice and principal of Mansfield College, Oxford, where she has founded a new human rights institute – escaped any 'discipline'; I really think the old judge wanted me to put her over my knee. He was an example of that dying generation who could not cope with women at the Bar, and certainly not in silk.

I made some law on the subject of professional kissing when a difficult client, upset to be told she had no case, complained to the Bar Council that

I had greeted her solicitor, Ruth Bundey, with a kiss. Indeed I had – Ruthie was an old friend whom I had not seen for a while, and the complaint was dismissed without a hearing. There was an appeal, to which I was not even asked to respond. The verdict in my favour established the rule (it was not found in *Boulton on Ethics*) that barristers may kiss their solicitor. I would not rely on it too much in these #MeToo days, except in the case of old friends. At Doughty Street we have a strict code of conduct which precludes inappropriate behaviour towards employees or pupils or juniors. The Bar's code of conduct is rather vague on the subject of advances to or from clients. I encountered the question only once, very early in my career, when propositioned by a glamorous porn star after a final speech that secured her acquittal. I asked around: would it be ethical, after the trial, to accept? 'Of course not,' my colleagues said. 'She's only attracted to you because of the power exerted by your professional persona.' 'She wants to repay you for your professional services – and you've already been paid by legal aid.' John Mortimer, however, saw no ethical difficulty. I did not accept the invitation, although more as a matter of prudence than ethics. These days you can telephone the Bar Council's Ethics Hotline to find out the answer before you disrobe.

Doughty Street's first major case was *Pratt & Morgan v Jamaica* (described in Chapter Eleven), which led to mass commutations of death penalties in the Caribbean, and my colleagues in chambers had it accepted by courts in East Africa and even Zimbabwe (where, as a result, you cannot be hanged after death row delays). Another early case produced a change in English law – recognition of 'battered woman syndrome', which induces women to react to longstanding violent abuse by eventually lashing out and even killing the abusive partner. English common law, fashioned by men down the centuries, had never allowed for post-traumatic stress disorder, or for the slow burn of anger that can finally erupt in furious retribution. Women who killed brutal lovers were guilty of murder and jailed for life – one of them, Ruth Ellis, was the last to be executed in Britain.

The woman in my case was Kiranjit Ahluwalia, whom I had met first in prison in 1991, two years into her life sentence. She was a small and frail

Indian mother with the saddest eyes I have ever seen. Her early hopes of a career after university had been shattered when her family insisted on an arranged marriage with a man named Deepak, whom she had never met. He beat her almost every day and, despite court orders intended to put an end to his violence, threatened to kill her with a knife and on one occasion tried to run her over. The only reason she could give for staying with him was her two young children, but another reason, given by our psychiatric experts, was that he had reduced her to a state of learnt helplessness – she was totally in his power. I read to the court an abject letter she had written to Deepak after he had gone off for a few days with another woman:

> *Deepak, if you come back I promise you – I won't touch black coffee again, I won't go town every week, I won't eat green chilli, I am ready to leave Chandigarh and all my friends, I won't go near Goodie Mohan's house again. Even I am not going to attend Bully's wedding, I eat too much or all the time so I can get fat, I won't laugh if you don't like, I won't dye my hair even, I don't go to my neighbour's house, I won't ask you for any help.*

In this pathetic state, she awaited his return. She put her child to bed (the other was with friends) and made her husband's dinner. Deepak threatened to beat her if she did not give him money, and held a hot iron next to her face before he fell into a drunken sleep. Several hours later she took a bucketful of petrol and a lit candle, and threw them onto his bed. Rushing to her child's bedroom, she picked him up and stood at his window in a daze, shouting to neighbours, 'I am waiting for my husband.'

Deepak died of his burns, and by the end of the year Kiranjit had been convicted of his murder. (I was not acting for her at this stage.) The court heard little of her mental state, other than from a prosecution expert who said she suffered from 'endogenous depression'. I wonder whether anyone looked up the meaning of 'endogenous' ('very deep').

At the appeal, where I appeared with my (very) learned junior, Andy (now Sir Andrew) Nicol, our six experts verified the existence of the state of learnt helplessness. The Chief Justice agreed that this could amount to a defence of diminished responsibility, which would reduce murder to manslaughter, thereby enabling Kiranjit's immediate release – to the cheers of the women's groups who had supported us.[60]

It was a precedent that would help other women in her predicament avoid a soul-destroying life sentence. I was not exactly Billy Flynn (the flamboyant death row lawyer in *Chicago* who gets Roxie Hart off her murder charge by manipulating the media), but Kiranjit's case was made into a movie, *Provoked*, with Miranda Richardson and various other stars. To my children's amusement, my character was played by Robbie Coltrane – for ever, to their minds, Hagrid in the *Harry Potter* movies.

*   *   *

Now that I was a head of chambers, I was deemed sufficiently respectable to be considered for the judiciary. Not as a High Court judge (I was too young, at forty-five, and doubted whether I wanted a full-time judicial career), but as a Recorder, a part-time judge who for four to six weeks each year conducts trials and passes sentence on the guilty. I went before a selection committee and was asked whether I had ever done anything which might be made a subject of scandal in the media. I told them I had never done and could never do anything of which my mother would disapprove. This seemed to satisfy them, but then I had to attend 'judge school', held in a hotel in the English countryside, where would-be judges are taught how to send people to prison. It was a little like *Lawyer's Got Talent* – you would be given the facts and then required to produce a sentence and a sentencing homily which was marked by three judges from the Court of Appeal, who failed you if you were over-merciful. The hotel was used for other training courses, and one of the waitresses confided, 'We like the judges best. They've all been to private schools so they know how to eat up their pud.'

I passed the course, and was soon presiding over my first trial. I was determined not to be the kind of judicial fuddy-duddy who would ask, 'Who are the Beatles?' My first case was about a fight between sex workers – the defendant, the prosecution alleged, had pulled out her rival's hair extensions. 'Er ... What are hair extensions?' the new judge had to ask. It was little comfort that the prosecutor did not know either: he had to call a women police officer to explain. I straightened my wig – my own hair extensions – to hide my embarrassment.

When my usher came in with the papers for my next case, I sniffed red meat. It was a computer thief, pleading guilty to nicking a large number of computers. I had recently had my own computer stolen in a burglary at my chambers, and I came into court fully determined to send this miscreant to prison.

'I am sorry, Your Honour,' said the prosecutor, 'I will have to ask you to stand down from this case.'

'Why on earth?' I was certainly not going to let this one be moved to a merciful colleague.

'The defendant has returned several of the stolen computers, and one of them is yours.'

I gave in – you cannot be a judge in your own cause or your own case. *The Guardian* ran the story under the headline 'BURGLAR MEETS VICTIM: HIS JUDGE'.

In the mid-1990s, Doughty Street came to political prominence, not only in the Commonwealth, where our Privy Council cases had stopped executions in many countries, but also in the United Kingdom itself, where my defence in the Matrix Churchill trial had exposed the arms-to-Iraq affair. As the plot unravelled in court, Doughty Street on occasion hosted the Labour Party front bench, who came for briefings. When the trial collapsed after Alan Clark admitted to being 'economical with the actualité', the Conservative government (now led by John Major) survived a censure motion by one vote. This was the era of 'Tory sleaze', which deepened when Neil Hamilton, then a junior government minister, sued *The Guardian* for alleging, in what was called the cash-for-questions scandal, that he had been paid to ask questions in Parliament by Mohamed Al Fayed, the proprietor of Harrods. I went to see Al Fayed and persuaded him to come up with evidence, not only against the minister but against six other Tory MPs. The libel action was withdrawn at the door of the court and 'Tory sleaze' helped to ensure Tony Blair's landslide victory in 1997.

The most bizarre – and most publicised – of my cases came in 1995, after a 'world exclusive' in the *Sunday Mirror* two years earlier: 'Di Spy Sensation – The Most Amazing Pictures You'll Ever See'. The photographs, spread over seven pages, were of Princess Diana exercising on a contraption called a leg press, taken by a camera sneakily hidden in the ceiling by the gym owner, Bryce Taylor, an impecunious New Zealander. The princess, out to prove herself after separation from Charles, was advised (badly, as it turned out) to go down in British history by issuing a novel action which would create a hitherto unrecognised civil wrong – invasion of privacy.[61]

The High Court judge who first heard her claim thought that such a dramatic change in the law should at least be contested – he extended legal aid to Bryce and asked me to represent him, which would mean cross-examining the people's princess. I would need to explore under cross-examination Diana's two-faced attitude to privacy – she had told the tawdry secrets of her marriage to journalist Andrew Morton for a book (*Diana: Her True Story*) which blackened Charles's name. A mock-up courtroom was constructed at Kensington Palace so she could prepare for my cross-examination, and 940 journalists applied for the seventy-five press seats in Court 36 of the Royal Courts of Justice. The courtroom artists, who produced what were meant to be accurate portraits of court proceedings but who were banned from sketching in court, had already painted our encounter: I was depicted, all jowls and splutter, pitted against the Queen of Hearts, radiant in the witness box.

I prepared for this case by doing something I had avoided throughout my life: joining a gym. I even learnt to 'cardio-funk', an exercise that Diana had been doing at Taylor's gym, which 'combines funky dance steps with aerobic moves set to hip-hop music'. I avoided her choreographed colonics, but learnt the art of toning my buttock muscles on instruments of torture called the life-cycle, the rotary torso, the lateral pull-down machine and the Concept2 rowing ergometer. As the tabloids rejoiced – salivated, in fact – over the upcoming courtroom clash, the establishment was wary: *The Times* described me as 'anti-establishment, republican and Australian', presumably in ascending order of horror. Journalists door-stepped my parents at our Sydney home – what advice would they give the princess? 'I would settle out of court,' said my father. And so she did – on the evening before 'the trial of the century'. There was a deal, and her lawyers withdrew her claim, reportedly after depositing a million dollars in Bryce's Swiss bank account. This was all swathed in secrecy, of course, so the princess could claim to have 'won', although it would be an odd sort of victory if the loser were to be rewarded with a sum greater than the 'winner' had claimed in damages. I cancelled my gym membership, forgot about cardio-funk and moved on, somewhat deflated, as always when a big case settles at the door of the court. It's a condition my wife called 'courtus interruptus'.

*   *   *

I published my memoir *The Justice Game* in 1998 – unusually, in mid-career, but that was the point. I wanted to look back on my profession while I was still part of it, with enough fire in my belly to argue for a Human Rights Act to put right some of the injustices I had encountered in my early days at the Bar. The Act was placed on the statute book by the Blair government later that year, and British law gradually became much the better for it. After my role in exposing Tory MPs in the arms-to-Iraq scandal and the cash-for-questions case, many assumed I would be made an attack dog for the new government: *Private Eye* pictured me in the new Cabinet as 'Persecutor General'. The call did not come, of course – Sir Humphrey would have disapproved and so would his political bosses. I was thrown one small crumb – the Minister for Culture and Sport nominated me for a position on the Royal Opera House board, although a fuss about the lack of diversity caused it to prefer Trevor McDonald, a newsreader born in Trinidad.

Not a single brief came to Doughty Street from the Labour government (if it had, they might have lost fewer cases) until Tony Blair himself was subjected to a police investigation alleging that he had hawked honours in return for large financial donations to the party (the cash-for-peerages scandal). At the party's request, I analysed the defective law – which had hardly been reformed since Lloyd George got away with it – and the defective police investigation, and pronounced the Prime Minister entirely innocent, as the law stood. My other contribution to his character was in respect of his invasion of Iraq (to which I was personally and legally opposed): I had to point out to the media that he was not guilty, as his ill-informed enemies would have it, of the crime of aggression. That, however, was because such a crime did not exist in English law, and because the international crime of aggression had not been brought into force. I added that it should be, with an urgency that is now manifest with the advent of Donald Trump.

Meanwhile, our children were growing up and going to school – there was a cubby and trampoline for them in the garden of our house at Swiss Cottage and the hamsters died unnatural deaths somewhere beneath the floorboards. We never had time for that normal perquisite of the middle-class metropolitan Londoner, a country cottage, although we took up John and Penny Mortimer's standing invitation to weekends in the Chilterns and we rented places in summer when our parents came to call. Kathy had by now been accepted, after a rough start, as part of the London literati, and was overwhelmed at being accorded an honorary degree from a university in Southampton – a Companion of Literature, which *Private Eye*, reporting her citation in cod Latin, abbreviated to a C. Lit. We did take advantage of my quiet flat in the Middle Temple for writing retreats, and I had a third home in the business-class compartments of long-haul jets, where I would mug up on the arguments I would have to present on landing. As my parents became too old to travel, I was impelled to find reasons – lectures, *Hypotheticals*, in 2014 even a stage show, *Dreaming Too Loud* – to visit them in Sydney. I acquired a second office in my brother's chambers – Tim was by now an SC, or Senior Counsel, as barristers in other countries prefer to say in preference to 'Queen's Counsel', which can give the wrong impression. It's one change that the English Bar will never make: how we love our sealed vellum parchment in its morocco-coloured pouch, signed (allegedly) by the Queen and describing us as her 'trusty and well-beloved' servants. We will all be KCs – King's Counsel – before too long, and for at least (given all the male heirs) another century.

* * *

It is one of the more arcane duties of a Queen's Counsel to advise the monarch, when called upon, free of charge. This may be a quid pro quo for a royal monopoly which allows us to double the fees we charge the common people. Nonetheless, becoming a silk is an important rite of passage – the effective bestowal of a 'Good Housekeeping Seal of Approval' by your profession upon your character and ability to argue the law. The decision as to when in your career to make the application is crucial, and most wait until they have notched up twenty years of trials and appeals; ever ambitious, I applied after twelve and was knocked back by Lord Chancellor Hailsham, a Tory grandee I had unwisely criticised in print. The following year, 1987, saw the appointment of the even-handed Lord Mackay, who in 1988 granted my letters patent. Then came a grand ceremony in the House of Lords for which we dressed in full-length wigs and new silk robes, wearing beneath them silk stockings and suspender belts. (I kid you not – this is a ceremony beloved by centuries of upper-class Englishmen.) We took our clerks, dressed in morning suits and proud smiles, our partners (Nigella accompanied me) and relatives (Tim came over for the occasion). The Lord Chancellor warned us not to get our names in the *News of the World* and invited us to order, for a modest fee, a videotape of the ceremony. It then became a bit silly, as we were required to parade in our robes through courts in which we practised, bowing three times to each presiding judge. It was exhausting (I practised in a lot of courts) and I went home for a sleep, almost missing my own party at the Wig and Pen Club, an ancient hostelry in Fleet Street where Henry VIII once disported himself.

I have yet to be called on to counsel Her Majesty free of charge, although I did advise her daughter-in-law's lover, James Hewitt. The press was in full pursuit after the story broke of his royal romance, so he hid in a converted pigsty in the south of France and then prevailed on an army pilot to helicopter him to north London, where he hid in our attic for a few days while I mulled over the 1351 Treason Act, which still punished with death any party to adultery with the wife of the monarch's eldest son and heir. James was bang to rights and Diana would have been guilty as an accomplice, although I had to doubt whether she would suffer the same fate as Anne Boleyn.

I have managed to rattle some royal ghosts – or, at least, their executors – in a curious case about royal wills. It is a longstanding tradition – almost a constitutional principle – that a will, once probated, is a public document: everyone is entitled to know, once we have shuffled off this mortal coil, how much we are worth and to whom we have left it. There has long been a law more or less to that effect, but the royals, since 1913, have been treated as exempt, although the law itself does not exempt them and until this particular case, nobody knew why, or how, the exemption had originated. The case was brought by a respectable and undoubtedly sane citizen – an accountant, indeed – who entertained the firm and fervent belief that he was the love child of Princess Margaret. He thought that his putative mother might have left him a legacy in her will, as might her mum, the good-hearted Queen Mother, and for this reason he sought to inspect these documents. He was acting in good faith, the courts said, but his belief was illusory – to this I did not demur. But what right did the royal executors have to deny him a look?

My researches uncovered a very English cover-up. Back in the early years of the twentieth century, Prince Francis of Teck made a will in which he left a favoured mistress some jewellery belonging to the Crown. Afraid of scandal, his sister, Queen Mary, arranged for the senior probate judge to order that the will be 'sealed' – kept secret from all but the executors, who were the royal family's solicitors. This convenient arrangement became a precedent, applied in the case of royal wills thereafter, without public discussion or even knowledge. Just a royal nod and wink to a senior judge, and an order made behind closed doors. I commenced a case – which still continues – arguing the public interest in unsealing royal wills, and the legitimate concerns of historians, journalists and especially the tax office to inspect them.[62] The royals have plenty of privileges in life and there is no good reason why they should claim a special privilege in death.

My contribution to making Britain safe for republicanism came in 2002, when *The Guardian* decided to mount a full-blooded campaign to abolish the royal family. This was illegal under the Treason Felony Act of 1848, passed in panic after the anti-monarchy insurgencies in Europe that had caused my own royal relatives to take ship to Sydney. It criminalised any attempt, by publishing, to 'imagine, invent, devise or depose our most Gracious Lady the Queen ... from her style, honour or royal name' and it applied to advocacy even of peaceful political change. Back in 1848, several Irish newspaper editors were convicted and transported to Botany Bay. Alan Rusbridger, *The Guardian*'s editor, did not actually lie sleepless in bed at night fearing arrest from Scotland Yard's Treason Squad, but he was concerned that this antiquated law was still retained by a number of Commonwealth countries and was being used in Zimbabwe, for example, to punish those who were imagining, inventing and devising the overthrow of Robert Mugabe. We sought a declaration that after the passing of the Human Rights Act it could no longer be used in Britain, and although the Law Lords did not see it as their function to keep the statute book up to date, they all said that any future prosecution would be irrational – the letter of the law of treason was pronounced dead, if not yet departed.[63]

* * *

In the year 2000 the Human Rights Act came into force in the United Kingdom, and to national astonishment its first beneficiary was the American boxer Mike Tyson. He was the youngest ever heavyweight champion of the world, at the age of twenty, and a convicted rapist a few years later. In 1995, aged twenty-eight, having served three years of his six-year sentence, he was released. Five years later, out to regain his heavyweight title from Lennox Lewis, Tyson fought a bout in Glasgow with American Lou Savarese on a freezing night in a hall packed with Scots baying for blood. It was not long in flowing – after twelve seconds Tyson floored Savarese, who went down for a count of eight. 'Fight on,' said the ref, unwisely – Savarese could barely stand. Tyson landed a left hook that shook him and then ('As every good boxer would be trained to do in these circumstances,' I found myself later telling the tribunal) went in for the knockout.

At this point the ref interposed himself and claimed to have said, 'Stop boxing,' but then, as a result of what I later described as 'inadvertent contact with Tyson's upper arm', the ref himself went down and Tyson kept hitting his opponent onto the ropes. After just thirty-eight seconds the fight ended, and the shaken referee declared Tyson the winner. As microphones were pushed in his face, the victor made some comments which were alleged to be 'detrimental to boxing and to the public interest'. Tyson was hauled before the British Boxing Board of Control, and the media had no doubt (the board's intention had been leaked) that his licence to fight would be cancelled, and he would be disqualified from title-fighting Lewis.

The case required a delicate examination of the role of 'hype', which had come to infect this particular sport – an expectation by promoters that boxers would sledge their future opponents to whet the bloodthirsty appetites of a potential audience and thus swell the 'gate' – their profit from the event. It had, in a way, started with Cassius Clay (*aka* Muhammad Ali) but his promises were poetic – to 'float like a butterfly, sting like a bee'. Tyson's declaration was, 'I'm coming for you, Lennox Lewis … I'm gonna rip your heart out and eat your children.'

My first defence, as reported in the press, was: 'Since Lennox Lewis has no children and boxing gloves do not rip through flesh, this comment is ludicrous and fantasised. Not even the law's measure of naïvety, the moron in a hurry, would take it seriously or imagine for a moment that it was intended as a threat.'

This argument did not seem to be convincing the tribunal, so I rolled out the new Human Rights Act, which by now had to be applied to all public bodies – including the British Boxing Board of Control. The Act gave particular importance to freedom of speech, which could only be curbed in the interests of public safety or preventing crime – not in the interests of boxing. To take away Tyson's livelihood and his chance to regain the title – punishing him for exercising his free-speech right to make tasteless but ridiculous remarks about a future opponent – would not only be unlawful but could open the board to a suit for damages. Besides which, Tyson's remarks were 'an ironic response to racist stereotyping – "You treat me as if I were a jungle savage, so I'll play along with your stereotype."' Here, I may have misattributed a degree of sophistication to my client – the truth is that he was so pumped up with adrenalin that in the few minutes after being declared victor he could have said anything. That is why there is a rule: radio and television interviews with boxers are not permitted in the ring following a contest – a rule that the steward on the night had blatantly breached by allowing the interview.

The case went on into the evening, and the board came back with merely a reprimand. I could not tell which argument had convinced them not to cancel Tyson's boxing licence, although the press reports of their decision were headlined 'Tyson Lands Human Rights Uppercut to Boxing Board'.[64] Thereafter, the Act would benefit many more worthy clients, but the case did make the point that human rights are for everyone – the good, the bad and the ugly.

*　　*　　*

One day in 2009 at Doughty Street we had a visitor who was to talk to us about her work at the Lebanon Tribunal, a court about which I had my doubts because George W. Bush had dreamed it up in the bath, after Prime Minister Hariri (the elected leader of the country) was blown up in a terrorist outrage. Bush, hitherto an enemy of international justice, said the US would support the creation of a court to try the perpetrators. The problem, of course, was that no one knew who they were – Hariri had so many enemies. The suspects were safe in Syria or un-extraditable to Lebanon.

Curiosity about the court brought me to the lecture, given by a young woman whose clever analysis and powerful presentation – quite apart from her fashion sense – made a big enough impression for me to suggest to my colleagues that she join Doughty Street. And so we offered Amal Alamuddin a tenancy. The first case we worked on together showed her calibre – it was a petition to the European Court of Human Rights on behalf of Yulia Tymoshenko, who had been Prime Minister of Ukraine and had led the 'Orange Revolution' against the Stalinists. Her enemy, the corrupt President Viktor Yanukovych, used his control of the judiciary to have her jailed on trumped-up charges: she was ill and in a prison hospital, her privacy grotesquely invaded as every move she made was videotaped. When Ukraine's human rights record was to be discussed at the Human Rights Committee in Geneva, Amal and I went off with Yulia's daughter, Eugenia, to lobby some of the delegations to mention her mother's case and deplore her unjust treatment. 'Oh, we can't possibly mention names,' said the British diplomats. 'It's against the rules.' But the next day, a number of the delegations did break the rules and condemn Yulia's maltreatment – the British, of course, squibbed, but the Americans spelled out her case and the Australians named her twice, perhaps because we had reminded them that Australia also, at the time, had a Julia (Gillard) as Prime Minister. I chaired a meeting at the Geneva Press Club, where Eugenia gave a moving account of her mother's sufferings and Amal provided an incisive analysis of Ukraine's breaches of international law. The court in Strasbourg decided in Tymoshenko's favour, and before long the mass demonstrations at Maidan Square saw Yanukovych flee to Moscow and Yulia freed from prison.

Amal is an exceptional lawyer and a loyal colleague, but the newspapers were more interested in another of her qualities, describing her as 'London's most beautiful barrister'. A mutual friend introduced her to George Clooney. After their much-publicised wedding in Venice, the paparazzi descended on Doughty Street – when we had lunch at Charles Dickens's coffee shop they would wait behind cars in the street for us to emerge, and then illuminate us with a lightning strike of flash bulbs. A bomb threat was phoned through to my extension at the chambers, and I wondered which of my cases had provoked it until I realised that it was probably a photographer hoping to empty the building so he could get his shot of Mrs Clooney. Amal uses her celebrity wisely and well, as a role model for young people who aspire to a professional career working for human rights, and in propelling a slothful United Nations to set up a court to punish the genocide that has been inflicted upon the Yazidis.

We appeared together in the Grand Chamber at Strasbourg, representing Armenia in *Perinçek v Switzerland*. Doğu Perinçek was a racist provocateur and fascist politician from Turkey, who went around countries which had genocide-denial laws, trying to get prosecuted for declaring that the Armenian genocide was a lie. The Swiss fell for his provocation and convicted him for genocide denial, and three judges in Strasbourg's lower court commented in passing that the reality of an Armenian genocide was an open question. I had recently pointed out in a book that, on the contrary, the Armenian genocide was proven beyond reasonable doubt, and Amal and I entered the fray on behalf of Armenia to have these ignorant comments in the lower court overridden by the appeal chamber. As far as Perinçek's conviction was concerned, we argued that it was unnecessary because nobody would bother about his opinion – it had not stirred up racial hatred or incited violence, and we were conscious of the need for free speech to protect Armenians and others who were being threatened with prosecution in Turkey for 'insulting Turkishness' by asserting the truth of the genocide.

The Grand Chamber of seventeen judges decided the case much as we had argued.[65] The paparazzi had been allowed into the chamber to photograph Amal and myself in our Ede & Ravenscroft outfits, and Amal's speech, setting out the facts of the genocide, must have been watched by every Armenian in the world. George tells the story of his regular Armenian car-park attendants at Los Angeles Airport – when he next left his car, one shouted to another, 'Hey. This guy is married to Amal. He gets to park for free!' I became a 'bonus point' on the BBC's *Brainbox Challenge* quiz show, hosted by my friend Clive Anderson. He showed a picture of us both, and asked, 'For two points, what is Amal Clooney's maiden name? And for a bonus point, what is the name of the old guy beside her?'

Another of my exercises with Amal was to examine whether international law regarding the right of nations to have their cultural property returned might develop far enough for the British Museum to be ordered to return to Athens its half of the Parthenon Marbles – sculptures of magnificent heritage illegally ripped from the walls of the Parthenon by British ambassador the Earl of Elgin at the beginning of the nineteenth century.

The Prime Minister of Greece invited us to come and inspect the new Acropolis Museum. It had been built beneath the Parthenon, and housed the other half of the marbles. They waited there, those dismembered gods and goddesses, to be reunited with the rest of their marbled bodies, stolen by Elgin. Our visit was much publicised and highly emotional – I found myself protecting Amal from all the old Greek ladies who wanted to hug her. We came away convinced of the case for reuniting the marbles, especially after seeing them in the British Museum at a secret visit, although by then it was difficult to do anything secret with Amal – she is always recognised and asked for selfies.

The marbles are an architectural wonder – an extraordinarily evocative picture of life in the first civilised society. Ordered by Pericles and sculptured by Phidias around 440 BC, they depict a procession of people walking and talking, playing sports and drinking wine. They are rightly regarded as a unique cultural treasure, not only for Greece but for Europe and the world. It was a crime to loot them: I studied the evidence carefully, and it is clear that their removal was contrary to Elgin's licence (which allowed him to take only 'stones' lying on the ground). He lied to Parliament when he said he had saved them from Turks whom he had observed stealing them – he did not arrive in Athens to observe anything until the thefts he had ordered were almost completed by his workmen. Nor has the British Museum kept them responsibly. It allowed them to be cleaned destructively (with carborundum rubber and copper chisels!) and now displays them in a gallery dedicated to Joseph Duveen, an art fraudster.

Reuniting them with the other marbles in the Acropolis Museum seemed to us a cultural imperative, and we thought that the Greek government had a reasonable chance of success in an international court. We wrote a lengthy opinion to this effect, but the government had changed by the time we came to deliver it, and said it would instead rely on diplomacy – a device that has failed Greece for more than 180 years (its first diplomatic demand was in 1833) and will always fail. One of the great things about Great Britain is that it usually complies with international law, and legal action in the International Court of Justice or the European Court is the only way that the two sets of marbles will ever be reunited. Unless, of course, the UK sells them to Europe to obtain a reduction in the cost of Brexit.

*   *   *

One court of great current controversy to which I occasionally travel is the European Court of Justice (ECJ), which interprets European Union law from a modern building in Luxembourg, a quick flip for British lawyers from City Airport. It's a boring little place compared to Strasbourg, without much call for advocacy (submissions are on paper and are first decided by an 'Advocate General' before you are allowed a short hearing to contest – or agree with – his or her opinion). But the judges, drawn from the twenty-seven European Union members, are apolitical and astute. Quite a few are academics, with training in the interpretation of rules and regulations cast in convoluted Euro-prose. On this subject only are their decisions binding on English courts, and they are usually respected as uncontroversial and correct.

My first experience of ECJ jurisprudence concerned a ban by UK customs on a German rubber sex doll, despite the fact that British rubber sex dolls were freely on sale in Soho. Quite rightly, despite squeals from the British (anxious, it would seem, to protect their perverts from foreign polythene playmates), the ECJ ruled the ban contrary to freedom of trade within the common market. Customs could not maintain a 'cordon sanitaire' against indecent products from member countries which were the same as those being produced and sold at home. It was as a consequence of this ruling that customs officers had to drop their absurd case against Gay's the Word for importing literature that would not be classed as obscene if published by UK publishers. Rulings such as this have knocked a little sense into British bureaucrats, and other decisions have forced them to comply with progressive standards on environmental regulation and data protection. The ECJ has gone so far, based on Edward Snowden's revelations, as to rule that American companies like Facebook and Google cannot transfer subscriber data to America because of the lack of safeguards against CIA interception. This goes too far (we have fewer safeguards against GCHQ interception when data sits on a server in Europe) but nonetheless the ECJ's intention of protecting the privacy of European citizens was worthy enough.

Having been ignored by the media for forty years, this court suddenly came to prominence in the Brexit debate. Shock and horror was evinced at a 'foreign' court that had power over British judges, even though its power could only be exercised in respect of European law, thereby relieving British judges of a task they did not want. It was an entirely benign institution, made a bogey by the ignorant populism of the Brexiteers.

The last case I did in Luxembourg concerned the dreadful conditions being experienced in Greece, where most refugees first land, at a time when that bankrupt nation could not afford to feed them or process their claims. That is what European law seemed to require – processing in the country of first arrival. But did the European Charter of Fundamental Rights, with its 'right to human dignity', change this position? We discussed the literary and philosophical origins of the right to dignity – I suggested the biblical parable of the Good Samaritan, Portia's speech on the quality of mercy and Emmanuel Kant's categorical imperative. It occurred to me, as I was addressing these judges, that over half came from nations that were run by, or had sided with, the Nazis – Germany, Austria, Italy and many of the Eastern European states. Their parents and grandparents would have witnessed, perhaps participated in, the miseries and atrocities inflicted, I told them, 'within living memory'. As I sat down, I reflected how far we had come, in little more than half a century, from the trial at Nuremberg to a case in this spacious and civilised courtroom, in which descendants of Nazis could join us in unravelling and applying a rule requiring human dignity. On any view this was progress, and it is a thousand pities that the UK will no longer be a part of it.

*   *   *

I am proud of starting Doughty Street Chambers and particularly proud of the 150 younger – mostly, much younger – barristers who have come to share its ethos and commitment. It is a postmodern invention in the sense that it has harnessed the two great attributes of the profession – brain power and independence – into a cooperative enterprise for developing human rights principles in legal doctrine and practice, in a rapidly changing society (changing, I might add, partly as a result of an increasing acceptance of those principles). The work is focused not only on English law: Doughty Street International, our global arm, led by Steven Powles, takes our members to all continents and many countries in the world to fight death penalties, torture, state repression and discrimination against women and minorities. At home, our teams deal not only with media and constitutional law, but with actions against the police, inquests, battles over housing and mental health, the rights of prisoners, of women, and of the LGBT community, race relations, environmental protection and the rights of children. The Doughty Street model has already spawned rivals and imitators – it is hard to believe how revolutionary it all seemed back in 1990. None of us ever expect to make fortunes, just a reasonable income without any profit share. On a turnover of about £25 million per year, that leaves enough money to sponsor human rights initiatives. Of course our premises do not compare with the lavish offices with water views, or the conference rooms with walls dripping with valuable art, in which big commercial law firms operate in Sydney, London and New York, where millionaire solicitor partners share in equity and profits. We are, at Doughty Street, individual barristers who have combined for progress rather than profit, while retaining our independence. We like it this way.

Chapter Thirteen

Spycatching

L ike all good spy stories, this one begins with a beautiful woman. MI5 attempted to recruit Jane Turnbull at Oxford, with the fabled 'tap on the shoulder'. No doubt they had satisfied themselves of her loyalty – her father was a bank executive, the family lived in a solidly conservative suburb outside London, and she had been recommended by one of her history tutors. However, they were evidently unaware that she was my girlfriend, attending all the *Oz* acquittal parties in London basements, and had a very fine sense of mischief. She declined the proffered career as a spy because she wanted to be a literary agent (which she still is). We occupied our own basement in Notting Hill for a while, until she sensibly left me for a poet (a published poet, I might add), but she followed my career and remembered my interest in using the law to challenge the power of the state. In 1985, by which time she was working for Heinemann, the publishing house, she called me up and invited me to Sunday lunch with her partner Brian Perman, Heinemann's CEO. We met at a pleasant restaurant overlooking Camden Lock. Jane was excited, Brian a bit apprehensive. He had bought the rights to a book called *Spycatcher* and wanted my advice. He had just been telephoned by John Bailey, the Treasury Solicitor (the government's legal chief) and warned against publishing it – or else. 'We have a bottomless purse,' Bailey had said: a threat to take injunctions and other actions which could bankrupt the company if it dared to publish.

I knew a little about the author, Peter Wright, a former assistant director of MI5, who had broken cover a year before with an interview for Granada

Television's *World in Action* from his retirement home in Tasmania, making allegations of treachery in the British secret service. I had been retained as an adviser to the Granada team to make a programme about the Australian Freedom of Information Act – an anodyne subject but one for which I arranged interviews with Gareth Evans (the Attorney General) and my barrister brother Tim, who was filmed using the Act to get information from the army, which he used to stop public parkland being used for a shooting range. All very worthy, no doubt, but hardly the cutting-edge material for which *World in Action* was famed. I discovered later that I had been used as a cover – when I went back to London, the team slipped down to Tasmania, in great secrecy, to interview Wright. Its brilliant director, Paul Greengrass (who went on to direct the *Bourne* movies), stayed on with Wright to ghost-write *Spycatcher*. I did not mind being used as a decoy – our documentary had given a fillip to the campaign for a Freedom of Information Act in Britain – and I watched the programme about Wright with some interest. He seemed a genuine whistleblower, even if he was partly motivated by anger at what he saw as a betrayal in denying him some pension rights. As a former senior member of MI5, his allegations had to be taken seriously.

Brian outlined them over lunch. The book he had bought would reveal that Wright – hired as an electrician – had been initially employed to burgle and bug his way around the foreign embassies in London (a breach of the Vienna Convention, but everyone did it). It told how he had then been promoted to an interrogator, and claimed to have unmasked many 'agents of influence' who had historical connections with Soviet diplomats. He had subsequently become convinced that his own boss, Roger Hollis, the director-general of MI5 from 1956 to 1965, was one of them. His accusations, he said, had not been properly investigated and he had been pensioned off, but without a satisfactory pension.

There was little doubt that publication of Wright's revelations as an 'insider' would breach the Official Secrets Act, which had a draconian section injuncting and punishing publication of the most anodyne of revelations – the number of cups of tea consumed in the Ministry of Defence, for example. It was used to ban *One Girl's War*, a Mills & Boon-style memoir by a former debutante who had obtained a job as a typist in MI5 during the war and fallen in love with her boss, only to find her romantic hopes dashed by the dawning realisation that he would be happier in the arms of men. Brian knew that the Treasury Solicitor's threat to bankrupt his company was overpowering: how on earth could he publish *Spycatcher*? Over coffee, I gave them an opinion, off the cuff, which went pretty much as follows:

1. Publication of Wright's memoirs was obviously in the public interest – in the *international* public interest – because Hollis had connections with the CIA and had travelled to Australia to advise the Australian Security Intelligence Organisation (ASIO). If, all that time, he was reporting to Moscow, and had never been called to account, this was certainly a matter about which the public ought to know. But there was no public interest defence to a breach of the Official Secrets Act, so the importance of the book was not a defence.

2. There was, however, a 'public domain' defence – i.e. that the information had already been made public – to an injunction based on breach of confidence, but British judges would simply decide that it was over-borne by the national interest in gagging spies and keeping intelligence service activity absolutely secret. It was certainly true that over previous years much had leaked to journalists and a lot of Wright's allegations could be found in books published by right-wing journalist Chapman Pincher, although this information had been leaked to Pincher by Wright himself. The further problem was that Wright was an insider, and a 'horse's mouth' allegation made in person by him had much more credibility than the same allegation made by a mere journalist from an unnamed source. For that reason, the public domain defence would not fly in an English court. An Australian court, however, might just uphold it.

3. It followed that the proposed publication in England would be injuncted by the Treasury Solicitor and that appeals would be unsuccessful – and very expensive, because his threat about the state's 'bottomless purse' was true. At this time, although the Cold War was past its peak, English judges had a knee-jerk propensity to uphold every government

claim based on 'national security' without inquiry as to whether it might be bogus.

4. Were Heinemann to publish in Australia, the company would have a reasonable prospect of beating off action by the UK authorities, depending on where the action was brought. Melbourne judges of the time tended to be Empire loyalists; in Sydney, the first-instance equity judges were unpredictable, but the new president of the Court of Appeal was Michael Kirby, who was sound on free speech, as were some of his colleagues. The High Court, if the case reached that far (and Mrs Thatcher would be determined that it should), could possibly decide that publication was in the Australian public interest (because of MI5's close connections with ASIO) or because Australia was a sovereign state, and under international law sovereign states did not enforce claims of a political nature at the behest of other states.

5. Win or lose, contesting an action in Australia, which Mrs Thatcher seemed determined to bring, would achieve massive publicity to whet the appetite of potential readers. It would be worth resisting to the hilt, so long as... (and this was the crucial bit)

6. ... A copy was sent, sold and secreted in the United States. Under the First Amendment, and most recently the Pentagon Papers case, publication there would be protected.

Brian was happy enough with my opinion to pay for lunch and in due course Heinemann's solicitor, David Hooper, instructed me to advise the company on its reasonable prospects of beating off any legal action by the British government in Australia. The government began one in September 1985, before the book had even been completed, and Mr Bailey foolishly refused David's sensible offer to remove anything that might damage national security: Mrs Thatcher was determined that Australian courts must apply the British Official Secrets Act and stop Wright from writing a word. This was not only a pig-headed refusal to compromise but reeked of colonial assumptions about Australia which were unacceptable at a time when that country was withdrawing from the Privy Council. So I was keen that the case should be fought and I believed it could and should be won.

Heinemann's multitude of Australian lawyers, however, did not seem to share my confidence. The publishers, based in Melbourne, had instructed a local firm, which took the mistaken view that different solicitors and counsel should be brought in to act for Wright, and, because the Brits had sued in Sydney, two more firms were retained there. At the first, merely formal, hearing, there were thirteen lawyers in court to represent Wright and eleven to represent Heinemann. This was ridiculous: the costs were exorbitant and the Australian silks were saying that we would have better prospects in the English courts. As we had no prospects there at all, Brian warned me that Paul Hamlyn, the eccentric millionaire philanthropist who owned Heinemann, was minded to throw in the towel.

By a remarkable, almost Dickensian, coincidence, I came to meet Paul shortly afterwards at the home of our mutual friends, Gordon and Mary Ellen Barton. I encouraged him to fight for free speech, but he was hesitant about the cost and the half-heartedness of the Australian lawyers. Another meeting *chez* Barton was arranged, however, and Paul arrived as a man transformed. He was giggling as he told us how he had just been approached by an emissary from 'the establishment', a rather down-at-heel Tory MP, who had passed on the message that Paul would be severely punished if *Spycatcher* were ever published. Paul would never receive the peerage he would otherwise be vouchsafed for his charitable works, and his wife would not thereby become a lady. Paul's eyes glistened mischievously as he thumped the table and declared, 'This has made up my mind for me. We are going to publish *Spycatcher* – whatever the consequences.'

Paul Hamlyn was the real hero of *Spycatcher*, and this heavy-handed threat, which doubtless came from Mrs Thatcher, was his turning point. I was about to leave on my annual Christmas visit to Sydney, and I promised Paul I would find a lawyer who would understand the politics of the case and mount the defence we had planned at a reasonable price. I thought I might pay a visit to an old friend, Little Malcolm.

I had christened him 'Little Malcolm' when he came up to Sydney University: the Dramatic Society was performing David Halliwell's play *Little Malcolm and His Struggle Against the Eunuchs*, about a young man planning from his bedsit to rule the world. Malcolm Turnbull always seemed to be struggling against eunuchs (and still is, by all accounts). He was working as a journalist while studying law and already had inordinate ambition. We met, in 1979, when he came to interview me while I held a visiting professorship at the University of New South Wales. We shared views on the social potential of law reform and got on like a house on fire. He desperately wanted a Rhodes scholarship and I was happy to be his referee. But he was in the doldrums about his application because of Rhodes's insistence in his will that scholars must have an interest in manly sports: 'They pick rugger buggers or cricketers,' moaned Malcolm.

'No, they don't – my sport was tennis. There must be some sport you can do.' We went through his pastimes, and alighted on surfing. 'But it's never been considered a manly sport – there are no precedents.'

'There soon will be.' I stayed up late that night writing his reference, with a disquisition on how surfing should be regarded, especially in Australia, as a muscular male activity. He was duly awarded the Rhodes, and while in Oxford he would visit me in Pembridge Crescent. On one delightful summer's day I stood in for his father-in-law, a Sydney QC, at a tiny Oxford church and gave his bride Lucy away. He stayed in London after his course, with a job at the *Sunday Times*, which was aborted because of a long strike by the print unions – an event that may have shaped his then-uncertain political allegiances. We were both Whitlamites, and it could not be predicted in which party he would choose to rise to power. He began working for Kerry Packer, sorting out Packer's rights to cricket teams and to *Playboy*, and I advised him to become independent – to go to the Bar. He did, but did not stick at it.

When I called to ask him to take on *Spycatcher*, his office was in the Packer building in Sydney's Park Street, where he had recently set up an in-house solicitors firm. Malcolm's political ambitions were in a bad way because he had just suffered attacks for being close to his boss, Kerry Packer. 'You need this case, for the sake of your career,' I said when we met. 'It's the best way of proving your free-speech credentials, and it will play well with republicans on the left – if you ever wanted to go that way – by standing up to the Brits. You are languishing here doing libel readings and suffering attacks from satirists.' (He had at some point morosely shown me a clip of a satire programme mocking Packer and his 'cat strangler' lawyer – more on this shortly.) 'This case will be fun – and, most important, it will be the making of you.' I cannot vouchsafe my words as verbatim, but that was the spirit of them, and they worked. Malcolm agreed to act for Heinemann at a low fee in the legal action being brought by the British government.

Heinemann, whose Australian headquarters were in Melbourne, had announced the publication of *Spycatcher* in Australia, and the British High Commission immediately obtained a temporary injunction. The court where they chose to file was in Sydney. This was a strategic mistake, probably made because their diplomats preferred to work from their favourite consulate in Kirribilli, overlooking the harbour. It was the first of many tactical blunders by Mrs Thatcher's legal army – so quick to bully but so weak and ill-informed when it came to a fair fight. Turnbull was beginning to relish it: 'It's a great case,' he faxed me. 'I am so grateful to that little turd Bailey for procuring it for us.' Little Malcolm saw himself as David pitted against Goliath, although David did not have a media mogul at his back: Kerry Packer had to approve – and did. He had taken on the British cricket establishment and won, and saw no problem with taking on the British intelligence establishment.

Meanwhile, from England I dispatched written opinions on the law and decided to hunt up some evidence. The Attorney General's writ had come with an affidavit by Sir Robert Armstrong, the Cabinet Secretary, claiming that in 1967 the Lord Chancellor had made a blanket prohibition on the release of any document making any reference to the security service. That Lord Chancellor was Lord Gardiner, my teenage idol who had defended *Lady Chatterley* and convinced Harold Wilson's government to abolish the death penalty and theatre censorship as well as the crimes of homosexuality and procuring abortion. It was a delight to meet him, and although he was in the advanced stages of Hodgkin's disease, his mind and memory were as precise as ever. Those electric blue eyes, which had once terrified witnesses like torches shone on rabbits at night, saw through Armstrong's claim. He signed an affidavit to say that a blanket ban on memoirs was not what Lord Chancellor Gardiner had meant at all.

I was also keeping an eye on the cases the Attorney General was bringing in Britain against newspapers which had reported any of the details in the book: predictably, the courts always ruled against them. One judgment was brought down on the day I took a flight to Australia – David Hooper quickly obtained a certified copy for me to carry to Malcolm, who was appearing in a pre-trial hearing two days later. The ever-gentlemanly silk the government had instructed told the judge that the British High Commission would have the certified judgments available for the court the following week. Turnbull stood, perhaps with the hint of a smile, or more probably with a broad grin (I don't know – like Macavity, I wasn't there), to say, 'Don't worry, Your Honour, I have the certified copies here.' He told me there was pandemonium from the team of British lawyers and spooks on the other side of the courtroom: how on earth had the certified copies come to Australia virtually overnight? Via the Soviet airline Aeroflot? Was Turnbull being assisted by the KGB? Mr Packer's fax machines at 60 Park Street were soon to show signs of interference.

Then, in England, a funny thing happened. Paul Hamlyn and I finally read a smuggled copy of the finished book. It did not really have the kind of public interest we had initially envisaged – quite the contrary. Peter Wright turned out to have no qualifications. Nepotism had taken him into the intelligence service (his father was one of their scientists) and having begun as an electrician fixing surveillance devices, which is where he should have remained – he was a competent enough bugger – somehow (probably because of his intense right-wing paranoia) he had become an interrogator, virtually an inquisitor, harassing and embarrassing left-wingers who had looked kindly on communism in the '30s, or at least until the invasion of Hungary in 1956. A number of his victims (including a Labour MP) had committed suicide after the stress of his McCarthyite interrogations. Wright believed the most incredible theories peddled by defectors (that the Sino-Soviet split was a cover story, for example). His case against Hollis had no real evidence – the man emerged as a dull but dutiful civil servant, who had aroused Wright's suspicions because he had spent some years in China in his youth and was having an affair with his secretary.

But wait – there *was* a real public interest here. It was that a man of Wright's malice and lack of judgement could ever become an assistant director of MI5. For me, this was the truly amazing revelation, together with its description of British 'intelligence' officials – pin-striped dunces who retired to their men-only clubs for well-wined lunches, topped off with a few double brandies before tottering back to their offices in Mayfair to gossip about sex scandals they might reveal involving 'lefties'. Wright (who had only two supporters on MI5's staff – an ex-policeman and an ex-army major) deduced that the organisation must have been infiltrated at the top because so many of their operations went wrong; he never considered the alternative hypothesis, that they were going wrong because of MI5's incompetence.

There were a few amusing stories in the book, such as the incident at the Buckingham Palace roundabout when an MI5 car trailing a car of Russia 'diplomats' came too close and crashed into it: the drivers, both spooks, got out and solemnly swapped their fake addresses. There was the argument about the 'watchers', male and female, who sat in cars outside houses and were expected to fall into each other's arms to allay suspicion when a suspect emerged – there had been a great internal debate about whether this might encourage infidelity. I think I had actually seen this happen once, when I was researching *Reluctant Judas* and had attracted MI5's attention. When I opened the front door unexpectedly, the woman in the car opposite frantically threw her arms around the driver's neck and started kissing him passionately. I had no idea that they might have been MI5 watchers, but the scene was so bizarre that it remained in my memory – years later, on reading *Spycatcher*, I was able to interpret it. There were also stories about a plot to assassinate Egypt's President Nasser and about a cabal of spooks who linked up with right-wing businessmen to plot the overthrow of Harold Wilson's government. But for any intelligent person, and any analyst reading it in Washington or Canberra, the message of the book was how incompetent MI5 had been in the '50s and '60s, running operations that did not operate and chasing its own tail by investigating its directors (not content with Hollis, the paranoid Wright also launched an inquiry into whether his deputy might be spying for Russia).

Peter Wright had unmasked himself (with the help of Paul Greengrass) as a highly disagreeable reactionary with no moral compass: he was in fact on quite a good pension but was bitter because he believed it should be better, so he had been selling secrets for several years to Chapman Pincher, earning £30,000 through a Swiss bank account. He had left England in 1975 to run a horse stud in Tasmania, telling friends that the motherland had 'too many blacks' (not a problem in Tasmania, where they had been wiped out by the British a century before).

My experience of Wright, when I spoke to him, was of a sour man who would do or say anything for money. He lived in a Little Buttercup world, where things were always the opposite of what they seemed. I told him I had been a board member of the National Council for Civil Liberties in the '70s when MI5 had tapped our phones. 'Yes, they did, they did, and that just proves how the organisation had been infiltrated by communists at the very top.'

How so? We were harmless.

'Exactly so, exactly so. The reds were in control of MI5. They took their resources away from bugging the Soviets, and deliberately wasted them on bugging insignificant organisations like the NCCL. Do you see?'

I did not – MI5 had a long-standing hostility to the left, ever since they had manipulated the defeat of Labour's first government back in 1924 by forging the Zinoviev letter, which suggested its ministers were allies of the Soviets. Wright was exhibit number one in a case against the kind of security services whose intolerance was incapable of protecting a tolerant state.

Back at the Bartons' dinner table, Paul Hamlyn had now convinced himself that he was publishing the book at the expense of his peerage because Wright himself, rather than Hollis, needed to be exposed and MI5 reformed. But this created a possible difficulty: Mrs Thatcher (the plaintiff was Michael Havers, her Attorney General) had sued both Wright and Heinemann, and the two were not on the same page. Wright was claiming public interest in exposing Hollis, while Heinemann, stepping back, could claim that, in any event, the public would be legitimately interested in judging Wright and his coterie in MI5. They were both represented by Malcolm at my suggestion – to save cost, and strategically to present a united front. One night Paul (a fastidious man) suddenly stuttered, 'I don't really want Turnbull representing my company. He's alienating people I know, and he's a bit...' (he reached for a word) '...uncouth.' There was a pause, and then he said, 'I would like you to represent the company.'

I doubted whether I had the 'couthness' he wanted, and this was a prospect I had never envisaged. I had been careful to keep my role, in what the Treasury Solicitor might otherwise see as a conspiracy to breach the Official Secrets Act, limited to opinions to solicitors and discussions in restaurants and behind the thick walls of the Bartons' establishment. I was applying for silk, which I needed to appear in Commonwealth courts, and had little doubt that the kind of reprisals Mrs Thatcher was threatening against Paul would be applied to his counsel. I could stomach that, but most importantly, I pointed out that it would be cheaper and tactically safer to let Malcolm continue to represent both parties, rather than opening up a second front which could be exploited to drive a wedge between Wright and Heinemann. (The company might be successfully defended, but if Wright was injuncted, it could not publish his book.) Paul, however, was adamant. The next day I took my concerns to my head of chambers, Emlyn Hooson, who thought reprisals likely but promised to do his best to protect me from them.

It was a measure of my naïvety about Malcolm that, despite my grave doubts about the tactical implications, I honestly thought he would be pleased with this turn of events. My appearance for the publisher would give him support while he argued the case for Wright. I would research the law (which I was doing already) and had an in-depth knowledge of security service 'dirty tricks' from other cases I had done, with which we could confound Sir Robert Armstrong. Malcolm would have a friend in court. It was with that feeling (hilarious, in retrospect) that I picked up the telephone to tell him.

Any spooks tapping Malcolm's or my telephone on 20 October 1986 would have been entranced at what they heard. Turnbull went into meltdown. I shall delete the expletives. He became furious, seemingly at the prospect that he would be sharing the limelight with someone else – especially me. 'You will take it over. You will get the publicity. You planned to betray me all along.'

Now, I have to say that if Malcolm had, quietly and reasonably, echoed my own concerns about separate representation, I would have agreed with him. But I was not prepared for this volatility, which ended, as I remember, with a furious threat to withdraw.

I was certain he would never let go of a case that would be the making of him, so I called him back that evening to see whether his rage had subsided. It had not. The trial was to come on in a few weeks, and Turnbull's threat, although obviously bluff, was an expression of insecurity that nobody needs in their lawyer. I went back to Paul with the advice that it was too late for me to act for Heinemann in the courtroom, and I felt that Turnbull's lust for glory might be a good thing – he would now have to work hard to win, and in any event keeping him on for Heinemann as well as Wright would prevent the government from exploiting the differences. I put his upset down to his recognition of how much the starring role in this case would help his career, which had been my argument for his taking it on in the first place.

Having convinced Paul to stick with his counsel of my choice, I went off to Singapore to do battle with Lee Kuan Yew (a tougher opponent than the British government) on behalf of the *Wall Street Journal,* and returned to fax some legal submissions for *Spycatcher* a few weeks later. Malcolm did the trial well, assisted by the foolish stuffed-shirt Sir Robert Armstrong, who caused a scandal at Heathrow as he was leaving for Sydney by assaulting a press photographer. In the witness box, Armstrong was unable to explain satisfactorily why the government had allowed so many of Wright's 'secrets' to be published through the right-wing mouthpiece of Chapman Pincher. He was also forced by Turnbull to admit that a part of his testimony had been 'economical with the truth'.

The judge was unimpressed: although no great jurist, he took the UK case apart and held for the defence on every argument except the one that nobody had given much chance, namely that Australian courts should not enforce the penal laws of a foreign country. I provided a brief in support of his judgment for the Court of Appeal, where Michael Kirby held in our favour with a splendid decision in favour of free speech. In the High Court, the judges very quickly and coolly decided that Australian courts should not enforce the penal laws of a foreign country by imposing the draconian British Official Secrets Act on an independent nation. *Spycatcher* could finally be published in Australia.[66]

But by now events had moved on. After our lunch, Brian had conveyed my advice to Paul Greengrass's literary agent, who arranged for a copy of the manuscript to move to the US. Jane Turnbull, from a public phone box in Bywater Street, Chelsea (the location John Le Carré uses for George Smiley's London flat), then sold the US rights to Viking/Penguin. MI5 did not move quickly enough, although two of its officials, with bowler hats and umbrellas, posed as sales tax inspectors to inspect the literary agency's offices in Doughty Street. They found nothing – the agent, Giles Gordon, had taken the Greengrass/Wright file home and hidden it under his bed.[67] Viking bided its time during the early publicity from the Australian proceedings and then announced it was publishing in America. A furious Mrs Thatcher was advised that under the First Amendment she could not injunct – all that could be done was to seize imported copies at UK ports and airports. This, of course, she obstinately did: the book, on sale at airport bookshops at Kennedy and LAX, and in Europe, sold like hot cakes to passengers on flights to Britain. Many were smuggled in bulk, and distributors sold them in the street. The judges loyally injuncted them; one Labour council was actually prosecuted and fined for placing a copy in its public library.

In the end, Viking sold the serial rights to the *Sunday Times*, which published a long précis of the book. It was, of course, sued – successfully. An end to these ridiculous legal actions funded by the 'bottomless purse' of the Treasury Solicitor came only when the European Court of Human Rights held that Mrs Thatcher's actions were an abuse of free speech. Her obsession with banning the book showed how counterproductive political (or any other) censorship can be. *Spycatcher* is a boring book which would not have sold well (and would only have sold in England) if her government had not intervened. Instead, it sold nearly two million copies and made £4 million for its publishers. (On contemplating my own paltry bill for advising them how to publish, I wondered whether barristers should be entitled to a success fee.) It also blasted Hollis's reputation – he could not mind because he was long dead, but his nephew ticked me off. 'What are you saying about Uncle Roger? He was the nicest, most decent, most loyal man you could ever imagine.' I am sure he was – thirty years on from publication of Peter Wright's paranoid fantasies, not a scintilla of evidence has emerged from KGB archives to suggest anything to the contrary.

I was then asked to protect Malcolm's burgeoning reputation in two libel cases in England. Chapman Pincher, using the services of Peter Carter-Ruck, a libel lawyer close to the intelligence services, sued him for defamation for comments he had made on breakfast television to the effect that Pincher still owed Wright money. Unfortunately for Pincher, Wright had kept all the letters in which he had, for profits that he shared with Pincher, spilt state secrets, and they were in our possession. I drafted a letter pointing out that a court might take the view that the evidence showed both of them implicated in a grave breach of the Official Secrets Act. We never heard from Carter-Ruck again, and several years later I had the pleasure of having Pincher's action struck out, with an order that he must pay all our costs. It was an interesting example of what is termed a 'gagging writ' – a false claim brought in an effort to suppress an uncomfortable truth.

The next time, it was Turnbull's turn to be defamed – by larger-than-life Canadian mogul Conrad Black. Black had fallen out with Malcolm when Black's Tourang consortium took over Fairfax Media in 1991. In his autobiography, published two years later, Conrad rehearsed with relish the Sydney scuttlebutt that Malcolm (in his much younger days) had threatened to kill his girlfriend's cat if she left him for another man. She did, and rumour had it that he killed the cat by strangling it with his bare hands. Black went one better: he alleged that Turnbull had put the cat in the freezer while she was out. I have to say the only evidence for any of this rubbish is a letter young Malcolm wrote to the cat, which was produced in a Sydney libel action: it is rather boyishly romantic, and contains no threat of cat-o-cide if its mistress remains cruel.[68] Black's claim that Turnbull was capable of some pussy-gulag was very defamatory – especially when published in England, this nation of animal lovers. I drafted a 'letter before action' which caused Black to withdraw the British and Australian editions of the book, but we had no power to have him remove the passage from the Canadian edition. There, some may really believe that the Australian

Prime Minister once murdered a cat, although since Canadians are more than happy to club baby seals to death, I don't suppose they think any the less of him for it.

*   *   *

The value of publishing Peter Wright's malicious memoirs was not merely to push Little Malcolm towards his destiny (and Paul Hamlyn was finally elevated to his peerage by a post-Thatcher government): it was to shake up – indeed, quickly reform – the British security service so that it was an effective force by the time of its next test, the surveillance of Islamic extremism. This took some time: in 1997, former MI5 officer David Shayler provided a story to the *Mail on Sunday* about how MI5 was still keeping files on leftist politicians, or at least refusing to destroy files kept on them in their socialist youth. I acted for the newspaper in the difficult business of fixing a payment to Shayler without it seeming an illegal inducement to spill state secrets. But Shayler needed money to go abroad and lie low and to instruct lawyers to defend his actions. I was happy to help – *Spycatcher* had shown an urgent need to depoliticise the intelligence services. Gerald Gardiner had told me how, even when he was Lord Chancellor under Harold Wilson, he would hold conversations with his Attorney General in a car with a friendly driver because he suspected the security services were bugging his offices to learn of and to leak these men's plans; Peter Wright's stories of MI5 plots against Wilson gave his fears some credence. MI5 had also been abusing its power to leak information about leftists to right-wing journalists like Pincher and to newspaper gossip columns. *Private Eye* was a favourite: the editor told me that he could always recognise their stories, impeccably typed on unheaded notepaper, written in the magazine's style to ridicule or damage some figure on the left. He always published them because he assumed they must be true.

Once, I was the target of the scoundrels who leaked this sort of scuttlebutt to the *Eye*. I had attended a weekend legal conference at Christ Church College, Oxford. The Attorney General, who was in attendance, was a weak man whom I had criticised in a number of articles in the *New*

Statesman, so I was surprised to be given the best room in the college. I suspected nothing and used it to entertain a female friend, who spoke about her political plans. A fortnight later some details which could only have been obtained by bugging the room were published in *Private Eye*. The editor left my name out because I had defended *Private Eye* in the past, but that did not lessen my friend's distress, or mine, at the invasion of her privacy. This experience was one of the factors that had persuaded me to fight to have *Spycatcher* published and it contributed to my view that absolute secrecy will come inevitably to cloak abuses of power; that the security services must be overseen by independent judges; and that its members must abide by a code of conduct.

Otherwise, my experiences with the security services have been relatively benign. I undertook cases where 'national security' was alleged to be involved and it was a common assumption that your telephone would be tapped. The best indication, so I was informed by someone who knew, was not (as everyone presumed) the sound of strange clicks or static on the line, but whether your telephone worked perfectly. Tapping was not necessarily detrimental to your client – when I was junior to the great Jeremy Hutchinson, defending Duncan Campbell, a journalist who was facing a long term of imprisonment for exposing the interception role of GCHQ, Jeremy and I would hold long, voluble telephone conversations, inventing defence witnesses and imagining tactics that would cause maximum embarrassment to the intelligence services. The listeners must have taken us seriously: Jeremy was soon invited to a dinner party at which he was placed next to a senior figure in MI6, who indicated they would accept a plea to a lesser charge that did not entail prison.

I did receive direct evidence that my telephone was tapped when I became too busy with the case to remember to pay my bill, ignoring repeated notices that unless I did so it would be cut off. Eventually I called the provider, British Telecom, to tell them that a cheque would be in the post. 'That's fine,' said the official. 'We'll reconnect your telephone as soon as we receive it.'

'Oh, it doesn't need reconnection. It hasn't been cut off yet.'

'Yes, it has.'

'No, it hasn't.'

'It most certainly has been.'

'It has not, I AM SPEAKING TO YOU ON IT.'

'Oh. Hmm. Just a minute…' The official took more than a minute, doubtless to consult a list marked 'intercepted telephones – not to be disconnected' and returned to say quickly, 'OK, just send the cheque.' I didn't until after the case had ended, having intuited that the state's appetite for information is greater than its appetite for money.

Don't think I am opposed to state surveillance. I welcomed police protection when I was defending Salman Rushdie, condemned to death by fatwa and with a bounty on his head. He was a friend, and Kathy and I put him up in our attic at one point, guarded by Scotland Yard's Special Branch. When I defended him in a blasphemy case brought by Muslim prosecutors, there was some concern that terrorists might despair of finding Salman and choose his barrister as a target instead. Special Branch said they would show us how to look for bombs placed under my car. We expected them to have high-tech equipment, but they brought us a mirror and showed us how to tie it to a broom. We did, and looked. 'But everything looks like a bomb under there,' Kathy wailed. We had some happy weekends with Salman and his police protectors at cottages in the English countryside – Kathy noticed that it was always the policemen who volunteered to do the washing up. One of them had an unreconstructed tendency to flash his gun when alone with our nanny, polishing the barrel very slowly.

One problem with surveillance – even when it is entirely legitimate – is that the spooks can jump to the wrong conclusion. In 1990, I acted for the Islamic extremist Yasin Abu Bakr, who had led 114 followers to attempt a coup in Trinidad, killing eight policemen and doing enormous damage. Abu Bakr and his men were all released from prison (see Chapter Eleven), and some years later I received a message that he was coming to Britain and wanted to see me. I did not believe that the authorities would ever let him into the country, but said that I would see him if they did – for no better reason than to urge him to pay my long-overdue fee, and, more importantly, the fee of my impecunious junior. To my amazement, he was allowed to enter, so I visited him at a hotel near Heathrow. I walked to his room along an empty corridor, and our discussion was brief: he wanted me to represent him in a case about his mosque. I said I would consider doing so, but only if he paid all his outstanding fees. That was the long and short of our conversation.

A few days later, my old friend Ramesh Maharaj, who was by then the Attorney General of Trinidad, called me up. 'I've just had a visit from the British High Commissioner. He wanted to know why my friend Mr Robertson was paying late-night visits to Abu Bakr!' The authorities obviously had surveillance in the corridor: if they had gone the whole hog and bugged the room, they would have discovered the reason. For spooks, a little knowledge can be a dangerous thing.

In the late 1980s, by way of a reality check, I experienced communist surveillance on my visits to Prague to help its leading dissident, Václav Havel, who was followed everywhere by secret police ready to arrest him and throw him back into prison for his philosophy and politics. I was followed too, and although I was not in danger like him (the worst that could happen to me was to be put back on a plane to London), it was a grubby experience. Every morning as I left the lobby of the hotel some sad stooge would drop the newspaper behind which he had been concealing himself, and tail me out. I took these policemen to museums in the hope of improving their education, and to visit Prague's Jewish cemetery, a maze of tall tombstones leaning at crazy angles behind which I would soon shake them off.

In due course the Soviet Union collapsed, the Cold War seemed to end and in the UK the IRA guns and bombs fell silent after the Good Friday Agreement. Now, the most dangerous terrorists were members of the Animal Liberation Front, who rescued smoking beagles and threatened scientists who used animals in their experiments (or at least used nice animals like dogs – they did not seem to mind scientists dismembering rats). But even in the halcyon period before Islamic extremism took hold, spooks in Britain did not always conduct themselves ethically: secret police from Scotland Yard's undercover squad hopped under the bedcovers of some of the women protesters they were surveilling, who subsequently became pregnant, at which point their secret police lovers decamped. It was a truly obscene example of how government spies, even in the most civilised country, will behave immorally if not carefully regulated. My chambers helped to expose the scandal and sued Scotland Yard for child maintenance on behalf of the unwitting mothers. (It paid up.)

Then, in the last decade, came the ethical dilemmas of dealing with suspects believed – sometimes rightly – to be very dangerous terrorists. Under George W. Bush, the CIA's way of dealing with them was by torture. How was British intelligence, bound by law to abjure torture, to turn a blind eye while continuing its important collaboration with the CIA? The issue arose in the case of Binyam Mohamed, an Ethiopian-born British resident who was arrested in Pakistan in 2002, handed over to US custody and denied access to a lawyer.[69] An MI5 man was sent to interview him, and the questions he asked made clear that he knew the prisoner's intended fate – he urged him to avoid it by confessing. Mohamed was then 'rendered' to a secret torture prison in Morocco, before being sent to Guantanamo, where British intelligence washed its hands of him. But had it been complicit in his torture? I was acting for the international media and we needed disclosure of the communications on his case between the CIA and MI5 and MI6: the British government resisted, citing an Anglo-American protocol which absolutely barred disclosure by either state if the other were to insist upon secrecy, as Washington did.

I contacted Morton Halperin, an old acquaintance who had served as a national security adviser to Presidents Johnson, Nixon and Clinton, and his evidence refuted the government claim: the protocol required each government to resist disclosure of the other's secrets, but if this was required by a court order, then the order should be complied with. The case eventually settled, but enough of the facts had emerged to illustrate the moral questions that arise for the security services of countries which of necessity now have to work in collaboration with those of a US President who has promised to bring back waterboarding, and who claims that torture works. It doesn't. The CIA discovered its primary clue to the hideout of Osama bin Laden not by torturing a suspect but after giving him a cup of tea.

I came to advise the then editor of *The Guardian*, Alan Rusbridger, when the paper first obtained documents from Edward Snowden, which seemed to show that Australian intelligence had been bugging the mobile phone of the wife of the Indonesian President. Australian lawyers said that these papers could not be published. I took a look at the documents – they were on DSD (Defence Signals Directorate) letterhead, and every page was stamped with a large coloured logo: 'Reveal their secrets. Protect our own.'

'Come on, Alan, this looks fake. This is Australian intelligence – they are intelligent Australians. I doubt very much whether they stamp such a corny motto on every page of their notepaper.' They do. Caesar's wife, or at least the wife of the President of Indonesia, should have been above suspicion. But spooks, or at least their political masters, love to lap up the kind of tittle-tattle that comes from mobile-phone intercepts, no matter how serious the breach of privacy.

Our allies were at it, too – Snowden revealed how the CIA had hacked into the cellphones of thirty-five heads of state, including Angela Merkel, who was not best pleased to find that the intelligence operatives had un-covered her takeaway orders for sausage and sauerkraut. Obama at least had the decency to apologise and promise not to do it again.

We have come a long way from tapping telephones. Secret policemen can find out all they need to know by analysing our metadata, our elec-tronic habits. And one problem with the collection of metadata is that there are no limits to who gets targeted. It's not confined, as it should be, to terrorist suspects and those believed to be engaged in serious crime. Take General Petraeus – he was America's most successful soldier, about to be appointed to head the CIA. But then, shock horror! His metadata revealed he had had a brief affair with a woman who was writing his biog-raphy. Infidelity meant, to puritanical Americans, 'Petraeus will betray us!' It was the premature end of a fine career.

So if you become a target of the spooks, whoever you are, you have no remedy and no defence. The problem – and it is a problem, throughout the West – is *quis custodiet?* Who guards the guardians? No country, no cohort of countries, has yet come up with a satisfactory system of over-sight. Such accountability as we have, in an unscientific, rough-and-ready way, comes from whistleblowers. They are dissidents, often, or trouble-makers like Julian Assange (see next chapter), but as the great historian

A. J. P. Taylor pointed out, 'All change in history, all advance, comes from the non-conformists. If there had been no troublemakers, no dissenters, we should still be living in caves.'

*   *   *

After all my years challenging state claims to national security, in courts and books and lecture rooms, I can offer only a few rather simple observations on the *quis custodiet?* question.

Surveillance and other forms of intelligence-gathering are necessary to combat terrorism and serious crime (including international paedophile networks, tax evasion and human trafficking). There can be no absolute right to privacy, and secret surveillance, by its very nature, must for a certain time remain secret.

The historical record of Western intelligence services, so far as we know it, demonstrates a capacity, sometimes a tendency, to yield to the temptation to abuse this power. Whether it is MI5 smearing and plotting against left-wingers, or the CIA planning to assassinate Castro with an exploding cigar, or ASIO bugging the wife of the Indonesian President, surveillance power is dangerous if used without independent oversight.

Oversight of the security services by politicians, whether ministers or committees, is useless: ministers are rubber stamps and do what their Sir Humphrey recommends, while parliamentary and congressional committees are lied to and kept in the dark. Oversight must be independent of the government and of the security services themselves.

The first means of achieving this is to require all surveillance warrants to be issued or approved by a judge. That is a protection which Britain refuses to provide, despite the fact that it has been strongly recommended by its own national security adviser. At present, warrants are issued by approval of the Home Secretary – a political pushover for the security services – who has no time or judicial capacity to vet their applications. Even with this reform, it would be what goes on in implementing the warrant that would remain beyond judicial supervision, and judges in any event tend to be partial to the intelligence services (the Foreign Intelligence Surveillance

Court in the USA, which issues warrants for FBI and NSA surveillance, has in thirty-three years turned down only eleven requests).

Where else to find guardians to guard the guardians? Never, I suspect, in the security services themselves, or in those who have been inculcated into believing that national security must always take precedence over civil liberties. We should be searching for patriotic sceptics, people like Alan Rusbridger and Helena Kennedy and AC Grayling, to place on oversight boards and commissions, citizens whose patriotism and decency is beyond question, who have an understanding of civil liberty and no predisposition to believe that everything the intelligence services say is true. (I could even describe myself as a patriotic sceptic, in the sense that I am loyal to both countries of which I am a citizen – except in cricket.)

Western intelligence agencies should have a published code of conduct, with disciplinary sanctions attached for its breach, and an independent tribunal to impose them. Lawyers, doctors and accountants have such a code – even estate agents, for heaven's sake, have their ethical standards. For spooks, however, you feel sometimes that the only rule is that the end justifies the means. I was rather taken with a memorandum supplied by Snowden of a secret meeting between UK–USA partners at GCHQ in Cheltenham a few years ago. The Americans suggested a dubious expedient be adopted and the Australians were enthusiastic. 'Oh no,' said the Canadians. 'We can't do that. We have a charter of rights.'

Chapter Fourteen

Assange in Ecuador

The Ecuadorian embassy is just beside Harrods, on the elevated ground floor of an Edwardian mansion block. It was the only safe place in London to leave your bicycle when for years it was staked out round the clock by teams of police doing nothing other than telling tourists the time. They were waiting for Julian Assange to lean so far over the balcony while addressing supporters that he might topple over it, into their outstretched arms, whereupon he would at that moment leave South America and instantaneously enter the United Kingdom. International law produces such miracles: embassy premises are 'inviolable' sovereign territory under the Vienna Convention, and one of Britain's best qualities is that it generally abides by international law. So across the threshold of this pied-à-terre in Kensington neither SAS unit nor Navy Seal may enter. When Scotland Yard picked up a rumour that Assange on dark nights would ascend to the roof to smoke Cuban cigars, they prepared a snatch squad, only to be told that Ecuadorian sovereignty extended skywards.

Inside the embassy, which I visit from time to time to see him, there are some reminders of Ecuador: a travel magazine on the front desk, a few toy llamas, a portrait of the incumbent President, and smatterings of conversational Spanish from the ambassador. At the end of a corridor is the refugee's lair, well stocked with books, computers, a sun lamp and an exercise machine. His bedroom is a converted toilet, a space that would rival in size the prison cell to which the government of the United States would wish him consigned for the rest of his life. But he is free, to do portentous things that keep his name in the headlines, like channelling Edward Snowden and exposing how the Democratic Party in the US dishonestly manipulated the presidential candidate selection process in favour of Hillary Clinton. That was in 2016, when the tergiversating Donald Trump tweeted, 'I love WikiLeaks'. Then he appointed as his CIA director one Mike Pompeo, who listed WikiLeaks as a 'hostile foreign intelligence agency', and an Attorney General, Jeff Sessions, who said that Assange's arrest was 'a priority'. In the musical chairs at the Trump White House, Pompeo is currently Secretary of State, likely to apply for the Australian's extradition should he venture out of the embassy.

What a long strange trip it has been (and continues to be) for this international man of mystery, whose baby face first glowed from the newswires in mid-2010, after he produced the 'collateral murder' tape, containing gunsight footage from a US Apache helicopter that showed US air crew shooting two Reuters reporters and several children. Assange's was no shoulder-slumped mugshot, but the visage of a dangerous cherub, beaming beneath a halo of blond hair, which hid a cranium that could outwit the most powerful country in the world. He had no money nor interest in acquiring any, which gave him a rock-star image among the internet generation in Europe as he sang his siren song of political transparency, justice and human rights. Just how mesmeric Assange had become by mid-August of that year may be measured by the front-page reporting, throughout the world, of the allegation that he had raped a woman in Stockholm. Within a few hours seven million people had clicked on the website of *Expressen*, the tabloid paper to which the story had been leaked. There was much less publicity a day or so later, when the senior prosecutor of Stockholm dropped the charge and said there was virtually nothing else to investigate.

Then, a week later, the charge was reinstated by a 'gender prosecutor' in another Swedish city, after a secret appeal by a politician acting for the complainant. Irrespective of the merit of the complaints, this was no way to run a legal system: prosecuting authorities should not be in the business of giving 'scoops' to tabloids and should not allow secret appeals to another prosecutor, from which hearing the suspect's lawyer is excluded. I said as much to a journalist, and in October I received a call from Assange, now back in London and in hiding as the threats from America and Sweden mounted. He was charming (save for a moment of pique when he lost an argument with my wife over the merits of Jane Austen) and when it turned out he had nowhere to stay for the next few nights it seemed only compatriotic to put him up.

Offering Julian Assange a bed for the night might have been hospitable, but it soon became clear that he was not going to sleep in it, or at all. He took up residence in the kitchen, computer on lap, curled up over it like a question mark. The only way I could get him to sleep – at 5 a.m. – was to indicate the kitchen's glass ceiling and to point out that any police helicopter could spot him a mile away. He instantly folded his computer and went off to bed. He was paranoid, of course, but he had every reason for paranoia, given the threats emanating from American politicians and now from Swedish prosecutors who vowed to issue a European Arrest Warrant (EAW) if he did not return to Stockholm for 'questioning' – after which there is no doubt they intended to charge him and consign him to prison with no right to bail.

The next day I took him for a walk in the autumnal serenity of Regents Park (its gnarled tree-trunks had been a favourite 'dead letter' drop for spies during the Cold War). He seemed genuinely horrified by the sex allegations – it was 'excruciating' even to talk about them. His mind was on higher things, but two women who announced that they 'wanted to teach him a lesson' had enlisted for this purpose the power of the Swedish state. He had gone to bed, separately, with each of them, at their initiative, but they later found out about each other and petulantly presented him with an ultimatum to have a blood test to prove he did not have HIV/AIDS, or else they would go to the police. He refused to be 'blackmailed' (as he put it) and the very next day one of them did go to the police. Soon the prosecutor's office was telling a tabloid that it was issuing a warrant for his arrest for rape. He had waited in Stockholm patiently for a month before returning to London in September, but now the Swedish prosecutors wanted him back and were pressing for his arrest. They would have succeeded, had they filled in the European Arrest Warrant forms correctly. While they corrected their mistake, Assange was allowed his moment of glory in London at the launch of 'Cablegate', when WikiLeaks began releasing classified cables from US embassies and consulates, exposing American diplomacy to a fascinated world.

In early December, the inevitable happened: Assange presented himself for arrest to the UK police and was taken to Wandsworth Prison, the first stage in his extradition to Sweden. By this time I was in Sydney, speaking at an international conference, and my client was not enjoying the petty restrictions of prison. My wife had sent him a Jane Austen novel, but he was not allowed access to the internet, and the latest issue of *Time* magazine was banned from the prison because it had his picture on the cover. His first bail hearing had not gone well. The Crown Prosecution Service (representing the Swedish prosecutor) endowed him with Houdini-like characteristics and suggested that well-connected supporters, such as US filmmaker Michael Moore, would be capable of spiriting him out of the country. So I was prevailed upon to give up a planned Christmas holiday on the beach with my family in order to make a new bail application in London. My old friend Richard Neville called before I left to impress upon me the importance of freeing Assange – I could scarcely believe it had been forty years since I had helped to get Neville out of the same prison after his conviction for publishing *Oz*.

The new bail hearing was jam-packed with journalists – hundreds attended from all over the world, straining and craning to see the human embodiment of internet freedom, captive in the court dock. I supported their request to allow, for the first time, tweeting from a courtroom, and it was granted: Assange's first legal precedent in favour of freedom of speech. The atmosphere was tense throughout, but the allegations were put in perspective and character witnesses refuted any idea that he was some kind of sex pest: bail was granted. The hundreds of tweets announcing his imminent release, however, proved premature: the Swedish 'gender prosecutor', demonstrating her determination to punish him, insisted on appealing to the High Court, a move that kept him in prison for a few more days. Her appeal failed and it was 6 p.m. on Thursday 16 December before Julian Assange emerged on the court steps – just in time for the evening news.

He stood beneath the gothic archway of London's High Court, his white hair dazzling in the television lights, speaking across the sheaf of microphones to a large crowd of supporters as light snow began to fall. I can be seen in the background, spoiling the iconic picture by looking at my watch (Assange can go on…). He spoke impressively, and after a week in which Cablegate revelations had wholly occupied the quality press of Western countries, this looked like his finest hour. A car to Norfolk had been laid on, and I told him to take it and lie low. A few hours later, I switched on *Newsnight*: there he was, live from Norfolk, clutching a cup of cocoa and trying to answer the questions I had advised him to avoid. He was attracted, like a moth, to TV lights.

The United States could not cope with his release of a quarter of a million of its diplomatic cables. There was a burst of hysteria against this alien, this peripatetic Australian, this blogosphere Machiavelli. Vice-President Biden labelled him 'a high-tech terrorist'. Mike Huckabee, on Fox News, suggested that he be assassinated. Shock jock Rush Limbaugh yearned for him 'to die of lead poisoning – from a bullet in the brain', while Sarah Palin, shooting from the lip, said 'he should be hunted down like Bin Laden' (which would at least have given him nine more years of freedom).

Later, visiting him in the Norfolk countryside while he was on bail, I would keep a wary eye open for Navy Seals. I received a few death threats from America for representing him, although since they came by email I did not take much notice. Assange, of course, had many more, one – from the US authorities – frighteningly real. A grand jury had been convened in secrecy in Maryland to consider charges under the Espionage Act, which would put him in a US 'supermax' prison for many years. I was not without contacts high in the Obama White House, and they told me, 'We don't want him, but the Pentagon does,' adding that the Pentagon usually gets its way. It kept its plans to punish him secret for some years – so successfully that many journalists and commentators in the UK derided Assange's fears – but in 2017 the US finally admitted that his arrest was 'a priority'. It had been ever since Cablegate.

*　　*　　*

It is worth going back, before going forward, to analyse why, exactly, America wants to incarcerate Assange for at least as long as it succeeded (until Obama mercifully interceded) in jailing his source, Chelsea Manning – which was for thirty-five years.

Assange was conceived off the coast of Townsville, on Magnetic Island. This is probably the only thing we have a common – he is a cyber geek and formerly a notorious hacker; I am a computer-phobic Luddite who still writes with a fountain pen (or at least a Montblanc biro). But, ironically, it is to the wisdom of the great Americans we have both turned for our free-speech arguments: to James Madison, urging for a First Amendment to create a nation 'where knowledge will forever govern ignorance, and a people who mean to be their own governors must arm themselves with the power that knowledge brings'. To Theodore Roosevelt, who called on 'muckrakers' to destroy what he described as 'the invisible government' – the corrupt links between business and politics. To the US Supreme Court, when it refused to injunct the publication of a top-secret leak, the 'Pentagon Papers', because it ruled that the only protection against abuse of power was an enlightened citizenry – enlightened by the *Post* and by the *New York Times*.

Julian Assange, the man from Magnetic Island, took the American legal aphorism that 'sunlight is the best disinfectant' seriously. He invented what might be termed an electronic dead-letter box, where sources could send him secret documents in complete confidence and remain anonymous because even he could not find out who they were. There would be no problem about protecting his sources – they could waterboard him for weeks and he could not tell because he would not know. All he could do would be to check the authenticity of the document – and WikiLeaks, so far as I know, has never published an inauthentic document.

So Assange became the latter-day Johnny Appleseed of information, scattering it far and wide, watching it inspire revolutions, expose crooked politicians and bent policemen, provoke policy debates and make us more knowledgeable about history and context. Now, hardly a week goes by without reference in some news story to a WikiLeaks revelation.

The organisation (using 'organisation' very loosely – WikiLeaks is basically Julian Assange, an inveterate loner, with a few assistants) began in 2006, publishing documents about the massive corruption in Daniel arap Moi's Kenya. Then documents were leaked exposing tax evasion through Cayman Island banks, then a document from the Church of Scientology, revealing malpractice. Then documents relating to banking fraud in Iceland; the dangers of a nuclear accident in Iran; and the greedy price-gouging of US and British contractors after the war in Iraq.

All these revelations were of obvious and immediate public interest and made him pretty popular. His exposés have not always benefited liberals or the left: WikiLeaks also helped to reveal 'Climategate', the apparent rigging of data by scientists. This gave a free kick to climate-change deniers, but it was true and WikiLeaks did not hesitate to host it.

After this came the material we now know to have been provided by Chelsea Manning. It is difficult to forget 'collateral murder', the tape that showed the aerial manslaughter of civilians by US forces. Then, in quick succession:

- The Afghan War Logs: revealing far higher civilian casualties from drone attacks than the US had been prepared to admit.
- Iraq-gate: no fewer than 400,000 filed reports, showing many thousands more civilian casualties than the US had admitted, and providing a treasure trove for war historians by revealing how the Iraq War had been fought on the ground, how blind eyes were turned to torture at Abu Ghraib and elsewhere, and how US forces would sometimes hand their prisoners over for torture and murder to pro-government death squads.

At this point, there had been only muted protest from the US government. But a number of other countries had become disturbed and had taken action to block all WikiLeaks-related websites, threatening to jail any of their citizens caught sending material to Assange. Which countries were these? Let me list them: China, Syria, North Korea, Russia, Thailand and Zimbabwe. These enemies of freedom sensed the danger, because dictators cannot cope with freedom of information.

Then, in November 2010, came Cablegate – the release of a quarter of a million American diplomatic cables. Hillary Clinton, then Secretary of State, warned foreign governments to be prepared for some unpleasant comments among the US government's supposedly private communications. They said, so she reported, 'Don't worry. You should see what we say about you.'

And so it came to pass that the people of Egypt and Tunisia discovered facts about the endogenous corruption of their rulers that helped to fuel the Arab Spring. That phenomenon has complex causes, but in Tunisia anger erupted among protesters when they read a cable from the US ambassador describing the Ben Ali regime, accurately, as a political kleptocracy. It was headed 'Corruption in Tunisia – what's yours is mine'. The most virulent attack on WikiLeaks came in the midst of Cablegate, on 14 January 2011. Assange was accused of leading the protesters in Tunis astray by false claims against their incorruptible President. That attack was made by Colonel Gaddafi.

Once he was on bail in Norfolk, Assange worked to transmit the cables to ninety different countries, alerting their people to misfeasance, hitherto hidden, in their public life. The cables revealed Hillary Clinton's plans to bug diplomats at the UN headquarters, and how Saudi Arabia and other Gulf States had urged the US to 'cut off the head of the snake' – the Iranian nuclear programme – by bombing Tehran.

But as Cablegate unfolded, it revealed, at least in my view, the most surprising secret of all: that US diplomacy is reasonably principled and pragmatic, and better informed and more objective than Western or locally based journalists. What WikiLeaks was doing, in some respects, was promulgating a CIA-sourced view of the world, ironically made to seem all the more credible by the US threats to silence Assange. The Cablegate releases certainly showed how heavy is the burden of world leadership that falls on the United States, under constant pressure from so many 'friendly' governments to bomb and brutalise, or at least protect them against their enemies.

Nonetheless, America was upset by dissemination of its diplomatic messages and the shrill, exaggerated voices calling for the messenger to be killed continued unhappily from the land of the First Amendment. American pride had been hurt by a pesky Australian, so they targeted him by grand jury proceedings and the military took out its anger on young Chelsea Manning, treating her abominably in prison until Hillary Clinton's press spokesman, P. J. Crowley, resigned in protest. Manning had been kept for eight months in solitary confinement, naked and without blanket or pillow, awoken every few minutes for a pretended 'suicide watch'. Her prosecutors hoped she would confess to being 'groomed' by Assange, and at one point, according to her lawyer, threatened her with the death penalty if she did not. Then came the CIA pressure on PayPal, MasterCard and Visa, to which they succumbed, to stop receiving donations for WikiLeaks or Assange. (You can still buy Nazi uniforms and Ku Klux Klan outfits with your Visa card but you can't donate to WikiLeaks.)

On what basis was Assange demonised? There is no doubt that the cables were of manifest public interest, revealing many examples of human rights violations and political corruption that American diplomats (with their CIA sources) were well aware of, but which had not been made public. But his accusers claimed that release of the cables had put 'lives at risk', and that he had 'blood on his hands'. However, over seven years have passed since Cablegate began, and five since all the cables were released. There has been no fatality causally related to their publication. Several US ambassadors and cable-authoring diplomats have had to be withdrawn because of their comments about their host country, but by August 2013, at the sentencing proceedings for Chelsea Manning, the Pentagon could produce no evidence that release of the cables had put any life in jeopardy, and was forced to retract an earlier claim that it had.

The lack of fatalities is unsurprising, and indeed to be expected, because none of the WikiLeaks cables was classified 'top secret' – the designation that diplomats must use if release would put lives at risk. The Pentagon Papers were classified 'top secret' and distributed only to a small circle of officials, but up to three million people, including 22-year-old soldiers, had access to the cables that Chelsea Manning uploaded on a Lady Gaga disc for Julian Assange. The fact that they were not classified as 'top secret' meant their authors did not expect any lethal reprisals if they were .

published, and none was in fact suffered, even after Assange published all the cables, including the parts 'redacted' by nervous newspapers.

We can all envisage situations where 'leaks' would be wrong and should be severely punished, because of the criminal way in which they are obtained – by bribery or duress or telephone hacking. Custodians of genuine secrets have a duty to classify them as such and to protect them, by 'top secret' classification, by encrypting or redacting their names, or simply by keeping them anonymous. It all comes back to a proper classification policy. If a 'top secret' class of harmful information does get out, then the first duty of government is to take steps to protect as best it can any persons whom the leak might put at risk, and then to make sure that its top-secret information is better protected in future. If it considers prosecuting the publisher – whether the *New York Times* or Julian Assange – it must only do so on evidence that they have procured the information by bribery or corruption or, at the very least, by inciting the leaker to reveal the information contrary to his duty, and always subject to a public interest defence if the information reveals serious abuse of power. There can be no criminal blame attached to journalists or publishers who receive state secrets from those who wish to divulge them. They have an ethical duty to protect their source, although if that source is caught through their own carelessness, he or she will have to suffer the legal consequences. (Chelsea Manning, for example, was caught because she confessed to someone who befriended her in an online chatroom.)

The issue of 'incitement' has been much discussed in relation to print journalism: there can be no criticism of a journalist who receives a secret document through the post from an unknown source, or meets a known source who, without encouragement other than a meal or a train fare home, hands over or reveals the secret information. Watergate's 'Deep Throat' (FBI associate director Mark Felt) would move a pot plant on his window ledge to signal to Bob Woodward and Carl Bernstein that he was ready to talk. Assange's arrangement for an electronic drop-box was the equivalent. In the Chelsea Manning proceedings, the prosecution suggested that the man Manning described as a 'crazy white-haired Aussie' and allegedly contacted online under the code name 'pressassociation' might have helped her navigate the contents of the Lady Gaga disc into the WikiLeaks electronic letter box, but the same principle would apply: Assange as journalist/publisher was not forcing or paying or inciting Manning to do what she very much wanted to do in any event.

There was no evidence against Assange to warrant opening the grand jury proceedings – an oppressive mechanism long abolished in England, in which prosecutors summon jurors and witnesses to a secret room where they alone hold court and there is no judge to exercise any independent or impartial control of proceedings. The jurors usually do what the prosecutor who has summoned them requests. 'A grand jury would indict a ham sandwich,' American lawyers say. The grand jury will return (or has, I suspect, already returned) a sealed indictment against Assange accusing him of Espionage Act crimes (so the US will be ready with an extradition application the minute Assange leaves the Ecuadorian embassy).

If the CIA gets its hands on Assange he will grow old in a US supermax prison, in order to deter other would-be publishers of US diplomatic data and military records. But WikiLeaks was not based in America and Assange owes it no national allegiance: he received the information outside the country and shared it with the media at the *Guardian* offices in London. Under the vague but broad provisions of the US Espionage Act of 1917, passed amid hysteria about spies in wartime, can a US grand jury's writ run anywhere in the world? We shall see. He was public enemy number one in Washington after Cablegate in 2010–11 and again in 2016–17 when he published leaked emails exposing chicanery within the Democratic Party, allegedly sent to him by Russian hackers. But he is really in no different position to any journalist who receives authentic information of public interest from a source who is willing to go to some lengths to give it, and who really wants it to be published.

It can only diminish US leadership and dim the beacon of the First Amendment to raise that old blunderbuss the Espionage Act and to aim it beyond the jurisdiction at a publisher who is a national of a friendly country, who disseminated information of public interest that was not 'top secret' and was in any event accessible to three million Americans. Yet this is what the Trump administration intends, by an interpretation of the Espionage Act that would give US courts an exorbitant jurisdiction over nationals of other countries for their operations outside America. Its new theory, to catch Assange, is that the First Amendment applies to protect only publishers who are American citizens. A ruling to this effect by Trump-appointed judges would be disastrous for free speech in the US and in the world.

If the CIA were really intelligent, it would feed Assange some information about the corruption of Putin and his clique, or that confirms Putin's order of the death by polonium poisoning in London of his enemy Alexander Litvinenko. This would test Assange's integrity, but I am pretty sure he would publish it.

*   *   *

In 2017, Sweden's 'gender prosecutor' finally withdrew her request for an extradition warrant to interview (and evidently to charge) Julian Assange with 'minor rape'. She did so under pressure from the Swedish courts, after her behaviour in refusing for six years his repeated offers to be interviewed in England was severely criticised by the UN Working Group on Arbitrary Detention. Her allegations have left a lingering pall over his character, but he has never been vouchsafed the right of having them tested before an open and impartial court – Sweden, as I shall explain, offered neither. I had them thoroughly investigated when I led his defence team at the hearing over the arrest warrant. For all the books, movies, documentaries and articles about him, the facts are never fairly stated. Let me summarise them.

Sweden has three classes of rape: extreme, serious and minor. Assange was charged with 'minor rape' – a contradiction in terms, but that is what the Swedes actually call the allegation against him. It amounted to having consensual sex without a condom, the use of which had been an implied condition of the consent. The maximum sentence for 'minor rape' is four years, and experts in Swedish sentencing law – which is merciful – told me that given the circumstances the likely penalty for Assange if he were convicted would be non-custodial.

In the case of both complainants, the police dossier confirms that the sexual engagements were not merely consensual but actively desired. Assange had come to Sweden at the invitation of a fringe political party to deliver a lecture on Saturday 14 August 2010. The first complainant, a 33-year-old Social Democrat politician, told the organisers that Assange could stay in her tiny one-room, one-bed flat, giving them an assurance that she would be out of Stockholm on the Friday evening – Friday the 13th, as it happens. She returned, however, for no apparent reason, and took him to dinner and then to bed – supplying a condom that she requested him to use, and he did.

One week later she alleged to police that at some point that evening he had torn it, or had torn it off. Oddly, given that this event was the basis of several molestation charges, she made no complaint the next morning, Saturday, when a colleague called to take Assange to his lecture. At that time she was proudly describing herself as his 'personal assistant', and tweeting to the world about how 'cool' and clever he was (tweets that she later removed). She also later removed her puerile blog, entitled '7 steps to legal revenge', which advised women on how to avenge themselves on 'cheating' men: 'You should use a punishment with sex involved, like getting his new partner to be unfaithful or ensure he gets a madman after him – the ideal is revenge as strong as possible.' Assange, for all his technical genius, does not appear to have looked at her blog before he permitted her to leap into bed. On Saturday afternoon, she volunteered to be his hostess at a 'crayfish party' (Swedes are inordinately fond of these lobster-and-liquor feasts) and arranged it for that evening in his honour. Witnesses confirm that she insisted he stay with her, despite others offering to put him up.

She did not complain to the police until one week later, after learning that he had spent the following Monday night in bed with the second complainant, a 26-year-old self-confessed 'groupie', who told police she had attended Assange's lecture in the hope of sexually attracting him – an objective in which she succeeded all too well.

This second complainant took him by train to her flat in the suburbs on the Monday night, and took him to bed, where he fell asleep and began to snore – to her annoyance, as she tweeted at the time to her rather voyeuristic friends. However, during the course of that night they had intercourse three or four times. On one occasion, when she was 'half asleep', as she put it, she asked whether he was 'wearing anything' and he laconically replied, 'I'm wearing you.' She did not object at the time but later inferred that he was not wearing a condom.

Her friends had read that he had spent some time in Africa, so they advised her to have him take a test for HIV/AIDS. Her only way of contact was to call his personal assistant – the aforesaid first complainant, the self-styled expert on revenge who was now given a motive for her own. That's when this 'personal assistant' called a journalist friend of Assange to make a menacing demand: unless he took a blood test for HIV/AIDS, both women would go to the police.

The journalist told police that he called Assange, who reacted with shock and said he was willing to take a blood test but did not want to do it as a result of blackmail. The next day (Friday 20 August) the first complainant directed the second to a police officer, who just happened to be her political colleague and Facebook friend.

In the course of the interview that ensued between this policewoman and the second complainant, the policewoman informed her that Assange would be charged with rape. She reacted to this news by fainting. Nonetheless, a few minutes later, an acting prosecutor, without further investigation, issued the warrant, and in breach of the rules revealed the fact to *Expressen*, a tabloid paper. Its scoop the next day – 'Assange Wanted for Rape' – went live to millions throughout the world. Two days later Stockholm's very experienced senior prosecutor cancelled the arrest warrant and publicly stated that there was no basis to pursue a charge of rape. This statement received little publicity.

I have given but a cursory summary of the 98-page police dossier – it can be downloaded in full on the internet, so readers can judge for themselves whether my analysis is fair. It included some eerie photographs of what looked like a jellyfish but was in fact a condom, supplied to the police by the first complainant, who said she had found it on the floor of her flat, two weeks after Assange had stayed on Friday the 13th, and it might have been the one he ripped, or ripped off. There was a lab report, from a lab

that reported that it had no experience of examining condoms but speculated that it could have been torn. This hardly amounted to corroboration
of the first complainant's story, but the photograph gets a surprised laugh
from the audience when it appears in the *We Steal Secrets* documentary
about WikiLeaks.

So this was not 'rape' as that term is normally understood. Whether
it was an offence did not matter for the purposes of EAW extradition
(Sweden had ticked the 'rape' box on the warrant, which was enough)
but the very use of the word 'rape' gave a false impression of malice
and violence.

I should make clear that I believe that it should be a sexual offence
for a man deliberately to deceive a sex partner whose consent has been
conditional upon his use of a condom. But in the Swedish police dossier
– the prosecution papers, so to speak – there was no clear evidence that
the second complainant had put any condition on her consent, nor indeed
any evidence (other than his equivocal reply) that he had not, in fact, worn
a condom. So how, after Stockholm's chief prosecutor had declared that
there was no evidence, did the case go any further?

Under Swedish law, victims are entitled from the outset to their own
lawyer, paid for by the state. The two complainants chose a controversial,
self-publicising Social Democrat politician, formerly Sweden's 'gender
ombudsman', who had called for a ban on football matches with Germany because the country had legalised prostitution. This man secretly
contacted the 'gender prosecutor' in another city, Gothenburg, who was
well known for her publicly stated view that prosecution of men charged
with sex crimes is socially worthwhile even in cases in which the defendant
is not found to be guilty.

Under a secret process, from which Assange's lawyer was entirely excluded, this 'gender prosecutor' reinstated the rape charge and then took
over the case. Assange obediently remained in Sweden throughout these
events, turning up voluntarily to the police station to answer questions
at an interview on 30 August. He denied the allegations, and waited in
Sweden until the new prosecutor informed his lawyer that he was free to
leave the country.

Back in London, he heard that the gender prosecutor wanted him to come back to Sweden to undergo a second police interview. He offered to answer police questions by telephone (the first complainant, after all, had made her complaint by telephone), by video-link from Scotland Yard's special video suite, by Skype or in person with police at the Australian or Swedish embassies in London. The prosecutor refused, although these methods of interview are regularly used in Sweden and other countries when witnesses and suspects are abroad. She was determined to get him back to Sweden, and there was little doubt that, whatever he said in that interview, she planned to arrest him immediately afterwards and to make a spectacle of his imprisonment. So she issued a European Arrest Warrant (EAW).

It is rare to overcome an EAW. The leading countries of Europe agreed, sensibly enough, to make extradition between them for criminal offences very easy. All that is required is for a judicial authority in one country to issue an EAW and send it to police in another country, who will arrest the suspect and, subject to any flaw in the warrant, or so long as that trial will not be flagrantly unfair, dispatch him or her to stand that trial. The technical points usually run by lawyers at these extradition hearings would be unlikely to avail Assange: the British prosecution authority had ironed out the initial mistakes and the Swedes had ticked all the right boxes. They had, for example, ticked the box on the form confirming the crime for which he was sought was 'rape'. We could not complain (although we tried) about the fact that he was only wanted at this stage for questioning, or about the fact that he had already been questioned, or about the rejection of his reasonable offer to undergo that questioning at Scotland Yard or at the Swedish or American embassies, or by Skype.

The only effective way to beat an EAW is by proving that the requesting state has some serious defect in its legal system – something that makes it fundamentally unfair by international human rights standards. At first, I thought this would be a hopeless line to run – no European justice system has a more squeaky-clean image than Sweden, a nice neutral nation that has given the world such treats as IKEA and ABBA. But a quick read of Stieg Larsson's novels suggested a darker underbelly, so I sent Jen Robinson to Stockholm to investigate what would happen to Julian if he were extradited and put on trial there. She returned with the startling information that his trial would be held in total secrecy, and even the judgment would omit the crucial factual details. There would be no jury, just a judge sitting with three 'lay judges' who would vote on the verdict, people not selected at random or from a professional magistracy, but nominated by the main political parties, for which reason they were often retired politicians. All leaders of these parties had by now condemned Assange – and the first complainant, her lawyer and her Facebook friend policewoman who decided to arrest, were all members of the main opposition, the Social Democrats. As the trial would be in secret, any bias shown by these superannuated politician-judges would be undetectable.

This had to be a winning point – I simply could not imagine our Supreme Court justices, however much they might personally wish the nation rid of Assange, ordering him forcibly deported to face a secret trial. The 'open justice' principle is engraved on their hearts – it is a constant and powerful rhetoric throughout English case law, usually quoting Jeremy Bentham: 'Publicity is the very soul of justice … It keeps the judge, while trying, under trial.'[70] If we could get the district judge to find as a fact that Assange faced a secret trial, the higher courts would have to prevent his extradition.

Secrecy was the basis of our main attack on the warrant. The 'gender prosecutor' actually conceded it, stating that the purpose is that 'the complainants may give evidence in confidence' – i.e. confident that their testimony, and any cross-examination that may undercut or demolish it, will never be revealed to the public. This means, to those familiar with the Anglo-American tradition of open courts, that justice will not be seen to be done, and may therefore not be done at all. It means that if lies are told, members of the public who know the truth will not come forward, because they will not know that those lies are being told. In Sweden, only the verdict is published, and sometimes the judge's legal reasoning, but because the evidence has not been heard or published, it will be impossible to know whether the reasoning is reasonable. While it is right that efforts should be made in rape cases to comfort alleged victims, that can best be done by limiting questions about their personal life and (in certain cases) granting them anonymity. Otherwise, open justice requires testimony in public. Sweden has the highest reported level of violent rape in Europe (a statistic that Amnesty International has deplored), and allowing complainants to give evidence in secret trials has not produced more convictions.

From society's standpoint, the Swedish practice is wrong – the public is entitled to details of the case, and publicity serves the deterrent purpose of criminal law, as well as providing accountability for police, lawyers and judges. To deny open justice to Assange would be not only unprincipled but absurd: statements by his accusers concerning his sexual behaviour, made in intimate detail, had been leaked to the media from the prosecution papers, published in skewed and selective detail by newspapers, and placed on the internet for anyone to access. No trial could be 'fair' unless it permitted the public to observe how Assange challenged that evidence, how he gave testimony himself and how his own witnesses testified, as well as how the lawyers and judges behaved.

Proof that Assange's trial in Sweden would not be fair was the key to keeping him in London. This depended on a finding of fact from the district judge to the effect that the evidence would be heard in secret. We knew that this was the invariable practice at rape trials in Sweden, although there was no statute that required it. It was at first blush surprising that the practice had never been challenged, either at appellate level or under the European Convention on Human Rights (which guarantees an open trial by independent and impartial judges), but there is a first time for everything.

At the hearing, we called a retired appeal judge from Stockholm and a senior Swedish prosecutor who testified that rape trials were indeed invariably held behind closed doors. The district judge in London accepted that this was the long-standing practice, 'certainly alien as far as our system is concerned'. Crucially, he concluded that:

Any trial in this case would be heard by four judges, one professional and three lay. The lay judges are chosen by political parties ... the evidence will almost certainly be heard privately. There has been considerable adverse publicity in Sweden for Mr Assange, in the popular press, on the television and in Parliament.

This factual finding was exactly what we wanted, even if the district judge failed to see that closed courts and political judges were not merely 'alien to our system' but should be alien to all systems. His reasoning was illogical and open to appeal. He said only that 'if the Swedish practice was a flagrant breach of human rights, I would expect there to be a body of cases against Sweden confirming that'.

This is a bad argument – novel cases are brought successfully all the time to challenge time-honoured practices as inconsistent with human rights rules. And there is a simple explanation for the failure to challenge secrecy, namely that almost all defendants in rape cases are very happy to have the sordid and brutal details of the evidence shielded from public view – that is why their lawyers do not complain. Moreover, although there had been no specific case brought against Sweden, the European Court has made many rulings against closed courts in other countries. Even in terrorist cases, where witnesses might be at risk, the court has said that publicity is 'indispensable' and in a recent case, concerning a public figure whose alleged sexual affairs had been discussed in the media, the court insisted that considerations of privacy or 'dignity of witnesses' could never justify closing the court doors, because it was in the interests of the general public that justice should be seen to be done. So the prospects of appeal success, on this ground, were very good indeed.

'Team Assange' – myself, John Jones (a brilliant junior, soon to take silk, and author of a textbook on extradition) and Amal Alamuddin (as she then was), and our solicitors Mark Stephens and Jen Robinson – concentrated on this winning point in writing the appeal submissions. It was the only ground on which I thought we would succeed, although there were more technical arguments. Necessarily, it invoked a full-blooded assault on Sweden for a fundamental error in its handling of rape and sexual assault cases – by ignoring the 'open justice' guarantee in all the human rights treaties it had ratified and allowing a bench mainly composed of superannuated politicians to decide them in secret. But after the grounds were filed, a strange thing happened – although it was normal enough with Assange, who has a long history of falling out with supporters and advisers. He had a meltdown about Mark Stephens, his dedicated solicitor, and sacked him. Then, with new lawyers, his legal strategy changed dramatically. He would no longer be making any criticism of Sweden or its legal system.

Although the 'open justice' argument was far and away his best shot, this ground was withdrawn.

Why did Assange throw away his trump card? I don't know, because I was not party to this change of strategy, which I thought ill-advised and indeed ridiculous. He instructed another solicitor, and took heed of other advisers, and it was announced (in a Bay Area newspaper in San Francisco, of all places) that he would no longer be making my criticism of the Swedish legal system. Media reports said that his strategy changed in the hope that the Swedish government and the two complainants might be mollified and would drop the extradition request. This seemed oddly optimistic, for a man famous for declaring that 'Sweden is the Saudi Arabia of feminism', and who had taken every opportunity to condemn, quite rightly, the country's justice system, on grounds including those that had now been withdrawn. It was also reported that overtures were made on his behalf to the two complainants after this radical change of tack, but they and their self-publicising lawyer (always available when the media wanted someone to attack Assange) proved unwilling to budge. Withdrawal of the open justice appeal grounds deprived him of the best answer to the question 'Why don't you go to Sweden – you will get a fair trial there?', namely that we had proven he would not get a fair trial there.

*   *   *

A few days before the surrender deadline, I met him and his rather gloomy Swedish lawyers at a farewell party thrown by Helena Kennedy. He did his best to be upbeat, giving a little speech of thanks, but his heart was not in it. I thought I detected fear in his eyes, the sort of fear I had seen in the faces of men as I had farewelled them on death row, although that might have been my imagination. But if there was fear in his eyes at that party, it was certainly not fear of Sweden. It was fear of ending his life in an American supermax.

Julian had always believed that Sweden would be his gateway to America. The WikiLeaks cables fed this belief: in them, US diplomats boasted that behind its pretence of neutrality, the right-wing Swedish government was strongly pro-American. At the time of his arrest on the EAW, it was being advised by none other than Karl Rove – 'Turd Blossom', as George W. Bush so fondly described his election guru. In 2006, Sweden had been caught illegally 'rendering' terrorist suspects to the CIA without allowing them any court process, and had been condemned by the European Parliament for so doing. There was good reason to think that the Swedes would be happy to comply with any request from the US Justice Department. Any onward extradition would, under EAW law, require the consent of the British government, but that consent would certainly be forthcoming. Assange, in other words, had a not unreasonable fear that, once in Sweden, whether he was acquitted or released after his sentence, he would be re-arrested before he could leave the country and held for extradition to the US. He would not be a free man before he was an old man.

I don't think that Assange planned his walk into the embassy of Ecuador the day before he had to surrender. He had struck up a good relationship with President Correa when he had interviewed him for his TV show the previous week, and he was doubtless aware of the possibility of asylum in an embassy protected by diplomatic immunity. Maybe he simply could not face entering that dark tunnel that had formed in his mind, down which he would go – to Sweden and thence inevitably to America and permanent loss of liberty.

Assange's arrival pleased the Ecuadorians, keen to flex a political muscle in Latin America, where everyone thought they had acted to defy the Yankees – and the US could not take reprisals or put on economic pressure because that would be an admission that they really did intend to take Assange should he go to Sweden. It even pleased Correa's opposition: his new friendship with media freedom meant he might stop persecuting the local press. What seemed at first merely a gamble to delay the inevitable soon took on a life of its own. By the beginning of 2018, Assange had served five and a half years (and still counting) of diplomatic incarceration. He has single-mindedly suffered the loss of his freedom of movement in return for retaining his freedom of speech.

I visit him from time to time. WikiLeaks continues to provoke, although he has copped a lot of flak from some supporters who think that his exposure of skulduggery in the Democratic Party helped Donald Trump win the US election in 2016. The CIA says that those emails originated from Russian hackers, which he disputes, although that would not breach Assange's principle of publishing anything of public interest. As I have said, I hope he would be principled enough to release any secret information he received about the corruption of Putin and his comrades, were the CIA smart enough to send him (anonymously, of course) the details.

The US Justice Department, in 2018, is still determined to put him in prison. What do they intend to charge him with? We know now, because a court has disclosed a warrant that the FBI obtained against Google to search the private emails of Assange and his assistants; they alleged that he violated five sections of the US Espionage Act 1917. The sentences for doing so add up to forty-five years.

That is Assange's reason for remaining in the Ecuadorian embassy after the Swedish proceedings against him were dropped. As soon as he emerges, the British police would arrest him for a breach of bail and although that is a minor offence (meriting at most a few weeks in prison) the US would immediately pounce and commence extradition proceedings, which would begin with his arrest and end two years later either with his release from prison in Britain (after a successful challenge to the extradition) or, if this failed, forced departure to Maryland for trial and (if convicted) incarceration for thirty-five or so years in an American supermax.

The Ecuadorian government, having granted him residency for over five years, at the beginning of 2018 made him an Ecuadorian citizen, and also appointed him as their political counsellor – a diplomatic position that normally carries with it immunity (and a salary). The UK has so far refused to recognise his diplomatic status – a change in its position since it automatically accepted the non-existent credentials of Dr Juffali. Ecuador claims this is a breach of the Vienna Convention. If the UK recognises his status it could then declare him 'persona non grata', which would require him to leave the embassy and the country but permit him to do so cloaked with immunity from US extradition requests, although there is no direct flight from London to Ecuador and Mr Pompeo might order the interception of any aircraft carrying his priority target. It's a story that will run and run, even if Assange stays put.

*   *   *

I don't share Assange's politics, but I agree with A. J. P. Taylor's maxim in that I think he's one of those gifted and mischievous eccentrics that society should learn to treat with a degree of toleration and even appreciation. I detected that he was somewhere on the autism spectrum before he accepted that he probably was, and my experience of my son's condition may also explain why I have stuck with him (despite losing several briefs from governments for doing so), while many of his supporters have fallen out. He is in many respects his own worst enemy and gives little thought to people other than himself, but his legion of critics – mostly journalists who have never met him – continue to overlook his genius and (actually) his courage. He is not a liberal's ideal of a 'nice' person when his sarcasm turns nasty or he turns against friends, and snobbish critics in England typically deplore his table manners (they accuse him of eating with his fingers) and always remind readers, as if it makes him the ultimate outsider, that he is an Australian. Without money or freedom, he is in no position to refute the calumnies. When not raging against enemies real and imaginary (but never including himself), he is charming, funny and autodidactically erudite.

Assange is an Australian publisher, whose actions all took place outside America – yet he's accused under the Espionage Act of disloyalty to America. He's not an American and owes it no allegiance, and despite unproven allegations of loyalty to Russia, I suspect (and hope) that he remains rather his own man. I'm not alone in that view – when *The Simpsons* made its 500th programme, they honoured not Mandela or Madonna, but Assange.

Kathy Lette was asked to write some dialogue, so when Assange cooks a BBQ for Homer, and Marge asks for the recipes for his delicious marinade, he replies, 'I'm sorry, but I never reveal my sauces.'

Chapter Fifteen

Freedom of Speech

<hr>

T he most common theme in my practice and writing, until it became
subsumed in my human rights work, was freedom of expression. In
the course of my career I have at some stage defended almost every newspaper, television and radio station, video game supplier and picture agency, in
trouble for what they had published or intended to publish. There were two
exceptions: the lawyers at *The Sun* and the *News of the World* never briefed
me (which I took as a compliment), nor did the lily-livered executives at
the BBC, always reluctant for a full-blooded fight against the government.
In the US, the First Amendment culture had created a mindset in which
media groups would make common cause to fight any restrictions, but in
Britain there was no organised lobby for freedom of speech.

After I gave a provocative speech at the Edinburgh Television Festival
about how broadcasters had supinely let Mrs Thatcher foist upon them a
new censorship body (chaired by William Rees-Mogg, who insisted that
'television must behave itself like a guest in the home'), a media defence
organisation was put together by John Birt and Barry Cox. It was a very
British organisation – about a dozen of us, exclusively male, chaired by
Lord McGregor (who had chaired a Royal Commission on the Press),
meeting over dinner at the men-only Garrick Club. It was not really my
scene as we politely wined and dined Thatcher ministers, although it did
have one important lobbying success when we persuaded Leon Brittan
to amend a new law increasing police powers so as to limit their ability to
seize journalistic material.[71]

Everyone seemed to agree with Tom Stoppard: 'I'm all for free speech. It's the newspapers I can't stand.' That was, in part, a problem caused by the state of media law prior to the Human Rights Act. 'The blind goddess of British justice raises her sword against the investigative journalist while her other hand fondles the Sunday muckraker,' I complained in my first of several books on the subject. Libel was and still is the worst constraint – the burden of proof, quite illogically (those who bring cases should prove them) and alone of all civil law actions, is placed on the media defendant. Contempt of court protected lawyers and judges and litigants from criticism; there was no defence to official secrets prosecutions, and breach of confidence was a growth area used to force newspapers to reveal their sources. On the other hand, there was absolutely no protection for privacy – English law had never acknowledged it as a right and the tabloid press was full of the grossest intrusions. There was a portentous organisation called the Press Council, paid for by the press proprietors with the object of staving off the advent of a privacy law by pretending to discipline the press. It was a confidence trick.

That, at least, was the conclusion of an inquiry into the Press Council I chaired in 1980, published as a book, *People Against the Press*.[72] The inquiry had been set up by the unions, although my colleagues were mostly liberal (they included Richard '*The Uses of Literacy*' Hoggart, Geoffrey Goodman, Katharine Whitehorn and Phillip Whitehead MP). We were all concerned at the demands for statutory regulation (coming, at that time, from the right) and I began with a simple refutation: 'Journalism is not a profession. It is the exercise by occupation of the right to free expression available to every citizen. That right, being available to all, cannot in principle be withdrawn from a few by a system of licensing or professional registration.' But it could be made the subject of criticism and correction, and we produced a 'Leveson Report' more than thirty years before Leveson, with some differences. His idea that the media should be forced by law to make apologies is ridiculous. (When Richard Ingrams was asked in court whether he had ever published falsehoods in *Private Eye*, he replied, 'Yes. The apologies.') Worse was his recommendation – which has actually made it into legislation (though the government has not yet dared to bring it into operation) that newspapers which do not sign up to a state regulator should pay the legal costs of claimants who make false claims against them. We recommended instead a law to protect privacy (which has now come to pass, thanks to the Human Rights Act) and a statutory right of reply for those subjected to demonisation and unfair attacks. This measure operates satisfactorily in some European countries and does not involve a threat to free speech: on the contrary, it permits abuses of free speech to be mitigated by ordering more free speech.

At first, I had found it difficult to work out a way to measure the success (or failure) of the Press Council, but then I hit upon the idea of asking its complainants. I wrote to everyone who had obtained an adjudication from the Press Council in the past five years. Those who'd had their complaints upheld were far more critical of its conduct that those whose complaints had been dismissed! It was obvious that 'self-regulation' was a sham and that a body – any body (whether called the Press Council or, later, the Press Complaints Commission or, currently, the Independent Press Standards Organisation) – funded by press proprietors would never really hold the press to account. There are, today, far fewer invasions of privacy, but that is not because of IPSO but because victims can sue for invasions of privacy, and receive damages (in the phone-hacking cases, for example, large damages from the tabloids) that the 'self-regulator' could never order.

The 'right of reply' has never been put into law, although it might do something to mitigate the real vice of the British press today, namely the way it passes off propaganda as 'news'. Stories are twisted to serve the editorial bias – in favour of Brexit, against Corbyn, and so on. IPSO made the mistake of declaring that editors have 'a right to be partisan' – which they do, in their editorials (which in consequence few bother to read). So editors have interpreted it as a right to denigrate unfairly, with stories based on anonymous sources (sometimes invented or exaggerated), confected quotations, dishonest headlines and prejudicial language. I was correct, back in 1980, to say that journalism is not a profession, and as a trade it is sometimes reckless and even contemptible, but I have never doubted the free-speech principle or the need to loosen the legal restraints over public interest reporting.

For that reason, I have become a trustee of the Bureau of Investigative Journalism – a body of reporters working with experts to understand and explain the problems caused by governmental and corporate malfeasance or negligence. The extraction of accurate information and its reliable analysis remain the greatest challenge for journalists today – making the news 'worthy' rather than 'fake'. Freedom of speech still relies on the philosophical foundation provided by the poet Milton – put everything in the public marketplace, and the good and the true will combat and drive out the bad and the false. An optimistic credo today, Milton's *Areopagitica*, but stirring nonetheless and worth repeating as often as possible.[73] I do not get too worked up by university students 'no-platforming' speakers who have ample mainstream outlets for their provocations and, *pace* Voltaire, I no longer think it necessary to fight to the death for expressions I do not like (there are too many of them). But John Stuart Mill's test remains valid – the state must not censor unless it can prove harm – and other rights (such as privacy, or confidentiality claimed by officials or corporations) must give way to the public interest in publication.

*   *   *

It was once famously said that freedom of speech in Britain depended on what 'a jury of shopkeepers' would allow – and that trial of media offences by juries was the best safeguard against government censorship. But that was said a long time ago, in relation to the printed word: once images were made to move on a screen, in cinemas and then on videos in a home, juries ceased to be trusted to keep the nation safe from bad pictures because, especially in the 1970s, they had a propensity to acquit. So for films and DVDs and PlayStation games and other forms of visual entertainment, the country has come to rely on a censor. It's called the British Board of Film Classification (BBFC), a little bureaucracy in Soho Square whose decisions are subject to its own appeals board, and occasionally to judicial review in the High Court. It has the unobjectionable task of 'certifying' films for various age classifications, but the more questionable role of banning an occasional video or visual game to show the tabloids (and the MPs they incite to outrage) that it really does protect the public from sex and violence. The first censor I met – a charming old man called John Trevelyan – admitted that its real purpose was to protect the profits of the distributors who paid for it. He did a deal with the DPP, who agreed not to prosecute any film certified by the board. This was sure-fire insurance, which protected movie distributors from the kind of obscenity prosecutions being brought against book publishers. In due course I came to work for – and then against – his successor, James Ferman, a paternalistic American who served as Britain's censor-in-chief for an excessive twenty-four years. I was able to observe the effects on the man of watching dirty movies for two decades: at first he wanted to cut them to pieces, then he seemed to become addicted to them, then he obsessively planned to release them to the public, which he achieved by devising an R18 certificate for what he termed 'good clean pornography'.

My first brief for the BBFC was to advise on the cause célèbre of the time, Gore Vidal's *Caligula*. The film starred Helen Mirren and Malcolm McDowell, treading their way gingerly through Roman orgies, staged by extras from porn films. Sir John Gielgud played Nerva – he had rejected the part with horror when it was first offered, but the cost of an extension to his home changed his mind, on condition that he was seen to die before the orgies began. The BBFC hired a number of senior counsel (I don't know the collective word for a group of QC's – a 'purse' of silks, I suppose) and Ferman was delighted when I spotted a scene which they had overlooked which had to be cut for legal reasons. It was a charming scene, of Roman matrons bottle-feeding their newborn babes, but my eagle eyes noted that each milk bottle was in the shape of a phallus – an indecent image in a scene with persons aged under sixteen (i.e. the babies). For a while I became a favourite adviser, giving a clean bill of health to *Lolita* (Jeremy Irons would have ended our friendship had I not – but his nymphet, unlike Nabokov's, was aged sixteen) and then to *The Last Temptation of Christ* – Hollywood's first take on the crucifixion. It was not blasphemous, and the most objectionable aspect of the movie was that all the bad characters – including the Devil – were played with English accents.

I fell out with Ferman when he banned *Visions of Ecstasy*, a harmless experimental film about the erotic trances of St Teresa of Ávila. He did this for political reasons, to show that he was sensitive to religious feelings after criticism for approving *The Last Temptation*. I appealed on behalf of the director, but he rigged the appeals committee by calling its most conservative members to hear the case, to which I responded by calling as an expert witness one of their discarded number, the novelist Fay Weldon. Notwithstanding her evidence, they found against us by 3–2, so off we went to Strasbourg, which at that time had a commission of sixteen legal experts to give a preliminary decision. They came down 14–2 in our favour, on the ground that upset to Catholic devotees of St Teresa did not provide a reason for stopping the sale of visions of her ecstasies to those who wished to see them. Ferman appealed to the court, where a preponderance of Catholic judges decided not that the movie was indecent but that a ban on it in Britain was within the state's 'margin of appreciation' – a cop-out they use to avoid deciding controversial moral issues.

Even so, I was annoyed with Ferman using the law of blasphemy at a time when it was being used in some primitive countries to jail (and even execute) disbelievers. It was not acceptable for Britain's censor to give blasphemy laws a seal of approval. But Ferman was intoxicated by his power to ban films by reference to arcane laws which ought to have been abolished long ago, and next he banned *International Guerrillas* – a ludicrous James Bond-style fantasy from Pakistan about the hunt for Salman Rushdie, whom it depicted as a sadistic terrorist. Ferman said it was a criminal libel on Rushdie, so I had Salman over to my home and we laughed our way through it. He wrote a witness statement condemning Ferman for censoring the movie, and this time the appeals committee unanimously voted to unban it.

The problem with the BBFC (as with the Press Council) was that it was set up to placate public anxieties and to keep its paymasters away from any problems with the criminal law. That meant it was vulnerable to political pressure at a time of moral panic. The first, in the early '80s, came over what the *Daily Mail* dubbed 'video nasties' – a genre of horror movies with some grisly titles like *The Evil Dead* and *I Spit on Your Grave*. The *Mail* began a campaign that terrified the BBFC, with stories claiming, '37 per cent of children aged under 7 have seen a video nasty' and 'The video nasty has replaced the conjurer at children's birthday parties'. Panicked MPs passed a special law to give the BBFC more power, and the DPP disgracefully issued a blacklist – an index of eighty-four titles that he demanded should be removed from sale, although no jury had convicted them. I defended several (including *The Evil Dead* and *Andy Warhol's Frankenstein*) successfully. I failed, however, with *Nightmares in a Damaged Brain*, about the cinematic merit of which my expert (*Guardian* film critic Derek Malcolm) was lukewarm. 'It's very well executed,' he told the jury. 'So was the Nazi invasion of Belgium!' exploded the judge. 'That didn't mean it had merit.' After a couple of years the *Daily Mail*'s research was shown to be flawed, juries began to acquit and the moral panic subsided as quickly as it had arisen: movies on the DPP's blacklist could be hired from Blockbuster by twelve-year-olds.

The next moral panic came in 1997, over video games, which had just become popular. The best were of British design and manufacture and I defended in the test case, over *Carmageddon*, a computer product of Stainless Games' creative technology and black humour, which had sold in hundreds of thousands in fifty-seven countries and was classified '15' in Australia and New Zealand. The BBFC refused to certify it as fit for any age, even for adults, cowed by pressure from the tabloids ('Ban Killer Car Game: MPs Enraged By Sick Computer Game'). It was good dodgem car-style fun, at least for an old revhead like me, as you earned points by running over mad digitised cows and crazy blobs ('sprites') which squeaked when hit and splattered green 'blood' on your windshield. Ferman banned what he said was 'a game which gives the player permission to carry out atrocious acts of carnage in this safely contained world of the PC screen ... well heeled, laddish young men will take great delight in savage delinquency...'

This was the sort of nonsense that emanated from James in his overheated later period, but his long-overdue departure from the BBFC did not usher in a new era of common sense: in 2006 I was defending *Grand Theft Auto* and *Manhunt II*. The latter game was banned because gamers could 'make use of a full range of weaponry, including axes, a mace, a baseball bat, plastic bags, Uzi submachine-guns, night-sticks, an iron maiden, an industrial compressor and toilet cistern lids'. I pointed out to the appeals committee that the game required the players to show some skill (e.g. an ability to disable an enemy with a toilet seat) and it accepted my arguments. The board petulantly protested to the Divisional Court, which asked the appeals committee to reconsider its decision, but it stuck to its guns (and its toilet seats). By this time, the BBFC had been hoisted by its own research: it commissioned an extensive study, 'Video Games', which found no connection between playing interactive games and a propensity to act out the violence in real life. Its conclusion, which should have been obvious to the board from the beginning, was: 'Gamers play games because they enjoy it.'

*   *   *

My early days at the Bar coincided with a moral panic about pornography – although what passed for porn then was a lot less arousing than what that word denotes today. As I open the latest *Sunday Times* wealth list, I see names I defended in the mid-1970s, like that young London University graduate David Sullivan, first prosecuted for sending porn-in-the-post, although he could have been done for fraud: he would advertise magazines called *Women and Horses!* and send his punters pictures of stately equestriennes. After his bust he instructed me to keep the committal proceedings going as long as possible – I read the lay justices my Oxford thesis on obscenity – and by the time we reached the Old Bailey, eighteen months later, he had made enough money to retain both Jeremy Hutchinson and John Mortimer to lead me. 'If the fine is more than £250,000, I'll have to ask for time to pay,' he told us at the court door. He was lucky in his judge, as well as his lawyers, and was fined £25. He went on to buy a newspaper (if you call the *Daily Sport* a newspaper), a football team and a chain of sex shops, and was soon to celebrate (on television, with Germaine Greer) his sale of one million vibrators.

Ralph and David Gold were other future multimillionaires; I defended them at Stoke Newington Crown Court before jurors who would go for lunch at the local pub, which featured strip shows more lurid than their magazines. (David's daughter, Jacqueline Gold, now has the Ann Summers franchise.) British policemen in this period discovered that it was much more pleasant reading porn than capturing burglars: they would raid the local newsagents and carefully read and index all the top-shelf publications (a task that would take months) and then apply for a destruction order at the local magistrates court. I would travel there with the psychotherapist Phillip Hodson, who was editor of *Forum* (a reasonably genuine sex education magazine). We would take as an expert witness for its 'public good' defence a most distinguished cleric, the Reverend Chad Varah OBE, founder of the Samaritans, whose name one Old Bailey prosecutor insisted on pronouncing 'Chad Guevara'. I did cause a shock in the courtroom after Chad had volunteered the fact that he had read the top-shelf magazines in bed the previous night. 'And did you masturbate?' I asked as innocently as possible, to the horror of the judge. Chad let a few beats pass before replying, 'Alas, no.' – with the emphasis on 'Alas'. The jurors empathised, and quickly acquitted. Alex Comfort's *The Joy of Sex* – subsequently (and still) a bestseller – did come to grief in Liverpool, before its very old stipendiary, one Mr Pugh, after it had been seized from the local WH Smith. He listened to me talk about the benefits of sex education for a while, and then interjected, 'But this book is about perversion … it has a chapter on … [he whispered] oral sex.' I produced a recent report which showed that a majority of married couples in Britain were admitting some indulgence in the practice. Mr Pugh sighed, and said in a voice of infinite sadness, 'If that is really so, Mr Robertson, I'm glad I do not have long to live.'

*   *   *

There was another aspect of freedom of speech which found more favour, at least from the higher judiciary. It was the 'open justice' principle, and I often appeared on behalf of newspapers when it was breached by lower courts. There was no law that said that courts must be open, but they always had been, since medieval times when trials were ill-conducted public meetings. Then Jeremy Bentham formulated the principle that would have saved Assange from Sweden, namely that justice must be seen to be done: 'Publicity is the very soul of justice. It keeps the judge, while trying, under trial.' I quoted it repeatedly in applications to the High Court to remedy errors made by magistrates who had, for example, tried to suppress the name of a drug-addicted witness because she was a relative of Sir Winston Churchill, or the address of a defendant, a former Tory MP, who did not wish his ex-wife to learn it. However, courts were always trying to breach the rule. In Felixstowe, for example, the court announced a policy of withholding the names of individual JPs who tried controversial cases, and this 'policy' was quickly adopted by other courts. When I challenged it on behalf of *Guardian* journalist David Leigh, the High Court handed down a splendid judgment describing court reporters as 'the watchdogs of justice' and declaring that 'there is no such person known to the law as the anonymous JP'. It added: 'A magistrate will be more anxious to give a correct decision if he knows that his reasons must justify themselves at the bar of public opinion.' That case – *R v Felixstowe Justices ex parte Leigh* – was hailed in its time (1987) as a landmark victory for court reporting. But I was recently struck by the shortness of the memory of those – i.e. court reporters – it was meant to benefit.[74] Cliff Richard's home was raided on a warrant that should not (at least in my opinion) have been issued, while a BBC helicopter filmed from above. Reporters asked for the name of the JP, but Sheffield Magistrates' Court said it had a policy of not identifying them, and no newspaper thought (or could afford) to challenge this unlawful refusal.

Open justice by way of television is still resisted by many lawyers and judges, afraid (to be frank) that it will show them up or lead to criticism. It may, and for good reason (remember the hopeless Judge Lance Ito from the OJ Simpson trial?), but the interesting thing about televising OJ was the studies that emerged in the US showing that it has encouraged more people to do jury service and encouraged jurors to listen more critically to lawyers. There is an old English law dating from 1925 which bans photography in court, but this is no bar to televising public inquiries. You would think that the very fact that it is a *public* inquiry would encourage judges to let it be seen by the public, but television stations are often afraid to ask. I appeared for CNN to gain permission from a sensible judge to televise parts of the inquiry into Dr Harold Shipman, who had killed several hundred of his patients, but I could not move Lord Hutton, on behalf of ITV, to permit cameras to cover the inquest into the death of Dr David Kelly, who had been the source for how the Iraq dossier had been 'sexed up'. He said the main witnesses might be intimidated by having to give evidence in front of the cameras, although since they comprised Tony Blair, Alastair Campbell and Geoff Hoon, I beg to doubt this very much.

My commitment to freedom of expression brought me strange forensic bedfellows – none more so than Sir James Goldsmith – a fanatically Europhobic billionaire – and Phyllis Bowman, head of the anti-abortion group the Society for the Protection of Unborn Children (SPUC). Sir James was first to realise, back in the days of Labour's landslide 1997 election, that the only way to leave Europe would be via a referendum, so he formed the Referendum Party and stood over 600 candidates, one in almost every constituency, with Brexit as their only policy. Mainstream parties were allowed five ten-minute party political broadcasts, but the BBC/ITV committee that made such decisions gave the Referendum Party one measly five minutes, on the ground that it did not yet have any seats. How on earth could a new party come to power through the ballot box, I asked the High Court rhetorically, if it was not allowed to get its message across by as many television broadcasts as its opponents? The court did not grasp the principle of equality, and simply relied on the so-called expertise of the BBC/ITV 'experts', although they were all rather intellectually self-satisfied characters to whom Brexit did not seem of any importance.[75] I was enthusiastically supporting Labour in 1997 but saw no difficulty in arguing the case for Sir James. We got on very well – he was dying of cancer at the time, but was fighting ferociously for his political beliefs, and I saluted his courage.

Phyllis Bowman, too, was the nicest of clients – a dear, devoted grandmother – although her anti-abortion beliefs would have cruel consequences and her way of promoting them – by publishing pictures of foetuses on 'how to vote' leaflets – undoubtedly offensive to many members of the public to whom they were handed. But that did not mean she should have been prosecuted under an absurd election law, which limited 'third-party' (i.e. pressure group) campaigning to the ridiculously low sum of £5 per constituency. This prevented not only SPUC but also Greenpeace, Friends of the Earth, Charter 88, CND and other campaigning groups from exercising their democratic right to participate meaningfully in elections. After having Phyllis's prosecution dismissed on technical grounds, I took the case to Strasbourg, where we easily won – the British law was contrary both to the free-speech right under Article 10 (you could not buy much 'free' speech for £5) and to the right to participate in elections.[76] Parliament was forced to change the law, which it did in 2000. (The limit is currently £2,000 per constituency.) Where human rights principles are concerned, you cannot pick and choose: Mrs Bowman's victory benefited all pressure groups, including those supporting a woman's right to choose.

*   *   *

It was (and still is) the law of libel that makes Britain a country where 'free speech' can become expensive speech. Libel lawyers operate on the principle 'If in doubt, cut it out' and trials for defamation can be occasions when the temple of law turns into a casino, as juries (before they were virtually abolished in 2015) awarded vast sums in tax-free damages, usually to plaintiffs who were already wealthy, against newspapers over allegations that could well have been true, although they could not be proved true, especially if sources were reluctant to come forward. In libel, for no logical reason and alone of all civil law actions, the burden of proof falls on the defence, which means that the claimant seeking damages does not have to prove his case: the defendant newspaper has to disprove it. Until recently, libel law had no defence for public interest investigative journalism, or for publications that had been properly researched and were reasonably believed to be true.

All this was antithetical to the First Amendment of the US constitution, which protected speech unless it was made with malice (i.e. in circumstances where the publication was reckless – making an allegation without caring whether it was true). So there was a conflict between American and English standards, which became acute when US newspapers and magazines were published in the UK. London became the libel capital of the world – 'A town named Sue', they called it, as American public figures took action here to protect a reputation they could not possess at home. In a global village, it hardly makes sense for plaintiffs to have different reputations in different parts of town, but US publishers were afraid of the expense of a British libel action: Daniel Moynihan's famous jibe about Henry Kissinger – 'Henry doesn't lie because it's in his interests, he lies because it's in his nature' – was solemnly edited out of US books about contemporary politics, and even from *Time* magazine, before they were published in Britain. I had to advise William Shawcross to make twenty-two cuts in his book *Sideshow* – a masterful account of Kissinger's role in Nixon's bombing of Cambodia – before it could be published in the UK: despite the public interest in reading all of a book already acclaimed in America, the ruinous cost of an English libel action left its publisher with no alternative. All that Americans and Russians needed to sue their critics in London's claimant-friendly courts was a 'reputation' – i.e. that some people here had heard of them.

Texan oilman Oscar Wyatt, on whom J. R. Ewing's character in *Dallas* was based, went so far as to claim he had a reputation to protect in England because his son was the first to have committed adultery with the Duchess of York and he had once been invited to dine at Buckingham Palace (I had his case against *Forbes* magazine dismissed: although he had been invited to dine at the palace, this happened only because the Queen was away).[77] If the defendant newspaper had no office or property in London, successful plaintiffs at first tried to enforce their judgment in America. But not after a New York case in 1992, in which I was an expert witness on the inadequacies of English law: to enforce it, ruled the judge, would be 'antithetical to the First Amendment' because of the unfairness of putting the burden of proof on the defence.[78] But international celebrity plaintiffs did not really need libel damages – what they wanted, by suing in London, was to chill any investigations into their own misconduct and to prevent or punish any publication about it.

The wonders of English libel law were touted abroad by English solicitors like Peter Carter-Ruck (his firm was the model for *Private Eye*'s 'Sue, Grabbit and Runne'). So after the American forum shoppers came the Russian oligarchs, anxious to punish American newspapers guilty of probing their past. They would stash their wives in Chelsea mansions, their children at English private schools and their mistresses in Mayfair and seek to develop connections (often with second-class royals, available for hire) which would give them the standing to sue by claiming close connections with the local establishment and a consequent reputation in the UK that would be damaged by any published exposure, even in an American paper which sold only a handful of copies in London. They were men of enormous wealth, profiteers from the break-up of the Soviet Union under the corrupt Boris Yeltsin, and without moral scruple. One, who had stolen money allocated to buy shoes for peasant children, left a message on my answering machine – the sound of machine-gun fire. It was almost impossible to obtain evidence from Russia admissible in an English courtroom – with Dow Jones's American lawyers Bob Sack and Stuart Karle, Mark Stephens and I went to Moscow to investigate one oligarch claimant, but we found that everything was up for sale (including KGB records) and would be regarded in an English court as tainted evidence.

The most important case was brought by the oligarch Boris Berezovsky. He sued *Forbes* magazine over an article about his KGB background and corrupt links with Yeltsin. It was written by a conscientious American journalist, Paul Klebnikov: Paul and I had no difficulty putting together a defence proving that Berezovsky was a gangster with a 'roof' (i.e. a protection squad) of murderous Chechens, and was deeply involved in fraud and political corruption. But *Forbes* had introduced Paul's article with a comment about the 'trail of corpses' behind Berezovsky, and we could not prove on the balance of probabilities (i.e. that it was more likely than not) that he was a murderer. So we argued *forum non conveniens* – that the case did not belong in London: the facts in the article were entirely Moscow-centric, *Forbes* sold a million copies in the US but only 1,000 in England, and our courts should not arrogate to themselves the role of libel globo-cops for foreigners with little real connection to this country. We lost in the House of Lords, although narrowly (3–2), with the most persuasive judgments the two in our favour.[79] The case settled, but the following year, in July 2004, Paul Klebnikov was assassinated in Moscow. It was suspected that Berezovsky had directed his execution, which was certainly a reprisal killing, but this could not be proved. Paul was one of a number of journalists murdered for looking too closely into oligarchs, and particularly into the biggest of them all, Vladimir Putin, who later turned on Berezovsky and tried to have him extradited. One day, Berezovsky was found dead in his Berkshire mansion. It looked (or had been made to look) like suicide. Nobody, including the coroner, could be sure.

Bill Browder, another of my clients, was a successful American business-man based in Moscow, until corrupt police used his company for a tax scam and arrested his lawyer, Sergei Magnitsky, who had blown the whistle on them. Magnitsky was killed in prison, and in his memory Bill devoted his time and money to promote 'Magnitsky Laws', which punish human rights violators by preventing them enjoying their ill-gotten gains – freezing their assets in Western banks, and denying them entry to Western countries and casinos that are their favourite haunts (see Chapter Seventeen). Bill's book *Red Notice: A True Story of High Finance, Murder and One Man's Fight for Justice* was a bestseller. The Russians did not come for him with polonium or a poisoned umbrella, but with a writ for libel – brought by one of the cops he had implicated in Magnitsky's death. This claimant hired expen-sive British lawyers and hunkered down for a trial that would have lasted for months and cost him millions, although he was on an annual police salary of US$15,000! State money was obviously behind him, as well as the KGB. I prepared our defence, using the testimony of Russian exiles (this time, I decided not to go to Moscow). Eventually the judge decided that the policeman had insufficient connection with England to be allowed to sue here, and was told to find his remedy in the Moscow courts. They were, of course, rigged in his favour: they had already convicted Bill, along with Sergei (even though he was dead), on trumped-up charges of fraud. They tried to have Interpol issue a 'red notice' against Bill to constrain his travel – hence the title of his book.

* * *

I have always, I suppose, been a journalist manqué. Early in my London life, when I was writing for the *New Statesman*, I actually considered abandoning the harsh discipline of the Bar in favour of the louche life of a hack, but I was deterred by the editor, who wanted to retain my inside take on the legal profession. But I spent a lot of time with journos, as friends or clients or both, and I had no doubt that helping to create a public interest defence to defamation would be a good thing for free speech. An even better thing would be to provide a legal right to protect journalists' sources of information. When I began practising, English common law provided no help at all: it allowed police, but nobody else, to withhold the names of their informers, and for editors this could produce a crisis of conscience.

It happened to Peter Preston, a friend who edited *The Guardian* in the '80s. In 1983, secret documents from the Ministry of Defence came to his office in a brown envelope, revealing the date when nuclear Cruise missiles would arrive at Greenham Common, an RAF camp in Berkshire. A women's protest group was permanently encamped there, waiting for this unpredictable day, so the actual date was big news. When it was published by *The Guardian*, the state pounced and the Treasury Solicitor, that baleful presence in the *Spycatcher* case, obtained a court order on the newspaper to hand over the original documents, which had markings directing MI5 to the very desk in the Ministry of Defence from which they had been sent. Peter was badly advised by his lawyer and instead of destroying the documents before the order was issued, he held on to them and objected that the order would force him to reveal his sources. The judges simply laughed – that was exactly why the order had been imposed, and if he did not comply they would fine the paper a massive sum for every day he disobeyed. He had little choice, and soon the 'mole' in the ministry was flushed out: a 23-year-old clerk named Sarah Tisdall. I went to court to see her sentenced – a tiny, weeping presence huddled in the huge dock of Court No. 1 of the Old Bailey. She was sent to prison, and Peter, whom I saw afterwards, was devastated. He felt responsible, and he was – but the law had left him little choice other than the liquidation of *The Guardian*. Should it not assist journalists to protect their sources?

I was certain that it should. Although a good journalist will have skills of analysis and research and (like a barrister) an ability to master a complicated subject in a short time, one critical qualification (at least for an investigative journalist) is the ability to cultivate sources of information. Much of the news that gets published is fed to journalists by public relations departments, press releases and press conferences – British government departments employ more than 5,000 professional PR people, and corporations have many thousands more. They are really professional propagandists, putting the spin on their stories that is most favourable to their employer. This makes it important, if 'news' is to be worthy of that word, for journalists to have sources – whistleblowers, leakers, insiders or whatever – who can tell them the truth. Were it not for 'unofficial sources' talking off the record to journalists, there would be far fewer facts for discussion in democratic society. If journalists betray their sources, and those sources are in consequence sent to prison, then information for investigative news reports will start to dry up, and what is published will be less reliable. That is why journalists cultivate sources by promising them anonymity. This must be a solemn promise, made in the service of the greater public interest, and it binds the conscience of the individual journalist as well as the conscience of their editor and – if he has a conscience – their proprietor. But moral rights are worthless unless reflected in legal rights, and unless a legal right could be extrapolated from the principle of freedom of expression in the European Convention on Human Rights, there would be no protection at all for journalists faced with court orders to reveal their sources.

In the early 1990s, a brief arrived from Geoffrey Bindman that enabled us to change the law, thanks to the courage of a young journalist named Bill Goodwin. He was working as a graduate trainee for a business magazine when he received information about a much-promoted company which revealed that it was in financial difficulties. He called the company, like a good journalist, to discuss the report, whereupon it went into meltdown and obtained a court order for Bill to reveal his source. I appeared for him before Lennie Hoffman, a first-class Chancery judge – my old tutor at Oxford, as a matter of fact – who treated my argument with the disdain he had no doubt treated my essays. He was sympathetic, but there was no way out – Bill was ordered to reveal his source, which the company insisted must be one of its high-level executives. Bill refused, so we went to the Court of Appeal, which offered him a Faustian bargain: put the name of your source in an envelope, which will not be opened unless you lose in the highest court. The highest court in England, they stipulated – I suspect they knew we were going to take this case all the way to the European Court of Human Rights in Strasbourg.

Of course we lost in the Court of Appeal, and in the final court the Law Lords were unsympathetic. The presiding judge gave me a condescending lecture: 'Mr Robertson, legal argument proceeds by building on precedents and statute law. You have cited no precedents and keep giving us this airy-fairy theory about free speech.' Well, exactly. There were no precedents. We lost, 5–0. We set off for a final appeal. The European Convention on Human Rights had been ratified by the free nations of Europe after the war, and during the Wilson government the great Lord Chancellor Gerald Gardiner had given individual litigants the right to petition its court. If their complaint was upheld, Britain had a duty to change its law to comply with the judgment. So off we went, to argue that Bill's conviction was a breach of Article 10 of the ECHR: 'Everyone has the right to freedom of expression. This right shall include freedom to hold opinions and to receive and impart information and ideas without interference by public authority…'

My submissions rolled on for 100 pages – but they took us over all the preliminary hurdles until we reached the Grand Chamber, of seventeen judges sitting around a long semi-circular bench.

Advocacy in Strasbourg is pretty easy – it is mainly done on written submissions, which counsel on each side has half an hour to develop in their argument, after which judges ask their questions. We then adjourn for coffee, and return to speak for fifteen minutes to answer those questions. Then we adjourn for an as-long-as-you-want lunch, in a city of Michelin-starred restaurants. It's probably the most pleasurable experience legal practice has to offer, so I invited John Mortimer and Bob Sack, as well as Kathy, who brought Georgina, aged one month. We drove to nearby Colmar for lunch at what was – and may still be – the best restaurant in the world. L'Auberge de l'Ill is set by the River Ill, in a village with chimney tops on which sit brooding storks. In its window is its guest book, open on a page for a day in 1956 where the signatures of the Queen Mother and Simone de Beauvoir are displayed, although I doubt they dined together. Inside, the presence of baby Georgie was greeted with delight and she was passed, gurgling, around the tables (this would never happen in an English restaurant). After coffee and petits fours by the river, we left in the late afternoon to catch 'the little Fokker' back to London.

Some months later, the judgment came down. We had won. The court ruled that Bill's conviction was a breach of Article 10 because of the importance, overlooked by our English judges, of 'having regard [for the] ... protection of journalistic sources for press freedom in a democratic society and the potentially chilling effect an order for source disclosure has on the exercise of that freedom'. It accepted our argument, which had been unanimously rejected at every court level in Britain:

> Protection of journalistic sources is one of the basic conditions for press freedom ... without such protection, sources may be deterred from assisting the press in informing the public on matters of public interest. As a result the vital public watchdog role of the press may be undermined and the ability of the press to provide accurate and reliable information may be adversely affected.[80]

This ruling became part of UK law in 1998, when the Blair government incorporated the European Convention as part of its Human Rights Act. It has given journalists in England stronger legal protection for their sources than journalists in the US – they can now give concrete undertakings to their sources that they will not be ordered by courts to identify them. This should be binding in conscience on newspaper proprietors, but in what was arguably the most shocking breach of ethics in newspaper history, Rupert Murdoch directed that the names of the sources of the journalists working for his papers *The Sun* and the *News of the World* should be handed over to the police. This arose during the phone-hacking scandal, when it emerged that tabloid papers had been illegally intercepting telephone calls and messages. It was said that Murdoch was advised by his American lawyers that unless he fully cooperated with the police there might be repercussions for his US media ownerships. Murdoch directed that all dealings with sources, logged on their computers, should be handed over to the police team that had been invited to take up residence at the News International offices in Wapping. This led to the prosecution of dozens of journalists and their sources: some of the latter had not been paid but were in government employ (all were sacked, whether or not the prosecution succeeded) and many who were paid had divulged information of public importance, such as how the Ministry of Defence was sending soldiers into battle without adequate equipment.

Murdoch's journalists and their sources were subjected to dawn raids and the heartache of waiting several years for trials. The mass betrayal of sources was not against the law, of course – there is nothing but a proprietor's own integrity to stop him or her from flouting the code of conduct that all papers purport to uphold. ('Journalists have a moral obligation to protect confidential sources of information.') But Murdoch's conduct, in throwing his journalists' sources (as well as his journalists) to the wolves, was unconscionable. I said so in an article I was commissioned to write by the news editor of *The Times* – the very fact that I was invited shows the depth of moral outrage among journalists at News Ltd's serious papers.[81]

* * *

I did a lot of work in the '90s for Dow Jones – the *American Lawyer* journal profiled me as 'Dow Jones's man about the Commonwealth' – in cases in which I defended its journalists from intemperate governments in countries where speech was not free. This was Dow Jones before Murdoch took it over – the editorials in the *Wall Street Journal* were generally conservative, but the paper and others in its stable prided themselves on objective reporting and in particular on standing up for free-speech principles whenever their journalists were endangered. I went to court in Singapore to defend Barry Wain, the editor of the *Wall Street Journal Asia*, for the crime of publishing a polite criticism of its courts (it is contempt to suggest in Singapore that its judges have in any way gone wrong). In Malaysia, I teamed up with its best advocate, Muhammad Shafee Abdullah, to engage in legal jousts with its Prime Minister, the bullying Dr Mahathir, when he tried to expel two

Wall Street journalists. When he lost, unlike Lee and Mugabe, he accepted the verdict – but then sacked the judges who delivered it.

By the turn of the century, the media was into the internet age, and one great legal issue was where you could sue a publication that was available on the web. Was it where the alleged defamation was put on the server (usually in the country where the publisher was established), or where it was downloaded (which could mean liability for the publisher in many countries)? We discussed this a lot – Dow Jones's US lawyers were Bob Sack, a brilliant exponent of defamation (*Sack on Libel*), now a US federal judge on the Second Circuit, and Stuart Karle, the in-house counsel dedicated to the company's free-speech mission. We wanted the paper to be judged by the standards of the First Amendment. We looked for a test case in a court outside the US, which could decide that internet downloading from a US site of a US newspaper article should be judged by the standards of US law. I gave them the worst advice I have ever delivered: 'Let's have the test case in Australia. They have a really progressive High Court.'

The case we would take to my really progressive High Court soon came up, in the form of an article in *Barron's*, a serious Dow Jones financial magazine, about one Joe Gutnick, a Melbourne identity known for his generosity to synagogues and Jewish charities of extreme orthodoxy, and most prominently for his ownership of a local Melbourne football club. He was trying to move into the New York stock market, and *Barron's* subjected him to a piece of US-style investigative journalism which he had never experienced from the Australian press, constrained by libel law inherited from England. Although the magazine had sold just two print copies in Victoria, the article had been downloaded by his Melbourne stockbrokers and members of his synagogue, and he brought an action for defamation in the Supreme Court of Victoria.

We objected that this court had no jurisdiction over an American publication which had been electronically extracted by Australians from New Jersey, where it was sitting on the Dow Jones server. We called a lot of very technical evidence which, to be simplistic, showed that downloading electronic messages involved sending electronic impulses from Melbourne to the New Jersey server, where they captured the article in its electronic form and brought it back to Victoria for reassembling. So it was as if Gutnick had sent a servant to America to buy a copy of the paper and bring it back: the actual 'publication', i.e. the handover of the information, technically took place in New Jersey, so the decision as to whether it defamed the businessman should be taken by New Jersey law. The judge in Victoria did not understand my arguments and took great exception to my encomia to free speech – platitudes that I had uttered in the House of Lords, the Privy Council and in courts around the Commonwealth, but which he seemed to think unfit to be heard in Melbourne. His judgment's infelicities were sufficient for me to persuade three High Court judges that the case should be considered by the full High Court.

The problem we had, once again, was the novelty of our argument: it had theory, philosophy and practical sense but no precedents, certainly none from Australia, which had no Bill of Rights that I could invoke. The judges, seven good black-letter lawyers, could find no black letters to assemble in our favour.[82] They were not bothered about the threat to free speech if wealthy plaintiffs could bring libel actions in any country, even in, say, Russia or Singapore. It was, however, an enjoyable experience to go briefly through a door I had never opened, to the court where I would doubtless have practiced, had it not been for the largesse of Cecil Rhodes. I was particularly struck by the quickness and erudition of the clerks (three per judge), who were the smartest people in the room.

The High Court sent the case back to Melbourne for trial, and we prepared for a lengthy one, but mediation saved the day. Sir Laurence Street, Australia's top mediator, settled it in a morning, without any damages to be paid by Dow Jones. The High Court's decision stood in the law books and was initially followed in Britain, but in time its flaws became apparent and it has been 'distinguished' – the polite word that judges use when they think a decision is totally wrong.

*   *   *

Mediation, sometimes confused with meditation, is the art of separating clients from their lawyers and convincing them that compromise is cheaper and better for their mental health than gambling on a favourable outcome in court. It's a mark of professionalism to encourage your client to embark on a process that could settle a case that would bring you fame and fees were it to go to trial. Both sides benefit, even when they think (as they usually do) that they are in the absolute right. That was the position as we prepared to fight for free speech over a disputed moment in the magical mystery tour of the Beatles.

The Beatles provided the music for my generation, and the muzak thereafter. Despite my friendship with George and Olivia Harrison, and a visit to Liverpool on a Beatles bus tour with Jules – I had a twinge of nostalgia on seeing the road signs for 'Penny Lane' and 'Strawberry Field' – I was never much into memories of the 'swinging '60s'. I arrived in Britain too late – in 1970 – and was soon defending them (in the *Oz* trial) rather than enjoying them. I regularly find Beatlemania irritating because my route to work takes me down Abbey Road, where my car is usually blocked by fans taking selfies at the iconic crossing in front of the recording studios. But in 2008 I found myself investigating events in the lives of the band in 1968, when they had fallen under the spell of a yogi called the Maharishi (dubbed by *Private Eye* the 'Veririchi Lotsamoney Yogi Bear') and had followed him to his ashram at Rishikesh in India to learn more from his Hindu teachings. Other worshippers joined them – Mike Love of the Beach Boys, Donovan, Mia Farrow and her sister, but the visit was not a success.

Ringo left early, unable to stomach Indian food. Then 'Magic Alex', one of John's hangers-on, claimed to have observed the sage in sexual congress with a female devotee. This for some reason upset John and George, who also decided to depart. 'What have I done?' implored the bewildered yogi as they took their taxis to the airport. 'If you're so cosmic, you'll know,' was John's withering reply. He even wrote a song, 'Maharishi', about the incident: 'Maharishi – what have you done? You made a fool of everyone.' The opening words (and the song title) were later changed to 'Sexy Sadie' at George's request – he was beginning to doubt the truth of the allegation Magic Alex had made. (As, later, did John, since Magic Alex had an ulterior motive for breaking them up with the guru, namely to restore his own influence over the band.)

So how, forty years later, did I come to study this alleged, if all too common, case of a spiritual leader interacting sexually with an adoring follower? My client, the *New York Times*, had published an obituary of the Maharishi.[83] It recounted the above facts, noting that the Beatles had been at their most creative (*The White Album*) under the Maharishi's benign influence, and may well have stayed together had they remained his disciples. Entirely legitimate speculation to make in an obituary written by a distinguished musicologist, one would have thought, but not if one were Alex Mardas, *aka* Magic Alex. He emerged from decades of obscurity as a rather seedy businessman in Athens, with an effective London lawyer in tow, to sue the *New York Times* for the imputation that he was a 'charlatan' (they had so described him) and a rumour-monger.

Initially I had his case dismissed on the grounds that it belonged, if anywhere, in New York (only a handful of copies of the paper had been distributed in London). However, we lost on appeal – English judges are jealous of their reputation as libel globo-cops – and there was nothing for it but to prepare for what would inevitably turn into a trial for historical sex abuse, with a parade of famous if faded pop stars.

It was not difficult to prove that Alex was a charlatan. He had come to London in the '60s and found work as a television repairman, but with the aid of a vivid imagination and a copy of *Popular Science* magazine he had convinced the Fab Four – John, in particular – that he was a genius – indeed a genie – who could produce fantastical electronic inventions. They would include:

- An X-ray camera that could take photographs through walls;
- A force field that would surround their homes with coloured smoke so the paparazzi could not intrude;
- A house which would hover in the air, suspended on an invisible beam;
- The artificial sun which would hover over the 'Apple Boutique' in Baker Street and light up the sky;
- Magic paint which would make objects painted with it invisible;
- A flying saucer made from the V-12 engines of George Harrison's Ferrari and John Lennon's Rolls-Royce;

- A 72-track recording studio more technologically advanced than EMI could offer at Abbey Road.

Dubbing him 'Magic Alex', the Beatles paid him a large amount of money to proceed with these inventions, none of which came to pass. The 72-track recording studio at Apple headquarters in Savile Row was built, but when they went there to record 'Let It Be' it did not work, and they were soon back at Abbey Road with a furious George Martin, their producer, who could not believe their gullibility. All the stories about the imagination and incompetence of Alex Mardas actually added a phrase to English scientific language: the 'Mardas Gap' is now used to describe the disparity between a designer's promise and what that designer can achieve. So Mardas did have a reputation – as something of a charlatan.

But the problem remained that the burden of proving truth is squarely on the defence in libel actions. And how, after forty years, could we prove a negative – that the swami did not meditate erotically with a female follower? Like all such rumours, those who had heard it at the time had conflicting memories: was he meant to have groped Mia Farrow, or her sister Prudence, or a blonde nurse named Pat who was there as a hanger-on to one of the celebrity guests? She was the likely victim in Paul McCartney's memory: he recalled John saying, 'Maharishi made a pass at her,' to which Paul replied, 'What's wrong with that?' To which John indignantly replied, 'Well, you know, he's just a bloody old letch like everybody else. What the fuck, we can't go following that!'

In time, and after more rational meditation, both John and George concluded that the Maharishi was innocent of an allegation Mardas had made to get them away from the guru's influence and his ashram. But both Beatles were dead by the time of the libel action, and although there were former devotees scattered around the world who were prepared to come to London to testify as to the unlikelihood of the allegation, my evidence fell short of proving that the holy man had refrained from sin.

Had Mardas been suing a British newspaper, the case would have been simple to settle: a quick negotiation, a small published apology for any distress he had suffered, with moderate payment towards his legal costs.

But the *New York Times* was unlike any other newspaper. Its venerated publisher, Adolph S. Ochs, had decreed as long ago as 1922 that the paper would fight every libel action to the death – a policy which had served to deter gold-diggers and had produced in 1964 the famous Supreme Court decision in *New York Times v Sullivan*, in which the First Amendment was interpreted to protect any journalism that was absent of malice. The edict, in his own handwriting, hung framed in the newspaper's boardroom – copies were faxed to any recalcitrant counsel who dared to suggest a settlement. Much as I valued the paper as a client, I advised that the Mardas case was not worth the candle. I had sent my colleague Jen Robinson around the US to dig out musical legends of my generation: the old rockers, hippies and hangers-on (many still unreconstructed) would have provided public entertainment for weeks and 'Magic Alex' might have been laughed out of court. But it would cost millions, so the *New York Times* agreed this time to relax its policy far enough to permit mediation.

The mediator usually shuttles back and forth between the parties trying to find some common ground, and Lennie (by now Lord) Hoffmann did this for us in an arbitration suite in Athens. The parties are meant to stay apart, but I bumped into Magic Alex in person when he came out of his team's room for a cigarette. We had a friend in common, which started our conversation – in no time he was telling me that, for reasons of his future business, what he wanted was a statement that the paper did not intend to brand him a confidence trickster. He didn't care about the Maharishi or money, and on that basis the deal was quickly sealed: the paper agreed to state that it had not meant to imply that Mardas was a confidence trickster, and his action was withdrawn. And having met him, in actual fact I do not think he was. A charlatan of sorts, but one who was deluded about his own incompetence and inability to achieve his inventions, rather than a crook who took the Beatles for a ride, in a flying saucer provided by their V-12 engines.

*   *   *

In 1984, I co-authored (with Andrew Nicol) a textbook, *Media Law*. It began as a slim volume which we were tempted to call *The Journalist's*

Toothbrush, because so many reporters were being advised to carry an overnight bag when summoned to court, in case they were sent to prison. Now in its sixth edition, it runs to 1,044 pages, and has always argued in favour of a public interest defence of 'reasonable publication' in libel cases.[84] I was first able to argue for this defence in court when defending the *Telegraph* against a libel claim brought by the then unknown Saif Gaddafi, favourite son of the colonel. It is not clear why he took action under English law, although it may have stemmed from advice I had given his father some years earlier. A novel had been published called *The Fifth Horseman* (i.e. of the Apocalypse) about Colonel Gaddafi's fictitious plot to blow up Manhattan with a nuclear device, and I was summoned to the Libyan embassy in St James's Square to tell the colonel what could be done about it. Speaking through a translator to a client somewhere in a desert tent, I pronounced the book extremely defamatory (which it was – Gaddafi was not a nuclear terrorist) and said I would be happy to act for him at a reasonable fee to obtain large damages. We would issue a writ and all he would have to do would be to fold up his tent and come to London to swear (he might even be allowed to swear an oath on his Green Book) that he would never dream of acquiring weapons of mass destruction.

I did not hear from the colonel again, but he may have passed on to his son, a student at the London School of Economics, something of the wonders of English libel law. Saif sued the *Telegraph* over an article which tied him to a complicated currency fraud. The piece began 'Like father, like son', which was the only sentence – although it was plainly defamatory – to which he did not take exception. The article was probably true, but since it had come from intelligence sources, we could never prove that in court. Our only chance was to pioneer a public interest defence, based on a free-speech right to publish important stories with reasonable care. There were few precedents, but enough straws in the legal wind to argue for the *Telegraph*'s right to tell an important story, reasonably believed to be true, about the Libyan dictator's son and heir.

Before the trial started, young Gaddafi went off to visit the Barrier Reef, with an entourage of retainers, who picked up most of the prostitutes in Cairns and took them on a sex- and drugs-fuelled cruise to shoot at sharks.

This provided ammunition for cross-examination, although I concentrated on 'Like father, like son' and on probing why Saif was so proud of the comparison. He came across as arrogant and brutal – the jury did not like him – and it was no surprise that, come the adjournment, his lawyers made a good offer to settle. It was accepted, and over a drink to celebrate I told the proprietor, Conrad Black, of my regret – we would have made legal history had he turned down the offer and gone eventually on appeal to ask the judges to create a public interest defence. He roared with laughter: 'Let Rupert make new law – that's the sort of thing he likes.'

I acted for for *The Times* – i.e. for Rupert – when it was sued by Michael Ashcroft, then Tory Party treasurer, over allegations that he had been using banks in the Caribbean as fronts for money laundering and drug trafficking. I put on a public interest defence which Ashcroft's counsel, George Carman, tried to strike out. As we were arguing hammer and tongs in the courtroom, we were passed a note from our solicitors, saying that Ashcroft had met Rupert on a golf course in Florida and that they had decided to settle. ('The buggers,' said George under his breath. 'I haven't agreed my brief fee.') I could understand Rupert's decision. It is usually better to settle lawsuits rather than old scores. Ashcroft is very wealthy and donated prize money to Britain's Political Book Awards. In 2015 I won 'Polemic of the Year' for my book on the Armenian genocide, and had no hesitation in accepting the prize from him – like MI5's Roger Hollis, he had been the victim of false allegations made by incompetent spooks (in Ashcroft's case, at the US Drug Enforcement Agency), which is why there was nonetheless an arguable public interest in publishing them.

Proprietors were not keen to pay to reform libel law through the courts (understandably – the cost of taking a case to the highest court adds up to over a million pounds in legal fees). But American editors at the *Wall Street Journal* had no such inhibitions, political or financial, and were happy to extend the principles of First Amendment freedom to Britain, the country whose repressive sedition laws, used against America's founding fathers, had inspired them to pass the First Amendment in the first place.

The plaintiff in the crucial case I took for the *Journal* in 2006, Mohammed Jameel, was a man in the motor trade in Saudi Arabia, where he owned most of the Toyota dealerships and was a multi-billionaire. In the aftermath of 9/11 it became an anxious international question as to whether Saudi Arabia – whence the Bin Ladens and most of the hijackers had come – would cooperate with the US in efforts to clamp down on terrorists. The *Wall Street Journal* was first to report that it was cooperating, to the extent of monitoring, at the CIA's request, some of their leading businessmen. Among the names included on its list, published in the *Journal*, was that of Mohammed Jameel. He sued, and was awarded damages for the implied defamation that he had come under suspicion – the lower courts said the *Journal*'s story would have been the same if the names had been left out. That just showed how little the judges knew about news-gathering: the very fact that the names were of important public figures close to the regime gave verisimilitude to the story and confirmed that Saudi Arabia really was cooperating with the US. We had to go to the House of Lords to establish that the public interest in news could override an incidental defamation, so long as the journalist had acted responsibly in checking facts as far as they could be checked. It was a great leap forward for news reporting.[85]

When I had first come to the Bar, I had observed a Ugandan princess, Elizabeth of Toro, collecting large sums in damages from every British newspaper. She had been Idi Amin's Foreign Minister but was sacked because he said that she had been found having sex in a toilet at France's Orly Airport. The republication of Amin's defamatory accusation was obviously in the public interest (as a sign of his madness, for a start), yet after her victory newspapers did not dare publish other attacks on public figures for fear that they would be similarly mulcted in libel damages. *Jameel v Wall Street Journal Europe* at last freed newspapers from this threat, in cases where what was newsworthy was not the truth of a statement but the fact that it had been made.

* * *

Taking American First Amendment values to courts outside America was easy enough when it meant defending worthwhile investigative journalism, but more difficult when it came to investigative journalism interleaved with naked women. This had been Hugh Hefner's trick with *Playboy* magazine to confound the censors, and it was copied by *Penthouse* founder Bob Guccione – the journalism in his magazine was harder, but so were the photos. Those were the days of sexual repression, when porn was seen as liberating by early feminists: its enemies were supporters of Lord Longford and Mary Whitehouse. By the late '70s I had become, through my textbook on the subject and Old Bailey cases, a world expert on censorship, and was dispatched to liberate a country even more sexually backward than Australia – New Zealand. It had its own Mary Whitehouse equivalent, named Patricia Bartlett, with whom I did battle on several occasions before New Zealand's Indecent Publications Board. The Kiwis took these cases very seriously and came down with guidelines precisely detailing what could be shown in magazines – at one point, I complained that they were splitting pubic hairs (but nobody laughed). I defended some trashy magazines, but I also acted for the publishers of banned works of literature and genuine sex educational material (Alex Comfort's *The Joy of Sex* again) and in 1979 won a judgment that liberalised the customs rules, permitting entry to New Zealand of an Australian novel which had just been prohibited: *Puberty Blues*, co-authored by one Kathy Lette.

My successes with New Zealand customs brought a call to strategise an attack on Canadian customs, which despite propinquity to the US had banned some editions of *Penthouse* because they had references to cunnilingus. The Canadian Customs Department had by law to give reasons for its decision, and incautiously stated in a letter to the publishers, 'Canadians are not in favour of oral sex.' This struck me as such an absurd statement – by then it was 1980 – that I advised my clients simply to take out full-page advertisements in Canadian newspapers quoting it, and inviting Canadians to disagree. Some newspapers accepted the advertisement, and the government began to look ridiculous. Canadian television then staged a great debate between its defender of decency – the Attorney General and political tough guy Roy McMurtry – and Bob Guccione. Their interlocutor pointed out that both these macho men were wearing the same brand of cowboy boots to debate whether Canadian women were in favour of oral sex, and the interview became surreal. Bob and Roy saw eye to eye, as well as toe to toe, and the ban was never imposed again. Ridicule turned out to be much better advice than to challenge the ban in court, where po-faced judges would probably have upheld it.

From the mid-1970s onwards, I was crossing the pond quite regularly to work on media law cases with American lawyers. It renewed my fascination with the land of the free, or at least the land that was then more free than the UK. There was a particular thrill about just being in America, even if it was only to watch on television from a hotel room the Jimmy Carter nomination acceptance speech when he quoted Bob Dylan ('America is busy being born, not busy dying') or Obama walking out, with that bottle of Fiji Water, into a Chicago park on his election night to proclaim, 'Yes, we did'.

As the T-shirt says, I love NY. The experimental theatre was better than in London, there were revivals of my favourite Broadway musicals, and there was – always and for ever – the Met. My son loved seeing the crazy polar bears in the Central Park Zoo – in his autistic imagination his real father is Steve Martin and I am actually a polar bear who disappears at night into the freezer; or, when I am in the Caribbean, I am with my climate-challenged family in the North Pole. I chose to stay at the raffish Elysée, where Tennessee Williams and Harold Robbins had worked on their drafts. When Kathy came along it would be the Algonquin, where her heroine Dorothy Parker once punned across the round table.

This was the difference, before the UK adopted its Human Rights Act, between the two legal systems: English common law was malleable, its rules always having exceptions which judges could seize upon and twist to comport with their own subjective prejudices. US legal principles – especially those derived from the constitution – were absolute. Its First Amendment struck down laws restricting freedom of expression, so in Britain a free-speech lawyer has to fight cases which could never be contemplated in America, where expression of fact or opinion can never be a crime (unless you are Julian Assange and can be prosecuted as a spy).

An obvious example is how jurors in the US may speak out after their verdict, give interviews and even write books about their experience. In the UK, the merest recollection of what happened during jury deliberations may incur a jail sentence of up to two years. This was the unlooked-for consequence of a case which arose from the prosecution of the Liberal Party leader Jeremy Thorpe for attempting to shut up a gay boyfriend, Norman Scott, by having him murdered. The chief witness for the prosecution was an MP colleague, whose evidence of Thorpe's murderous intentions was credible, except for the fact that he had already sold his story to the *Telegraph* for a £25,000 down payment and a bonus of a further £25,000 if Thorpe was convicted on his testimony. It was a disgraceful deal, and when jurors were interviewed by journalist David Leigh and a colleague, they said that it was the main reason they had acquitted Thorpe. The editor of the *New Statesman* was keen to publish the interview, and I advised him he could do so – it had manifest public interest (if only to show the dangers of allowing the media to buy up trial witnesses) and there was no law against interviewing jurors. There was, of course, an ill-defined law of contempt of court, which allowed judges to punish actions which tended to pervert justice, but the action that had perverted justice in the Thorpe trial was that of the *Telegraph*, not of the *New Statesman* in exposing its consequence. Disgracefully, if typically, Conservative Attorney General Michael Havers decided to prosecute the *New Statesman*, and not the Conservative-supporting *Telegraph*.

I had only been a barrister for five years, and expected the journal would hire a QC for its defence. I reckoned without the sense – or sense of humour – of Bruce Page, its editor: 'You advised us to publish, so you should be the best person to defend your decision.' (Also, I was the cheapest.) It is the sort of honour that lies heavily upon you – barristers often advise against publication (in which case they cannot be proved wrong) but here I had stuck my neck out – the judges should not, in my view, twist their contempt power to create a new criminal offence, and although they would be sorely tempted, I believed they would have fidelity to law.

Nonetheless, many lawyers were horrified at the prospect that talking jurors might expose inadequacy in lawyers, and indeed in the jury system itself. I threw myself into research at the British Library – difficult, before the internet – and came up with fifty-seven interviews and articles by jurors about their experiences which had been published over the years.

Some were truly insightful – Graham Greene, Simon Hoggart and Alan Coren were among the authors – and, as I emphasised to the court, all were reassuring and supportive of the system of jury trial. It was for Parliament, not the judges, to create new penal law, especially if it meant muzzling thousands of citizens who did jury service each year. To my surprise, the Chief Justice – the formerly fearsome Lord Widgery – had begun to suffer from dementia, and was asking odd questions ('Who is Mr Bruce Page?' 'He is the defendant, m'lud') and reading his papers upside down. Fortunately, the colleague who covered for him was a good common lawyer, and accepted my arguments. The *New Statesman* (and inferentially, its legal adviser) was acquitted.[86]

I thought this decision a great victory, although I was given pause when I heard that the irresponsible Lord Denning, at Temple dinners, was condemning the Attorney General for not appealing it. ('They are saying there's no law against it. They should have appealed to me. I would have made one.') But the spectre of newspapers interviewing jurors after celebrated trials outraged QC MPs (there were a lot of them in Parliament at the time) and they procured a draconian amendment to the Contempt of Court Act which made it an imprisonable crime for any juror to dare whisper any detail of what had gone on in the jury room, no matter how much the revelation might be in the public interest. Their object, quite unashamedly, was to protect the institution of jury trial from informed criticism, and this law has even stopped scientific and beneficial research on how juries reach their verdicts. I would have no objection to a law that prevented jurors from selling their secrets, or identifying fellow jurors, but this is a dragnet offence which prevents revelation of serious impropriety or injustice in the jury room. It is yet another example of a British penchant for sweeping distasteful truths about much-loved institutions – whether the jury or the monarchy – under the carpet.

Another example of a British taboo, where law puts its fingers to its lips and goes 'Shh...', is on the subject of suicide. I had to fight a court battle to free information on the subject when I was counsel to the Voluntary Euthanasia Society, which had begun a battle – which continues – to abolish the crime of aiding or abetting suicide.

393

For many centuries English law laid down that bodies of suicide should be buried at night at crossroads, with a stake through their heart and a stone on their heads. This antipathy was given its rationale by the eighteenth-century jurist Blackstone: it was punishment for the presumption of 'invading the prerogative of the almighty, and rushing into his immediate presence uncalled for'. Self-murder was a serious crime, and would-be suicides were prosecuted for botching their own demise – a Gilbertian law providing comedy in *The Mikado*, but not repealed until 1961. The Suicide Act of that year exonerated the victim, but perpetrated the punishment (up to fourteen years' imprisonment) for aiding or counselling anyone who needs help to effectuate a wish to die with dignity. This was a time when compassionate doctors who complied with requests to shorten the life of a dying patient were prosecuted, and MPs blanched at requests to further reform the law – as they still do today.

In the 1980s, a few of the society's more enthusiastic euthanasiasts were fed up, and became revved up. They changed their name to EXIT, and offered a kind of take-away suicide service. A telephone call from a potential suicide would, after some brief enquiry, be handed over to a 'dispatcher', an elderly gentleman who would turn up at the given address with the necessary sleeping pills and a plastic bag to put over the head to curtail breathing. After some deaths, he was prosecuted at the Old Bailey together with Nicholas Reed, the secretary of EXIT, who became my client. Some of the evidence was heart-rending – the service had been a boon to a number of terminally ill people, and to their families, when doctors had refused to ease the pain. But a few of the cases – of depression, rather than terminal illness – were less clear-cut and we failed (despite the eloquence of John Mortimer, who appeared for the 'dispatcher') to achieve a sympathy verdict.[87]

I had more success, however, with the society's 'do it yourself' instruction manual entitled *A Guide to Self-Deliverance*. It came with a philosophical foreword by Arthur Koestler and set out the arguments against committing suicide before proceeding to detail five sure-fire ways of accomplishing it without resorting to desperate and unreliable measures such as wrist-slitting or drug overdosing. In the hostile climate of the time, I advised that distribution should be confined to members of the society, and thousands joined in order to obtain it.

After thirty-five members had dispatched themselves with its guidance (it was in some cases found beside the body, the relevant passages underlined), the Attorney General came under pressure to act. He was reluctant to bring criminal charges against the executives of the society – they had not personally assisted anyone's suicide, but had merely made accurate information available for individual choice, and they were highly respectable people who were likely to be acquitted by an Old Bailey jury. So, instead, the government mounted a civil action, running to a High Court judge in the hope that he would declare the publication a crime and thus force the society to withdraw it. As with the *New Statesman* case, it was slightly nerve-racking to appear in court to defend your own advice – you engage as objectively as you can in a proceeding in which your own mind is on trial. Fortunately, the judge was Harry Woolf, an independent and excellent jurist (and, later, a fine Chief Justice). He accepted my argument that the government could not usurp jury trial and have judges declare that certain conduct was criminal, if there was no specific law against it. Especially in the case of a literate and even-handed booklet, with a foreword by Arthur Koestler which might actually deter some readers from the fatal action.[88]

After our victory, I had earnest discussions with my clients over whether the booklet should now be put on sale to the public. In 1984, this issue really bothered me – as a matter of personal morality rather than law, I told them I would not like to see *A Guide to Self-Deliverance* on sale at WH Smiths, available to any temporarily depressed teenager. They agreed, and the booklet was made available only to their members. Now, thirty years on, you can download its methods from the internet.

* * *

Although my reputation was mainly as a defender of free speech, I had no difficulty accepting briefs to act against foul speech by suing reckless or negligent newspapers. Large damages were won by Helen Mirren, for example, over a story that she was impossible to work with – a story invented by a malicious journalist to whom she had refused an interview. A libel action is generally to be avoided, but becomes a necessity if a lie strikes at your integrity. My friend Michael Foot, himself a renowned journalist, always advised MPs not to sue, but after he became leader of the Labour Party the *Sunday Times* published a front page he could not ignore. Its headline screamed 'KGB: MICHAEL FOOT WAS OUR AGENT'. At one level, this was ridiculous and regarded as such: Foot was the epitome of a patriotic Englishman, notwithstanding (actually, because of) his left-wing views, which drew him to the Levellers and Chartists and other proudly English socialist movements. *Private Eye* aroused laughter throughout the land with a picture of Michael and his dog ('Disraeli') hunting for dead-letter boxes on Hampstead Heath. But since being a KGB agent is an act of treason, Michael had to sue. The allegation was a beat-up from a book the *Sunday Times* had bought for serialisation, and there was no evidence to back it other than that KGB agents would sometimes attend fundraising parties for *Tribune*, Michael's left-wing newspaper, and leave a contribution.

If I wanted to find the person really responsible for the publication of this falsehood, I did not have far to look. But in libel law, hardly ever did you sue proprietors personally. That was because you had to prove they were the 'moving spirit' of the paper and that they had caused the words to be published. My solicitor, David Price, did some investigation, and discovered that Murdoch would call the editors of his British Sunday papers every Thursday. He would ask what they intended to publish on the front page and he would question them intensively about whether they were getting value for the money paid for any serialisation rights. He would therefore have known of, and approved, 'KGB: MICHAEL FOOT WAS OUR AGENT'.

So we did sue Rupert Murdoch personally. His lawyers tried to deflect the writ, claiming that the story was the responsibility of the editor, but we replied that on the *Sunday Times* front page, 'splash' stories like this were subject to approval by a proprietor who was its 'moving spirit'. I was looking forward to cross-examining Rupert, but it was not to be. Like Princess Diana, he settled at the door of the court – in this case, by agreeing to pay a six-figure sum to Michael in damages. I had another bad case of 'courtus interruptus'. Nonetheless, we trooped off with Michael to celebrate at the Soho haunt of London's old left intelligentsia, the Gay Hussar (named before 'gay' acquired another meaning).

I had tried to stop Murdoch from buying the *Sunday Times* to begin with. He was anxious to purchase Times Newspapers – *The Times* itself was losing money but its sister paper, the *Sunday Times*, was not, and for that reason the law required his purchase of that paper to be referred to the Monopolies and Mergers Commission. Rupert did not want this, and Mrs Thatcher's government broke the law to accommodate him. He went privately to see her and afterwards her Trade Secretary announced that the deal would go through without referral.

I was brought in to act for *Sunday Times* journalists who did not want Murdoch as their boss. I was led by Lennie Hoffman, the then top Chancery silk, and we were pretty certain of success – our expert accountants all verified that the *Sunday Times* was viable as a going concern. We could not guarantee victory, of course, and our solicitor said something to the journalists about a danger of losing by one vote in the final appeal court and having to mortgage their houses. The majority took fright and voted to withdraw the case and accept Murdoch as their proprietor in return for his promise to set up an 'independent' board to protect editorial integrity – a laughable ruse for which all but nineteen of them fell.

Thereafter Murdoch got rid of two editors (Harold Evans and Andrew Neil) whom he thought too independent, and published sensational lies such as the 'Hitler Diaries' and the Foot–KGB story. It was at that point I coined an aphorism that became my only entry in the *Australian Dictionary of Quotations*: 'Rupert Murdoch is a great Australian, in the sense that Attila is a great Hun.'

That said, some years later I was pleased to introduce Rupert to twenty-year-old Georgie, at the after-show party for the Sydney premiere of the film of *Les Misérables*. 'Were you moved by the movie, Mr Murdoch?' she asked sweetly.

'Oh yes, I was very moved,' he beamed.

'Those poor radical students killed on the barricades – didn't it make you want to cry?' (Georgie was a student leader at SOAS.)

'It did. Actually I dropped a few tears before the happy ending.'

Then, a steely rising voice: 'And how, Mr Murdoch, do you think Fox News would have covered that protest? On the side of the police repression, of course, as it always is. Fox News is…'

Rupert turned his deaf ear to her diatribe (a tactic he deploys when berated by parliamentary committees). He moved away, in the direction of Hugh Jackman and Russell Crowe, muttering, 'I love Fox News.'

Chapter Sixteen

Struggling for Global Justice

B y the time the millennium approached, my schoolboy career goal of addressing Old Bailey juries had been achieved. I even had my own locker in that holy of holies, the QCs' dressing room, where each morning the studs were inserted into the wing collar – carefully, to avoid that vulnerable gland in the neck – before sashaying down the spiral staircase, silk gown flapping, to the appointed court. It was a sign of my age that the judges were more polite, and the policemen younger. This was a self-contained world, in which you could pass pleasantries with your opponent of a morning when standing at the robing room urinals, before dumping on his arguments in a court below. There were frequent visits to the law courts in the Strand for libel cases or actions against the government – as the Human Rights Act took hold after 1998, these became more likely to succeed.

There were also my visits to the Privy Council in Downing Street and to the countries for which it was the final appeal, and missions for Amnesty International to places as varied as apartheid South Africa, post-conflict Vietnam and communist Czechoslovakia. Grave violations of human rights were occurring to dissidents in each country, far graver than those I was fighting in Britain, and they began to draw me away, more and more, from my locker in the silks' robing room at London's Central Criminal Court.

The rights themselves needed no new definition. They had been settled back in 1948, when Eleanor Roosevelt handed the Universal Declaration of Human Rights (the 'Magna Carta of all mankind') to the president of the UN General Assembly, Australia's H. V. 'Doc' Evatt. At the same time came the Genocide Convention and then the Geneva Conventions, requiring humane treatment for prisoners of war. What this great post-war triptych did not have was an enforcement procedure – a system to bring violators to trial and punishment. As a result, global justice was just smoke in the pipe dreams of professors. I am what is called a 'positivist' in jurisprudence: I hold that a rule is one of law not because it can be found in a treaty or a textbook but because there is at least a slim prospect that somewhere someday someone will be arrested for its breach. Amnesty missions were a good education about the need for enforceability, and I was inspired by victims I met in each country.

For instance, there was the sad-eyed old 'student' in a Vietnamese 're-education' camp. He had been a civil servant in South Vietnam, the government for which America had fought and lost, leaving its allies to communist revenge. 'Re-education' was a euphemism for indefinite detention, in a prison where the library had books by only one author – V. I. Lenin. The prisoner was routinely tortured, to make sure he had read them, but his main concern was for his children, who, as the offspring of a 'disloyal citizen', were themselves denied education, food and work (reprisals against the family members of dissidents are a particularly nasty feature of communist regimes, as they were of the Nazis').

There was the poet Robert Ratshitanga, the prisoner of Venda, a Ban-tustan puppet state invented by the government of South Africa to pretend that black people had some degree of independence. His crime had been to give a plate of porridge to starving ANC guerrillas, and he was facing a mandatory five-year sentence in a malaria-ridden prison. But – and prob-ably because an Amnesty observer was present – the prosecution offered him a deal which would have him released in a few months. All he had to do was to plead guilty to committing an act 'with an intention to impair the sovereignty of the state of Venda'. He refused, despite suffering from a serious illness which would see him dead before his sentence was finished. 'There is no way,' he told me, 'absolutely no way, that I can bring myself to acknowledge the existence of the state of Venda.' He had extraordinary presence and dignity, and I failed to convince him to save his own life by uttering the artificial words demanded by the state – the state, of course, of South Africa. It was a true act of conscience, to decline to receive mercy at the hands of a country in which he did not believe. On my nomination, Amnesty made him a prisoner of conscience.

There are ethical problems which can arise on the kinds of 'fact-finding' missions I conducted for Amnesty and other human rights organisations: you can never find facts from a prisoner when a guard is in earshot – indeed, you should never put the prisoner in peril by inviting him to criticise his captors in those circumstances, because he will probably be punished after you leave. You must beware of government translators, and watch out for the power structure in refugee camps, which are usually run by a political faction which will have a 'line' about the events at home which refugee claimants will be coached to repeat.

You must never put your interviewees in peril, which means obeying the local law, no matter how absurd. This was brought home to me the first time I took Václav Havel to lunch – he was on bail and could have been returned to prison at any time. I had just arrived and did not have any of the devalued local currency, and assumed I could pay in US dollars, which were accepted with alacrity everywhere in Prague. Havel explained that if I did he would be arrested by the secret police watching from a far table (they always sit near the window) and charged with being an accomplice in 'black marketeering' – a rule enforced only against enemies of the state. 'This is the first rule of being a dissident – you must scrupulously obey the law.'

Sometimes, this can be difficult. When I was observing trials for Amnesty International in the puppet homeland of Venda, I would arrive at Johannesburg Airport at 5 a.m., hire a car and drive for several hours up a straight road (bringing out what my wife called my 'Australian male revhead tendencies') before turning off to the courtroom. Inevitably, on one occasion I fell into a speed trap where a slightly apologetic policeman issued me a ticket, which I paid on the spot. When I mentioned this to Amnesty, they took it very seriously and a top-level meeting was called on the question of whether they should reimburse me. They decided to do so – but I would not rely on this as a precedent.

More serious difficulties can arise over confidentiality. I always interviewed judges and prosecutors, inducing them to talk with a letter from
Amnesty's Secretary General promising to keep their comments confidential. One of my missions to apartheid South Africa was to consider
the correctness of the convictions of the 'Sharpeville Six' – half a dozen
protesters who had been sentenced to death under the now discredited
'common purpose' doctrine: they had been part of a crowd which had
witnessed the 'necklacing' of an informer although they had no direct part
in this grisly reprisal. They had been convicted and sentenced by a judge
somewhat inappropriately named Human. I confronted him at his house,
and found a rather lonely old racist, dying of alcohol poisoning, but who
needed to talk. He took me for drinks at the Pretoria Club, which he
boasted was very progressive ('We even admit Jews,' he said, although not
blacks or women). After a few more drinks, he made some admissions
to me that might have founded an appeal. Had the prisoners not been
reprieved, would I have broken my promise of confidentiality in order to
save their necks? I would need to consult with Amnesty, but ultimately
my conscience would probably have made me speak out: after all, as every
equity lawyer knows, there can be no confidence in iniquity.

I visited Václav Havel regularly in the run-up to the Velvet Revolution
which brought him to the presidency. In this period, as the leader of the
dissident group Charter 77, this great philosopher-playwright-politician
was under constant surveillance from the communist government, and
regularly taken back to prison. Czechoslovakia was sometimes a truly Kaf-
kaesque experience in those dog-days of Warsaw Pact communism. The
government actually prosecuted the Jazz Society, which had been raising
money to honour John Lennon's memory, pretending that it had been
profiteering, although it was a non-profit-making organisation. I don't
particularly like jazz (you keep thinking it will turn into a tune, but it
doesn't); however, the prosecution of Karel Srp, the Jazz Society president,
was an opportunity to experience 'telephone justice', which operated in
most communist countries. The judge, a party worker, was telephoned by
the party boss the night before the trial and told to convict and how long to
make the sentence. It was what everyone calls a 'kangaroo court' (everyone

except me, because as an Australian I cannot bring myself to use the phrase – I do not know what our beloved marsupial has done to become a symbol for injustice). The Jazz Society trial ended with a two-year prison sentence for the leader, less than it would have been if we had not fomented an international fuss. As I came out of the court building in Prague's Charles Square with Havel, we were seen by several hundred young protesters, who struck up a ragged chorus of 'We shall overcome'. 'That's impressive,' I said to Václav. 'Yes,' he replied, 'and on these occasions you can always spot the secret police – they are the ones who know all the words.'

* * *

In Europe, a ray of human rights hope had started to shine some years before Havel's Velvet Revolution in 1989. The European Convention on Human Rights, drafted by British lawyers and ratified in 1951 by Western European countries, aimed to be a bulwark against the encroachment of communism. It had a court in Strasbourg where individuals could petition, and any government found in breach of the Convention had to change its law in order to comply. I had first appeared in the court to win a right of appeal for the media (the Channel 4 case – see Chapter Nine) and in 1988 I brought a case against Denmark which had international consequences. I acted for Mogens Hauschildt, a dealer in silver bullion – 'the silver king' of Denmark, notorious there for an alleged fraud. He had been arrested and denied bail by a judge who had looked at the evidence and decided that he might flee because he was likely to be found guilty at his trial. A few months later the very same judge presided at his trial and, surprise surprise, found him guilty. Obviously this judge did not have an open mind – he had prejudged the case at the bail application, and had gone on to fulfil his own prophecy. The Human Rights Convention guarantees everyone an 'independent and impartial judge' and this judge was patently not impartial.

The importance of the case was that Denmark, like some other European countries, had what is termed an 'inquisitorial' system of criminal justice, where a judge does the investigating (or supervises the police investigators). Britain and America have the 'adversarial' system, in which the prosecution do the investigation and present its case in a court where a judge who has had nothing to do with it previously presides, and the final decision is left to a jury. In Demark, however, the judge who supervised the prosecution process – granting search warrants, denying bail and so on – would also act as the trial judge, sitting without a jury. It was a system dating back to the Grand Inquisitors of the Spanish Inquisition, and the Danish government could not understand my argument about why it gave rise to a perception that the judge was biased. It was so confident of victory that it offered a free trip for any law student who wanted to observe its success, and over a hundred took up the offer. I had brought only my new secret weapon, a brilliant young junior, Keir Starmer. It was his first trip abroad, and he forgot his passport: my first argument in Strasbourg was to convince the *gendarmerie* to allow the future shadow Brexit Secretary to enter Europe.

For a barrister there is nothing more important than securing an impartial judge and I warmed to the subject with some passion at the hearing. Logic too was on our side – my forensic radar told me that the Danish case, based on its traditional way of working and the difficulty of changing it, was coming apart at the seams. In due course the court held that a judge who conducts the investigative stage against a defendant cannot preside at his trial.[89] *Hauschildt v Denmark* is now a leading authority, from a court which gained in power a couple of years later when the Soviet Union collapsed and all its client states – led by Czechoslovakia under President Havel – signed up to its Convention. It now has jurisdiction over forty-seven countries (including Turkey and Russia) and lays down basic standards for due process and fair trial.

The Hauschildt case was probably the most influential result of all my trips to Strasbourg. In retrospect, it is hard to imagine how any justice system could think a trial judge impartial who had repeatedly made pre-trial decisions on the basis that the defendant was likely to be found guilty. I have no quibble at all about the constitutional system which places a judge – an 'investigating magistrate', in charge of, or at least supervising, police inquiries into the suspect. British police could certainly benefit from such oversight, and it might be thought that there are fewer wrongful convictions – and certainly fewer wrongful acquittals – in France and Denmark than in the UK. What is crucial, however, and now accepted throughout Europe as a result of the Hauschildt case, is that the judge at the trial itself must not be the same judge who has authorised the police investigations into the suspect on the basis that he is likely to be guilty, or has charged him on that basis. The English principle that justice must be seen to be done, and therefore the trial judge must have made no pre-judgment on the suspect, has come to be internationally accepted: every human rights convention, and most constitutions, guarantee the right to an impartial judge.

This was never the case in communist countries, which practised 'telephone justice'. Nor is it the case in Brazil, where investigating judges act as trial judges, and are free to declare their pre-trial suspicions about the defendant before he or she goes on trial. In 2016 I had to observe the conduct of one such judge, an anti-corruption campaigner named Sérgio Moro, as he started an avalanche of prejudice against his target, the former President of Brazil, Luiz Inácio Lula da Silva, known to his people, and throughout the world, as 'Lula'. Moro and his prosecution team went to lengths that no judge in England or on the Continent would ever contemplate to convict a defendant, and I took Lula's case to an international tribunal, the UN's Human Rights Committee in Geneva, to complain that he was not being tried in accordance with its standards. Corruption is a serious charge, and common enough in Brazil that prosecutions for it are very much in the public interest. But only if they are fair – and Moro's are not.

Lula is something of a phenomenon who has inspired working-class men and women throughout the third world. He was born in desperate poverty in a shanty town, and went to work to support his family at the age of eight, selling peanuts on the street. At fourteen he passed his only exam, about how to operate a lathe, and worked at that trade until his charisma and concern for fellow workers led to an invitation to become an official of his trade union, and, soon, the leader. His lack of schooling turned out to be an advantage, as he imbibed none of the revolutionary agendas fashionable at universities in the 1960s – he was interested only in improving the terrible condition of workers in Brazil and reducing the poverty of its people. He decided, to that end, that the trade unions should have their own political force – the Workers' Party – and stood for President as its leader. He was elected in 2002 with 52 million votes, and again in 2008 with 58 million, which made him at the time, as President Obama joked, the most popular politician in the world. His presidency was a fine time for Brazil: aided by a favourable economic climate, some 20 million people were helped out of poverty by policies that are recommended today by the UN, involving family allowance to mothers if their children are schooled and inoculated. He could not constitutionally stand for the next presidential election in 2010, and stood aside for his Workers' Party protégée Dilma Rousseff.

Thereafter, like many Western ex-leaders, he made his living by giving speeches for money – most of which was donated to an institute to promote his ideas on poverty relief. He lives very modestly in a small apartment in a nondescript building outside São Paolo. I visited – to subject the home to my own test for corrupt people, i.e. whether there were gold taps in the bathroom. There were none – he was well-known to live, without luxury, a workaholic life for workers and for the Workers' Party.

I was under no professional obligation to take Lula's case to Geneva, so I investigated its background, which was set against the endemic corruption (which had started long before Lula) in parts of Brazil's public life. This particular part concerned bribes allegedly given by construction and engineering companies to win contracts with Petrobras, the nationalised oil company: some of this money had supposedly been funnelled to political parties, including the Workers' Party. I could find no evidence that Lula had instigated or personally benefited from this corruption, and nor could Sérgio Moro, the judge determined to convict him. Moro's taskforce of scores of police and prosecutors found no suspect money in Lula's accounts (none of them overseas) nor any receipts that had not been declared and taxed.

Unlike some other politicians and businessmen sucked into Moro's 'Operation Carwash' (so called because it started in the discovery of money laundered through a garage within Moro's jurisdiction), the actual charges against Lula were quite minor, for example that his family had used, half a dozen times a year, a country property belonging to wealthy friends (given Tony Blair's habit of taking holidays on the property of friends ranging from the Bee Gees to Silvio Berlusconi, this hardly seemed a crime). The first and main charge was that his wife had bought a share in a beachfront apartment from a housing co-op which had been taken over by a 'Carwash' contractor: it had offered them an upgrade to a more spacious apartment, and the contractor made some £200,000 worth of improvements to entice them to move in. But Lula never did, and the legal title remained in the name of the contractor. I was quite willing to believe that an unscrupulous developer might do a favour like this to ingratiate itself with a once and future President (Lula was entitled to stand again in 2018) but there was no evidence that Lula had done anything, or offered to do anything, in return – there was no quid pro quo that is necessary to prove bribery. He was out of office at the time, had no power to award contracts and there was no evidence that he had promised to do anything for them. So I thought Lula was probably innocent, but even had I thought him probably guilty I would have taken the case – an appeal to the UN Human Rights Committee – because of the abuses he had suffered at Moro's hands.

This 'investigating judge', before he turned himself into Lula's trial judge, had taken liberties that would have him removed from the case in countries that uphold the rule of law. Moro had used his power to authorise interceptions of Lula's telephone conversations and those of his family, his friends and even his lawyer. Under Brazilian law, these must be kept secret. But Judge Moro gave the audio tapes of the intercepts to the media, which published them with relish. Then, his zeal took him a step too far. He stopped the intercepts, but contrary to his order they continued, and recorded a conversation with President Rousseff. These tapes, illegally recorded against his own order, Moro decided he should release for public delectation. This lawbreaking was too much for Brazil's supine Supreme Court, and Moro had to concede ungraciously that his judgement might have been incorrect. Still the Supreme Court did not remove him from the case. In no other advanced country would a judge be permitted to whip up public animosity against a suspect he was about to try – he would inevitably be removed from his victim's case. But Moro was untouchable – under Brazil's anomalous criminal procedure, he is the judge on the case, who orders investigative procedures against a suspect, charges him and then turns around to try him, without a jury or assessors. It is as if the policeman who investigates, arrests and charges you suddenly takes off his helmet, puts on a wig and finds you guilty.

In the run-up to the trial, Moro's team worked hard to create a public expectation of guilt. His chief prosecutor took a ninety-minute slot on national television to explain to the public why Lula should be convicted. So much for the presumption of innocence – Brazil has no contempt-of-court law, nor any rule that stops prosecutors and judges from attacking suspects before or during their trial. The chief prosecutor even published his own book, detailing his case against Lula, in the middle of the trial. Meanwhile, Moro attended the launch of a book that defamed and condemned Lula, signing copies and posing for press photographs. He publicly congratulated right-wing demonstrators who sang his praises in the street, and it was impossible to go into a bookshop without seeing his photograph, in an Eliot Ness pose, on the covers of books and magazines. The media, dominated by the giant Globo franchise, assumed Lula's guilt and faked pictures of him in prison clothing: these are reproduced on balloons and life-size rubber dolls, held aloft at demonstrations against the workers' party. All this is made possible by an unfair system of investigation and trial in which there is no effective distinction between prosecutorial and judicial functions and no protection for the presumption of innocence.

When first invited, I did not particularly want to visit Brazil – the Zika virus was at its height and it was not warm enough to swim at Copacabana. I did have a sneaking desire to see whether Rio really does have a more beautiful harbour than Sydney (on closer inspection, it does not). I am glad I went, however, and have gone back, not only because of the dedication and courage of Lula's beleaguered defence attorneys, but for the opportunity to survey a legal system constructed in such a primitive way that gives me renewed confidence in – and actually gratitude for – our own. I am not complacent about it, having strived over the years for reform, but I do think we should always strive for a system that provides, as far as humanly possible (and sometimes it is not possible), a fair trial before an impartial judge.

In July 2017, Judge Moro predictably convicted Lula and sentenced him over the beach apartment to a jail term of nine and a half years in prison. He appealed to the Federal Court in the southern city of Porto Alegre, whose Chief Justice immediately announced that Moro's judgement was 'impeccable'. I doubt that he had the time to read it, but this is a court which abandoned from the outset even the appearance of impartiality. Shortly before the appeal was heard, the Chief Justice's registrar posted on her Facebook page her wish that Lula be sent to prison, urging her friends to support her. The Chief Justice refused to criticise her, and indeed endorsed her right to prejudge the man who was seeking justice from his court.

I attended, with a translator, the so-called appeal hearing in January 2018. There were meant to be three judges, but there seemed to be four. The fourth turned out to be the chief prosecutor, sitting on the right hand of the presiding judge and retiring with them for lunch and coffee. He turned to his colleagues to make the prosecution's submissions, for half an hour, whereupon Lula's lawyer had fifteen minutes to respond. The judges asked no questions; they simply pulled out their judgments, already written and typed, and read them – for the next six hours. The 'hearing' was a farce – they had come to it not with an open mind, but with a decision – to reject the appeal and to increase the sentence to twelve years – already agreed.

The little lathe-worker divides this nation of 210 million people very much on class lines: the wealthy, the professional classes, the Globo media (more right-wing than the Murdoch media) and the judges (among the best-paid in the world) all oppose him: the workers love him, as do most of those falling between the cracks of the favelas. The truth, probably, is that Lula could never be tried fairly in Brazil. Which is why it was necessary to bring aspects of his case to an impartial UN tribunal. It may well decline to hear the case until all his appeals are decided, and he will have to serve some time in prison (he surrendered to Moro's arrest warrant in March 2018) and perhaps suffer disqualification from standing again for

President. However, by bringing the complaint to Geneva we did something to highlight the injustices he has suffered so far. He is now in prison for a crime he did not commit – a 'bribe' of an upgraded apartment that he never accepted and in any event did nothing for in return.

Political corruption is a curse – the seamy side of democracy, by which business people steal from the public purse and politicians profit – and it does not matter that the profits are not for themselves but for their party (even if it is the Workers' Party). But you cannot combat corruption effectively unless you prosecute it fairly. Otherwise, convictions will be counterproductive, because they will not be accepted as just, and the rule of law will suffer.

There are several inquiry models that Brazil could adopt, none more successful than the Independent Commission Against Corruption (ICAC), pioneered in Hong Kong and now a regular feature of parliamentary democracy in Singapore, Sydney and elsewhere. It involves a permanent and well-resourced body tasked to investigate wrongdoing by politicians, public servants and state enterprises, with full powers of surveillance and arrest and public hearings (at which suspects are represented) overseen by a distinguished committee to ensure its work does not become politically partisan. Those of its reports which allege criminal behaviour are referred to prosecutors and the evidence is tested at trial by impartial judges who have not been involved in the process of gathering it. The accountability of public officials is achieved not by leaks to the media but at public hearings where the other side of the story may be heard: any charge that results is subsequently the subject of a fair trial. There are other effective models, none of which rely on public demeaning of suspects by an all-powerful judge-prosecutor working hand-in-glove with the media to create an expectation that the suspect will be found guilty – a prophecy that the judge-prosecutor is then empowered to fulfil.

Lula deserves respect for his achievements, but not immunity. If there is evidence that he personally benefited from corruption, he must answer it, but before an impartial judge and in proceedings that give him a fair opportunity to do so. Judge Moro and the prejudice whipped up by the Globo media have made this impossible: as the prison-garb Lula dolls and balloons waving in the streets demonstrate, Operation Car Wash has turned into a kind of lynch law aimed at pulling down the most successful symbol of workers' power in Latin America. That is why it must be exposed – not for the sake of corrupt congressmen or thieving construction bosses, but for respect for human rights, and protection against prosecutions that turn into persecutions.

*　　*　　*

The job that really opened my eyes to the need to combat corruption effectively came many years before my experience of Brazil. In 1990, I was appointed as counsel to a Royal Commission which uncovered a plot that belonged in a James Bond movie. It was hatched in Antigua, a small tourist island with 365 beaches ('one for every day of the year') and an obsessive love for cricket inspired by its legendary batsman, Viv Richards. It was still ruled by the trade unionist who had led it to independence from Britain in 1981, one V. C. Bird, who gave his name to its airport, its main street and many of its enterprises, the most wicked of which was a project of his son, Vere Bird Jr, Minister for National Security. Vere Bird Jr was in the pay of the Medellín cartel – led by Pablo Escobar and Rodríguez Gacha – who needed some up-to-date weapons for their murders. Vere Jr placed an order with Israeli Military Industries for Uzi sub-machine guns and Galil assault rifles, and arranged for them to be shipped to Antigua and deposited in a container at the dock of St John's, the capital. The very night of their arrival on the docks, a tramp steamer owned by Escobar slipped into the harbour, loaded the container and took it off to Colombia, where one of the rifles was used to kill a presidential candidate. The assassin dropped the rifle, which was identified as coming from Israeli Military Industries. Colombia accused Israel of dealing with the cartel and Israel accused Antigua. Under pressure from the USA and Britain, Antigua set up a Royal Commission under Sir Louis Blom-Cooper, who asked me to act as its counsel to investigate where the truth lay.[90]

It lay with the utterly corrupt Vere Bird Jr, although this venal and stupid character had been played upon by some Israeli mercenaries who had been training Escobar's terrorist militia in Colombia. They had not only arranged the gun shipments but had agreed with Vere to move the terrorist training to Antigua, using the facilities of the local defence force. The drug trafficking cartel, in other words, at war with a democratically elected government and busy killing judges and journalists courageous enough to oppose them, would have their vicious army trained by Israeli mercenaries (and a few drop-outs from the SAS) with facilities on the island which had unwittingly been provided by the UK and America, which funded the Antiguan defence force. Fortunately, the conspirators were incompetent and the plot took little time to unravel: their telephone records showed them making calls to Medellín that they could not explain. They had lazily relied on their secretaries to implement the details, church-going women who told the truth under oath when summoned to give evidence. Our proceedings were televised, and the people of Antigua were able to see, under cross-examination, just how rotten their government was. They dubbed me 'the Silver Fox' because of my hair colour – these days, my sobriquet would be 'the mangy grey fox'. (At least it was an improvement on 'the Rottweiler', the tag given me by the *Daily Mail* when it was thought I would cross-examine Diana.)

International law had let down the people of Colombia, and of Antigua. The world was beginning to be concerned about weapons of mass destruction, but most innocent victims of organised crime and marauding armies die from bullets fired from conventional weapons like assault rifles and sub-machine guns. I went to Washington to present to a Senate committee our commission's recommendations for a convention to control the sale and supply of conventional arms. We received strong support from Senator Sam Nunn, who recognised the ease with which they fall into the hands of narco-traffickers and terrorists, but it was another twenty years before member states of the UN, the most powerful of them steeped in the arms trade, could muster the numbers to support even a weak convention against the trafficking of conventional weapons.

The work in Antigua was difficult and dangerous. We lived in a beach-front villa guarded around the clock by armed police who feared for our safety from cartel hitmen. Their fears were not entirely fanciful and I paid many a silent tribute to all the judges and prosecutors who have been killed for fidelity to their profession, in Colombia by the cartel and in Italy by the Mafia. We enjoyed the calypso competitions, however, an art form which combines political satire and catchy music – clues to corruption on the island were contained in the songs, the bitter journalism of the shanty towns that tourist dollars, creamed off into politicians' pockets, rarely reached. This is a familiar story: corrupt regimes run government as a private business, leaving schools and hospitals and social services starved of funds: tourism profits and foreign investment rarely percolate down to their people.

*   *   *

One contribution to international law arose from the coup in Fiji led by George Speight in 2000. The country had recently agreed, after years of democratic consultation, on a new constitution and had held an election based on preferential voting which had given the People's Coalition fifty-eight out of the seventy-one seats in the House of Representatives. It was led by an Indian, Mahendra Chaudhry, and contained many Indian MPs. This displeased the indigenous Fijians of the extreme nationalist Taukei movement, who demanded a return to an earlier constitution which had discriminated in their favour. Speight and some armed thugs entered Parliament, assaulted the Prime Minister and held MPs hostage while demanding abrogation of the new constitution. The army's strongman, Commander Bainimarama (in a Boris Johnson moment, I pronounced him 'Commander Bananarama'), had the hostages released and Speight arrested, but then himself purported to abolish the constitution and install a government led by members of the indigenous faction. They drafted another constitution to discriminate in favour of ethnic Fijians, reserving the main positions in government for those of their race. This was merely 'ethnic apartheid' said the London QC brought in at great expense by the temporary government to defend these actions in court. It was unlawful apartheid, I said, and a breach of an international law against the over-throw of democracy.

We argued the case in the Court of Appeal of Fiji, which resembled an international tribunal. There were two New Zealand judges, one Tongan, the Chief Justice of Papua New Guinea and a judge of the NSW Supreme Court – who later joked that I had addressed a sixth judge, namely the television camera transmitting the hearing to the public (as almost all the people on the island were watching to see justice done, that would not have been inappropriate). The court rejected the new government's argument that 'might makes right' and ordered it to dissolve itself and bring back Mr Chaudhry, despite its offer to hold elections some time in the future (this is usually an idle promise. Emergency rule becomes a way of life – only Cincinnatus returned to his farm).

The court's decision gave support to our contention that although there was no international right to democracy (see China), there was nonetheless a legal presumption that peoples who have enjoyed democratic government cannot have it removed by force.[91] No military junta or 'interim' power that overthrows a democratic government and lawful constitution should be recognised unless it can prove that it has popular acceptance and support – which of course Fiji's new government did not. At least it complied with the court's order and self-dissolved, bringing back Mr Chaudhry until he was replaced by another coup and the country ended up under the virtual dictatorship of Commander Bainimarama. I asked the UN to reconsider the use of Fijian troops as peacekeepers and urged President Obama to stop drinking Fiji Water because of its connection with the military regime. These appeals had no effect, but at least the case had helped to create a precedent, a presumption in international law that once a democracy, always a democracy.

This presumption did not appeal to the Australian government when it recolonised Norfolk Island in 2016, destroying the qualified democracy which had been granted back in 1979. Norfolk Island has only 2,000 inhabitants, half directly descended from Tahitian women who coupled with Fletcher Christian and his *Bounty* mates after they had jettisoned Captain Bligh. While Australia looked after their international affairs, its people enjoyed a good measure of self-government, which was uncontroversial and conservative – they forbore from legalising cannabis or euthanasia or same-sex marriage, encouraging instead a community ethos and custodian-ship of the *Bounty* relics and a world heritage site which displays the relics of the most brutal of Britain's prisons. After the recolonisation, their Parliament was locked up and the islanders were told to stop singing 'God Save the Queen' – where else in the world could that be a revolutionary anthem?

I visited, at their invitation, to consider whether Australia's recolonisation could be undone. The people of Norfolk had forebears oppressed by Bligh and were now being crushed by an Australian government led by Malcolm Bligh Turnbull (named in honour of the cantankerous captain). I found an obscure UN committee on decolonisation which agreed to accept their petition. Norfolk is a unique place, full of history, with its trademark pine trees framing two of the best beaches in the Pacific, and off its shores I rediscovered the joy of fishing (and the special excitement of getting the catch into the boat before it is taken off the hook by a shark). Of course, its constitutional arrangements were anomalous and idiosyn-cratic and as such unacceptable to bureaucrats in Canberra, who want to turn this unique place into just another seaside town in New South Wales, under NSW law but without any rights to vote in its elections. This is the problem with bureaucracies – the inability to tolerate difference, even when that difference has deep cultural and historical foundations.

*   *   *

Norfolk Island is a shared part of both Australian and British history: it was first used as a prison – an extension of the convict settlement at Sydney, under the rule of the first Governor, Captain Arthur Phillip. Of all the characters in that shared history, Phillip has always struck me as the most extraordinary. He was a humanitarian, far ahead of his time. A poor boy trained by the British Navy, he grew up to be one of Nelson's captains and with amazing seamanship took his little floating prison, the First Fleet, in 1787 on a 12,000-mile voyage beyond the known world. He was a true egal-itarian, sharing his own rations with the convicts when times were grim, and his survival skills kept the little colony going. He drafted the first law for a settlement that only he dreamed might ever become a nation: 'There can be no slavery in a free land.' He refused to carry out his instructions from the Home Office to acquire brides by force for the male convicts (seven for every female offender) from the indigenous women, and he did his best to foster good relations with the Aboriginals – refusing reprisals after they had speared him in the shoulder, punishing soldiers who mistreated them, and adopting two young Aboriginal men – Bennelong and Yemmerrawanne – whom he took back to England with him in 1792. On arrival, Bennelong sensibly took the next ship home, but Yemmerrawanne stayed – he was the first Australian expatriate – and died of pneumonia in the English winter. Phillip bought him an expensive tombstone which may still be viewed at the churchyard in Eltham, south London, just opposite the bus stop where Stephen Lawrence was murdered.

Despite his amazing achievements as white Australia's founding father, Phillip was ignored by the British establishment: he was not vouchsafed burial in Westminster Abbey or even Bath Abbey (where he lived) but given a crummy grave somewhere in the church at Bathampton. In a fit of expatriate patriotism, I persuaded the premier of New South Wales that we should uplift both Phillip and Yemmerrawanne, bring them home and give them a state funeral and bury them under a monument overlooking Sydney Harbour. I was appointed a secret agent of the New South Wales government to negotiate with the relevant bishops to effectuate the removals. The Church of England's consistory court had just made a ruling that permitted foreign heroes buried in English cemeteries to be taken back to the place of their heroism, and I saw no reason why it could not apply to Englishmen valued in another country but not at all in England. The Bishop of Bath and Wells could not have been more helpful, and arranged for the church's exhumation expert to report on uplifting Captain Phillip. The Bishop of South London was very helpful, too: he immediately promised to locate Yemmerrawanne's bones beneath the headstone. A week later, he called with bad news: the good parishioners of Eltham had needed more burial space, and the remains of the Aboriginal had been the first to be thrown out. The headstone had been propped up against the wall, and there was nothing beneath it. 'We do have a lot of spare bones,' said the Bishop, rather hopefully, I thought (he was looking forward to visiting Sydney), but I resisted the temptation – DNA testing would have caught us out.

The people of NSW would have to make do with Governor Phillip. But then came a second, final blow to my great plan: the exhumation expert could not find Phillip's coffin. It was not where a notice in the church tells Australian tourists that it is, and it could not be located anywhere in the crypt beneath the building. The Church of England had lost the plot. It had, in fact, lost two plots, and my mission to bring the bones back to where they might be venerated could not be fulfilled.

There were other Aussie bones in London, however – those of Aboriginals slaughtered by British marines and convicts in Tasmania in the 1820s, in 'black wars' which wiped out almost the entire native population. A House of Commons Select Committee on Aborigines reported in 1836 that British occupation of the island 'could not be reconciled with feelings of humanity or even with principles of justice or sound policy' and that 'it could not fail to leave an indelible stain upon the British government'. That 'indelible stain' is now, of course, called 'genocide'. But a sordid by-product was a trade in Aboriginal skulls and bones: graves were robbed and some natives may actually have been killed to supply Victorian mantel-pieces with skeletal curios: the British Governor's wife, Lady Franklin, was a particularly avid collector. In time, most of these human relics came into the hands of the Natural History Museum. There they sat in shoeboxes for upwards of a century, until 2009, when the Australian government (at the behest of its indigenous people) asked for them back. That was when the museum's scientists suddenly took an interest, and announced that before they could be returned for proper burial they must first be subjected to 'destructive testing': they planned to cut teeth and some sections from the skulls in DNA laboratories and dissolve them in acid. This mutilation of their forebears outraged the Tasmanian Aboriginal Centre (TAC): I could feel the fury in the voice of its head, my old friend Michael Mansell, as he called to tell me how this would breach cultural taboos, torture the spirits of the deceased, and subject his people to desecration and disrespect. He was calling me on Thursday night (London time) to ask me to stop the testing, which was to be carried out on the Monday.

I was keen to help, but there is no property in a dead body and the museum had possession, traditionally nine-tenths of the law, although the odds had shortened thanks to the Human Rights Act (which requires some respect for religion and for family). The museum had ignored it, and had behaved arrogantly and unethically by not even attempting to consult with descendants or their representatives, the TAC. By Sunday I had put together the case for an injunction, which went before the 'weekend judge' on the High Court – coincidentally, its only black judge, Linda Dobbs. She granted the injunction, which the museum rushed into court on Monday to try to discharge it. Their counsel waxed indignant: these skulls were museum property, and its scientists were only going 'to cut them about a bit'. That was an unfortunate turn of phrase: 'What they are going to do, my Lord, is to experiment on the bones of victims of genocide.'

We held the injunction and the judge, taken aback at all the novel legal issues the case raised, begged us to try mediation. The museum at first refused, until it felt the pressure from donors disturbed at the prospect of 'genetic prospecting' on genocide victims. So the case did go to mediation, before the former Chief Justice of England and the former Chief Justice of NSW. The museum scientists were hard put to identify any positive value in the information they might glean through processes contrary to Aboriginal law, lore and religious belief concerning the treatment of the dead, requiring their remains to be lain to rest with customary ceremony in traditional lands.

My skeleton argument on behalf of the skeletons pointed out that Tasmanian Aboriginals are a minority group under international law, which gives a special status to their identity, culture and religion. There is an emerging principle of free, prior and informed consent by indigenous people to policies affecting their rights, and this principle had deliberately been ignored by museum scientists who believed (as did Dr Mengele, I suppose) that the pursuit of knowledge is an overriding good in itself. In this case, the scientists should have been aware that they were seeking to extract data from the remains of human beings killed in British genocide, unlawfully brought to Britain as the result of grave robberies and massacres, and that their experiments were intended to measure racial characteristics. These experimenters were looking for 'natural abnormalities' to put Aboriginals on the lower rung of the ladder of 'human diversity': after two centuries of stigmatic denigration by British scientists who portrayed them as 'primitives' with small brains, heavy brows and flat heads, it is little wonder that my Aboriginal clients were suspicious of the museum's projected research.

The mediation took a whole week of anxious ethical wrangling, and it must be said that the museum representatives, so sure of their position at the outset, were slowly but sincerely won over to the indigenous viewpoint and eventually agreed to all the TAC demands. The remains of the lost tribe were returned for burial in their ancestral lands in Tasmania, where they can rest in peace safe from the carving knives of scientists, unless those scientists can convince the TAC that further knowledge really is worth acquiring. It was a result of some significance for the ethical duties of museums: I am not normally on the side of traditions and superstitions when they interfere with science, but there are moral limits to the acquisition of knowledge. Certainly where it involves an assault on human dignity expressed in burial customs, where no clear advantage can be predicted, and further racial degradation is on the cards.[92]

*   *   *

One request for a legal opinion turned into a book. It came from a group of Armenians who were upset by UK government statements that the evidence about massacres of Armenians at the hands of the Ottoman Turks in 1915 was 'not sufficiently unequivocal' to amount to genocide. What did I think? I had to warn them that as an independent QC I would have to make up my own mind on the issue and that no matter how much they paid me (in fact, very little) I might well decide that the killings did not fit the definition of 'genocide' at all. They were prepared to take the risk, and it was a pleasure to have the excuse to immerse myself in history books as well as law books to come up with the answer. There was no doubt at all: in 1915 the Ottomans had solved 'the Armenian question' by eliminating the Armenians, a Christian enclave whom they viewed as likely to support Britain rather than the Germans, with whom the Turks had opportunistically allied in the war. There were some two million Armenians within their borders, and the Young Turk government killed over half. They began by rounding up and murdering the intellectual leaders – politicians, professors, lawyers and the like – then conscripting able-bodied men, who were worked to death. Then they ordered the women, children and old men to march without food and medicine through the desert to places we only hear of now because they have recently been occupied by ISIS. Hundreds of thousands died from starvation and disease, as the government seized their homes and businesses and confiscated their property.

Since this extermination of part of a race on religious or racial grounds obviously satisfied the Genocide Convention definition, why was the UK government denying it? The answer was found in secret Foreign Office records, which it only disgorged after persistent enquiries under the Freedom of Information Act. The FCO told ministers – correctly – that Turkey was 'neuralgic' about the genocide, and that 'HMG is open to criticism in terms of the ethical dimension. But given the importance of our relations (political, strategic and commercial) with Turkey … the current line is the only feasible option.'[93]

In other words, this had become 'An Inconvenient Genocide' (the title of my book): because of Turkey's 'neuralgia' and because of its strategic and political importance, the truth could not be admitted.[94] It still cannot, as Turkey remains a vital NATO ally and continues to threaten reprisals should the UK call the 1915 massacres by their proper name. Britain has, however, dropped the dishonest statement that the evidence is 'not sufficiently unequivocal'; it now says that the question is for a court, knowing that there is no court to decide it. I am fortified by the fact that most authorities now accept the truth – it was pleasing to hear Pope Francis describe it as 'the first genocide of the twentieth century'. (Popes are not infallible, however, and it was in fact the second genocide – the first was the massacre of the Herero people in modern-day Namibia, by German troops under the command of Herman Göring's grandfather, in the first decade of the century.)

My absorption in Armenian history led me to take up the cause of its people who live in Nagorno-Karabakh, a delightful little country in the clouds, its mountain ranges full of ancient Christian churches (the Armenians were first to convert, back in 303 AD). Because of its land dispute with Azerbaijan, which has closed its airport, I have to take a bumpy six-hour car trip skirting Mount Ararat (resting place of Noah's legendary Ark) and dodge bullets fired at random by the Azeri Army marshalled at the 'line of contact' – a line over which Armenian and Azeri soldiers have been shooting at each other for thirty years. Karabakh is one of those small countries (there are several of them in this region) whose right to exist is powerfully opposed by armed neighbours, and where the international community has dismally failed to broker peace. There were pogroms in the past, and both sides fought fiercely for their cause, although the siege of Stepanakert in 1991–92, where the Azeri planes and guns brutally targeted Armenian schools and hospitals, was a mini-Guernica. The background to the conflict is too complex even to sketch, but the foreground is all too apparent: what I see when I visit is young men and women whose lives are put on hold while they serve compulsorily for years in the armed forces. They are not tortured, of course, and only occasionally shot, but the waste of their young lives for want of a political solution is shameful.

Armenia, a country of three million people without oil wealth like Azerbaijan, or political importance like Turkey, could not survive without the help of its diaspora, concentrated in California, where I find myself every April reminding them of the genocide – though they need no reminding, only the consolation of knowing that others share their sorrow, and their anger that Turkey still denies history by refusing to apply the 'g' word to the Ottoman massacres.

* * *

As may be gathered from the cases in this chapter, my legal career had moved on from the worlds of Rumpole, John Mortimer and Jeremy Hutchinson, and seemed based, in the twenty-first century, at the departure terminal at Heathrow. I was not alone: the chambers formed Doughty Street International, with an office in The Hague to cater for members involved in cases in courts based there – the International Court of Justice, the International Criminal Court and various UN war crimes tribunals. I missed the congeniality and companionship in the Bar Mess of the Bailey, but there were prisoners in greater peril elsewhere in the world who claimed my attention.

My wife was not too bothered by my human rights work – it kept me out of the house. Sometimes, however, she was heard to express the wish that they would hang my clients quickly so my services would no longer be needed. She learnt her lesson, I think, early in our marriage when she did cut up rough about my devoting a weekend of fathering time to helping the only opposition MP in the Parliament of Mauritius, Navin Ramgoolam, under illegal attack from right-wing enemies. Some months later, tickets to Mauritius dropped through the post with a note from Navin saying that he had won the election, and indeed his party had won every seat in the house. Could I come and advise his government on law reform, and bring the family? So our family holidays – they were beach holidays for the family, while I drafted new laws, in that delightful island over the years of the Ramgoolam premiership – made up for my sojourns in less serene places. I was not allowed to take the kids to Africa after a trip to the Gambia, when I led them, under the tutelage of a dreadlocked Rasta guide, to a mysterious, gaseous lake to pat some rather large crocodiles. They were soporific from the gas, but with jaws large enough to swallow Georgie should they decide to yawn. I had faith in the magic of the lake, which had never had a fatality, but Kathy decided that working holidays should thereafter be confined to Mauritius and the Caribbean.

Of course, it is one consequence of acting for oppositionists that some of them eventually come to power and summon you back to help; this time you are accorded VIP treatment, sometimes from the same police who monitored you when you were acting against the government. My children became fond of the armed police who escorted them when I came to advise the government of Trinidad – they took Jules and Georgie to a funfair, and the kids took great delight in the fact that their guards were too frightened to join them on the ghost train.

My literary partnership with Kathy seemed to work – I would take the first draft of her novels with me to a death row, or to a dreary Holiday

Inn in Sarasota near Jules's tennis training camp, to wrestle their plots into some sort of shape. Kathy in return would take my drafts to the hairdresser's and try to add some jokes, although she had to admit defeat with *Crimes Against Humanity*. She had fled school at age fifteen, and her quicksilver mind was untouched by university, so we were sometimes at cross-purposes. 'You write here, "She felt she was in a Rousseau-like state of nature." Don't you know that Hobbes was the state of nature, while Rousseau was the social contract?'

'But I was thinking of the painter, who depicted women in those jungles.'

And so on, into the night.

Chapter Seventeen

The World's Fight

It might be thought that the stars aligned at the time of my birth, the very time when the judges at Nuremberg pronounced a verdict that created international criminal law. I first noticed the coincidence when I began work on *Crimes Against Humanity* half a century later. I had decided to write a book about the prospects of enforcing human rights law, in the hope that the book might actually advance these prospects. The time seemed propitious: the European Court of Human Rights was expanding its jurisdiction, there were some good judgments from the Inter-American Human Rights Court that served Latin America, and the Privy Council was developing a human rights jurisprudence for the Commonwealth, at least in respect of death sentences and trial fairness. National courts had delivered some important judgments on torture and on free speech; there were cases stretching back centuries on the law of war ('international humanitarian law', as it is confusingly called); the UN had set up war crimes courts for the nations that had emerged from what had been Yugoslavia; a court had been instituted in Tanzania to prosecute the perpetrators of the Rwandan genocide. There had even been a conference in 1998 to establish an International Criminal Court. My book attempted to weave together these *fin de siècle* developments as indicative of a historic shift, from appeasement to justice, in international relations. No longer would tyrants, I posited, be allowed to leave the bloody stage with amnesties in their back pocket and their Swiss bank accounts intact: they could be indicted by international prosecutors and tried in international courts.

The problem with prosecuting tyrants, however, was that they were usually heads of states, who had immunity from prosecution. I argued in the book that the key to puncturing the 'state sovereignty' that gave them immunity would be to charge them with a 'crime against humanity'. The worst of such crimes was genocide, which the world had a duty, under the UN Genocide Convention, to punish. But mass murder, torture and rape would be elevated into international crimes if committed systematically or over a widespread area, and pardons and amnesties granted under local law could not shield rulers from punishment by international courts. *Crimes Against Humanity: The Struggle for Global Justice* was both an exposition of human rights law as it had developed thus far and a clarion call for a binding obligation on all states, including America, to submit to international justice. The book's advocacy of a global justice movement was described by John Bolton, George Bush's future UN ambassador and now Donald Trump's national security adviser, as 'a threat to American sovereignty'.

It was published on 24 March 1999, the day the House of Lords ordered retired Chilean dictator General Augusto Pinochet to be extradited to Spain for trial as a torturer, and the day that NATO bombed Serbia to stop its ethnic cleansing in Kosovo. The age of enforcement had begun, at the fag-end of a century in which more than 150 million lives had been lost to war and genocide. The book had 450 pages in its first edition; the fourth, which I wrote in 2012, had over 1,000, a measure both of the craving for global justice and the complications of delivering it.

The first test of the main thesis in my book came with the arrest in London of General Pinochet. I had written to him, without answer, of course, as an Amnesty member, back in 1973 when his coup overthrew the democratically elected Salvador Allende. Pinochet had murdered Allende's supporters (including Pablo Neruda), 'disappeared' 4,000 dissidents, and set up torture chambers to break opposition to his military rule and spread terror. So confident was he that no law could catch up with him that he allowed his state torture to become public knowledge. It generally involved the infliction of pain by electric shocks, accompanied in many cases by degradation through rape and bestiality, often in front of family members, who themselves were induced to confess to stop the agonies of a wife or daughter.

Pinochet retired as commander in chief of the army in 1998, festooned with amnesties he had arranged for himself. Preserved by that cloak of immunity which international law bestowed on former heads of state, he decided to come to London – to have his back treated at a clinic in Harley Street. He had been given red-carpet treatment on previous visits (the Ministry of Defence was hopeful Chile would buy British arms) and had openly supped around town. My friend Ruthie Rogers (whose husband Richard, one of the world's leading architects, had designed the court in Strasbourg) ran the fashionable River Café restaurant, and was so horrified at the sight of Pinochet's name on the gold card print-out that she donated the amount he had paid for his meal to Amnesty International. On his arrival at Heathrow on this visit he was, as usual, given VIP treatment, and the next day it was reported that the ageing mass murderer 'took tea' (I am reliably informed it was whisky) with his good friend Lady Thatcher. He then attended his private clinic, from where his presence in London was leaked to *The Guardian*.

That is when Baltasar Garzón, Spain's judge in charge of terrorist investigations who had for years been gathering evidence of Pinochet's guilt, asked Scotland Yard to arrest him for extradition to Spain under a European convention that facilitated the processing of criminal suspects wanted for trial in member states (this was the European Arrest Warrant – EAW – used to arrest Julian Assange). Obedient to European law, London's anti-terrorist squad pulled off one of its finest operations, surrounding the bed of the recumbent torturer just a few hours before he was scheduled to fly home. His arrest produced an international sensation: the Pope, Henry Kissinger and George Bush Sr joined Lady Thatcher in demanding his release – so too did his mortal enemy Fidel Castro, anxiously urging respect for Latin-American dictators (like himself). Pinochet's arrest was immediately challenged in court. At the initial stage, three judges (and they were good English lawyers) ordered his release: they could not understand how an allegation of torture, which could be made against so many state visitors to London, could puncture Pinochet's immunity. Garzón appealed to the House of Lords, and both Amnesty and Human Rights Watch entered the proceedings to explain how those who committed crimes against humanity should have no hiding place.[95]

I was briefed by Human Rights Watch, which gave me an opportunity to put some passages in my new book into a legal submission, to the effect that immunities should apply to heads of state only in relation to their exercise of legitimate state functions, and by no stretch of the imagination could widespread and systematic torture – a crime against humanity in international law – be regarded as a legitimate state function.

The verdict from the House of Lords, televised live, had all the thrill of a football penalty shootout, as the five Law Lords rose in turn to announce their decision. The first two put their balls firmly through our goalposts: it was 0–2 to the torture team. Then one, and another, scored for Garzón – the international justice game stood at 2–2. That was when Lennie Hoffmann, by now a Law Lord, stood to declare that Mr Pinochet had no immunity – the torturer must go to trial. There was pandemonium in the square outside, full of his victims who had come to London in the hope of seeing international justice done: for the first time since Nuremberg, it was. But it was also British justice, which is adamant that no judge should in any way be perceived to be affected by any private interest. Lord Hoffmann had helped, free of charge, a charitable trust set up by Amnesty, which had made itself a party to the case, and so was disqualified. The judgment was set aside and a new panel of seven Law Lords had to be found, none of whom must have any connection with human rights. They were, in the main, commercial lawyers whose experience was largely concerned with interpreting contracts. They focused on the Torture Convention – one of those unenforced and hitherto unenforceable documents that most governments had signed without dreaming it would have any effect. But it had imposed a duty on them 'to try or to extradite for trial' credibly suspected torturers, and our literal-minded Law Lords took those words to mean what they said. The final score in the return match was 6–1 to human rights.

Pinochet spent eighteen months under house arrest (well, mansion house arrest) in England before, with a mercy the general had never shown his victims, the Home Secretary allowed him to return home due to medical evidence that he was unfit for trial. Once back in Chile he had the most amazing recovery since Lazarus, but spent his last years tormented by legal actions and prosecutions for his newly discovered corruption. The Pinochet precedent entered international law – and was used to further the prosecutions of Slobodan Milošević, Charles Taylor, Radovan Karadžić, Ratko Mladić, Hissène Habré and other mass-murdering leaders and generals.

In London, the Pinochet case was for several months the main political controversy, and I went around TV studios arguing that his crimes against humanity could not admit of human forgiveness. My opponents – usually Norman Lamont, once Mrs Thatcher's Chancellor of the Exchequer – had to acknowledge the evidence of the viciousness of Pinochet's torture regime; they claimed that retribution should be left to history (which depends, as Richard Nixon pointed out, on who writes it) or to God (but in an increasingly secular society, belief in a torture camp named 'Hell' was no longer universal).

The loudest ploy of the Pinoshits was to accuse us of 'destabilising Chile's fragile democracy'. This was soon proved to be nonsense – Michelle Bachelet, whose father (an air force general loyal to Allende) had been killed by Pinochet, was elected President. The country settled down and showed no lingering fondness for its dictator, especially when he was revealed to have stolen a lot of its money. The Blair government at least played a straight bat – 'We must let the law take its course.' The course it took was a matter of some bewilderment to Australia's Prime Minister. 'I was not taught that this sort of thing could happen when I was at law school,' remarked a bemused John Howard.

*   *   *

It is one thing to formulate a theory about international justice, and another to put it into practice. That real challenge came in 2002, when I was invited by the United Nations to become an appeal judge at its latest war crimes court, in war-torn Sierra Leone, and was made the court's first president. At the time, Sierra Leone (named by fifteenth-century Portuguese navigators after the lion-shaped mountains they could see from its shores) was the poorest country in the world. Many of its people had been captured by early slave traders, but the capital, Freetown, had been established by British abolitionists as a haven for the slaves they had freed, and for the American slaves who had fought for Britain during the war of independence. In due course the country's mineral wealth – notably its diamonds – was despoiled by my benefactor Cecil Rhodes and the De Beers corporation, and until the 1960s it had been run by colonial administrators. Graham Greene, stationed there during World War II, gives a memorable account of the country in *The Heart of the Matter*. It was a peaceful place until it achieved independence in 1961, when it was disrupted by army coups and became for a while the regulation one-party state. The eleven years from 1991 saw it dissolve into the most brutal civil war between rival armed factions, fighting each other as well as a government returned after a UN-sponsored democratic election.

One such faction, the Revolutionary United Front (RUF), was led by a pathological killer named Foday Sankoh, and backed by Charles Taylor (President of neighbouring Liberia). The two had met at a terrorist training camp in Tripoli in the early '90s, hosted by Colonel Gaddafi, whose malign hand was detectable behind brutal RUF incursions into Sierra Leone from across the Liberian border. The RUF devised a new entry in the human rights chamber of horrors, called 'chopping'. The slogan of the UN-brokered election was that the people had 'power in their hands'. So, those who had voted were asked in which hand they had held their pen, and that hand was then chopped off. Mutilation proved successful as a means of terrifying and degrading the population, so the group devised more devilish tortures, such as lopping off legs as well as arms, sewing up vaginas with fishing lines, cutting open the stomachs of pregnant women and padlocking mouths. It recruited children, drugged, trained and armed them with AK-47s, 'blooded' them by forcing them to shoot their own relatives and had them execute village chiefs in the main square. It attacked Freetown in an operation called 'No Living Thing', which lived down to its name.

My appointment as a UN appeal judge was welcomed by the High Commissioner for Sierra Leone, who assured me that it would not take up too much of my time – just an occasional appeal a few years hence, after the trials had finished. Of course it did not work out that way: my fellow judges elected me as the court's first president and I had to be on hand regularly for the difficult work of getting the court up and running, interspersed with visits to the UN in New York to report progress and ask for more funds in order to progress further. But I made the time, and although my duties in Sierra Leone disrupted my life and my practice for five years, I thought that duty had, in some indefinable way, called. If justice could conduce to peace, after Africa's most barbaric war in its poorest and most inhospitable country, there would be some proof of my book's thesis.

I arrived in Freetown in 2002 to a city that bore little resemblance to Graham Greene's description – it was full of burned-out buildings and the ravages left by Operation No Living Thing. It was a dangerous, unpleasant place – some visitors, like Tony Blair, simply stayed at the airport, made a speech and returned home on the same plane. To enter the city involved a lengthy ferry trip over a long stretch of water or else a hair-raising flight in one of the old Ukrainian helicopters used by the UN, with young Ukrainian pilots. Two of them crashed while I was there, losing more than twenty lives on each occasion.

To provide justice for victims of the atrocities, the special court was to comprise three institutions – the registry, the office of the prosecutor, and the judiciary – two chambers for trials and one for appeals. I presided over the Appeal Court. We had an American prosecutor, David Crane; a British deputy, Desmond de Silva QC; a British registrar, Robin Vincent; and my fellow judges. They were a mixed bag, ranging from a fine and upstanding Nigerian jurist to a local judge who drove Robin mad by demanding employment for his relatives and provision of court cars to take his wife shopping. They had the flaws of being UN appointees nominated by member states, rather than being meritocratically selected. Some were lazy (one trial court rarely managed to start on time) and venal, forever wanting me to use my powers of advocacy at the UN to increase their perfectly adequate salaries.

The war had ended in an uneasy peace and we were guarded around the clock by a contingent of UN 'Blue Helmets', alert for threats from Charles Taylor and from factions which had not yet laid down their arms. The city was rife with rumours of excursions by Taylor's death squads (he was still in power in next-door Liberia) and by al-Qaeda operatives seeking diamonds for their own financing of terrorism elsewhere on the continent. There was a more immediate threat, too: as I was ushered into the decaying 'VIP room' at the airport on my arrival, I noticed the first malarial mosquito. Almost every person at the court went down at some point with this recurring disease, the carriers of which I kept at bay by a foul-smelling repellent called DEET (diethyltoluamide). I succumbed on one occasion, and tried the remedy I remembered from my Biggles books, namely quinine, immediately sozzling myself in gin and tonic (only later was I reminded that quinine was in the tonic, not the gin). Fortunately, Robin had obtained some of the mysterious herbal pills which the Vietcong had developed to cure their malaria, and it cured mine – nobody knew how.

The war had taken 75,000 lives and left many more in various states of mutilation – our court sponsored a disabled football team, all members on roller-boards, without arms or legs or both. It was heart-rending to hear, at the court's official opening (graced by Kofi Annan, then the UN Secretary General, and Harriet Harman, UK Solicitor General), the children's choir from the Milton Margai School for the Blind: all these kids had been deliberately and viciously blinded by the RUF during the war. Victims were everywhere, as were those who had mutilated them. The only persons we could put on trial were those perpetrators who 'bore most responsibility' for the atrocities. A dozen of the faction leaders were rounded up and put in our prison, including Chief Samuel Hinga Norman, whose tribal militia, the Civil Defence Force, had actually fought for, and saved, the elected government. The American prosecutor decided to charge him for recruiting child soldiers, which was ironic since Norman himself had been recruited into the British Army at the age of fourteen. He was a respected figure in the community and had been made Home Affairs minister in the post-war government – he was arrested on the way to a Cabinet meeting, and when he reached the prison the guards saluted.

This was a reflection of our biggest challenge – we were the first of the new international courts to sit, as the army said, 'in theatre' – in the very place where the crimes had been committed and where many of their perpetrators were still at large. The judges for atrocities in the former

Yugoslavia sat in safety at The Hague, and *genocidaires* in Rwanda were on trial in Arusha, in peaceful Tanzania. But we wanted to let victims see justice being done on those most responsible for their sufferings, and we did so publicly, notwithstanding the danger and the inconvenience. People oppressed for years by the most primitive savagery saw their oppressors arrested and brought from a new jail to a new court to which they could come and hear evidence of their sufferings being used to punish their torturers. When Charles Taylor was apprehended and brought by helicopter to Freetown, almost every citizen clambered to the rooftops of the city to watch. However, the UN deemed it too dangerous to try him in 'theatre': the court moved (by which time I had left it) to the safety of The Hague.

Delivering on the Nuremberg legacy after a civil war in Africa had other problems. As the Nuremberg prosecutor had said, 'We succeeded because of the Teutonic habit of writing everything down.' But the warring factions in Sierra Leone had kept no incriminating records, and guilt had to be proved by laborious excavations of clues from mass graves and by testimony from informants who needed protection – some had to be given new identities and a new life in other countries. There were many novel questions that my appeal court of five judges had to consider. And because 'fair trial' concepts had moved on since Nuremberg, we had to make improvements. For example, under the Nuremberg model the prosecutor was an 'organ' of the court, along with the judges and the registrar, but there was no provision for the defence. I had always felt that this was unfair, so I instituted an independent defence office, which could ensure that all prisoners were competently – sometimes outstandingly – represented, and this initiative was later adopted by the International Criminal Court.

Our first task was to build a court. I approached Richard Rogers. As a believer in international justice, he agreed, without taking a fee, to design a world-class structure for Sierra Leone. But all financial decisions were made by a UN committee in New York, and when his tender came in – at only $100,000 more than a firm which had built a Crown Court at Wolverhampton – I could not convince the bean-counters to leave Sierra Leone with an architectural legacy. Certainly the Americans (the Bush regime) were opposed to any form of legacy – they wanted our defendants convicted as quickly and as cheaply as possible. I had to explain that justice need not be exquisite, but must not be rough: if they failed to provide enough money to pay for the trials, and particularly for the defence office, we would pull up stumps and depart. In the end the funds were provided, a serviceable court was built and the trials proceeded as fairly as possible.

This was in no small measure due to Robin Vincent, the epitome of an honest and imaginative administrator. He was an English cricket obsessive, and we spent our spare time happily sledging each other. His calmness and cunning came through in dealing with the UN bureaucracy and in overcoming all the frustrations in getting the court up and running. At one point he sent a list of essential demands to Kofi Annan, with a threat to resign if they were not met. 'You shouldn't resign, old chap,' said a visiting stuffed-shirt from the British Foreign Office. 'You won't get your K.' (FO-speak for knighthood.) 'I don't give a damn about my K,' replied Robin. 'I only care about my court.' Annan came through with the resources, and the UK did come through with his K before Sir Robin died of cancer in 2011, shortly after his term of duty had ended.[96]

In 2004, I took the judges to the Middle Temple for a week to settle the 'Rules of Evidence and Procedure' and our prosecutor indicted Charles Taylor. The court was in business, and soon in session. But did international law even allow us to indict a sitting head of state? A week of Appeal Court hearings was scheduled to settle this and other unsettled questions, such as whether it was an international crime to recruit child soldiers and whether an amnesty could be valid for a crime against humanity. Taylor remained safe at first as dictator of Liberia – we had kept his indictment a secret, but when he left for a conference in Ghana the prosecutor opened it and asked the government to arrest him. Instead, it warned him and assisted his flight back to Liberia. He was overthrown, but fled to Nigeria where he was allowed to stay as a paying (i.e. bribing) guest, but our prosecutor managed to freeze his Swiss bank accounts and ultimately, thanks to US pressure, Nigeria handed him over. He had, in the meantime, sent a team of lawyers to our Appeal Court to argue that, wherever he was, he was beyond our jurisdiction, because he possessed the immunity traditionally given to heads of state. We rejected this argument and decided that credible allegations of crimes against humanity might be tried in an international court irrespective of any claims of immunity, which were binding only on domestic courts.

We refused to be bound by the amnesty that the defendants had all been given by a peace agreement signed at Lomé in Togo, where peace negotiations had taken place in 1999. This took international law a step further than had been reached by the Pinochet precedent, which had invalidated only the amnesties that Pinochet had given to himself. Our decision invalidated all amnesties given for crimes against humanity. Amnesty International applauded the judgment and I suggested that it should change its name – to 'No Amnesty International'. It was in this case that I had the sensation which must be felt by many appellate judges, of rejecting the legal submissions I had once fervently made when a barrister. The arguments I had canvassed to uphold the amnesty and save the lives of the Muslimeen in Trinidad did not apply to the Revolutionary United Front, which had continued to kill and mutilate.

Our most ground-breaking judgment was to declare that it was a crime to recruit child soldiers. This was the first prosecution of its kind anywhere in the world, and it was appropriate to initiate it in Sierra Leone, where over 10,000 children under the age of fifteen had been enlisted to serve in the armies of the warring factions. Many were killed or wounded and others were forced by guns or induced by drugs to kill and maim their victims, including members of their own community and even their own relatives. For survivors, the consequences were traumatic – they suffered reprisals from the villagers they had been ordered to attack and later exhibited behavioural problems and psychological difficulties.

The evidence before the court about child recruitment was abhorrent, but abhorrence does not create an international law crime. The principle of legality – the rule against retrospective law-making – requires that a defendant, at the time of committing the acts alleged to amount to an offence, must be in a position to know, or at least readily establish, that those acts would entail punishment, no matter how grotesque they might appear to decent people. That stage was certainly reached by the time the convention establishing the International Criminal Court came into force in 2002, with its prohibition on child recruitment, but in my opinion it had not been reached by 1996, the year that Samuel Hinga Norman was charged with recruiting children to his force, which was defending the government, because at that point no country had made child recruitment an offence. Our court split on this question (my opinion was endorsed by later cases and textbook writers), but the difference did not matter: we were at last, and to this extent unanimously, declaring that henceforth forcing children to fight was an international crime.[97]

There were more novel decisions: how to deal with a 'Truth Commission' which wanted to interrogate our defendants before we could put them on trial; whether to order human rights researchers and journalists to give evidence for the prosecution and to disclose their sources – our decisions on those issues have also found their way into textbooks. At one point, three defendants from the RUF objected to my hearing their appeals because I had previously written critically about this faction (taking my facts from Kofi Annan's reports to the Security Council). I was happy to stand down from their cases because their defence seemed to be that the RUF had not committed the crimes that Annan and various commissions had imputed to it, so they might perceive me as biased. But they went further and tried to remove me permanently from the court – in which endeavour they failed. At trial, of course, these defendants admitted all the RUF atrocities – their unsuccessful defence was that they personally were not involved.

They might have done better had I heard their appeals. Over the five years I was a member of the court, my colleagues held in favour of the prosecution in every appeal, and I was the only judge to rule, on several occasions, for the defence. I would probably have upheld the appeal of Sam Hinga Norman (and of his co-defendants) had he not died before the verdict. His co-defendants were convicted on the same facts, by two trial judges against one. I had left the court by the time of their appeal, but it always strikes me as a matter of logic that if one of three judges thinks a defendant innocent, there must be a reasonable doubt about his guilt.

Charles Taylor's trial received more publicity than any other when Naomi Campbell and Mia Farrow stepped into the witness box to tell how Taylor had given Campbell uncut 'blood diamonds' from Sierra Leone at a dinner party in South Africa hosted by Nelson Mandela. Taylor had denied being paid in diamonds for the arms he had supplied to the RUF, and had even denied ever possessing them, so the evidence was relevant. Naomi Campbell was a reluctant witness and had told Oprah Winfrey on her TV show that she was afraid to attend, so her appearance was a mark of the authority of the court. Taylor was convicted of aiding and abetting crimes against humanity ranging from terrorism, rape and murder of civilians to recruiting child soldiers and sex slaves. The evidence set out in blood-curdling detail the crimes of the mass-murdering and mass-mutilating rebels he supported, although from his presidential palace in Liberia he had no direct involvement with the atrocities. He knew about them, however, at least from reading newspapers, and he supported the perpetrators with money and munitions. His conviction should serve as a warning to other political and military leaders who send assistance to brutal factions in a civil war, with knowledge that they will use that assistance to commit crimes against humanity.

Taylor's appeal was given short shrift, and in May 2012 he was sentenced to fifty years' imprisonment, which he is serving in Britain. I had left the Appeal Court by this time, but I certainly would not have upheld the length of this sentence – as he was sixty-four at the time, he will die well before his release date. Sentencing convicts to serve more-than-life terms is a cruel American habit which is antipathetic to sensible penology – even the likes of Charles Taylor should be sentenced to a prison, not a mortuary.

I served for five years on the UN War Crimes Court and it was not an easy ride. I spent many hours looking down over the endless sands of the Sahara before smearing myself with DEET as we touched down. Petty theft was a daily problem – I had my robes stolen (much good that must have done the thief) and my suit was neatly extracted from its suit-carrier, so I had to appear at the court's opening in Robin's ill-fitting clothes. However, I do have some pleasant memories – of the zest for life of the limbless victims, of the court coffee shop, where I could mingle with young lawyers on prosecution and defence teams, and court staff and NGO visitors to discuss the way forward for the global justice movement. And I will never forget the friendship of Robin Vincent.

Every time we visited Freetown there was some improvement – a lick of paint on the customs office, a new newspaper on the streets, a new asphalt road from the landing pad. The court contributed to a reduction in superstition, by putting a feared juju man on trial and showing him to be a fraud – grown men, as well as child soldiers, had believed that the potions of these priests, smeared on their bodies, would protect them from enemy bullets. (General Butt Naked was one of these foolish fighters in Sierra Leone, convinced of his juju invulnerability – his name was adapted for a character in *The Book of Mormon*).[98] It was heartening to see how democracy had begun to take hold among a people who had always enjoyed peace until army coups had replaced the rule of law and tribal rivalries had been whipped up by leaders greedy for power and for diamonds. By putting those leaders on public trial, the court contributed to the peace, and gave some meaning to the slogan 'No Peace without Justice'.

Sierra Leone also afforded an insight into the practicalities of international justice. It is one thing to write academic treatises on the subject; on the ground, the complexities and challenges are extremely arduous. We were unable to overcome the costs and the delays that have dogged other international courts, but ours was generally hailed as a success, and its 'hybrid' model (with a significant minority of judges, lawyers and staff recruited from the locality) is sometimes suggested for other countries. I remain convinced that a war crimes court is most effective if it sits in the country recently torn apart by the war: it becomes one of the institutions that can help put the nation together again.

In 2010, I was invited to Nuremberg's iconic courtroom by the German Foreign Ministry, which had decided to make it more than simply a tourist attraction: they wanted to fund a centre to promote 'the Nuremberg legacy' – putting tyrants on trial for crimes against their own and other people. I sat in my judicial robes on the very bench where the judges had glared at Göring and Ribbentrop, and where Spencer Tracy had been pictured in the movie *Judgment at Nuremberg*. I was full of ideas of how this historic court could be used to bring the legacy alive: we could televise a mock trial of my relative, the Kaiser, for invading Belgium and ordering unrestricted submarine warfare, or we could arraign some long-dead German diplomats and Turkish politicians for connivance with the Armenian genocide.

The dour German officials blanched, more noticeably when I suggested some modern trials, of George W. Bush for invading Iraq, for instance, or Vladimir Putin for aggression in Ukraine. They took fright, and decided that it should be turned into just another un-embarrassing 'academy' for academics. I was invited to speak at the opening, where I made one last desperate suggestion – to stage a trial of Sep Blatter for the corruption of FIFA. It was no use. The historic court at Nuremberg will not be the stage for anything interesting any time soon.

*   *   *

Everyone who hopes for peace and justice in the world pins their faith on the United Nations. The organisation is the best we can do, although it is never good enough thanks to its structural weaknesses, most notably the Great Powers' veto in the Security Council, which gives Russia and China, and sometimes America, the ability to dishonour their proclaimed 'responsibility to protect' victims of crimes against humanity.

I first entered the UN building in New York at the request of its Staff Association. Its members, most of whom had made personal sacrifices to work for the organisation, were not being treated fairly. The internal disciplinary and employment law procedures had not been updated since 1947, management was entitled to behave as it liked, and nepotism – the abiding problem of an organisation with its officials appointed by governments of member states – was rife. I chaired a commission which recommended the appointment of a full-time independent judiciary to deal with all internal problems and to stand between management and staff in order to resolve the frequent internal disputes that were damaging the UN's work. In 2008, these recommendations were finally implemented and the Staff Association elected me as their 'distinguished jurist' member to sit on the new Internal Dispute Tribunal, which would supervise the new system and nominate the judges, chaired by Kate O'Regan, formerly of the South African Constitutional Court.

Our first task was how to have them appointed in a way that would avoid the drawbacks of state nomination. We decided to advertise for candidates internationally in *The Economist* and *Le Monde*: they had to have been judges for a decade or so, and to send us examples of their work. This produced about 400 applications. We called the best thirty candidates to The Hague, not only for an interview but also (to their horror) for a three-hour examination in which they had to write a judgment on given facts, which would show their juristic ability. It was fascinating to see how the competitive examination, that mainstay of the old English civil service and the merit-based mandarin bureaucracy of China, really sorted the sheep from the goats. Some of these lawyers, although long-time judges in their own countries, seemed unable to write with any clarity. The examples they had sent us earlier must have been written by their clerks or their associates.

The most important safeguard for human rights, both in national and international courts, is access to justice delivered by judges who are both independent of government and impartial towards the parties. By 2017, when I was invited to deliver a keynote speech on the subject at the International Bar Association annual conference back in Sydney, I had become something of an expert. I had successfully defended the Chief Justice of Trinidad when its government tried for political reasons to remove him, reported in favour of the Chief Justice of Sri Lanka when her government impeached her for a decision in favour of the Tamils, and even obtained a Privy Council verdict for a judge who had been unfairly disciplined for drinking.[99] I have written extensively on the problems of political appointments to the bench, and on the current danger of populist movements and governments seeking dependent judges – legal lickspittles who will do their bidding. From Poland (where the government intends to sack Supreme Court judges and replace them with cronies) to Venezuela (where hardline judges do the government's dirty work by ordering the arrest of political opponents) to America (where Donald Trump appoints only judges who share the 'values' of his base) to Britain (where pro-Brexit tabloids condemn honest judges as 'enemies of the people'), judicial independence is under threat. It is ironic that this long-time critic of judges should become their defender, but they are no good at defending themselves and the times call for an explanation of why, so long as they remain impartial, their independence is essential to democracy, no matter how unpopular their decisions.

*   *   *

As a former UN appeal judge, I sometimes receive requests to investigate and adjudicate quasi-judicial controversies that the UN and its member states lack the political courage to undertake. In 2009, the Washington-based Boroumand Foundation ('Human Rights and Democracy for Iran') asked me to report on a massacre of which I had not previously been aware: the mass killing of political prisoners and atheists in Iran in 1988. I conducted interviews with survivors and witnesses in the US and in European cities, examined the Iranian press at the time, and found that these killings constituted the worst crime against humanity committed against prisoners since World War II – comparable in wickedness to the killings in Srebrenica and to the death marches of Australian and American prisoners by the Japanese.

The Supreme Leader of Iran, Ayatollah Khomeini, and his President (and now Supreme Leader) Ali Khamenei had ordered that the many thousands of prisoners in Iranian jails who supported a left-wing opposition should be destroyed. The signal was given and the prisons went into lockdown: these young men and women were blindfolded and ordered to join a conga line which led straight to the gallows. They were hanged from cranes, four at a time or in groups of six; or from ropes in front of stages at assembly halls; some were taken to army barracks at night, directed to make their wills and then shot by firing squad. Their bodies were doused with disinfectant, packed in refrigerated trucks and buried by night in mass graves. Two months later, the same process was applied to male prisoners who were atheists – female atheists were (for abstruse theological reasons) whipped five times a day until they either converted or died. Families were not allowed to know where their loved ones were buried and even today are not allowed to mourn them. Many thousands were killed in this way by Iran's theocratic state – without trial, without appeal and utterly without mercy.

My report was the first detailed account of this atrocity to be published.[100] It identified the perpetrators, many of whom are now in high positions in the Iranian state (the Minister of Justice at the time of writing this was a main organiser). These men deserve to be prosecuted for crimes against humanity, and their interest in obtaining nuclear weapons must be stopped at all costs (even at the cost of maintaining Obama's Iran deal, which I criticised at the time for not being made contingent on an improvement in the country's human rights record). I warned about this dangerous theocratic state in my book *Mullahs without Mercy: Human Rights and Nuclear Weapons*, published in 2012, and my hostility to the regime remains undimmed, notwithstanding the election of a more liberal president – who remains under the thumb of his cruel Supreme Leader and the Revolutionary Guards. I have sometimes found myself acquainted with strange bedfellows – on conference platforms between Rudy Giuliani and John Bolton, for example – but on this subject if on few others we are on the same side (although my reasoning is different).

In 2009, I wrote a book about a very different kind of state – the Vatican, which should not be a state at all – and how it has connived at the torture, through sexual abuse, of children. The project began with a call from Christopher Hitchens, an old friend who knew of my interest in crimes against humanity – I had discussed them in a documentary inspired by his book about Henry Kissinger. What did I think about the reports emerging from Ireland and Boston about paedophile priests and the apparently endemic child abuse in Catholic institutions? Did I think that this might amount to an international crime? I said to Hitch that I would get back to him, and I did, some months later, after studying court reports and the available psychiatric evidence and immersing myself in the mysteries of canon law and the law relating to statehood.

My response was *The Case of the Pope: Vatican Accountability for Human Rights Abuse*.[101] There was no doubt that paedophile priests, and other clergy who took advantage of kids trained to revere them as the agents of God, had bewitched, buggered and bewildered hundreds of thousands of children in their care, in a scandal covered up by bishops and cardinals throughout the world to avoid reputational and financial damage to the church. Overseen by a special commission in the Vatican responsible for canon law (headed by Cardinal Ratzinger, later Pope Benedict), they had kept these crimes a secret from local police, while abusive priests had quietly been moved to other parishes, where they had reoffended.

Pope Benedict had become an enemy of human rights by exploiting the UN decision to grant 'statehood' to the Vatican (which did not, in my legal opinion, qualify for it – for one thing it's a 'country' where no children are born, except by accident). He insisted on vetoing all UN initiatives for family planning, contraception, and what he called 'the sinister ideology of women's empowerment'. He regarded homosexuality as 'evil'. He had rallied the Catholic countries of Latin America to make common cause with Muslim states like Libya and Iran to veto, for example, the UN's projected 'right to sexual health'. But his responsibility for widespread and systematic child abuse made him a candidate for criminal investigation. 'Put the Pope in the Dock' was how *The Guardian* headlined my findings,[102] although I insisted on calling the book *The Case of*, rather than *against* – readers could judge for themselves.

My book provided evidence relied upon by the UN Committee on the Rights of the Child, which in 2014 condemned the Vatican for putting children in peril. Ratzinger, the ostrich Pope, retired when he became too old to cope and was replaced by a better man. Pope Francis has not, however, brought in the reforms that are essential if the scourge of child abuse is to be stopped. That will require the church to raise the age of communion and confession from seven (at which age kids are so readily brainwashed into reverence for the priesthood) to thirteen or fourteen, when they are more capable of resisting sexual advances and may have more confidence to report them. It will also require an end to the secrecy of the confessional, as the Australian Royal Commission on child abuse has recommended, at least in respect of priests who hear confessions from fellow priests about abusing children. I have noticed, however, some recent changes – at La Madeleine, the majestic cathedral in Paris, confession boxes have been replaced by glass offices, where priests sit in open view, their hands on the table, to hear confessions.

*　　*　　*

Bangladesh is a Commonwealth country where my books are on the law syllabus and my arguments for prosecuting those responsible for the hideous genocide of 1971 have been well received – so well that they have set up the International Crimes Tribunal to try the Islamists who collaborated with the Pakistani Army in killing all the students, intellectuals and teachers who might have led this breakaway state, as well as slaughtering hundreds of thousands of Hindus. I applauded the determination of the government to provide a reckoning, even forty years later, and although the worst culprits were depraved and dissolute Pakistani generals, there is no doubt that they were assisted by members of local Islamist factions, some of whom rose to be ministers in later governments and were now opposition leaders. What I did not applaud was the fact that the 'International Crimes Tribunal' has no international judges or lawyers and that it sentences almost everyone it convicts to hang by the neck until they are dead. Most of the defendants are political enemies of the current government, which doubly delights in sending them to the gallows. It was ironic to read the first appeal decision by the Bangladesh Supreme Court, which justified the tribunal's existence with lengthy quotes from *Crimes Against Humanity*, yet ended by deciding that all its convicted prisoners should be executed. I wrote a report for a human rights organisation which emphasised the legal and political folly of imposing death sentences.[103] (After most executions, there are riots in which numbers of citizens are killed.) My efforts were not appreciated and one minister publicly called on the government to arrange for my 'punishment'. I am not sure how this is to be administered, but I doubt that I will be returning to find out.

Then there was Sri Lanka, on which I reported for the Bar Association of England and Wales. In 2009, government forces – especially its navy – had launched a massive bombardment of the Tamil community in the north, killing up to 70,000 (mostly civilians) and displacing 350,000. The government of Mahinda Rajapaksa banned the media and denied any wrongdoing, but soon the truth emerged, captured in fleeting and grainy images on cellphone cameras, of summary executions; naked female bodies on the beach violated and drowned; lines of captives in handcuffs, shot where they were standing. The undoubted viciousness of the Tamil Tigers could not justify these government-ordered reprisals against Tamil civilians and my report urged the establishment of a war crimes court.

The nation's Chief Justice had ruled in favour of Tamils in a dispute with the government, and Rajapaksa, in fury, insisted on her dismissal. He had a majority in Parliament and his MPs, lacking all integrity, voted to impeach her on charges which were obviously false and fabricated. The Sri Lankan Navy celebrated her dismissal with a firework display. It was nonetheless an outrageous attack on judicial independence, a value that protects all citizens. My report concluded that she was not guilty of the charges.[104] She was reinstated as Chief Justice when Rajapaksa was overthrown, but I felt some sanctions were in order for his MPs who had colluded in her removal.

*   *   *

I have been involved in designing and participating in court systems that can deliver on the Nuremberg legacy of punishing perpetrators of crimes against humanity. There has been some progress since the Pinochet precedent, but the system's stumbling block is the inability of the pole-axed UN Security Council to agree on taking action against violating states and their leaders. The worst example is Syria. In May 2011, I wrote an article, 'Assad Should Face International Justice', pointing out that the Syrian President's deliberate decision to use tanks, machine guns and poison gas over seven weeks against unarmed civilians already amounted to a crime against humanity.[105] Only 800 protesters had been killed at that stage, but as the toll mounted to more than 500,000 over the subsequent seven years, the Security Council always declined to refer Assad to the prosecutor of the International Criminal Court because Russia blocked any action against its ally.

What is to be done when international law (Article 2(4) of the Covenant of the United Nations) prohibits attacks on sovereign states other than in self-defence, subject (it may be) to a narrowly defined right of humanitarian intervention? Occasional Western air strikes on Syrian bases in response to the use of chemical weapons make no difference, other than to ruffle international relations and increase the resolve of Assad and his people. As for Russia, it is too powerful to attack for annexing Crimea or for assassinating its enemies abroad. The West must find another way, more sophisticated than brute force, which takes advantage of globalisation – the intertwining and interdependence of actors, whether business people, parastatals, corporations or ecumenical churches, or simply family connections. There must be a reckoning for abuses of human rights by sovereign states or sovereign statesmen, and their cronies and supporters and even their fellow nationals may have to suffer for their crimes. Not just by trade sanctions, but by banning them entirely from doing business or using banks, expelling them and seizing their property, and ousting their children from private schools. As a deterrent to commission of crimes against humanity, depriving the criminals and their friends and their supporters of the proceeds, and of their psychological well-being, is a better deterrent than Trump's preference for bomb craters.

One such measure I have been advocating is a 'Magnitsky Law'.[106] This is named in memory of Sergei Magnitsky, a lawyer and whistleblower who complained to the authorities in Moscow about how companies belonging to his client, Bill Browder, had been scammed by highly placed police and tax officials. Magnitsky was immediately arrested and thrown in prison, where judges ordered him to remain for a year despite serious illness. He was tortured, and died in his prison cell. To be clear, Vladimir Putin – rootin' tootin' shootin' Putin – did not kill Sergei Magnitsky. He was killed by middle-ranking officials of Putin's corrupt state apparatus – by a criminal gang of policemen and tax officials, with the help of tame judges and prosecutors. The judges were like the train drivers to Auschwitz, turning a blind eye to the inhumanity they were helping to perpetrate, denying bail to a sick man wrongly detained by corrupt police. These criminals and their accomplices were safe in Russia, of course, but that's not where they wanted to keep or spend the proceeds of their crime. So Browder led an international campaign to stop them enjoying their ill-gotten gains – to freeze their assets in Western banks and deny them entry to countries with the casinos that were their favourite haunts.

President Obama signed the Global Magnitsky Act in 2012, targeting several Russian judges along with the crooked police and tax officials. Putin's furious first response was to stop the adoption of Russian orphans by American families. Then, more logically, he introduced his own Magnitsky

Law, which targeted American officials who ran Guantanamo Bay, although they had no money in Russian banks and Dick Cheney is unlikely to want to holiday in the Kremlin.

A Magnitsky Law cannot reach heads of state or diplomats who enjoy privileges and immunities, but it may deter those who carry out their orders, who profit from crimes against humanity and want to stash their cash in more stable countries where their families can have access to good doctors and Western schooling. The idea is now being taken up by the European Parliament: if you can identify human rights violators abroad, you should act to stop them enjoying their gains in your country, by banning them from entering. Also – and this is important – deny them access to your banks and medical facilities and schools. Of course, normally we try not to visit the sins of the father on the children, but in the case of corrupt and brutal officials, I don't see why not, because they are very often motivated by a desire to benefit their family. The nastiest man I have ever investigated – an Israeli general who had been profiting from illegal arms sales to the Medellín drugs cartel – once pleaded with me not to name him. 'I only did it for my family. For the sake of my children.' If their families are denied medical treatment in the West, if their children are barred from the playing fields of Eton, that seems only fair.

But we cannot pretend that human rights will overcome race venom, or religious hatred, or lust for power or money. It was particularly tragic that the first political protesters to be killed in Syria back in 2011 held banners demanding 'Assad to The Hague'. Their expectations of international justice were far too high. After a few thousand deaths they turned violent, and were violently supported by al-Qaeda and then by ISIS, while Assad was lent violent support by Iran and then Russia. Now there is no end to the violence, and no end to the refugees (by 2017, half of Syria's population). ISIS has committed genocide against Yazidis and Coptic Christians, while NATO has been afraid to put boots on the ground. The UN has quietly offered to set up a Sierra Leone-style court in Baghdad to try captured ISIS leaders, but the Iraqi government has refused to cooperate because the court will be unable to pass death sentences.

'Don't you despair?' people often ask. I do not, because belief in human rights takes hold in small places, and slowly spreads, from Nagorno-Karabakh to Norfolk Island. I have observed how far the UK has moved since I began practising here, to embrace ideas that were then barely thinkable. I have seen how the tyrants to whom we once wrote pathetic letters have been arrested for their tyranny; how members of the gay community, discriminated against for so long, are finally allowed to marry; how electronic communication has brought into being the global witness, and I have watched how those of my children's generation have come to support the rights of people with whom, at their age, I was never concerned. And for all the enormity of our present problems – refugees, terrorism, climate change, Trump et al. – the life I have sketched in this book has left me with faith in the one quality that ultimately identifies us as human. Not our power to speak or reason or love, or to subdue base instincts or achieve autonomy or worship gods, but our counterfactual capacity for kindness. Human rights standards reflect our ability to care for others and for future others. That is why I believe they are worth fighting for.

As for global justice, I have always seen it as a struggle that will continue for many years, as two steps forward are followed by one step back. For fifty years we failed to deliver on the Nuremberg legacy, and only since the turn of the century have we made any sort of start. There is a long way to go, but we will go in the right direction if we maintain the rage against atrocities inflicted on human beings anywhere in the world, and by making sure that the perpetrators do not profit.

Epilogue

———

By the close of 2015, Doughty Street Chambers had been operating for twenty-five years. We hired Shakespeare's Globe to celebrate, with by now over 100 barristers (half of them women) and thirty-four QCs (eleven women), with thirty support staff, occupying five houses alongside and opposite the Dickens Museum. My co-heads of chambers over the quarter-century had personally progressed: Peter Thornton was Chief Coroner, Keir Starmer an MP and Ed Fitzgerald was generally rated as the best public lawyer in the land. Helena Kennedy was now a baroness and a truly doughty fighter for justice, while several of my old juniors had gone on to become High Court and circuit judges, and even a Lord Justice of Appeal. Sir Louis Blom-Cooper, the most distinguished of our original associates, was about to turn ninety, still engaged on his lifelong crusade to reform the law of murder.

The Globe that night was heaving, and I didn't need a jukebox, because this time I had a stage, from which to declaim Shakespeare's lines about refugees from a scene he wrote for *Sir Thomas More*, which is never performed (because he did not write the rest of it). The London mob is protesting against the city taking refugees – Dutch Protestants, fleeing the Inquisition. They are led by George Betts, an Elizabethan shock jock, who says to the Chancellor, 'The removing of the strangers cannot choose but much advantage the poor handicrafts of the city' (i.e. British jobs for British workers). More's response:

Grant them removed, and grant that this your noise

Hath chid down all the majesty of England;

Imagine that you see the wretched strangers,

Their babies at their backs and their poor luggage,

Plodding to th' ports and coasts for transportation,

And that you sit as kings in your desires,

Authority quite silenced by your brawl,

And you in ruff of your opinions clothed;

What had you got? I'll tell you: you had taught

How insolence and strong hand should prevail,

How order should be quelled; and by this pattern

Not one of you should live an aged man,

For other ruffians, as their fancies wrought,

With self same hand, self reasons, and self right,

Would shark on you, and men like ravenous fishes

Would feed on one another.

Shakespeare's answer, it seemed, to Nigel Farage. The following year came my seventieth birthday – the Bible's 'three score years and ten' – although I was rushing around the world, increasingly to see my ageing parents in Sydney and doing cases in international courts while taking pride in the achievements of my children. I gave no thought to old age, let alone to death. There were a few funerals, of friends like Snoo Wilson and Alan Rickman, but Jeremy Hutchinson reached his century. I gave the speech at his birthday celebration, reliving the ABC case and *The Romans in Britain*, thirty-five years before, as if they were yesterday. Jeremy always said that the life of a barrister is ephemeral – full of sound and fury, signifying nothing – but his own provides a refutation.[107]

Then, inevitably, came the expatriate's nightmare, which I had been spared for so many years – to be woken by telephone in the small hours and told that a parent was dying. It was Christmas and the flights to Sydney were full, even on Malaysia Airlines, but I managed to find the last seat on Singapore Airlines – first-class only – leaving in a few hours' time. It was expensive, but if you can't drown your sorrows in

Krug and caviar, flying 12,000 miles to your mother's deathbed, when can you?

Although I have seen bullet-ridden bodies in my human rights work, I had never been at a deathbed. I assumed it would be like the last scene in *La bohème* – the heroine, reclining and declining, singing in a lower register, the tenor turning his back to gaze out the window while his friends are first to realise that the fat lady will not sing again. A modern version would have doctors and social workers – the real 'grief counsellors', I suppose – singing to relatives their resigned aria 'Miracles Do Not Happen'. I teased them by telling about my grandmother, who at the age of seventy-three stepped on a rusty garden rake and developed tetanus, from which all the doctors advised she would shortly die. 'She's had a good innings,' they said (for those days, she actually had) and offered an easeful death. For some reason my parents refused their offer to turn off her life support, and she recovered to live to a sprightly ninety-six. 'Oh, but her case was written up in the medical textbooks,' they said, as if that made all the difference.

Public hospitals are now predisposed towards the 'easeful death' philosophy of Peter Singer, a philosophy I had championed when I acted for the Voluntary Euthanasia Society. That did not stop me from questioning it, although in my mother's case it was a no-contest. She had left us clear instructions to end the kind of pain that I had watched her endure over the past two nights. She died on Christmas Day – an auspicious date for death, so the Eastern Orthodox Christians believe, because it signifies a fast track to heaven. This is a theological superstition, but one I could not help mentioning at her funeral. My eulogy raised a few laughs at my brother Graeme's expense (particularly from his children) when I told how Mum had wrestled with the dilemma of what to do about the cannabis plant that, as a rebellious teenager, he had grown in her beloved garden. Should she uproot it, or should she report it to the police? In the end, she decided to leave it. 'But I am certainly not going to water it!'

We knew the risk – when one long-term partner dies, the other often follows within a few weeks. My father evinced that intention by the simple expedient of refusing to eat. Before long he was being treated in hospital – with enough success for me to return to England for a few weeks and leave my brother to hold the fort. The medical bulletins from Sydney were optimistic at first, but then came another refusal to eat, and a return to hospital for force-feeding, then home again, and the doctors' use of the 'p' word – 'palliative care', which seems to mean nothing except basic care until death. I made plans for an early return, disrupted by a bout of bronchial pneumonia picked up in the freeze of the English winter. The inevitable email arrived: my father had died peacefully in his sleep – and it was off to Heathrow again. I arrived the night before his funeral and painfully coughed my way through the eulogy.

We had been through it all so recently, this ritual in the crematorium chapel, the arguments over the music and which photographs to put on the memorial card, the rounding up of grandchildren for the funeral readings. It's not an ordeal I want my own (currently hypothetical) grandchildren to go through: if I have any forewarning of my own death I shall choose the music (the judge's song from Gilbert & Sullivan's *Trial by Jury*, the human rights duet from *Don Carlo*, 'Love Me, I'm a Liberal' by Phil Ochs and Wagner's 'Liebestod'), the place (a small theatre, or perhaps a rented courtroom – definitely not a church), and (be warned) I will if possible pre-record my own eulogy – my final speech, so to speak, although there is something to be said for ending with a blast. The best conclusion to a commemoration that I have attended was for Sir Tom Bingham, that brilliant Law Lord, in Westminster Abbey. After all the gloomy reminiscences (at seventy-five, he was too young to die) there emerged from behind the catafalque a fully-fledged New Orleans jazz band belting out 'When the Saints Go Marching In'.

After my father's funeral, I walked into the leafy grounds to observe the resting place of my parents' ashes, beneath a straggling shrub that needed watering. There was space for more containers, the crematorium official heavily hinted – perhaps I might purchase a place? I have always been a bit leery of ending up as ashes, ever since a client – a defendant in the massive 'Operation Julie' LSD bust – had the container on his desk seized by police, who sent it off for forensic analysis believing that the substance inside would be some exotic drug. It was, however, his mother. Ashes cannot be spread in the Old Bailey (although perhaps someone could climb up and leave mine in her scales). I was as a child much taken by Robin Hood, who roused himself from his deathbed, called for his trusty bow and one arrow, and used the last of his strength to shoot it into Sherwood Forest. 'Bury me where you find it' was his dying instruction to Friar Tuck, presumably his executor. But I have always fancied a tombstone, which could elliptically be inscribed 'Rather his own man'. Spike Milligan has an appropriate epitaph: 'I told you I was ill.' Novelist Kathy Lette wants on hers 'At last, a good plot.'

* * *

Back in Britain, life had never been so boring. 'Brexit' was an IQ test that its citizens failed, and for the next few years we will be condemned to hearing of all these tedious negotiations with Europe about the terms for departure. I had a bet on the result with the philosopher AC Grayling some months before the referendum. 'Oh, the British are far too intelligent to vote to leave,' he had declared.

'They will,' I countered. 'I'm Australian and I know how Anglo-Saxons can panic at the prospect of swarthy people in boats coming towards them.'

There would be lots of refugees in boats on the Med in the summer, just when the referendum was to be held. AC bet me a dinner, which I accepted. But he's smart and was first to ask where I would take him when he won. 'Oh,' I said expansively (and expensively). 'To Skye Gyngell's new restaurant at Somerset House. Where will you take me?'

'To the Garrick,' AC replied, referring to his men-only club which serves overcooked meat followed by spotted dick. I have not bothered to collect my winnings.

Meanwhile, I have watched the lemming-like progress of the Great British nation over the white cliffs of Brexit. I blame David Cameron for promising the referendum in the first place, and then for failing to make its result conditional upon achieving a majority of the electorate (Leave obtained support from only 37 per cent of the voting public, against 35 per cent for Remain, and 28 per cent who did not vote at all) or a two-thirds majority of actual voters or a majority in all parts of the UK (Scotland and

Northern Ireland voted to remain). These are the sort of conditions that other countries which make political decisions by referendums generally apply. Instead, this referendum was merely 'advisory' – a fact about which the ignorant media, the BBC in particular, failed to inform voters: they presented the referendum as if its verdict would be binding, thus arousing the general expectation that the result would be conclusive and that the UK would be bound to exit. This was such a common belief in the days following the result that I penned a comment for *The Guardian* pointing out that as a matter of law Parliament was not bound by an advisory result and that MPs had a duty to decide for themselves:

> Our democracy does not allow, much less require, decision-making by referendum. That role belongs to the representatives of the people and not to the people themselves. Democracy has never meant the tyranny of the simple majority, much less the tyranny of the mob (otherwise, we might still have capital punishment). Democracy entails an elected government, subject to certain checks and balances such as the common law and the courts, and an executive ultimately responsible to parliament, whose members are entitled to vote according to conscience and common sense.

This opinion trended astonishingly, as if some new take on democracy, although it merely echoed the views of eighteenth-century conservatives like Edmund Burke. When the Court of Appeal judges more or less agreed, and ruled that Parliament must take the decision to leave, they were demonised in the *Daily Mail* as 'enemies of the people'. In which case, count me in.

As I suspected when I made my bet with AC Grayling, fear of refugees was an important factor – Nigel Farage, a man whose bonhomie hides a nasty racist streak, played up in UKIP propaganda the prospect of an influx of people with dark skin. This is a fear that works for governments which promise to 'turn back the boats' from my native Australia, and its impact should come as no surprise in Britain – after all, 35 per cent of French voters backed Marine Le Pen. But there were other factors, quite apart from the Russian bloggers who now appear to have been active in pursuit of anarchy in the West. It was interesting, after the Leveson Report and all the attempts to encourage a fair press, to note how journalists on *The Sun* and the *Mail* and even the *Telegraph* abandoned all pretence of professionalism and simply became political propagandists. (Murdoch cunningly allowed *The Times* – his 'paper for intelligent people' – to be fair to the case for Remain.) It was a complicated issue, of course, and the Leave case was simple, and supported by simple lies (£350 million a week for the NHS!), while the Remain camp was complacent and ineffective. It failed to reassure that class of protest voters who made the difference for Leave and for Trump – who had seen their standards of living and of life reduce and could not envisage them improving by sticking with Brussels or with Hillary. Things could not get worse, they thought, but they were wrong.

The nation has no notion of how to 'Brexicate' – to extricate itself from the referendum result. With a few exceptions, MPs who know very well that Britain's best interests are to stay, or at least to secure a 'soft' departure, dare not speak out against the lie that 'the British people' voted to leave, when only 37 per cent did. The Prime Minister, a recent convert once she realised she could not be Prime Minister unless she converted, talks about achieving a 'good deal' and of her revulsion at the prospect of a 'bad deal'– the idea of a 'fair deal' does not seem to have occurred to her as the only way forward. As for her ministers, Andrea 'down with experts' Leadsom seems the worst, although rivalled by Chris Grayling, who was a truly awful Lord Chancellor, depriving prisoners of books and legal aid of money, and having little understanding of the principles of fairness that must underpin any Department of Justice. His successor, Michael Gove, did understand those principles and is a man I quite like: at private dinners he strikes me as an enthusiastic and clever ex-journalist teeming with ideas – some good, some bad, and one terrible. That one is Brexit.

For some years, while Boris Johnson was editing *The Spectator*, we had been neighbours in Doughty Street – I came close to running him over as my car dodged his bike. We have had some enjoyable encounters, none more so than at a celebration on the night he was first elected Mayor of London. He came down a long line of Tory well-wishers, his trademark ebullience dimmed as he was forced to shake hands and utter replies of no consequence. Then he came to Kathy Lette: 'I can't think of you as a Mayor, Boris. To me, you'll always be a stallion.' His face lifted, his lips salivated and he was about to make a suitably obscene reply when suddenly he disappeared: enclosed by his minders, directed by Lynton Crosby to remove him immediately from the temptation to be his old self.

He proved a feckless Foreign Secretary. I had been advising the Reuters Foundation about the plight of Nazanin Zaghari-Ratcliffe, a British-Iranian dual citizen who worked for its charity and who had been arrested in Iran when she went back to show her new baby to her parents. She was jailed for five years on a bogus charge of spying, and for fifteen months the FCO did absolutely nothing to support her – not even uttering a diplomatic protest when, contrary to the Vienna Convention, the Iranians denied her any visits from the British consul. After a year, this inaction so infuriated me that for the first time in my life I took the last resort of a pompous Englishman when the steam rises out of his ears – a letter to *The Times*. It had absolutely no effect.

Meanwhile, the other saga making Britain a laughing stock had arisen, as usual, from a moral panic – in this case, from the revelation that Mrs Thatcher's favourite celebrity, Jimmy Savile, had been a serial paedophile. So, in the fevered imagination of the tabloids, must be other famous men accused by fantasists of dismembering small boys in drug-crazed satanic rituals in Westminster apartments and guesthouses in Pimlico back in the '70s and '80s. So profoundly did these stories of high-level 'cover-ups', orchestrated by the then Attorney General Michael Havers, take hold that the government set up an Independent Inquiry into Child Sexual Abuse (IICSA) to investigate, marking its 'independence' by appointing a redoubtable ex-judge, Dame Elizabeth Butler-Sloss, as its chair – until it realised that she was the sister of the late Sir Michael. After replacing her with another worthy woman (it must, illogically, be a woman) who turned out to be a friend of another prime suspect, the Home Office hired at vast expense a female judge from New Zealand. It could have established (as I did) by a few calls to local lawyers that this lady was the least esteemed member of the New Zealand judiciary. The IICSA wasted eighteen months under her chairmanship – she resigned after admitted unfamiliarity with relevant English law and a disinclination to learn it (although she could have mugged up on it during all her taxpayer-funded trips back to New Zealand).

I kept an eye on this unfolding disaster because I had some evidence to offer: the only example I had ever encountered of a cover-up of the crimes of a high-ranking paedophile. Back in the early '80s, I had received a brief to appear for executive members of an organisation called the Paedophile Information Exchange (PIE), at committal proceedings to examine whether conspiracy charges (to send indecent letters by post) should put them on trial. I was something of an expert on conspiracy law, with a duty to accept this unattractive task (a taxi on the rank has sometimes to drive to dark suburbs) and at least the 'stipe' (stipendiary magistrate) listed to hear the case was one of my favourites. Mr Branson SM was an austere but fair man who would not suffer any prosecutorial impropriety. We spent a week examining the evidence: PIE was essentially a perverts' correspondence club, where members wrote to each other, in sickening detail, their fantasies about grooming and abusing children, in copperplate schoolmasterly (many were in fact schoolmasters) handwriting. The legal issue, at the committal, was whether they had done so by agreement with the defendants, and so the letter-writers had to be called and cross-examined. They cut pathetic figures, these old men in crumpled suits and dandruffed collars who had all been required to plead guilty to an offence of sending indecent material through the post before they testified. Now they were paraded in shame before Mr Branson, forced to admit to their depraved imaginations and answer my questions. There was, however, one great curiosity about the prosecution case: the most prolific offender, the hub of this daisy-chain of pornographic penmanship, whose writings I found stomach-turning and slightly sinister, had not been arrested or called to give evidence. His name, the police assured us, was Mr Henderson and they were unable to trace him.

Looking back, I think my rat-smelling antennae, so vital for a defence counsel, may have been dulled by disgust at the effusions of these PIE-men. Mr Branson committed them for trial – he was a principled enough beak to have refused to do so had the abuse of process revealed later come to his attention at the time. Only when the trial (at which I did not appear) was over did a whistleblower – an outraged policeman, I suspect – leak to *Private Eye* the fact that a decision had been taken 'at a high level' that the key figure in the case, whose name was not in fact Henderson, should not be identified or prosecuted. His name was Sir Peter Hayman and he had recently retired as British High Commissioner in Canada after a long and distinguished career in MI6, in which he had served as a deputy director (and where he should have been recognised as a proselytising paedophile). The story caused some scandal, and to hose it down the DPP put out a misleading press statement, claiming that Hayman had not been given preferential treatment (he had: unlike his fellow paedophiles, he had not been prosecuted or called to give evidence or put in a position where his central role could be examined by Mr Branson). It was, indeed, a classic British cover-up, which continued in this way after it had been uncov-ered.[108] I trust that the IICSA will manage to find out how and by whom Sir Peter Hayman was protected – from me, and from Richard Branson's dad.

Otherwise, its work might do some good by refuting all the absurd stories about cabals of distinguished conservatives killing small boys after beating and buggering them in Pimlico apartments. I acted (very briefly) for *Scally-wag*, a scurrilous magazine which dreamed up much of this scuttlebutt in the early '90s. No one paid any notice until it alleged that the then Prime Minister, John Major, was having an affair with a Downing Street caterer, and the story 'went viral' (as we did not say in the days before the internet). The *New Statesman* then commented on the phenomenon of how 'The Strange Case of John Major's Mistress' had become an overnight urban legend. It did not endorse the story, and when Major sued I thought it had a good defence – I could convince a jury that a serious political magazine was simply discussing the role of rumour in Whitehall, and not accusing John Major, that scion of 'family values', of adultery. Major's lawyers pulled a fast one by choosing to sue WH Smith, the *Statesman*'s distributors, as well: its board immediately grovelled and settled by paying Major a large six-figure sum (which the *New Statesman* by contract had to reimburse, even though it maintained that the article was not libellous). The *Statesman* was snookered, and ended the case by offering Major the libel raspberry – the sum of £1, which he was happy to accept. I thought we should have pressed on to trial, to defend the right of journalists to discuss politically significant allegations without endorsing them. Had we done so, of course, we might have proved that John Major did indeed have a mistress – not the rather nice caterer alleged by *Scallywag* but the altogether more embarrassing personage of his Cabinet minister Edwina Currie, who later wrote about their sex life in excruciating detail in her autobiography.

Scallywag's inventions, twenty years later, were picked up and passed off by fantasists whose stories found a ready audience among senior policemen. One stood outside Ted Heath's old home, declaring the allegations 'credible and true', while other senior officers – including a chief constable – gave similar endorsement to stories about a murderous 'No. 10 paedophile ring'. How did it come about that those senior police officers took leave of their senses and authorised raids on the homes of old and sick (in Leon Brittan's case, dying) public figures of yesteryear? The moral panic induced by Savile was one explanation, as was a 'trust the victims' approach to historical abuse claims (notwithstanding that such a claim can bring compensation – a ready motive for some false allegations). There is another reason, which I gave incautiously to a radio news programme which interviewed me 'live' after a good dinner: 'Britain has the most stupid police force in the advanced world.' I should not have put it like that, although police I met afterwards had been amused and thought I had a point, and Home Office boffins earnestly contacted me for more details. The truth is that we do not like our police to be too clever: Constable Dogberry and Gilbert and Sullivan's policemen of Penzance are more to our liking, and the BBC is always there to give reassurance – the intelligent Inspector Morse, who usually gets his man (or woman), is about as realistic as Dixon of Dock Green was back in the '60s. The IICSA has yet to make headway on its more urgent task of reviewing child abuse in churches (especially the Catholic Church) and church schools, and recommending the safeguarding measures (no communion or confession for children until they are teenagers, for example) that *The Case of the Pope* demonstrates to be necessary. It has just announced that its 2019 inquiry will be into the 'VIP paedophile ring' – it is depressing to think that for the next few years, the British media will be full of Brexit and VIP sex abuse and (no doubt) royal babies.

*   *   *

This is a prospect that makes me wonder whether I should bother to stay in my adopted country, or to return 'home' now I have reached three score years and ten, the biblical allotment of sentient life. As a boy I had always assumed I would follow the Australian retirement dream of 'travelling north', to a home on a beach to fish and listen to the cricket until the inevitable heart attack. It is a measure of medical progress over my lifetime that my inspiration these days is Donald Trump, who does so much (well, so much damage) at my age. I have been fortunate in having Australia, that sane and beautiful and relatively happy country, as a fall-back, and was touched in 2018 to be awarded its equivalent of a knighthood, an 'Order of Australia' – I am entitled to call myself an AO, although people here would think it stands for 'adults only'. Although I sometimes discourse over the back fence with my neighbour in north London, Dame Edna Everage, about Sydney retirement homes where we could spend our dementia years, I shall stick with my fantasy of good old liberal England for a few years yet.

And it is still an endearing and enduring country, for all its current craziness. As I conclude this book, I am summoned to the palace. A party for the Commonwealth – usually a pleasant occasion to meet fellow expatriates who have contributed a lot to British culture as authors and singers and journalists and arts administrators. Of them, tonight, there is no sign – only High Commissioners and business people and (oddly) Theresa and Philip May and senior members of the Cabinet. The penny drops – the royals have been co-opted in the quest for post-Brexit trade deals. The Queen is her seemingly eternal self – we reminisce about Kathy's corgi dress, which she remembers well. Her husband ('Phil the Greek' we called him at school) is not present, so I cannot chat to him about the days when he 'sat' for Stephen Ward. Prince Charles is there, as an added attraction, looking confident of becoming the next head of the Commonwealth (I do not reveal my preference for Obama). We mingle, and I avoid the Prime Minister (as Home Secretary, she made distasteful remarks about human rights lawyers), but I collar Boris to ask the latest on Nazanin Zaghari-Ratcliffe, whose case he was forced to take up after making some mistaken remarks about her being a journalist (whereupon the Iranians gleefully proposed to add another five years to her sentence as a spy). 'Privy Councillor terms, old chap, Privy Councillor terms,' he insisted (apparently unaware that I was not a Privy Councillor), but revealed nothing more than I already knew. We were in the Long Gallery at the palace, and it was an opportunity to view the Queen's art collection – those remarkable Rubenses and Poussins so wisely recommended by her adviser, Sir Anthony Blunt. He could have been executed as a traitor before his appointment, as he had been a Soviet spy, but MI6, his former employer, covered up his crime. As, perhaps, they did for Sir Peter Hayman.

Nonetheless, as the bus pass and the pension serve to remind, I am entering my final act – and in life, as in opera, the final act is always the shortest. So this might be a good time to hang up the wig and gown for ever and revert to some of the wishful projects of my younger days, abandoned whenever my cab was hailed to take me to the Old Bailey or away to some far-off courtroom. I once started a crime novel featuring (of course) an international lawyer, and a play with music on the life of the '60s troubadour Phil Ochs. I wrote a screenplay about John André, the brilliant spymaster who almost won the war of independence for Britain when he engineered the defection of Benedict Arnold, Washington's best general, with the help of the general's wife, a judge's daughter. André was hanged by the Americans despite intercession from Hamilton, now of eponymous musical fame. The ending on the gallows, Kathy says, is moving, but the sex scenes are dreadful. As I was wondering whether to revert to these projects, I suddenly realised that I could not stop thinking in the language of the lawyer ('revert' being the word they use when they promise – usually insincerely – to get back to you). Then came a call from Lula for help in Brazil, a request from Qatar for an opinion on the legality of its blockade, a victim of Harvey Weinstein wanting to challenge non-disclosure orders, and the prospect of an oil and gas arbitration in Paris in the spring – so the appearance of this memoir does not mean my trials are at an end. I will remain a cab on the rank, although more mindful of the adage on John Mortimer's coffee cup: 'Old lawyers never die. They just lose their appeal.'

461

Acknowledgements

This book began in 2016 as a way of saying farewell to my parents: I sat beside them listening to their memories, and the early chapters came with their assistance. My family – Kathy, Georgie and Jules (with his amazing recall) – vetted and abetted my recollection. My greatest debt, of course, is to clients who granted me the privilege of taking their cases and have allowed me to tell the tale, and to my work colleagues – pupils and juniors, clerks and solicitors – who have been my companions in the lists. Particular thanks must go to Richard Bayliss, my faithful clerk for the last quarter-century. My gratitude for overseeing this volume goes to Olivia Beattie, managing editor of Biteback, who has subjected my manuscript to the same scrupulous scrutiny as when publishing my other works on subjects as diverse as Iran, nuclear weaponry and the Armenian genocide. The earlier Australian edition of this book benefited from expert editing by Catherine Hill, assisted by Amanda O'Connell and supervised by Nikki Christer. Alex Courtnage, my brilliant personal assistant, researched facts and interpreted my handwriting, as did his successor, Erin Leach. Tim Robertson, Giampaolo Pertosi, Lesley Holden, Mary Ellen Barton and Patrick George have helped, while John Fairley and Andrew Robertson provided family photographs. All errors are down to me. Some of the cases I recount have been misreported in the media and some of the people I recall have been demonised in the press: my take on them provides another perspective – the view, so to speak, from the robing room.

Endnotes

Chapter One: Who Do I Think I Am? (pp. 1–23)

1   Belinda Dettmann and Jane Stevens, *Agnes the Secret Princess: An Australian Story* (Sydney: Newport, 2015).

2   Geoffrey Robertson, *Dreaming Too Loud*: 'For a Tumut schoolteacher, blown up at Bapaume', (Sydney: Vintage, 2013), Chapter 12.

3   After her death in 2016 we discovered – from anxious calls to the family home from charities for the poor – that she had for years been anonymously donating generously to them.

4   Barrie Cassidy, 'The RAAF trainee who crashed landed on a roof', The Drum, ABC News, 24 April 2015.

5   The poem, 'High Flight', was written by John Gillespie Magee Jr, a young Anglo-American airman serving with the Royal Canadian Air Force, a few weeks before his death in an aerial collision in Britain in 1941. I found a handwritten copy in a letter my father sent to his mother from the front line in 1943, doubtless to console her if he were to suffer the same fate.

Chapter Two: Baby Boomer (pp. 25–57)

6   C. H. Rolph (ed.), *The Trial of Lady Chatterley: Regina v Penguin Books Ltd* (London: Penguin Books, 1990).

7   Car rallies were absurdly popular in '50s Australia, especially the 'Redex Trial', in which familiar-brand vehicles were driven around the country. It was a big deal to be taken, age seven, to gawk at cars you could see on the streets, lined up before the start of the 1953 Redex Trial. I had completely forgotten my excitement until Peter Carey's novel about it, *A Long Way From Home* (London: Faber, 2017), stirred my memory.

8   See *Summerhill* (CBBC, January 2008).

Chapter Three: Student Power (pp. 59–75)

9   *Four Corners*, 'Great Economic Lecture' (ABC TV, April 1967).

Chapter Four: Learning the Law (pp. 77–106)

10   I never dared to venture into this tiny space – the description is by Mary Gaudron, quoted in Pamela Burton, *From Moree to Mabo: The Mary Gaudron Story* (Perth: UWA Press, 2010), pp. 45–6.

11   G. Hawkins and N. Morris, The Honest Politician's Guide to Crime Control (Illinois: University of Chicago Press, 1969).

12   In 1996, the House of Commons passed a Bill to remove the need for allegations of fault, but it was never implemented. As recently as February 2018, the Justice Secretary, an obscure

commercial solicitor named David Gauke, said he was 'studying the evidence for change' but would not 'rush to a conclusion' – see Francis Gibb, 'Justice Secretary pledges to review divorce laws', *The Times*, 5 February 2018, p. 4.

13   See Ken Inglis, *The Stuart Case* (Melbourne: Black Inc., 2002).

14   See G. R. Robertson and J. C. Carrick, 'The Trial of Nancy Young' (*Australian Quarterly*, June 1970), pp. 34ff.

15   For an example see Sir Louis Blom-Cooper QC, *Power of Persuasion* (London: Hart Publishing, 2017), p. 341.

16   See Larry Writer, *Pitched Battle: In the Frontline of the 1971 Springbok Tour of Australia* (Sydney: Scribe, 2016), pp. 56–70.

Chapter Five: Must Rhodes Fall? (pp. 107–134)

17   'Interview with the Warden of Wadham' (*Cherwell*, 1971)

18   Philip Ziegler, *Legacy: Cecil Rhodes, the Rhodes Trust and Rhodes Scholarships* (Connecticut: Yale University Press, 2008), p. 252.

19   Starr Jameson (of 'Jameson Raid' infamy) was closest to Rhodes, and thought 'he would turn in his grave' at the prospect of a black beneficiary: see Ziegler, p. 64.

20   This is a current scandal, encapsulated in the *Guardian* headline in October 2017: 'Oxford accused of "social apartheid" over admissions – one in three colleges failed to admit black British A-Level students in 2015' (*Guardian Weekly*, 27 October 2017, p. 25).

21   Ziegler, op. cit., p. 299.

22   My detailed account of the Oz trial can be found in Chapter 2 of The Justice Game (London: Vintage, 1998).

Chapter Six: Down at the Old Bailey (pp. 135–156)

23   *DPP v Stonehouse* (1978) AC 55.

24   *Home Office v Harman* (1983) 1 AC 280.

25   Geoffrey Robertson, 'Michael Gove's Magna Carta' (*Standpoint*, July/August 2015, Issue 74).

Chapter Seven: Trial by Jury (pp. 157–186)

26   And may continue – the rapist, Kirk Reid, is being considered for release by the Parole Board, according to newspapers in 2018.

27   Geoffrey Robertson, *The Justice Game*, op. cit., p. 313. See also David Leigh, *Betrayed: The Real Story of the Matrix Churchill Trial* (London: Bloomsbury, 1993).

28   See Frances Gibb, 'Dozens jailed over evidence failures, warns watchdog', *The Times*, 5 February 2018. Richard Foster, chairman of the Criminal Cases Review Commission, said that failures to disclosure 'amounted to hundreds of cases over the years'.

29   *The Justice Game*, op. cit., Chapter 5.

30   Sian Griffiths, 'Drugs are rife, says woman jailed over death of top Tory's daughter', *Sunday Times*, 11 February 2018, p. 5.

31   Geoffrey Robertson, *Stephen Ward Was Innocent OK: The Case for Overturning His Conviction* (London: Biteback Publishing, 2013).

32   *R v Chief Stipendiary Magistrate ex p Choudhury* (1991) 1 All ER 306.

33   See, for example, 'British Barrister Accused of Child Abuse' (*The Guardian*, 3 February 2017).

Chapter Eight: Family and Friends (pp. 187–210)

34   Geoffrey Robertson, *Reluctant Judas: Life and Death of the Special Branch Informer Kenneth Lennon* (London: Maurice Temple Smith, 1976).

35   *Earl Pratt and Ivan Morgan v Attorney General of Jamaica* (1994) 2 AC 1.

36   Geoffrey Robertson, *Mullahs Without Mercy: Human Rights and Nuclear Weapons* (London: Biteback Publishing, 2012); 'The Massacre of Prisoners in Iran' (Boroumand Foundation, 2010).

37   *Geoffrey Robertson's Hypotheticals*, 'All in the Family' (ABC TV, 5 February 1989).

38   SOAS is the School of Oriental and African Studies, a part of the University of London. I am now one of its trustees.

39   Maria Stenmark, *Mum's the Word* (New South Wales: North Rocks Press, 1986).

Chapter Nine: Hypotheticals (pp. 211–227)

40   The full transcript is found in Geoffrey Robertson, *Dreaming Too Loud*, op. cit., Chapter 20.

41   *W v Edgell* (1989) EWCA Civ 13; (1990) 2 WLR 471.

42   *Hodgson and Channel 4 v UK*, Decision on Admissibility, 9 March 1987, 51 DR 136.

43   Intelligence Squared, 'It's Time to End the War on Drugs' (13 March 2012). Available at: https://www.intelligencesquared.com/events/versus-drugs/

Chapter Ten: Hard Cases (pp. 229–257)

44   *R v McCann & Others* (1991) 92 Cr App R 239.

45   See Clive Borrell, 'Yard Inquiry into Agent Provocateur Allegations', *Sunday Times*, 2 August 1976, p. 1. See also *R v Ameer & Lucas CCC* (1977) Crim L R 104, & G. Robertson, 'Entrapment Evidence: Manna from Heaven, or Fruit of the Poisoned Tree?' (1994) Crim LR 805.

46   Thomas Harding, *Blood on the Page: A Murder, a Secret Trial, a Search for the Truth* (London: William Heinemann, 2018).

Chapter Eleven: In the Privy (pp. 259–287)

47   https://deathpenaltyinfo.org/deterrence-states-without-death-penalty-have-had-consistently-lower-murder-rates, accessed 5 April 2018.

48   Michael X was also charged with the murder of Gale Benson but was never prosecuted on that count; two of his followers were later convicted. There was some evidence to suggest provocation (which would have reduced murder to manslaughter) but this was not explored at his trial.

49   *Earl Pratt and Ivan Morgan v Attorney General of Jamaica* (1993) UKPC 1; (1994) 2 AC 1.

50   Kris's appeal has been delayed because US authorities – the FBI and CIA – are refusing to disclose information that the victims were killed on Escobar's orders. Commendably (although after staying silent for so long), the UK government has filed an 'amicus' brief in the US Southern District Court supporting disclosure: see Jacqui Goddard, 'UK demand US release documents that could free Kris Maharaj after 32 years in prison' (*The Times*, 20 April 2018).

51   *Phillip (Lennox) v Director of Public Prosecutions* (1992) 1 AC 545 (PC).

52   *AG of Trinidad and Tobago v Phillip* (1995) 1 AC 396 (PC).

53   Louis Blom-Cooper, *Guns for Antigua* (London: Gerald Duckworth & Co Ltd, 1988).

54   *Antigua Power v Baldwin Spencer & Others* (2013) UKPC 23.

55   This was the purpose of bringing the case, which we did not win because the tribunal applied an English rule that you could not sue on a corruptly obtained contract, rather than the European rule that all circumstances relating to such a contract should be taken into account. The arbitrators imagined that this English rule would deter corruption – but on the contrary it only ensures that corruption will never be exposed – there would be no point in a plaintiff admitting it if they would thereby lose the case! See *World Duty Free Company Ltd v The Republic of Kenya* (ICSID Case No. ARB/00/7).

56   See Geoffrey Robertson, 'Criminal Justice' (*The Spectator*, 22 June 2002).

57   Patrón is now the top-selling luxury tequila brand and the third largest-selling tequila in the US – *Wine Spectator*, 30 November 2017, p.56. George Clooney tells me that his brand, Casamigos, is superior.

58   There is a presumption that those appointed to ambassadorial positions that carry immunity should be nationals of the sending state – unless, exceptionally, they have some connection or qualification which justifies their appointment. Dr Juffali had none. The government was later to claim that he had offered to set up a medical centre on the island. Philanthropy might justify his appointment as an envoy or honorary consul, posts which carry no immunity, but not an ambassadorship purchased by his wealth in order to evade his personal obligations to his wife and child. St Lucia had a duty to waive his immunity and allow matrimonial justice to take its course, rather than to place him above the law so he could avoid obligations to support his family.

Chapter Twelve: Doughty Street Chambers (pp. 289–313)

59   Geoffrey Robertson, *The Tyrannicide Brief* (London: Chatto & Windus, 2005).

60   *R v Ahluwalia* (1993) 96 Cr App R 133.

61 For more detail about this case, see *The Justice Game*, op. cit., Chapter 17.
62 See *Brown v Executors of the Estates of HM Queen Elizabeth, the Queen Mother & of HRH the Princess Margaret* (2007) EWHC 1607 (Fam) and (2008) EWCA Civ 56, and *Brown v Information Commissioner & the Attorney General* (2015) UKUT 393 (AAC).
63 See *Rusbridger & Toynbee v Attorney General* (2003) UKHL 38 (House of Lords) and (2002) EWCA Civ 397 (Court of Appeal).
64 Tyson did fight Lewis for the title in 2002 but was knocked out in the eighth round. The celebrity audience included Tom Cruise, Britney Spears, Hugh Hefner, Michael Jordan, Ben Affleck, Halle Berry and Morgan Freeman, as well as Donald Trump and Alec Baldwin (who has been playing the President on *Saturday Night Live*).
65 *Perinçek v Switzerland*, No. 27510/08 ECHR 2015.

Chapter Thirteen: Spycatching (pp. 315–336)
66 *Spycatcher: The Candid Autobiography of a Senior Intelligence Officer* by Peter Wright (with Paul Greengrass) was published in Australia in 1987 by William Heinemann. Malcolm Turnbull's *The Spycatcher Trial* was published by Heinemann in 1988.
67 Giles Gordon, *Aren't We Due a Royalty Statement?* (London: Chatto & Windus, 1993), pp. 304–5.
68 There are many different versions of the false story of Malcolm killing the cat: one has him putting the pet in a freezer. See Richard Ackland: https://www.crikey.com.au/2009/06/18/loves-letter-lost-malcolm-turnbulls-dead-cat-scrawl-unearthed/, accessed 7 April 2018.
69 *Mohamed, R v The Secretary of State* (No. 2) (2010) EWCA Civ 158.

Chapter Fourteen: Assange in Ecuador (pp. 337–359)
70 Jeremy Bentham, *Draught of a New Plan for the organisation of the Judicial Establishment in France* (London, 1790), pp. 25–6.

Chapter Fifteen: Freedom of Speech (pp. 361–398)
71 See Police and Criminal Evidence Act 1984.
72 Geoffrey Robertson, *People Against the Press* (London: Quartet, 1980).
73 'The attempt to keep out evil doctrine by licensing is like the exploit of that gallant man who thought to keep out the cows by shutting his park gate … Lords and Commons of England, consider what nation it is whereof ye are, a nation not dull and slow, but of a quick, ingenious and piercing spirit. It must not be shackled or restricted. Give me the liberty to know, to utter, and to argue freely according to conscience, above all liberties.'
74 *R v Felixstowe Justices ex p Leigh* (1987) QBD 582.
75 *R v BBC & ITC ex p Referendum Party* (1997) EMLR 605.
76 *Bowman v UK* (1998) 26 EHRR 1.
77 *Wyatt v Forbes* (unreported) (2 December 1997), Morland J.
78 *Bachchan v India Abroad Publications* (1992) 585 NYS 2d 661.
79 *Berezovsky v Forbes* (2000) EMLR 643.
80 *Goodwin v UK* (1996) 22 EHRR 123, para 39.
81 Geoffrey Robertson, 'Protecting Sources Is a Legal and Moral Duty' (*The Times*, 15 February 2012).
82 *Dow Jones & Company Inc. v Gutnick* (2002) 210 CLR 575.
83 Allan Kozinn, 'Meditation on the Man Who saved the Beatles' (*New York Times*, 7 February 2008).
84 Geoffrey Robertson and Andrew Nicol, *Robertson and Nicol on Media Law*, fifth edition (London: Penguin, 2007).
85 *Jameel & Another v Wall Street Journal Europe* (No. 2) (HL) (2006) UKHL 44.
86 *Attorney General v New Statesman & Nation Publishing Co. Ltd* (1981) QB1.
87 *R v Reed* (Nicholas) (1982) Crim LR 819.
88 *AG v Able* (1984) 1 All ER 277.

Chapter Sixteen: Struggling for Global Justice (pp. 399–423)
89 *Hauschildt v Denmark*, Application No. 10486/83 Series A, No. 154 (1990) 12 EHRR 266.

90   See Louis Blom-Cooper, *Guns to Antigua* (London: Duckworth, 1991), and Geoffrey Robertson, *The Justice Game*, op. cit., Chapter 2.
91   See *Republic of Fiji v Prasad, Melbourne Journal of International Law* (Volume 2, Issue 1, 2001).
92   See Geoffrey Robertson, *Dreaming Too Loud*, op. cit., Chapter 8.
93   Memorandum from the FCO Eastern Department to Minister Joyce Quin and others, 12 April 1999. See Geoffrey Robertson, *An Inconvenient Genocide: Who Now Remembers the Armenians?* (London: Biteback Publishing, 2014), pp. 162–3.
94   *An Inconvenient Genocide*, op. cit.

Chapter Seventeen: The World's Fight (pp. 425–448)

95   For the full story, see 'The Pinochet Precedent' in Geoffrey Robertson, *Crimes Against Humanity* (London: Penguin, 2012), pp. 435–45.
96   Geoffrey Robertson, 'Robin Vincent obituary', *The Guardian*, 22 June 2011; www.theguardian.com/law/2011/jun/22/robin-vincent-obituary, accessed 9 April 2018.
97   Prosecutor Lee Norman (child soldiers case) SCSL-04-14-AR72, 31 May 2004.
98   See Desmond de Silva, *Madame, Where are your Mangoes?* (London: Quartet, 2017), p. 14.
99   *Rees & Others v Crane* (1994) 2 AC 173.
100 'The Massacre of Political Prisoners in Iran', 1988 report of an inquiry conducted by Geoffrey Robertson QC (Washington: Boroumand Foundation, 2010).
101 Geoffrey Robertson, *The Case of the Pope* (London: Penguin, 2010).
102 *The Guardian*, 2 April 2010.
103 'Report on the International Crimes Tribunal of Bangladesh' (International Forum for Democracy and Human Rights, 2015).
104 'Report on the Impeachment of Sri Lanka's Chief Justice' (Bar Human Rights Committee, 2013).
105 'Assad Should Face International Justice' (*The Independent*, 12 May 2011).
106 See Geoffrey Robertson, 'Europe needs a Magnitsky Law', in Elena Servettaz (ed.), *Why Europe Needs a Magnitsky Law* (2013).

Epilogue (pp. 449–461)

107 See Thomas Grant, *Jeremy Hutchinson's Case Histories* (London: John Murray, 2015), and *Guardian* obituary.
108 The DPP gave a highly questionable account of why Hayman was not prosecuted, which did not in any event explain why he was allowed a false name and not, like other correspondents, called to give evidence. See *The Times*, 11 May 1981, and 'Pain, Anguish and the DPP' in the *Sunday Times*, 22 March 1991. More accurate reports of the cover-up will be found in *The Guardian* and *Private Eye* in this period.

Index